Cryptology for Engineers

An Application-Oriented Mathematical Introduction

Cryptology for Engineers

An Application-Oriented Mathematical Introduction

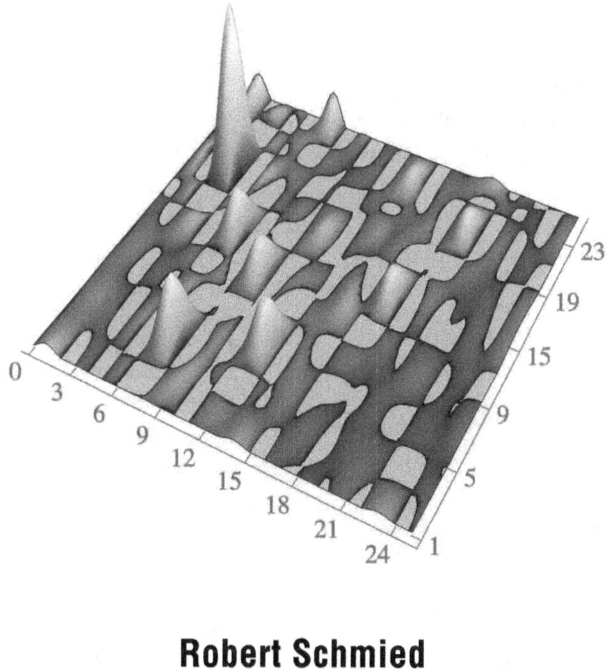

Robert Schmied

Bundeswehr University Munich, Germany

World Scientific

NEW JERSEY • LONDON • SINGAPORE • BEIJING • SHANGHAI • HONG KONG • TAIPEI • CHENNAI • TOKYO

Published by

World Scientific Publishing Co. Pte. Ltd.
5 Toh Tuck Link, Singapore 596224
USA office: 27 Warren Street, Suite 401-402, Hackensack, NJ 07601
UK office: 57 Shelton Street, Covent Garden, London WC2H 9HE

Library of Congress Control Number: 2020011861

British Library Cataloguing-in-Publication Data
A catalogue record for this book is available from the British Library.

First published 2020 (hardcover)
Reprinted 2026 (in paperback edition)
ISBN 978-981-98-3275-0 (pbk)

CRYPTOLOGY FOR ENGINEERS
An Application-Oriented Mathematical Introduction

ISBN 978-981-120-804-1 (hardcover)
ISBN 978-981-120-805-8 (ebook for institutions)
ISBN 978-981-120-806-5 (ebook for individuals)

For any available supplementary material, please visit
https://www.worldscientific.com/worldscibooks/10.1142/11492#t=suppl

Desk Editor: Amanda Yun

Typeset by Stallion Press
Email: enquiries@stallionpress.com

Preface

Cryptology has become an indispensable part of everyday life in today's transparent and digital world. Cryptology originally involved encrypting messages to ensure communication security, and this has been extended to a multitude of areas, especially in engineering involving computerization and continued research on various topics. These topics have at least two things in common: they are embedded into connected systems and they have to guarantee maximum security. For these reasons, we need to address different security services to ensure security goals. Security services are static parts of a cryptosystem that are enriched by clearly defined sequences of action for their application. A cryptosystem is a main part of a so-called encrypter that ensures security of any kind of message in a communication system. Such a cryptosystem must be negotiated between the participants of the communication, i.e., the sender and the receiver. Therefore, the same components on the sender side of the messages are also established on the receiver side.

This book focuses mainly on the various basic algorithms needed to ensure today's security goals. This requires a deep introduction to its mathematical background, which is important for understanding difficult algorithms. Each chapter is enriched by examples; many can be done by hand and a few with computer support. The algorithms are correct and directly implementable. However, a one-to-one implementation is not intended for use because the focus here lies on comprehension and not on the implementation of security against an attacker.

Figure A: schematically shows the topics that are briefly mentioned here. The numbers in white circles indicate the chapters in which these topics are suitably introduced and primarily discussed.

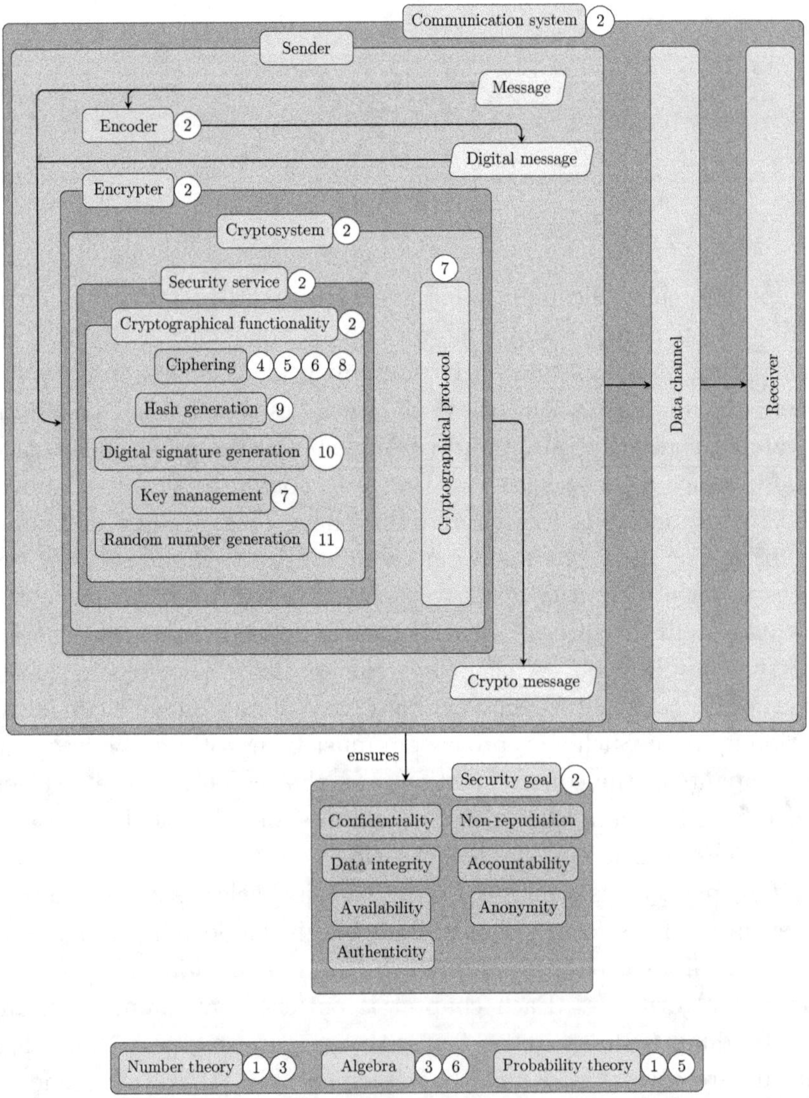

Figure A: An overview of the covered topics, denoted by chapter numbers in white circles.

About the Author

Robert Schmied is a scientist at Bundeswehr University Munich, Department of Electrical Engineering and Information Technology. Since his doctoral graduation he has been gaining experience in teaching cryptology and data science for many years which are both his work priorities and main fields of research at the chair of mathematics. In data science he is influenced by the ideas of exploratory data analysis which is more relevant than ever in a new guise. In cryptology, he deals with Shannon entropy-based, statistical text analysis.

Contents

List of Algorithms

List of Figures

List of Tables

Chapter 1

Basics on Number Theory and Probability Theory

Note 1.1. In this chapter, the requirements are:

- being able to add and multiply numbers,
- being able to order numbers by relations of less than ($<$ or $\leq$),
- knowing that every non-empty subset of $\mathbb{N}$ has a smallest element,
- knowing that for each $n \in \mathbb{N}$ there is only a finite number of elements $z \in \mathbb{Z}$ applying $|z| \leq n$, and
- being able to deal with mappings.

Selected literature: See (Applebaum, 2008; Hardy *et al.*, 2008; Hoffstein *et al.*, 2008; Ross, 2014).

Every application that uses one or more services concerning cryptology takes advantage of results from number theory. Furthermore, modern security concepts apply outcomes from probability theory. Therefore, it is important to develop this theory.[1]

1.1 Euclid's Fundamental Theorem of Arithmetic

This section deals with the sets
$\mathbb{N} = \{1, 2, 3, \ldots\}$, $\mathbb{N}_0 = \{0, 1, 2, \ldots\}$, $\mathbb{Z} = \{0, \pm 1, \pm 2, \pm 3, \ldots\}$ and $\mathbb{R}$.

[1]See (Hoffstein *et al.*, 2008) or (Hardy *et al.*, 2008) for some introductory sections.

1.1.1 *Division with remainder*

Cryptosystems, which we will discuss later,[2] are commonly used to provide a requirement for the confidentiality of transmitted messages. Before demonstrating examples of cryptosystems, we have to understand the principles of number theory. Modular arithmetic, namely the theory of congruences on finite sets, will be addressed. The arithmetic on finite sets can be addressed by addition and multiplication rules. Initially, each calculation rule is collected in terms of a so-called *Cayley table*,[3] for example,[4] as $n = 3$ and the set $\{0, 1, 2\}$

$+_3$	0	1	2
0	0	1	2
1	1	2	0
2	2	0	1

$\cdot_3$	0	1	2
0	0	0	0
1	0	1	2
2	0	2	1

This table is generalized because it is too complex to record all the possible $n \in \mathbb{N}$. Therefore, the concept of integer division with remainder is needed. However, we are not always able to divide some integer $z \in \mathbb{Z}$ by a natural number $n \in \mathbb{N}$, but the remainder is exactly determined. Let

$$\lfloor . \rfloor : \mathbb{R} \to \mathbb{Z},\ x \mapsto \lfloor x \rfloor := \max\{q \in \mathbb{Z};\ q \leq x\}$$

be the *floor function*, i.e., $\lfloor \frac{22}{7} \rfloor = 3$ and $\lfloor -\frac{22}{7} \rfloor = -4$.

Theorem 1.2 (Division with remainder in $\mathbb{Z}$). *Let $z \in \mathbb{Z}$ and $n \in \mathbb{N}$. Then, there are determined numbers $q \in \mathbb{Z}$ and $r \in \{0, 1, \ldots, n-1\}$ satisfying*

$$z = q \cdot n + r.$$

In this situation, q is the quotient and r is the remainder of dividing z by n.

---

[2]The term is discussed in Convention 2.24.
[3]Arthur Cayley (1821–1895).
[4]According to the Examples 3.12 and 3.16.

Proof. Existence: let $q := \lfloor z/n \rfloor \in \mathbb{Z}$ and $r := z - q \cdot n \in \mathbb{Z}$. As $q \leq z/n < q+1$,

$$\begin{aligned} q \leq z/n < q+1 &\Leftrightarrow q \cdot n \leq z < q \cdot n + n \\ &\Leftrightarrow 0 \leq \underbrace{z - q \cdot n}_{r} < n \end{aligned}$$

and hence $0 \leq r < n$. Therefore, $z = q \cdot n + r$.

Uniqueness: it is $0 \leq r/n = z/n - q < 1$ and thereby $z/n - 1 < q \leq z/n$, yielding the uniqueness of q. □

Similarly, the remainder[5] r from dividing z by n (manner of speaking: remainder *modulo* n) is unique and denoted by

$$r = z \bmod n.$$

The natural number n is called the *modulus*. We can define a mapping

$$\rho_n : \mathbb{Z} \to \{0, \ldots, n-1\}, \; z = q \cdot n + r \mapsto r := z \bmod n, \tag{1.1}$$

in order to express this process.

Example 1.3. $n = 7$:

z	$q \cdot n + r$	$\rho_n(z)$
$-22 =$	$(-4) \cdot 7 + 6$	6
$-14 =$	$(-2) \cdot 7 + 0$	0
$0 =$	$0 \cdot 7 + 0$	0
$1 =$	$0 \cdot 7 + 1$	1
$9 =$	$1 \cdot 7 + 2$	2
$23 =$	$3 \cdot 7 + 2$	2

Remark 1.4. n is easily chosen from $\mathbb{Z} \backslash \{0\}$ in Theorem 1.2. If $n < 0$, we just have to work with $|n| = -n$, and finally, $-q$ is used instead of q. For example, $9 = (-1) \cdot (-7) + 2$ or $-14 = 2 \cdot (-7)$. In terms of denoting a remainder modulo n, this n must be a natural number.

[5] Alternatively, the remainder is called residue, e.g., in (Dixon *et al.*, 2010).

In the case of two positive integers, the following simple algorithm is used:

Algorithm 1.1: Division algorithm for positive integers

Require: Positive integers $z, n \in \mathbb{N}$.
Ensure: $q \in \mathbb{N}$ and $r \in \{0, \ldots, n-1\}$ with $z = q \cdot n + r$.

$q := 0$, $r := z$.
while $r \geq n$ **do**
  $r := r - n$.
  $q := q + 1$.
end while
return (q, r).

If the remainder r is zero, $z = q \cdot n$. This special case is important and has its own term.

Definition 1.5 (Divisor and multiple). Let $a, z \in \mathbb{Z}$. We denote

$$a \mid z \;:\Longleftrightarrow\; \exists q \in \mathbb{Z} : z = q \cdot a.$$

as "a divides z". In doing so, a is called a *divisor* of z and z is a *multiple* of a.

In the event that a is not a divisor of z, we denote $a \nmid n$. All divisors of $z \in \mathbb{Z}$ that are natural numbers are collected as

$$D_z := \{a \in \mathbb{N};\ a \mid z\}.$$

For any D_z, $1 \in D_z$, because for any $z \in \mathbb{Z}$ the simple equation $z = z \cdot 1$ is valid, thus $1 \mid z$. Moreover, every $z \in \mathbb{Z}\backslash\{0\}$ divides itself due to $z = 1 \cdot z = \pm 1 \cdot\ |z|$. Hence, the corresponding D_z contains at least the elements 1 and $|z|$, and D_z is a finite set because from $a \mid z$, $z = q \cdot a$ for some $q \in \mathbb{Z}$ and $1 \leq a \leq z$. A special case is $D_0 = \mathbb{N}$ because $0 = 0 \cdot a$ for all $a \in \mathbb{N}$.

Example 1.6.

$$60 = 1 \cdot 60 = 2 \cdot 30 = 3 \cdot 20 = 4 \cdot 15 = 5 \cdot 12 = 6 \cdot 10$$
$$\Rightarrow D_{60} = \{1, 2, 3, 4, 5, 6, 10, 12, 15, 20, 30, 60\}.$$

Two or more numbers $z_1, \ldots, z_k \in \mathbb{Z}\backslash\{0\}$ that are different from zero have at least one divisor in common, 1. The set of *common divisors* is determined by

$$D_{z_1} \cap D_{z_2} \cap \ldots \cap D_{z_k}.$$

Due to the finite number of elements in the sets D_{z_i}, there always exists a largest number.

Definition 1.7 (Greatest common divisor). Let $z_1, \ldots, z_k \in \mathbb{Z}$. Then, the value

$$\mathrm{GCD}(z_1, \ldots, z_k) := \begin{cases} \max D_{z_1} \cap \ldots \cap D_{z_k}, & \text{at least one } z_i \neq 0, \\ 0, & \text{all } z_i = 0, \end{cases}$$

based on a mapping $\mathrm{GCD} : \mathbb{Z}^k \to \mathbb{N}_0$ is called the *greatest common divisor* of $z_1, \ldots, z_k$. If $\mathrm{GCD}(z_1, z_2) = 1$, then z_1 and z_2 are called *relatively prime* numbers.

Let

$$\mathcal{L}(z_1, \ldots, z_k) := \{\lambda_1 \cdot z_1 + \ldots + \lambda_k \cdot z_k;\ \lambda_i \in \mathbb{Z} \text{ for all } i = 1, \ldots, k\} \tag{1.2}$$

be the set of integer linear combinations of integers $z_1, \ldots, z_k \in \mathbb{Z}\backslash\{0\}$. $\mathcal{L}(z_1, \ldots, z_k)$ is a subset of $\mathbb{Z}$ that contains $\pm z_i$ and thus, it has a smallest positive element, for example, $d = \mu_1 \cdot z_1 + \ldots + \mu_k \cdot z_k$. If $t \in \mathbb{N}$ is a common divisor of $z_1, \ldots, z_k$, $z_1 = q_1 \cdot t, \ldots, z_k = q_k \cdot t$, then t is a divisor of d because

$$\begin{aligned} d &= \mu_1 \cdot z_1 + \ldots + \mu_k \cdot z_k = \mu_1 \cdot (q_1 \cdot t) + \ldots + \mu_k \cdot (q_k \cdot t) \\ &= (\mu_1 \cdot q_1 + \ldots + \mu_k \cdot q_k) \cdot t. \end{aligned}$$

Suppose d is not a divisor of z_1. Then $z_1 = q \cdot d + r$, $r \in \{1, \ldots, d-1\}$ and

$$\begin{aligned} r = z_1 - q \cdot d &= z_1 - q \cdot (\mu_1 \cdot z_1 + \ldots + \mu_k \cdot z_k) \\ &= (1 - q \cdot \mu_1) \cdot z_1 + (-q \cdot \mu_2) \cdot z_2 \\ &\quad + \ldots + (-q \cdot \mu_k) \cdot z_k \in \mathcal{L}(z_1, \ldots, z_k). \end{aligned}$$

However, the positive integer r would be smaller than d, contrary to the assumption of d being the smallest in $\mathcal{L}(z_1, \ldots, z_k)$. Therefore, $d \mid z_1$. By passing the role of z_1 serially to the remaining z_i's, d divides $z_2, \ldots, z_k$. Hence, d is a common divisor of $z_1, \ldots, z_k$. Since all common divisors of $z_1, \ldots, z_k$ are divisors of d, d is the unique greatest common divisor of $z_1, \ldots, z_k$.

Example 1.8.

$$\begin{aligned} D_{14} = \{1, 2, 7, 14\},\ D_{49} = \{1, 7, 49\} &\Rightarrow D_{14} \cap D_{49} = \{1, 7\}, \\ &\Rightarrow \text{GCD}(14, 49) = 7, \\ \mathbf{1} = -5 \cdot 11 + 4 \cdot 14 &\Rightarrow \text{GCD}(11, 14) = 1, \\ \mathcal{L}(10, 15, 20) = \{\ldots, -10, -5, 0, \mathbf{5}, 10, \ldots\} &\Rightarrow \text{GCD}(10, 15, 20) = 5. \end{aligned}$$

Since $d \in \mathcal{L}(z_1, \ldots, z_k)$ and $d = \mu_1 \cdot z_1 + \ldots + \mu_k \cdot z_k$, any multiple $u \cdot d = (u \cdot \mu_1) \cdot z_1 + \ldots + (u \cdot \mu_k) \cdot z_k$ of d also belongs to $\mathcal{L}(z_1, \ldots, z_k)$. Alternatively, every $k \in \mathcal{L}(z_1, \ldots, z_k)$ belongs to $\mathcal{L}(d)$ because $k = \lambda_1 \cdot z_1 + \ldots + \lambda_k \cdot z_k = (\lambda_1 \cdot \mu_1) \cdot d + \ldots + (\lambda_k \cdot \mu_k) \cdot d = (\lambda_1 \cdot \mu_1 + \ldots + \lambda_k \cdot \mu_k) \cdot d$. Together, $\mathcal{L}(d) = \mathcal{L}(z_1, \ldots, z_k)$.

Corollary 1.9. *If* $d = GCD(z_1, \ldots, z_k)$, *then*

$$\mathcal{L}(d) = \mathcal{L}(z_1, \ldots, z_k).$$

Given $z_1, z_2, z_3 \in \mathbb{Z}$, suppose $z_1 \mid z_2 \cdot z_3$, that is $z_2 \cdot z_3 = \lambda_1 \cdot z_1$. Let $d = \text{GCD}(z_1, z_2) = 1$. Then

$$\begin{aligned} z_3 = z_3 \cdot 1 = z_3 \cdot d &= z_3 \cdot (\mu_1 \cdot z_1 + \mu_2 \cdot z_2) \\ &= (z_3 \cdot \mu_1) \cdot z_1 + (\mu_2 \cdot \lambda_1) \cdot z_1 = (z_3 \cdot \mu_1 + \mu_2 \cdot \lambda_1) \cdot z_1 \Rightarrow z_1 | z_3. \end{aligned}$$

Corollary 1.10. *Given $z_1, z_2, z_3 \in \mathbb{Z}$, suppose $z_1 \mid z_2 \cdot z_3$. If z_1 and z_2 are relatively prime numbers, then $z_1 \mid z_3$.*

Example 1.11.

$$\begin{array}{ll} 11 \mid 308 = 14 \cdot 22,\ \mathrm{GCD}(11, 14) = 1 & \Rightarrow 11 \mid 22 \\ 14 \mid 98 = 49 \cdot 2, \quad 14 \nmid 2 & \Rightarrow \mathrm{GCD}(14, 49) \neq 1 \end{array}$$

The integers $z_1, \ldots, z_k \in \mathbb{Z}\backslash\{0\}$ possess at least one positive common multiple, in particular $z_1 \cdot \ldots \cdot z_k$, where each of the sets $\mathcal{L}(z_i)$ contains $z_1 \cdot \ldots \cdot z_k$. The intersection $\mathcal{L}(z_1) \cap \ldots \cap \mathcal{L}(z_k)$ contains all common multiples of $z_1, \ldots, z_k$.

Definition 1.12 (Least common multiple). Let $z_1, \ldots, z_k \in \mathbb{Z}\backslash\{0\}$ be k non-zero integers. Then, with $U := \mathcal{L}(z_1) \cap \ldots \cap \mathcal{L}(z_k)$, the value

$$\mathrm{LCM}(z_1, \ldots, z_k) := \min \mathbb{N} \cap U$$

is called the *least common multiple* of $z_1, \ldots, z_k$.

Let $v = \mathrm{LCM}(z_1, \ldots, z_k)$, $v = \nu_j \cdot z_j$ for some $\nu_j \in \mathbb{Z}$. Then, $u \cdot v = (u \cdot \nu_j) \cdot z_j \in \mathcal{L}(z_j)$ for $u \in \mathbb{Z}$. Thus, $\mathcal{L}(v) \subseteq U$. Alternatively, from Theorem 1.2 there is a $q \in \mathbb{Z}$ satisfying $0 \leq k - q \cdot v < v$ for any $k \in U$. But we know that $k \in U$ and $q \cdot v \in U$, such that $k - q \cdot v \in U$. Since v is the smallest positive element of U, we obtain $k - q \cdot v = 0$ and $U \subseteq \mathcal{L}(v)$. Together, $U = \mathcal{L}(v)$.

Corollary 1.13. *If $v = LCM(z_1, \ldots, z_k)$, then*

$$\mathcal{L}(v) = \mathcal{L}(z_1) \cap \ldots \cap \mathcal{L}(z_k).$$

Example 1.14.

$$\begin{aligned} \mathrm{LCM}(14, 49) &= \min\{14, 28, 42, 56, 70, 84, 98, \ldots\} \cap \{49, 98, \ldots\} \\ &= 98, \\ \mathrm{LCM}(15, 20) &= \min\{15, 30, 45, 60, \ldots\} \cap \{20, 40, 60, \ldots\} = 60. \end{aligned}$$

Let $z_1, z_2 \in \mathbb{Z}\backslash\{0\}$ be integers and $d = \mathrm{GCD}(z_1, z_2)$, $d = \mu_1 z_1 + \mu_2 z_2$, $z_1 = q_1 d$, $z_2 = q_2 d$ and $v = \mathrm{LCM}(z_1, z_2)$, $v = \nu_1 z_1 = \nu_2 z_2$. Then,

$$z_1 \mid z_1 q_2 = q_1 d q_2,\ z_2 \mid z_2 q_1 = q_2 d q_1 \Rightarrow v \mid q_1 d q_2$$

because each common multiple of z_1 and z_2 is divided by v. It follows

$$dv \mid dq_1 dq_2 = z_1 z_2 \Rightarrow z_1 z_2 = m_1(dv),\ m_1 \in \mathbb{Z}.$$

Alternatively,

$$\begin{aligned} dv &= (\mu_1 z_1 + \mu_2 z_2)v = \mu_1 z_1 \nu_2 z_2 + \mu_2 z_2 \nu_1 z_1 \\ &= \underbrace{(\mu_1 \nu_2 + \mu_2 \nu_1)}_{m_2 \in \mathbb{Z}} z_1 z_2 \Rightarrow z_1 z_2 \mid dv. \end{aligned}$$

Thus,

$$dv = m_2(z_1 z_2) = m_2 m_1 (dv) \Rightarrow m_1 m_2 = 1.$$

Either $m_1 = m_2 = 1$ or $m_1 = m_2 = -1$.

Corollary 1.15. *Given $z_1, z_2 \in \mathbb{Z}\backslash\{0\}$, then*

$$GCD(z_1, z_2) \cdot LCM(z_1, z_2) = |z_1 z_2|.$$

Example 1.16. Look at LCM(14, 49) and LCM(15, 20) again:

$$\mathrm{LCM}(14, 49) = \frac{14 \cdot 49}{\mathrm{GCD}(14, 49)} = \frac{14 \cdot 49}{7} = 98,$$

$$\mathrm{LCM}(15, 20) = \frac{15 \cdot 20}{\mathrm{GCD}(15, 20)} = \frac{15 \cdot 20}{5} = 60.$$

1.1.2 *Prime numbers*

There are natural numbers possessing special properties that are useful for cryptosystems. These numbers occur in almost every modern cryptography technique.

Definition 1.17 (Prime number). A natural number $n \in \mathbb{N}$ is called a *prime number* or *prime* if $|D_n| = 2$. Such a number is denoted by p. If $n \in \mathbb{N}$ is not prime, then n is a *composite number*.

Remark 1.18.

(1) 1 is not a prime number due to $D_1 = \{1\}$ and $|D_1| = 1 \neq 2$.
(2) A divisor of n that is a prime number at the same time, is called a *prime divisor*.

Example 1.19. For $n = 120$,

$$D_{120} = \{1, 2, 3, 4, 5, 6, 8, 10, 12, 15, 20, 24, 30, 40, 60, 120\}.$$

In this case, the numbers 2, 3 and 5 are prime divisors.

Another example is $D_7 = \{1, 7\}$, where 7 is a prime number.

Remark 1.20. For p prime, $\mathrm{GCD}(a, p) = 1$ for all $a \in \{1, \ldots, p - 1\}$ and $\mathrm{GCD}(0, p) = p$.

Let a prime number p be a divisor of $a \cdot b$, $a, b \in \mathbb{Z}$. If $p \nmid a$, then a and p are relatively prime numbers and based on Corollary 1.10, $p \mid b$. Analogously, from $p \nmid b$, $p \mid a$.

Corollary 1.21. *Given $a, b \in \mathbb{Z}$ and p prime, suppose $p \mid a \cdot b$. Then $p \mid a$ or $p \mid b$.*

Example 1.22.

$$\begin{aligned}
&11 \mid 308 = 14 \cdot 22 \\
&11 \text{ prime} && \Rightarrow 11 \mid 14 \text{ or } 11 \mid 22 \\
&5 \nmid 11 \text{ and } 5 \nmid 14 && \Rightarrow 5 \nmid 154 = 11 \cdot 14
\end{aligned}$$

It is true that $1, n \in D_n$. Let $S = D_n \backslash \{1\}$. The smallest element $p \in S$ is prime because each positive divisor a of p, $p = q_2 \cdot a$, is a divisor of n: $n = q_1 \cdot p = (q_1 \cdot q_2) \cdot a$. However, the positive divisors of p are 1 and p.

Corollary 1.23. *Every $n \in \mathbb{N}$, where $n > 1$, has a prime divisor.*

A particular sequence $(a_n)_{n\in\mathbb{N}_0}$,

$$a_n = \frac{4^n - 1}{3}, \; n \in \mathbb{N}_0. \tag{1.3}$$

The first ten members of $(a_n)_{n\in\mathbb{N}_0}$ are

$$0, 1, 5, 21, 85, 341, 1365, 5461, 21845, 87381.$$

In preparation, we need to know the geometric progression

$$s_n = \sum_{i=0}^{n} x^i = \frac{x^{n+1} - 1}{x - 1}, \; x \in \mathbb{R}\backslash\{1\}, \tag{1.4}$$

which is valid from

$$\begin{aligned} s_n + x^{n+1} &= \sum_{i=0}^{n+1} x^i = x^0 + \sum_{i=1}^{n+1} x^i = 1 + \sum_{i=0}^{n} x^{i+1} \\ &= 1 + x \cdot \sum_{i=0}^{n} x^i = 1 + x \cdot s_n. \end{aligned}$$

Let $x = 4$, then

$$\begin{aligned} 1 + 4 + 16 + \ldots + 4^{n-1} &= \sum_{i=0}^{n-1} 4^i \overset{(1.4)}{=} \frac{4^n - 1}{3} = a_n \in \mathbb{N}_0 \\ &\Leftrightarrow 3 \mid 4^n - 1 = 2^{2n} - 1 = (2^n - 1) \cdot (2^n + 1). \end{aligned}$$

From Corollary 1.21, $3 \mid 2^n - 1$ or $3 \mid 2^n + 1$. If $n = 2k$, $k \in \mathbb{N}_0$, is an even non-negative integer and $3 \mid 4^k - 1$,

$$\begin{aligned} 3 &\mid 4^k - 1 = 2^{2k} - 1 = 2^n - 1 \\ &\Rightarrow a_n = \underbrace{\frac{2^n - 1}{3}}_{\in\mathbb{N}_0} \cdot (2^n + 1). \end{aligned}$$

Alternatively, if $n = 2k+1$, $k \in \mathbb{N}_0$, is an odd positive number, and $3 \mid 4^k - 1$,

$$2^n + 1 = 2^{2k+1} + 1 = 2 \cdot 2^{2k} + 1 = 2 \cdot 4^k - 2 + 2 + 1 = 2 \cdot (4^k - 1) + 3$$

where the relation $3 \mid 2^n + 1$ and hence

$$a_n = (2^n - 1) \cdot \underbrace{\frac{2^n + 1}{3}}_{\in \mathbb{N}_0}.$$

Overall, a_n is a composite number for $n > 2$.

Corollary 1.24. *Let $n \in \mathbb{N}_0$, $n > 2$. Then, $a_n = \frac{4^n - 1}{3}$ is not prime.*

Finally, the third to tenth members of $(a_n)_{n \in \mathbb{N}_0}$ can be written as

$$21 = 7 \cdot 3, 85 = 5 \cdot 17, 341 = 31 \cdot 11, 1365 = 21 \cdot 65,$$
$$5461 = 127 \cdot 43, 21845 = 85 \cdot 257, 87381 = 511 \cdot 171.$$

We will refer to this sequence in Section 11.1. Euclid[6] was the first to examine the amount of primes.

Theorem 1.25 (Euclid's theorem). *There are infinitely many prime numbers.*

Proof. Suppose there is a finite number of prime numbers $p_1, \ldots, p_n$. Let z be the product of all these prime numbers plus one,

$$z = p_1 \cdot \ldots \cdot p_n + 1 > \max\{p_1, \ldots, p_n\}.$$

z cannot be prime, which would contradict the proof's origin. From Corollary 1.23, there has to be a prime divisor of z. Assume $p_i \mid z$ for any $i = 1, \ldots, n$. But for each p_i, it applies

$$z - 1 = p_i \cdot \prod_{j \neq i} p_j, \; p_i \mid z - 1 \Rightarrow p_i \mid z - (z - 1) = 1.$$

[6]Euclid of Alexandria (about 300 BC).

Thus, p_i is a divisor of 1 and is not a prime number. Because of Corollary 1.23 there has to be another divisor that is a prime number. However, this would contradict the previous assumption. □

Example 1.26.

$2 \cdot 3 \cdot 5 \cdot 7 + 1 = 211$ (prime)
$2 \cdot 3 \cdot 5 \cdot 7 \cdot 11 + 1 = 2311$ (prime)
$2 \cdot 3 \cdot 5 \cdot 7 \cdot 11 \cdot 13 + 1 = 30031 = 59 \cdot 509$ (composite number)

An old method can be used to find primes smaller than a given $n \in \mathbb{N}$. The sieve of Eratosthenes[7] is a very simple algorithm. Firstly, all integers smaller than n are written, beginning with 2, and some integers will be removed. Therefore, starting at the first non-crossed out element m of the list, all of its multiples $k \cdot m$, $k = 1, \ldots, \lfloor \frac{n}{m} \rfloor$, are crossed out and this step is repeated until we reach an element m that satisfies $m^2 > n$. The remaining elements are primes.

Example 1.27 (Sieve of Erathostenes).

$$n = 27.$$

The following steps are performed:

2 3 4 5 6 7 8 9 10 11 12 13 14 15 16 17 18 19 20 21 22 23 24 25 26 27
2 : 2 3 ~~4~~ 5 ~~6~~ 7 ~~8~~ 9 ~~10~~ 11 ~~12~~ 13 ~~14~~ 15 ~~16~~ 17 ~~18~~ 19 ~~20~~ 21 ~~22~~ 23 ~~24~~ 25 ~~26~~ 27
3 : 2 3 ~~4~~ 5 ~~6~~ 7 ~~8~~ ~~9~~ ~~10~~ 11 ~~12~~ 13 ~~14~~ ~~15~~ ~~16~~ 17 ~~18~~ 19 ~~20~~ ~~21~~ ~~22~~ 23 ~~24~~ 25 ~~26~~ ~~27~~
5 : 2 3 ~~4~~ 5 ~~6~~ 7 ~~8~~ ~~9~~ ~~10~~ 11 ~~12~~ 13 ~~14~~ ~~15~~ ~~16~~ 17 ~~18~~ 19 ~~20~~ ~~21~~ ~~22~~ 23 ~~24~~ ~~25~~ ~~26~~ ~~27~~

Since $7^2 = 49 > 27$, the sieving process stops here and the remaining numbers $2, 3, 5, 7, 11, 13, 17, 19$ and 23 are primes.

A very interesting but hard to prove[8] result yields the *prime number theorem* that produces an estimate about the asymptotic distribution of the prime numbers among the positive integers.

[7] Eratosthenes of Cyrene (276 BC–*c.* 195/194 BC).
[8] See (Hardy *et al.*, 2008) for a detailed derivation of the proof.

Theorem 1.28 (Prime number theorem). *Let* $\pi(n)$ *be the number of primes smaller or equal to some* $n \in \mathbb{N}$. *For any arbitrarily small* $\epsilon > 0$ *and any corresponding large enough* n, *it applies that*

$$(1-\epsilon) \cdot \frac{n}{\ln(n)} \leq \pi(n) \leq (1+\epsilon) \cdot \frac{n}{\ln(n)}.$$

In other words: $\lim_{n\to\infty} \frac{\pi(n)}{n/\ln(n)} = 1$.

Every positive number greater than one can be written as a product of prime numbers. This is called *factorization* or *decomposition* of a number into prime factors.

Theorem 1.29 (Fundamental theorem of arithmetic). *For any positive integer* $n > 1$, *there exist prime numbers* $p_1, \ldots, p_s$ *satisfying* $n = 1 \cdot p_1 \cdot \ldots \cdot p_s$. *This representation is unique, except for its order.*

Proof. We can prove the existence by induction on n.

Basis: $n = 2$: $2 = 1 \cdot 2$.
Induction hypothesis: the statement applies for $n - 1$.
Induction step: the smallest divisor greater than 1 of n is a prime divisor according to Corollary 1.23. If $n/p = 1$, then $D_n = \{1, p\}$, and because p is prime, the statement is correct. If $f := n/p > 1$, it follows from the induction hypothesis ($f \leq n-1$) that f is a product of prime numbers. This ensures its existence.

For the uniqueness, assume

$$n = p_1 \cdot \ldots \cdot p_s \text{ and } n = q_1 \cdot \ldots \cdot q_t$$

to be different factorizations of n into prime divisors satisfying p_i, q_j prime for all $i = 1, \ldots, s$ and $j = 1, \ldots, t$. The statement is that p_1 is equal to one of the prime divisors $q_1, \ldots, q_t$. We prove this by induction on the number t of prime divisors.

Basis: $t = 1$ is clear since $p_1 \mid n = q_1$ and p_1, q_1 are prime.
Induction hypothesis: the statement applies for $t - 1$.

Induction step: it applies $p_1 \mid n = q_1 \cdot \ldots \cdot q_t$. By using brackets we have $p_1 | q_1 \cdot (q_2 \cdot \ldots \cdot q_t)$. From Corollary 1.21, $p_1 | q_1$ or $p_1 | q_2 \cdot \ldots \cdot q_t$. In the first case, the statement is verified since p_1, q_1 are prime. In the second case, we know that p_1 is a prime divisor of $m = q_2 \cdot \ldots \cdot q_t$ and m can be factorized by $t-1$ prime divisors. Hence, the induction hypothesis takes effect and p_1 is equal to one of the prime divisors $q_2, \ldots, q_t$.

Renumbering results in $p_1 = q_1$ and looking at n/p_1, or rather n/q_1, the induction hypothesis takes effect again. Now, it is $s = t$, or rather $p_i = q_i$, for all $i = 1, \ldots, s$ after renumbering. The factorization into prime numbers is unique, except for order. □

Any $z \in \mathbb{Z}\backslash\{0\}$ can be factorized by first factorizing $|z|$ and then, if $z < 0$, multiplying the product by -1. Calculating a factorization is difficult and will be addressed in Section 7.2.3. Summarizing the same prime divisors we obtain the representation

$$n = p_1^{\alpha_1} \cdot p_2^{\alpha_2} \cdot \ldots \cdot p_k^{\alpha_k}, \tag{1.5}$$

and n is said to be decomposed or factorized into prime factors. The set of all natural divisors of n can be written as

$$D_n = \{p_1^{\gamma_1} \cdot \ldots \cdot p_k^{\gamma_k};\ 0 \le \gamma_i \le \alpha_i,\ 1 \le i \le k\},\ |D_n| = \prod_{i=1}^{k} (\alpha_i + 1).$$

Example 1.30.

$$120 = 2^3 \cdot 3 \cdot 5 \Rightarrow |D_{120}| = 4 \cdot 2 \cdot 2 = 16.$$

There is a connection between the factorization of each of two (or any) numbers and their GCD and LCM. Let

$$\begin{aligned} a &= q_1^{r_1} \cdot q_2^{r_2} \cdot \ldots \cdot q_k^{r_k}, \\ b &= u_1^{s_1} \cdot u_2^{s_2} \cdot \ldots \cdot u_l^{s_l}. \end{aligned}$$

be factorized into prime divisors. We suppose that the sign of a and b is undiscriminatingly positive. Furthermore, let

$$D = \{p_1, \ldots, p_m\} = \{q_1, \ldots, q_k\} \cup \{u_1, \ldots, u_l\}$$

be the set of all prime divisors of a and b. If we look at

$$\begin{aligned} a &= p_1^{\alpha_1} \cdot \ldots \cdot p_m^{\alpha_m}, \\ b &= p_1^{\beta_1} \cdot \ldots \cdot p_m^{\beta_m}, \\ a \cdot b &= p_1^{\alpha_1+\beta_1} \cdot p_m^{\alpha_m+\beta_m}, \quad (\alpha_j, \beta_j \text{ could be zero}), \end{aligned}$$

then with $\gamma_j \leq \min\{\alpha_j, \beta_j\}$,

$$p_1^{\gamma_1} \cdot \ldots \cdot p_m^{\gamma_m} \mid a, b.$$

Since

$$d = p_1^{\min\{\alpha_1,\beta_1\}} \cdot \ldots \cdot p_m^{\min\{\alpha_m,\beta_m\}} \mid a, b$$

is also a divisor of a and b and is even the largest, $d = \mathrm{GCD}(a, b)$. Because of Corollary 1.15, $\mathrm{GCD}(a, b) \cdot \mathrm{LCM}(a, b) = a \cdot b$, and since $\min\{\alpha_j, \beta_j\} + \max\{\alpha_j, \beta_j\} = \alpha_j + \beta_j$,

$$p_1^{\min\{\alpha_1,\beta_1\}} \cdot \ldots \cdot p_m^{\min\{\alpha_m,\beta_m\}} \cdot p_1^{\max\{\alpha_1,\beta_1\}} \cdot \ldots \cdot p_m^{\max\{\alpha_m,\beta_m\}} = a \cdot b.$$

Corollary 1.31. *Let $a, b \in \mathbb{Z} \backslash \{0\}$ be factorized into prime numbers. Then,*

$$\underbrace{\prod_{j=1}^{m} p_j^{\min\{\alpha_j,\beta_j\}}}_{GCD(a,b)} \cdot \underbrace{\prod_{j=1}^{m} p_j^{\max\{\alpha_j,\beta_j\}}}_{LCM(a,b)} = |a \cdot b|.$$

Example 1.32.

$$15 = 3 \cdot 5, \ 20 = 2^2 \cdot 5 \Rightarrow D = \{2, 3, 5\}, \ \gamma_1 = \gamma_2 = 0, \gamma_3 = 1.$$

$\mathrm{GCD}(15, 20) = 2^0 \cdot 3^0 \cdot 5^1 = 5$ and $\mathrm{LCM}(15, 20) = 2^2 \cdot 3^1 \cdot 5^1 = 60$ and

$$(2^0 \cdot 3^0 \cdot 5^1) \cdot (2^2 \cdot 3^1 \cdot 5^1) = 300 = 15 \cdot 20.$$

1.2 Basic Concepts of Probability Theory

This section addresses *probability spaces*,[9] wherein a triple $(\Omega, \mathcal{F}, \mathbb{P})$ consisting of three integral parts that models an experiment containing non-deterministic elements.

1.2.1 *Probability spaces*

Experiments

- that are carried out according to predetermined rules,
- can be repeated as often as needed in theory, and
- whose output cannot be predicted,

are called *random experiments*. Thereby, Ω is the *sample space*, the non-empty set of possible outcomes of an experiment. $\mathcal{F}$ is a *set of events* and each event is a set of possible outcomes. Lastly, $\mathbb{P}$ is a mapping $\mathbb{P} : \mathcal{F} \to [0, 1]$ that maps a value between 0 and 1 to each event, the *probability measure*. Each member of Ω is called a *simple event*. An *event* is a set $A \subseteq \Omega$ that occurs if the outcome ω of the random experiment is a member of A, $\omega \in A$. The set of events is composed of all needed events. A commonly used example is the power set of Ω. The security of the occurrence of events needs to be assessed, which can be done by a mapping $\mathbb{P} : \mathcal{F} \to [0, 1]$ fulfilling the following properties:

- $\mathbb{P}(\emptyset) = 0$, $\mathbb{P}(\Omega) = 1$, $\mathbb{P}(A) \geq 0$,
- $1 = \mathbb{P}(\Omega) = \mathbb{P}(A \cup \bar{A}) = \mathbb{P}(A) + \mathbb{P}(\bar{A})$, $\bar{A} = \Omega \backslash A$,
- $\mathbb{P}(A \cup B) = \mathbb{P}(A) + \mathbb{P}(B)$ for $A \cap B = \emptyset$ and
- $\mathbb{P}\left(\bigcup_{i \in \mathbb{N}} A_i\right) = \sum_{i \in \mathbb{N}} \mathbb{P}(A_i)$ for mutually disjoint A_i.
- If $B \subseteq A$, $\mathbb{P}(B) \leq \mathbb{P}(A)$, which already follows from $\mathbb{P}(A) = \mathbb{P}(B \cup (A \backslash B)) = \mathbb{P}(B) + \mathbb{P}(A \backslash B)$.

Every mapping applying these properties assigns events to a *probability*. Unfortunately, the power set $\mathcal{P}(\mathbb{R})$ is not a valid set of events for the important standard case $\Omega = \mathbb{R}$. Therefore, no such mapping

[9]The presentation here is quite brief. For an extended introduction into probability theory see (Ross, 2014) or (Applebaum, 2008).

$\mathbb{P} : \mathcal{P}(\mathbb{R}) \to [0, 1]$ exists. However, the idea of such a mapping remains applicable and the required properties are plausible. The set of events $\mathcal{F}$ must be reduced such that all other considerations are remaining. A suitable set of events is the so-called σ-field.

Definition 1.33 (σ-field). A system of sets $\mathcal{F} \subseteq \mathcal{P}(\Omega)$ consisting of subsets of the sample space Ω is called a *σ-field* on Ω if it meets the following properties:

- $\Omega \in \mathcal{F}$,
- $\bar{A} \in \mathcal{F}$ for all $A \in \mathcal{F}$, and
- $\bigcup_{i \in \mathbb{N}} A_i \in \mathcal{F}$ for all $A_i \in \mathcal{F}$.

Every σ-field is a set of events. Based on a σ-field we can define a mapping that assigns events to probabilities.

Definition 1.34 (Probability mass function). Let $\mathcal{F}$ be a σ-field on a sample space Ω. A mapping $\mathbb{P} : \mathcal{F} \to \mathbb{R}$, which assigns a probability to every $A \in \mathcal{F}$, is called a *probability mass function* if it meets the following properties:

- $\mathbb{P}(A) \geq 0$ for all $A \in \mathcal{F}$,
- $\mathbb{P}(\Omega) = 1$ and
- $\mathbb{P}\left(\bigcup_{i \in \mathbb{N}} A_i\right) = \sum_{i \in \mathbb{N}} \mathbb{P}(A_i)$ for mutually disjoint A_i.

The axiomatic probability theory comes from Kolmogorow.[10] We modeled a random experiment by establishing the three mentioned building blocks $(\Omega, \mathcal{F}, \mathbb{P})$,

- Ω is a sample space,
- $\mathcal{F}$ is a σ-field on Ω and
- $\mathbb{P}$ is a probability mass function on $\mathcal{F}$.

If there is an at most countable set $T \in \mathcal{F}$ with $\mathbb{P}(T) = 1$, then T is called the *support* of $\mathbb{P}$ and the probability space is called

[10] Andrei Nikolajewitsch Kolmogorow (1903–1985).

discrete. Otherwise, it is called *continuous*. The pair $(\Omega, \mathcal{F})$ is called a *measurable space*. By a mapping $f : T \to [0,1]$ with $\mathbb{P}(\{\omega\}) = f(\omega)$, $\sum_{\omega \in T} f(\omega) = 1$, the discrete probability mass function is fully characterized. Considering that $\mathbb{P}(A) = \sum_{\omega \in A} f(\omega)$ for all subsets $A \subseteq T$, f is a *discrete density*.

1.2.2 *Conditional probabilities*

Let $(\Omega, \mathcal{F}, \mathbb{P})$ be a probability space and $(\Psi, \mathcal{P}(\Psi))$ a measurable space. A measurable mapping $X : \Omega \to \Psi$, i.e., $X^{-1}(A) \in \mathcal{F}$ for all $A \in \mathcal{P}(\Psi)$, is called a *random variable*. Consider now Ω and Ψ being at most countable. The probability that the so-called discrete random variable X takes on the value $x \in \Psi$ is denoted by

$$\mathbb{P}(X = x) := \mathbb{P}_X(\{x\}) := \mathbb{P}(X^{-1}(\{x\})) = \mathbb{P}(\underbrace{\{\omega \in \Omega;\ X(\omega) = x\}}_{\text{this is an event from } \mathcal{F}}), \tag{1.6}$$

in which $\mathbb{P}_X : \mathcal{P}(\Psi) \to [0,1]$ is the *pushforward measure*. We denote the *probability mass function* of X by $p_X : \Psi \to [0,1]$, $p_X(x) := \mathbb{P}(X = x)$. In the same way, for any $M \in \mathcal{P}(\Psi)$

$$\mathbb{P}(X \in M) := \mathbb{P}_X(M) = \mathbb{P}(\{\omega \in \Omega;\ X(\omega) \in M\}).$$

Since M is an at most countable set, we can calculate

$$\mathbb{P}(X \in M) = \mathbb{P}_X(M) = \sum_{m \in M} \mathbb{P}_X(\{m\}).$$

Now, let $X_i : \Omega \to \Psi_i$, $i = 1, \ldots, n$, be discrete random variables. Then, the *joint probability distribution* of $X_1, \ldots, X_n$ is defined by

$$\mathbb{P}_{X_1,\ldots,X_n}(\{(x_1, \ldots, x_n)\}) := \mathbb{P}((X_1 = x_1) \cap \ldots \cap (X_n = x_n)).$$

Therefore, the function value is the probability that $X_1(\omega) = x_1$ and $X_2(\omega) = x_2$ and ... and $X_n(\omega) = x_n$. The probability mass function is abbreviated as $p_{X_1,\ldots,X_n}(x_1, \ldots, x_n)$. By adding up all the values of Ψ_i, it follows

$$\sum_{x_i \in \Psi_i} \mathbb{P}_{X_1,\dots,X_n}(\{(x_1,\dots,x_n)\})$$
$$= \mathbb{P}_{X_1,\dots,X_{i-1},X_{i+1},\dots,X_n}(\{(x_1,\dots,x_{i-1},x_{i+1},\dots,x_n)\}).$$

By adding up the values of all variables except one consecutively, we get the *marginal distribution*. The random variables are called *independent* if

$$\mathbb{P}_{X_1,\dots,X_n}(\{(x_1,\dots,x_n)\}) = \mathbb{P}_{X_1}(\{x_1\}) \cdot \mathbb{P}_{X_2}(\{x_2\}) \cdot \dots \cdot \mathbb{P}_{X_n}(\{x_n\}),$$
$$p_{X_1,\dots,X_n}(x_1,\dots,x_n) = p_{X_1}(x_1) \cdot p_{X_2}(x_2) \cdot \dots \cdot p_{X_n}(x_n), \quad (1.7)$$

for all possible values $x_i \in \Psi_i$.

Suppose an event $A \in \mathcal{F}$ occurs with a probability of $\mathbb{P}(A)$. Now, if new information $B \in \mathcal{F}$ is assumed to occur, the probability of A has to be reassessed. Assuming $\mathbb{P}(B) > 0$, this is called the *conditional probability*

$$\mathbb{P}(A|B) := \frac{\mathbb{P}(A \cap B)}{\mathbb{P}(B)}. \quad (1.8)$$

The space Ω of possible outcomes can be reduced to B. If $(B_i)_{i \in I}$ is a partition of Ω for an at most countable set I, i.e.,

$$\bigcup_{i \in I} B_i = \Omega \text{ and } B_i \cap B_j = \emptyset, \quad i \neq j,$$

then

$$\sum_{i \in I} \mathbb{P}(A|B_i) \cdot \mathbb{P}(B_i) \overset{(1.8)}{=} \sum_{i \in I} \mathbb{P}(A \cap B_i) = \mathbb{P}\left(\bigcup_{i \in I} A \cap B_i\right) = \mathbb{P}(A). \quad (1.9)$$

This is called the *law of total probability*. In addition, if $\mathbb{P}(A) > 0$, *Bayes' theorem* is attained,

$$\mathbb{P}(B_i|A) \overset{(1.8)}{=} \frac{\mathbb{P}(B_i \cap A)}{\mathbb{P}(A)} \overset{(1.9)}{=} \frac{\mathbb{P}(A|B_i) \cdot \mathbb{P}(B_i)}{\sum_{i \in I} \mathbb{P}(A|B_i) \cdot \mathbb{P}(B_i)}. \quad (1.10)$$

The term $\mathbb{P}(A \cap B)$ is the probability of the joint of events A and B. Let $A_1, \ldots, A_n$ be events and $\mathbb{P}(A_1 \cap \ldots \cap A_n) > 0$. Since

$$0 < \mathbb{P}(A_1 \cap \ldots \cap A_n) \le \mathbb{P}(A_1 \cap \ldots \cap A_{n-1}) \le \ldots \le \mathbb{P}(A_1)$$

it follows

$$\begin{aligned}\mathbb{P}(A_1 \cap \ldots \cap A_n) &= \frac{\mathbb{P}(A_1 \cap \ldots \cap A_n)}{\mathbb{P}(A_1 \cap \ldots \cap A_{n-1})} \cdot \ldots \cdot \frac{\mathbb{P}(A_1 \cap A_2)}{\mathbb{P}(A_1)} \cdot \frac{\mathbb{P}(A_1)}{1} \\ &\overset{(1.8)}{=} \mathbb{P}(A_n | A_1 \cap \ldots \cap A_{n-1}) \cdot \ldots \cdot \mathbb{P}(A_2 | A_1) \cdot \mathbb{P}(A_1).\end{aligned} \tag{1.11}$$

This is called the *multiplication rule*. The conditional probability of random variables X_1, X_2 is the probability for $X_1 = x_1$, given $X_2 = x_2$ in which $\mathbb{P}_{X_2}(\{x_2\}) > 0$,

$$p_{X_1|X_2}(x_1|x_2) := \frac{\mathbb{P}_{X_1,X_2}(\{(x_1, x_2)\})}{\mathbb{P}_{X_2}(\{x_2\})} = \frac{p_{X_1,X_2}(x_1, x_2)}{p_{X_2}(x_2)}, \text{ and}$$

$$p_{X|Y,Z}(x|y,z) := \frac{\mathbb{P}_{X,Y,Z}(\{x, y, z\})}{\mathbb{P}_{Y,Z}(\{y, z\})} \overset{(1.8)}{=} \frac{p_{X,Y|Z}(x, y|z)}{p_{Y|Z}(y|z)}.$$

It follows

$$\sum_{x_1 \in \Psi_1} p_{X_1|X_2}(x_1|x_2) = \frac{\sum_{x_1 \in \Psi_1} p_{X_1,X_2}(x_1, x_2)}{p_{X_2}(x_2)} = \frac{p_{X_2}(x_2)}{p_{X_2}(x_2)} = 1.$$

The special case of $\mathbb{P}_{X_2}(\{x_2\}) = 0$ is treated in a flexible and appropriate manner, but considers the probability properties.

Expectation

The *expectation* of a discrete random variable $X : \Omega \to \Psi \subseteq \mathbb{R}$ is defined by

$$\mathbb{E}[X] := \sum_{\omega \in \Omega} X(\omega) \cdot p(\omega) = \sum_{x \in X(\Omega)} x \cdot p_X(x). \tag{1.12}$$

Consider a real-valued function $f : X(\Omega) \to \mathbb{R}$. The expectation of the corresponding random variable $Y : \Omega \to \mathbb{R}$, $Y = f(X)$ is

$$\mathbb{E}[Y] = \mathbb{E}[f(X)] \overset{(1.6)}{=} \sum_{x \in X(\Omega)} f(x) \cdot p_X(x).$$

In addition, the expectation of $f(X_1, \ldots, X_n)$ is

$$\mathbb{E}[f(X_1, \ldots, X_n)] = \sum_{x_1 \in X_1(\Omega)} \cdots \sum_{x_n \in X_n(\Omega)} f(x_1, \ldots, x_n) \cdot p_{X_1, \ldots, X_n}(x_1, \ldots, x_n).$$

We will refer to the results summarized here in Chapters 2, 5, 9 and 11.

Chapter 2

Security in Communication Systems

Note 2.1. In this chapter, the requirements are:

- being able to calculate a remainder modulo n, see Section 1.1, and
- being able to apply basic probability concepts, see Section 1.2.

Selected literature: See (Biggs, 2008; Martin, 2017; Proakis, 2008; Stinson, 2005).

From smartphones to fridges and wearable devices, more devices are interconnected or connected to the internet. Smartphones stream music to speakers over a wireless network, smart fridges can place orders for grocery items from a supermarket and fitness bands send heart rate data to a smartphone. These three processes are examples of a basic model of a *communication system*, as shown in Figure 2.1. A sender ("fridge") transmits data ("get me milk") over a channel ("internet") to the receiver ("supermarket"). This model is very simplified at this point, but is sufficient to recognize the main terms of the digitized world concerning security. Currently, more than 50% of the world's population is connected to the internet,[1] and the percentage is growing every year.

[1]Data in Figure 2.2 from http://www.internetworldstats.com/stats.htm.

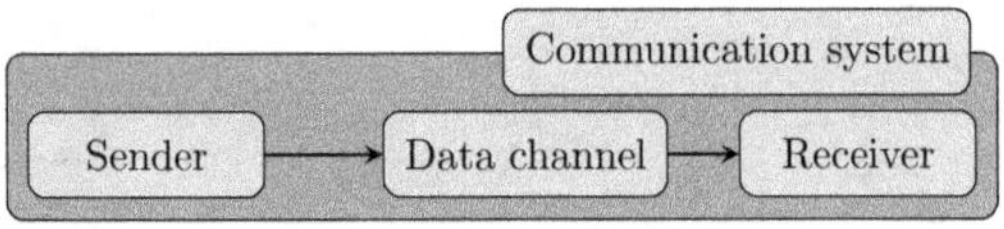

Figure 2.1 Basic communication system.

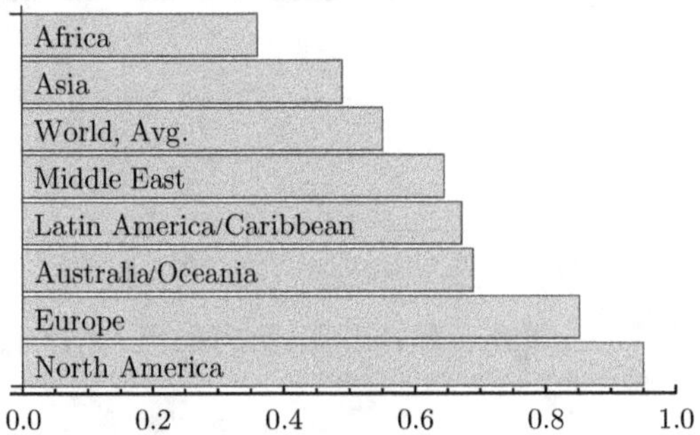

Figure 2.2 World internet penetration rates categorized by geographic regions, 2018.

2.1 Character Sets and Alphabets

Digitization[2] has come a long way since its basic principle, which can be traced to Braille's[3] tactile writing system that took its final form in 1837. Braile used cells of six possibly embossed dots to encode 26 letters (and more). Each cell was assigned a specific pattern. For example, the word "cryptography" is shown in Figure 2.3. All of the discernable Braille symbols form a finite set. A finite set is

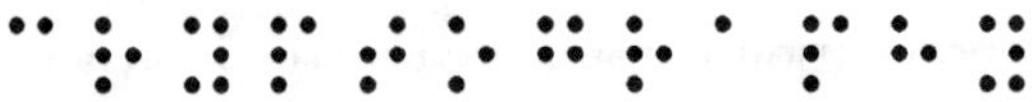

Figure 2.3 The word "cryptography" written in Braille.

[2]From the Latin word *digitus*: finger, property of the finger to be used for counting.

[3]Louis Braille (1809–1852).

called a *character set* and its elements are called *symbols*.[4] A binary character set contains exactly two symbols. For example, the Morse code[5] consists of a pair of two symbols, • and –. Again, the six dots of Braille's symbols are distributed over three rows and two columns, and are either embossed (1) or not (0). By writing this line by line, we obtain the tuple $(1,1,0,0,0,0)$, signing the letter c. Therefore, starting from the binary character set $\mathbb{Z}_2 := \{0,1\}$, we can create a new character set based on the Cartesian[6] product $\{0,1\}^k$, $k \in \mathbb{N}$, where $k = 6$. There are mappings from the set of small Latin letters to Braille's character set or $\{0,1\}^6$. Every injective mapping from one character set to another is called a *code*.

Example 2.2. Let

$$\mathbb{Z}_{26} := \{0, 1, \ldots, 25\}$$

be the set of the first 26 non-negative numbers,

$$\Sigma_{\text{lat}} := \{\text{a,b,c,d,e,f,g,h,i,j,k,l,m,n,o,p,q,r,s,t,u,v,w,x,y,z}\}$$

be the set of the small Latin letters and Σ_{Bra} the Braille's character set. The mappings

$$\mathbb{Z}_{26} \to \Sigma_{\text{lat}},\ 0 \mapsto \text{a}, 1 \mapsto \text{b}, 2 \mapsto \text{c}, \ldots, 25 \mapsto \text{z},$$

and

$\Sigma_{\text{lat}} \to \Sigma_{\text{Bra}}$, a ↦ ⠁, b ↦ ⠃, c ↦ ⠉, …, z ↦ ⠵,

are then codes.

From Example 2.2 it is clear that a code does not need to be a surjective function, i.e., the mapping $\Sigma_{\text{lat}} \to \Sigma_{\text{Bra}}$ does not reach each symbol in Σ_{Bra}. This is no surprise because $|\Sigma_{\text{Lat}}| = 26 < 64 = |\Sigma_{\text{Bra}}|$. Alternatively, after coding a symbol (encoding process), it is possible to reverse the process (decoding process). Thus, it is essential that a code has to be an injective mapping.

---

[4]See (Biggs, 2008).

[5]Samuel F. B. Morse (1791–1872).

[6]Named after René Descartes (1596–1650).

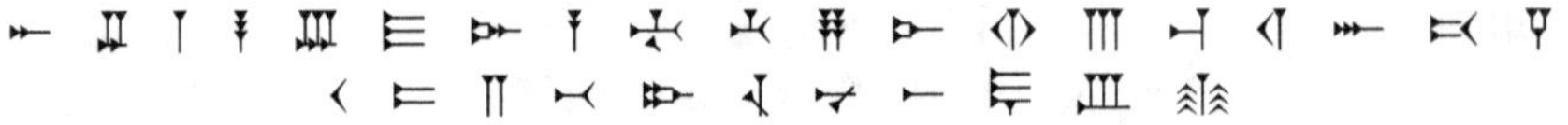

Figure 2.4 The Ugaritic alphabet.

It is often useful to review a sort order of symbols. In natural language, there are finite number of letters in an alphabet that are arranged in ascending order. For example, the Ugaritic alphabet that dates from about 1300 BC[7] was an alphabetical cuneiform. The Ugaritic letters are shown in Figure 2.4. The ordering is assumed to have originated from a poem that children learn by heart,[8] as reflected in the sorting of the alphabet at that time.[9] The people of the region commonly made lists, so they list their symbols and needed ordering. Additionally, primary school pupils routinely learn the symbols. However, the reason for special ordering is not clear. Finally, semantic ordering is hypothesized, or the ordering is based on the successive occurrence of the metaphors of the symbol in a life story. Today's alphabets are based on the ideas of such early alphabets, however, their natural ordering is not understood. Letters can be arranged in another way. For example, we can arrange the letters by counting their frequencies in a set of texts, which can be useful in frequency analysis (see page 48).

Example 2.3.
Let $\leq$ be the commonly known ordering of numbers. This order relation has some properties. For each x, y and $z \in \mathbb{Z}$,

- $x \leq y$ AND $y \leq z \Rightarrow x \leq z$ (transitivity),
- $x \leq y$ AND $y \leq x \Rightarrow x = y$ (antisymmetry) and
- $x \leq y$ OR $y \leq x$ (totality).

Such an order is called a *total order* on some set. It does not matter whether this order relation needs to be restricted on $\mathbb{Z}_{26}$. Therefore, these properties hold for every ordering of symbols.

---

[7] https://en.wikipedia.org/wiki/Ugaritic_alphabet.
[8] http://www.finse.dk/ugarit.htm.
[9] We follow the remarks of Küster (2006).

A character set Σ with a total order $\preceq$ on Σ, $(\Sigma, \preceq)$ is called an *alphabet*. Each symbol can be dedicated either to be preceding, following or equal to any other particular symbol in the alphabet. Moreover, the relation between the symbols is transitive: if one symbol precedes another symbol and this second symbol is preceding a third one, then the first symbol also precedes the third one. The indicated binary relation is depicted by a strict total order. For example, given the set

$$\mathbb{Z}_n := \{0, 1, \ldots, n-1\},\ n \in \mathbb{N}, \tag{2.1}$$

provided with the natural ordering $\leq$ of numbers, the tuple $(\mathbb{Z}_n, \leq)$ is an alphabet. Let $(\Sigma, \preceq)$ be a non-empty alphabet. For some fixed $k \in \mathbb{N}$, any tuple $(s_1, \ldots, s_k) \in \Sigma^k$ is said to be a *string* of length k over Σ. Building a finite sequence of symbols from an alphabet results in a string. There can be many strings generated from an alphabet. Thus, sometimes the set of allowed strings is restricted. The set of all strings over Σ is reduced by $\Sigma^* := \bigcup_{k=0}^{\infty} \Sigma^k$. Any subset $\mathcal{L}_\Sigma \subseteq \Sigma^*$ denotes the set of all possible words and is called *language* over Σ. Each $m \in \mathcal{L}_\Sigma$ denotes a single *message*.

We later distinguish between different types of algorithms for cryptographical purposes depending on the cardinality of an alphabet.

Example 2.4.

- $\Sigma_{\text{lat}} = \{$a, b, c, d, e, f, g, h, i, j, k, l, m, n, o, p, q, r, s, t, u, v, w, x, y, z$\}$ denotes the lowercase Latin alphabet using natural language ordering,
- $\Sigma_{\text{Lat}} := \{$A, B, C, D, E, F, G, H, I, J, K, L, M, N, O, P, Q, R, S, T, U, V, W, X, Y, Z$\}$ denotes the uppercase Latin alphabet using natural language ordering,
- $\Sigma_{\text{Latext}} := \Sigma_{\text{Lat}} \cup \{.,!,?,\ ,\ ,;,:\}$ denotes the uppercase Latin alphabet extended by punctuation marks using ordering given by the arrangement here,

- $\Sigma_{\text{dez}} := \{0,1,2,3,4,5,6,7,8,9\} = \mathbb{Z}_{10}$ denotes the alphabet of digits using natural ordering of numbers,
- $\Sigma_{\text{bool}} := \{0,1\} = \mathbb{Z}_2$ denotes the Boole's character set[10] with natural ordering of numbers to get an alphabet,
- $\Sigma_{\text{hex}} :=$ {0, 1, 2, 3, 4, 5, 6, 7, 8, 9, a, b, c, d, e, f} denotes the character set of the ordered hexadecimal numbers.

Remark 2.5.

- If the alphabet is clear, we can write $\mathcal{L}$ instead of $\mathcal{L}_\Sigma$.
- For formal reasons, the empty string contains no symbols and that denoted by ϵ is contained in Σ^*.
- For convenience, we can write messages in a shorter form. Instead of the string

$$(C, R, Y, P, T, O, G, R, A, P, H, Y) \in \Sigma_{\text{Lat}}^{12},$$

a string representation of this tuple is

"CRYPTOGRAPHY".

Moreover, we indicate splitting a string $(s_1, \ldots, s_l, s_{l+1}, \ldots, s_k)$ into a left and a right section by

$$\underbrace{s_1 \ldots s_l}_{L} || \underbrace{s_{l+1} \ldots s_k}_{R}.$$

Sometimes the left part (L) is called the *prefix* and the right part (R) is called the *suffix*.
- Each of the two symbols in Σ_{bool} is called a *bit*.

The catenation of two strings of any length, k and l, respectively, is specified by the mapping

$$\Sigma^* \times \Sigma^* \to \Sigma^*,\ ((s_1, \ldots, s_k), (\hat{s}_1, \ldots, \hat{s}_l)) \mapsto (s_1, \ldots, s_k, \hat{s}_1, \ldots, \hat{s}_l).$$

This operation is associative and non-commutative. The length of a message m denoted by $|m|$ is the number of symbols of m. The empty ϵ string has zero length.

[10] George Boole (1815–1864).

Example 2.6.

- The string $m = (C, R, Y, P, T, O, G, R, A, P, H, Y)$ has length $|m| = 12$,
- $m = (12, 0, 19, 7, 18) \in \mathbb{Z}_{26}^5$, $|m| = 5$,
- $\underbrace{0111}_{L} || \underbrace{0101}_{R} \in \mathcal{L}_{\Sigma_{\text{bool}}} := \Sigma_{\text{bool}}^8$, $|L| = |R| = 4$.

The exchange and storage of messages is of great importance in today's digitized world. A message consists of characters originating from a character set and it can usually be put together according to certain syntactic specifications. Only in a situational context does information arise from a message. We will define an amount of information in Section 5.2.2 and assume that messages are just one or more connected symbols that are not interpreted.

2.2 Digital Messages

The mathematician Claude Shannon[11] pioneered digitization in the publication of "A Mathematical Theory of Communication"[12] in 1948. In the last decades of the 20th century, computer technology and interconnectedness has rapidly developed. There is an urgent need to protect the enormous amounts of digital data.

Previously, mathematician George Stibitz[13] used the word "digital" in reference to the fast, electric pulses emitted by a device designed to operate anti-aircraft guns in 1942, similar to a sharp 0-1 separation. Considering a broader view of *digital messages* the value of a binary code of a message is often created by an encoding process of a message based on letters. Particularly, a *binary code* is used if the co-domain is based on the Cartesian product of Boole's alphabet. We abbreviate the term "digital message" as *data*.

[11]Claude E. Shannon (1916–2001).

[12]http://math.harvard.edu/~ctm/home/text/others/shannon/entropy/entropy.pdf.

[13]George R. Stibitz (1904–1995).

2.2.1 *Encoding messages*

Example 2.7.
From Example 2.2, we build the inverse function $\Sigma_{\text{lat}} \to \mathbb{Z}_{26}$,

$$\text{a} \mapsto 0, \text{b} \mapsto 1, \text{c} \mapsto 2, \ldots, \text{z} \mapsto 25.$$

The message (element of Σ_{lat}^*)

sec**u**rity||is||the||main||goal||of||cryptography

has the representation (element of $\mathbb{Z}_{26}^*$)

18, 4, 2, **20**, 17, 8, 19, 24 || 8, 18 || 19, 7, 4 || 12, 0, 8, 13 || 6, 14, 0, 11 || 14, 5 || 2, 17, 24, 15, 19, 14, 6, 17, 0, 15, 7, 24.

The code table of the American Standard Code for Information Interchange (ASCII)[14] is an example of a binary code with a constant string length. This means that every symbol has the same length in the binary character set.

Example 2.8.
In an example for a binary code, each code is assigned a symbol ("sym") and corresponding binary representation ("binary") as shown in Table 2.1. The message

sec**u**rity||is||the||main||goal||of||cryptography

has the following representation.

111001111001011100011**1110101**1110010110100111101001111001||
11010011110011||111010011010001100101||
1101101110000111010011101110||1100111110111111000011101100||
11011111100110||11000111110010111100111100001110100
1101111110011111100101100001111000011010001111001

There are $7 \cdot 35 = 245$ bits needed.

[14]cf. https://sltls.org/ASCII.

Table 2.1 ASCII-table or ISO 7-bit code.

dec	binary	sym	dec	binary	sym	dec	binary	sym	dec	binary	sym
0	0000000	NUL	32	0100000	SP	64	1000000	@	96	1100000	’
1	0000001	SOH	33	0100001	!	65	1000001	A	97	1100001	a
2	0000010	STX	34	0100010	“	66	1000010	B	98	1100010	b
3	0000011	ETX	35	0100011	#	67	1000011	C	99	1100011	c
4	0000100	EOT	36	0100100	$	68	1000100	D	100	1100100	d
5	0000101	ENQ	37	0100101	%	69	1000101	E	101	1100101	e
6	0000110	ACK	38	0100110	&	70	1000110	F	102	1100110	f
7	0000111	BEL	39	0100111	‘	71	1000111	G	103	1100111	g
8	0001000	BS	40	0101000	(	72	1001000	H	104	1101000	h
9	0001001	TAB	41	0101001	)	73	1001001	I	105	1101001	i
10	0001010	LF	42	0101010	*	74	1001010	J	106	1101010	j
11	0001011	VT	43	0101011	+	75	1001011	K	107	1101011	k
12	0001100	FF	44	0101100	,	76	1001100	L	108	1101100	l
13	0001101	CR	45	0101101	-	77	1001101	M	109	1101101	m
14	0001110	SO	46	0101110	.	78	1001110	N	110	1101110	n
15	0001111	SI	47	0101111	/	79	1001111	O	111	1101111	o
16	0010000	DLE	48	0110000	0	80	1010000	P	112	1110000	p
17	0010001	DC1	49	0110001	1	81	1010001	Q	113	1110001	q
18	0010010	DC2	50	0110010	2	82	1010010	R	114	1110010	r
19	0010011	DC3	51	0110011	3	83	1010011	S	115	1110011	s
20	0010100	DC4	52	0110100	4	84	1010100	T	116	1110100	t
21	0010101	NAK	53	0110101	5	85	1010101	U	**117**	**1110101**	**u**
22	0010110	SYN	54	0110110	6	86	1010110	V	118	1110110	v
23	0010111	ETB	55	0110111	7	87	1010111	W	119	1110111	w
24	0011000	CAN	56	0111000	8	88	1011000	X	120	1111000	x
25	0011001	EM	57	0111001	9	89	1011001	Y	121	1111001	y
26	0011010	SUB	58	0111010	:	90	1011010	Z	122	1111010	z
27	0011011	ESC	59	0111011	;	91	1011011	[	123	1111011	{
28	0011100	FS	60	0111100	<	92	1011100	\	124	1111100	|
29	0011101	GS	61	0111101	=	93	1011101	]	125	1111101	}
30	0011110	RS	62	0111110	>	94	1011110	^	126	1111110	~
31	0011111	US	63	0111111	?	95	1011111	_	127	1111111	DEL

In practical applications, it is necessary to create digital messages. This is mainly because of transmissions over today's data channels. Example 2.7 shows this process using the alphabet $\mathbb{Z}_{26}^*$. As observed, it is sometimes essential to convert integers from one number system to another. The set $\mathbb{Z}_p$ of the first p non-negative integers from (2.1) establishes a *p-adic* system's number

$$x_{(p)} = x_{n-1}x_{n-2}\dots x_{0(p)}$$

consisting of n digits $x_i \in \mathbb{Z}_p$ that can be represented by a decimal number

$$x_{(10)} = \sum_{i=0}^{n-1} x_i \cdot p^i = x_{n-1} \cdot p^{n-1} + x_{n-2} \cdot p^{n-2} \cdot \ldots \cdot x_0 \cdot p^0,$$
$$= (((x_i \cdot p + x_{i-1}) \cdot p + x_{i-1}) \cdot p + \ldots + x_1) \cdot p + x_0. \quad (2.2)$$

If the p-adic system the number is coming from is known, we can write just the digits. For example, the decimal number 215 is

$$215 = 215_{(10)}.$$

The last line in Equation (2.2) depicts the Horner's scheme.[15] To convert a p-adic system's number $y_{(p)}$ to a q-adic system's number $z_{(q)}$ we can use the Horner's scheme to represent a first step $y_{(p)}$ as a decimal number $x_{(10)}$, and then theoretically set the decimal number $x_{(10)}$ on base q:

$$x_{(10)} = (((z_i \cdot q + z_{i-1}) \cdot q + z_{i-1}) \cdot q + \ldots + z_1) \cdot q + z_0.$$

By dividing $x_{(10)}$ by q we get the remainder z_0 that is the last digit searched for. By dividing the quotient $((z_i \cdot q + z_{i-1}) \cdot q + z_{i-1}) \cdot q + \cdots + z_1$ by q, z_1 remains. We continue until the quotient becomes zero. Thus, we can iteratively obtain all the digits from behind, which is the second step.

Example 2.9.
The number $y_{(16)} = 75_{(16)}$ from the hexadecimal system is to be converted to a binary number.

First step:

$$x_{(10)} = 7 \cdot 16 + 5 = 117.$$

[15]William G. Horner (1786–1837).

Second step:

$$
\begin{aligned}
117 \,/\, 2 &= 58 \text{ remainder } 1\\
58 \,/\, 2 &= 29 \text{ remainder } 0\\
29 \,/\, 2 &= 14 \text{ remainder } 1\\
14 \,/\, 2 &= 7 \text{ remainder } 0\\
7 \,/\, 2 &= 3 \text{ remainder } 1\\
3 \,/\, 2 &= 1 \text{ remainder } 1\\
1 \,/\, 2 &= 0 \text{ remainder } 1
\end{aligned}
$$

It follows that $75_{(16)} = 117_{(10)} = 1110101_{(2)}$.

Example 2.10.
From Example 2.7 we can get a binary-coded representation of a letter from Σ_{lat}.

Σ_{lat}	$\mathbb{Z}_{26}$	$p = 10 \to q = 2$	$z_{(2)}$
u	$20_{(10)}$	$(1 \cdot 2^4 + 0 \cdot 2^3 + 1 \cdot 2^2 + 0 \cdot 2^1 + 0 \cdot 2^0)_{(10)}$	$10100_{(2)}$

Digital messages are to be represented in a binary-coded form based on the Boole's character set. Depending on the length of the underlying character set Σ, there is a maximum number l of bits to take:

$$l = \min\{k \in \mathbb{N};\ 2^k \geq |\Sigma|\} = \lceil \log_2 (|\Sigma|) \rceil,$$

in which $\lceil . \rceil : \mathbb{R} \to \mathbb{Z},\ x \mapsto \lceil x \rceil := \min\{q \in \mathbb{Z};\ q \geq x\}$ is the *ceiling function*. Thus, the letters from Σ_{lat} can be coded by five bits, e.g., by injective mapping

$$
\begin{aligned}
&c_5 : \Sigma_{\text{lat}} \to \Sigma_{\text{bool}}^5,\\
&a \mapsto 00000,\ b \mapsto 00001,\ c \mapsto 00010,\ \ldots,\ z \mapsto 11001.
\end{aligned}
$$

This is a coding with a constant length of bits.

Example 2.11.
The message

security||is||the||main||goal||of||cryptography

gets coded by

10010001000000101**10100**10001010001001111000||
0100010010||100110011100100||01100000000100001101||
00110011100000001011||0111000101||
00010100011100001111100110111000110100010000001111001111000.

The message requires $5 \cdot 35 = 175$ for encoding.

However, 26 letters are insufficient. In addition to the formerly used ASCII-codes (see Example 2.8), there are other code tables. The ISO 8859-1[16] standard uses 8 bits and can represent 191 of 256 possible symbols ($20_{(16)} - 7e_{(16)}$ and $a0_{(16)} - ff_{(16)}$). The internet standard, UTF-8,[17] is widely used. Each symbol gets a digital code and each code has a binary representation that has a maximum length of 4 bytes, i.e., 32 bits. The standard letters can be written by one byte, however, special characters require more than one byte. Thus, it is a coding with a variable length of bits.

Example 2.12.
The small Latin letters are coded by one byte. The message

sec**u**rity||is||the||main||goal||of||cryptography

has the following binary UTF-8 representation:

011100110110010101100011**01110101**011100100110100101110100
01111001||0110100101110011||011101000110100001100101||01101101
01100001011010010110111 0||01100111011011110110000101101100||
0110111101100110||0110001101110010011110010111000001110100
01101111011001110111001001100001011100000110100001111001

UTF-8 is the ASCII code with a leading zero. Here, we obtain $8 \cdot 35 = 280$ bits.

2.2.2 *Blockwise and variable-length encoding*

A binary code yields a large amount of bits to code a message, which requires a lot of memory and increases its transmission time. Thus, a binary code needs to require less bits. One possibility to reduce

[16]http://www.iso.org/iso/catalogue_detail.htm?csnumber=28245, 1998.
[17]Defined in RFC3629: http://tools.ietf.org/html/rfc3629, 2003.

the number of bits is through *blockwise coding*. In doing so, a constant count of symbols is coded together. Considering a p-adic number system with n digits, there are p^n different numbers available. Therefore, the number of q-adic digits necessary to represent all these numbers are

$$l = \min\{l \in \mathbb{N};\ q^l \geq p^n\} = \lceil \log_q (p^n) \rceil = \left\lceil n \cdot \frac{\ln(p)}{\ln(q)} \right\rceil$$

digits.

Example 2.13.
The known message

sec**u**rity||is||the||main||goal||of||cryptography

consists of 35 letters. If we decide on seven blocks each with five small Latin letters, all the blocks have to be represented as a 26-adic number. Lastly, these numbers have to be converted into a binary code. This encoding yields $\lceil \log_2 (26^5) \rceil = 24$ bits each.

Block	Coding in $\mathbb{Z}_{26}^5$ $(x_4, x_3, x_2, x_1, x_0)$	$x_4 \cdot 26^4 + x_3 \cdot 26^3 + x_2 \cdot 26^2 + x_1 \cdot 26^1 + x_0 \cdot 26^0$	Binary representation
sec**u**r	(18, 4, 2, **20**, 17)	8297761	**0**11111101001110100100001
ityis	(8, 19, 24, 8, 18)	4006202	**00**1111010010000100111010
thema	(19, 7, 4, 12, 0)	8808592	100001100110100010010000
ingoa	(8, 13, 6, 14, 0)	3888716	**00**1110110101011001001100
lofcr	(11, 14, 5, 2, 17)	5276249	**0**10100001000001001011001
yptog	(24, 15, 19, 14, 6)	11244278	101010111001001011110110
raphy	(17, 0, 15, 7, 24)	7778938	**0**11101101011001001111010

The bold zeros extend the short sequences of bits to produce a block size of equal length. Otherwise, the sequence would be ambiguous. By taking the first 24 bits of this sequence without leading zeros, we would get back the senseless string "bkifpj":

$$111111010011101001000011 \rightarrow 16595523 \rightarrow (1, 10, 8, 5, 15, 9).$$

Instead of obtaining 175 bits while coding each individual letter in $\mathbb{Z}_{26}$, we obtain $7 \cdot 24 = 168$ bits. By coding the whole message as one single block, we achieve $\lceil \log_2 (26^{35}) \rceil = 165$ bits as the best case scenario.

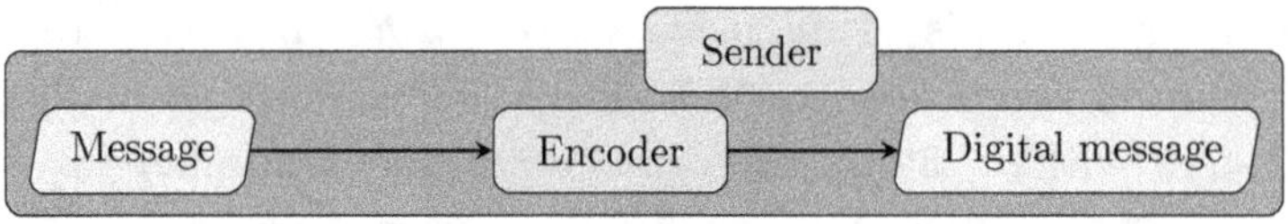

Figure 2.5 Extended communication system on the sender's side.

The blockwise coding establishes a *code table* that is impractical to write down, as can be seen in the computing in Example 2.13. There are many ways to get a digital message. For example, an efficient binary coding method is the *Huffman code*,[18] which is a lossless message compression scheme based on Shannon's work on information theory. A Huffman code is a variable-length code.[19] With this, the basic communication model from Figure 2.1 can be extended. The sender often has to digitize the message in an encoding process as shown in Figure 2.5. The receiver must reverse the process.

Digital messages, or synonymously, data, may be copied as often as needed without any loss. Every participant of the digital world has to use an architecture for managing the life cycle of data. Such an architecture is called an *information system*. Two main tasks of an information system are storing and distributing data. When accessing data in accordance with those tasks, we have to establish an electronic communication for every possibility, and it must be ensured that not everyone has access to the data.

2.3 Security in Technical Information Systems

Digital messages are an integral part of modern communication and data keeping. Therefore, we will look at two types of technical information systems: (1) a communication system that ensures the exchange of data between at least two participants called *entities*,

[18]David A. Huffman (1925–1999).

[19]More information on coding is provided in (Proakis, 2008).

and (2) a *data keeping system* that ensures the working storage of and access to data.

2.3.1 *Security goals*

When processing data, a system has to guarantee full user satisfaction at all times. For this reason, the system provides some services for different purposes.

Convention 2.14 (Service). A *service* is a technical unit of a system that bundles and provides related functionalities on a clearly predefined interface.

A system has to meet different types of requirements to satisfy all involved entities. Alternatively, if we want the system to function smoothly, we demand that it does everything the way it should. It is like comparing the actual value with the target value. Similarly, the system needs to be operationally reliable. We call these two aspects, *safety*.

The data involved should be protected against outside entities. If two separate entities are communicating, they usually do not want external viewers. This is especially true in the case of sensitive information, and many countries have implemented regulations. These aspects relate to *privacy*.

Protection is a term used to get a system into states to deny access from third parties. Here, access concerns all existing data and system states. The entities are interested in setting who may use the data and system states in an existing computer system.

The most important term in our context is *security*, which means saving a system from any loss and avoiding abuse. Security of data concerns all characteristics of named systems and is a generic term in this context. In data keeping, an entity wants to ensure no unauthorized access. While communicating, the data should also remain unaffected. However, it is not only the data. The communication itself may be completely hidden from third parties. The need for protection was recognized very early. For example, the Greek historian Plutarch[20] wrote in the biography of Lysander[21] that during the Peloponnesian War[22] he foiled an *attack* from the Persians by issuing a warning message that was encrypted by a *scytale*. A scytale is an example of a transposition cipher that will be explained in Section 4.2.2.

Every data keeping system is a communication system, as everything concerning access to or the management of data is related to communication. For example, the storage of data requires confidential interaction between the data owner and the data keeping system, which also covers communication systems. Thus, it sufficiently addresses only communication systems. To achieve security in communication systems, we have to identify abstract goals.

Convention 2.15 (Security goal). A (technical) *security goal* is a desired state of a technical system that guarantees security of the data.

In general, there are some important security goals:

- *Confidentiality*: the assurance that the data cannot be viewed by an unauthorized entity.
- *Data integrity*: the assurance that the data has not been changed in an unauthorized way.
- *Availability*: the assurance that a service is working properly at any times.
- *Authenticity*: the assurance that an entity is permitted to be currently active in a communication session.
- *Non-repudiation*: the assurance that an entity cannot deny a previous action about the data to a third entity.
- *Accountability*: the assurance that a given entity can be attributed to be the original source of the data.

[20] Plutarch (46–120).
[21] Very little is known about Lysander's life. He died in 395 BC.
[22] Dated 431 BC to 404 BC.

- *Anonymity*: the assurance that an entity's identity is hidden from other entities.

Example 2.16 (Confidentiality). Many people use services over a wireless connection. The most important technique is connecting over a wireless local area network (WLAN), and is used for increasing convenience. Alternatively, this convenience leads to a higher risk of being attacked from a third party. An entity within the range of this connection could monitor and alter the sent data. Therefore, this data should be confidential.

If no unauthorized information acquisition from data is possible, a system guarantees confidentiality. Thus, a communication system has a defined number of participants and no one else is granted access to the system. In other words, a system has to restrict the availability of data (transmitted or saved) to achieve confidentiality. As Steven Bucci wrote in *USA Today* on 10 June 2013: "[...] Individuals don't get to decide for themselves what should be classified. If an individual knowingly has given classified material to unauthorized person, it's a grave breach of trust and law."[23]

Example 2.17 (Data integrity). We can download software from some websites by clicking on a download link. After downloading, it is possible to check whether the downloaded file was correctly transmitted by comparing a checksum from the website with the one calculated from the downloaded file. If they match, we can assume that data integrity was ensured.

In 2016, the German newspaper *Süddeutsche Zeitung* (often abbreviated as "SZ") publicly denounced the methods of the Volkswagen-subsidiary, Audi. They wrote that Audi had manipulated the exhaust gas cleaning data of diesel cars in the US to its

[23]https://www.usatoday.com/story/opinion/2013/06/10/edward-snowden-heritage-foundation-editorials-debates/2410213/, 10 June 2013.

favor.[24] After starting the car, the operating temperature of the catalyst was reached much faster via a special program, and so less emissions were recorded in the test phase.

The communicated exhaust gas cleaning data was not correct from the view of the customers. However, in cryptology, if no unauthorized and unnoticed tampering is performed, a system maintains its integrity. Unintentional or intentional changes on data have to be recognized.

Example 2.18 (Availability).
In countries with a high affinity to digital technologies, a majority of the population uses smartphones. However, the smartphone must dial in to the telecommunications network with its unique SIM card. A failure of this network completely blocks communication and service is not available.

On 29 November 2016, about 900,000 customers of Deutsche Telekom (a German telecommunications company headquartered in Bonn) could not use their internet router because a British citizen had successfully hacked into consumer routing devices.[25] A system guarantees its availability if authenticated and authorized participants are not affected in access and use of their permitted services of a system. All the services of a system should be available and operating properly.

Three terms—confidentiality, integrity and availability—build the core of the security of a system.

Example 2.19 (Authenticity).
Gaining access to data on a computer normally requires authentication. That is part of a log-on process. The entity needs some

[24] http://www.sueddeutsche.de/wirtschaft/abgas-affaere-wie-audi-die-pruefer-austrickste-1.3245094, November 11, 2016.
[25] https://www.dw.com/en/deutsche-telekom-hacker-very-sorry-for-botnet-attack-on-a-million-internet-users/a-39877386.

credentials such as a user name and a password to sign in. At this exact moment, the authenticity is clear and acts as a form of proof at a certain time. However, a replay of the credentials may later be carried out by a third party. Therefore, the aspect of time is essential.

The malware Dridex[26] was used to eavesdrop on victims' computers to steal personal banking information, which could be used to siphon off money. The two masterminds were condemned by a London court at the end of 2016.

The term "authenticity" refers to the credibility of a part of the system that can be checked by a unique identity and characteristic properties. A synonym for this process is entity authentication. Unfortunately, for Dridex, the mechanism for authentication turned out to be weak.

Another aspect of authentication concerns *data origin authentication*, which includes both the authentication of the data source and the integrity of the data itself. The difference between entity authentication and data authentication also concerns time aspects. A successful data origin authentication does not reveal much about the timeliness of the data. However, a successful entity authentication has to be up-to-date information. There has to be a timestamp or a unique random number, known in cryptology as *nonce*,[27] inside the process.

Example 2.20 (Non-repudiation).
Buying something from an online shop establishes a binding legal transaction between the seller and purchaser. The seller is interested in obligating the purchaser to pay for the ware. The purchaser must not deny its part in the legal transaction.

A system ensures non-repudiation if it is not possible for an entity to deny a certain action afterwards. In the context of electronic

[26]https://en.wikipedia.org/wiki/Dridex.

[27]Abbreviation for "**n**umber used **o**nly **once**".

commerce or electronic business, this concept is very important to ensure the transaction is legally binding.

> **Example 2.21 (Accountability).**
> Forwarding an email on behalf of another demands the receiver to prove the origins of the email. This does not depend on the time at which this happens.

It is possible to identify the entity that is responsible for a specific event, which is called accountability. Determining who performed an action of opening the door sometimes is difficult. For example, the owner of a computer account must not allow others to use this account, which helps the owner prevent harmful operations by third parties.

This example shows that accountability has to be stronger than data integrity because we cannot assume that the data has remained unchanged and therefore cannot be sure of its origins. Therefore, accountability includes data integrity. Furthermore, there is no need for authentication in the email forwarding process. What matters is that its origins are clear.

> **Example 2.22 (Anonymity).**
> Some people do not want to make their activities on the internet public. This is especially relevant for journalists working in dangerous countries such as in countries suppressing free reporting.

It is difficult to hide a sender's information from third parties. Sent data may be confidential but it is possible to backtrace the sender's IP. As a result, it is very difficult to reach perfect anonymity in this context.

2.3.2 *Cryptosystems*

Cryptology is one of the main disciplines that emphasizes design and analysis of methods for security goals. This domain is divided into two sub-domains. Cryptography concerns the designing of methods, while cryptanalysis deals with the analysis of the benefits of such methods.

Convention 2.23 (Security service). A *security service* is a service that achieves at least one security goal.

Such services are the "basic generic tools" in a security toolkit provided by the discipline cryptology.[28]

Convention 2.24 (Cryptosystem). An implemented system including exact procedures and security services that are necessary for reaching predefined security goals is called a *cryptosystem*, as schematically shown in Figure 2.6.

There are several steps needed to establish a situation reflecting the predefined goals. In a communication system, a sequence of data is created that forms a process and is called a cryptographical protocol,[29] corresponding to those in processes mentioned in Convention 2.24. Five different properties are claimed for a cryptographic protocol. Three claims concern the entities, i.e., any participant of the process has to

- know the whole process and its steps and data structures,
- accept the by-the-definition execution of the process and
- be detained from doing undesired actions to gain additional information.

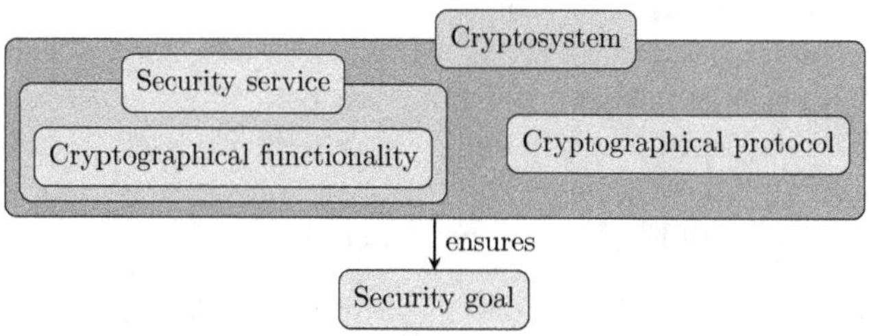

Figure 2.6 Components of a cryptosystem.

[28]Stated in (Martin, 2017). He calls it "cryptographic primitives".
[29]See Convention 2.30 and this is more detailed in (Mahalingam, 2014).

The last two claims concern the process itself, i.e., the protocol has to

- be complete; each possible case has to be reflected in advance, and
- be unambiguous and well-defined.

2.4 Classical Cryptosystems

The term "*classical cryptosystem*" encompasses all encryption and decryption procedures, including their functionalities used up to the middle of the 20th century. We present a selection of these procedures to prepare for the mathematically calculations. Cryptology deals with the protection of data against unauthorized access. Translated from ancient Greek, we study the "science of hiding".[30] However, this definition is now too narrow. The field of cryptology is divided into two sub-areas. In its original meaning, cryptography[31] deals with the transformation of readable texts (*plaintexts*) into unreadable texts (*ciphertexts*), and vice versa with the help of a secret key. The forming process is modeled using a mapping. For this purpose, we must define the domain, the co-domain and the mapping itself.

In his work "Divus Iulius", the poet Suetonius[32] describes how Caesar[33] enciphered messages:

> "Epistulae quoque eius ad senatum exstant quas primum videtur ad paginas et formam memorialis libelli convertisse, cum antea consules et duces non nisi transversa charta scriptas mitterent. Exstant et ad Ciceronem, item ad familiares domesticis de rebus, in quibus, si qua occultius perferenda erant, per notas scripsit, id est sic structo litterarum ordine ut nullum verbum effici posset: quae si qui investigare et persequi velit, quartam elementorum litteram, id est D, pro A et perinde reliquas commutet."

"A" is replaced by "D", and generally every letter is replaced by the one that is three positions behind it in the alphabet, starting

[30]Derived from the words ὁ λογος, τὸ κρύπτειν.
[31]τὸ γράφειν.
[32]Gaius Suetonius Tranquillus (70–122 AD), see (Tranquillus, 1918, Section 56.6).
[33]Gaius Iulius Caesar (100–44 BC).

from the beginning when the end is reached. The following principle reflects the process:

$$\begin{pmatrix} ABCDEFGHIJKLMNOPQRSTUVWXYZ \\ DEFGHIJKLMNOPQRSTUVWXYZABC \end{pmatrix}. \tag{2.3}$$

The top row of symbols are encrypted to the bottom row symbols and conversely. Caesar used this type of encryption for various situations. During his campaigns, he sent encrypted messages that were additionally encoded by Greek letters to Cicero[34] who was able to decrypt the messages. If each letter is replaced by exactly one letter, it is a *simple monoalphabetic substitution cipher*, and the original text can likely be recovered.

Example 2.25 (Caesar cipher). In applying the *Caesar cipher*,[35] we replace an uppercase letter using the principle of shifting shown in (2.3) and define the mapping

$$e_3 : \Sigma_{\text{Lat}} \to \Sigma_{\text{Lat}},\ A \mapsto D, B \mapsto E, C \mapsto F, \ldots, X \mapsto A, \\ Y \mapsto B, Z \mapsto C$$

for encryption. The three-shift value represents the key for this cipher. The string "FUBSWRJUDSKB" is obtained by encrypting the readable string "CRYPTOGRAPHY". A slightly longer text sample is the beginning of the Gospel according to Saint Mark[36]:

"THE BEGINNING OF THE GOSPEL OF JESUS CHRIST THE SON OF GOD AS IT IS WRITTEN IN ISAIAH THE PROPHET BEHOLD I SEND MY MESSENGER BEFORE YOUR FACE WHO WILL PREPARE YOUR WAY THE VOICE OF ONE CRYING IN THE WILDERNESS PREPARE THE WAY OF THE LORD MAKE HIS PATHS STRAIGHT JOHN APPEARED BAPTIZING IN THE WILDERNESS AND PROCLAIMING A BAPTISM OF REPENTANCE FOR THE FORGIVENESS OF SINS AND ALL THE COUNTRY OF JUDEA AND ALL JERUSALEM WERE

[34]Marcus Tullius Cicero (106–43 BC).
[35]To about 50 BC.
[36]Saint Mark the Evangelist 1, 1–20, source: https://www.bibleserver.com/text/ESV/Mark1.

GOING OUT TO HIM AND WERE BEING BAPTIZED BY HIM IN THE RIVER JORDAN CONFESSING THEIR SINS NOW JOHN WAS CLOTHED WITH CAMELS HAIR AND WORE A LEATHER BELT AROUND HIS WAIST AND ATE LOCUSTS AND WILD HONEY AND HE PREACHED SAYING AFTER ME COMES HE WHO IS MIGHTIER THAN I THE STRAP OF WHOSE SANDALS I AM NOT WORTHY TO STOOP DOWN AND UNTIE I HAVE BAPTIZED YOU WITH WATER BUT HE WILL BAPTIZE YOU WITH THE HOLY SPIRIT IN THOSE DAYS JESUS CAME FROM NAZARETH OF GALILEE AND WAS BAPTIZED BY JOHN IN THE JORDAN AND WHEN HE CAME UP OUT OF THE WATER IMMEDIATELY HE SAW THE HEAVENS BEING TORN OPEN AND THE SPIRIT DESCENDING ON HIM LIKE A DOVE AND A VOICE CAME FROM HEAVEN YOU ARE MY BELOVED SON WITH YOU I AM WELL PLEASED THE SPIRIT IMMEDIATELY DROVE HIM OUT INTO THE WILDERNESS AND HE WAS IN THE WILDERNESS FORTY DAYS BEING TEMPTED BY SATAN AND HE WAS WITH THE WILD ANIMALS AND THE ANGELS WERE MINISTERING TO HIM NOW AFTER JOHN WAS ARRESTED JESUS CAME INTO GALILEE PROCLAIMING THE GOSPEL OF GOD AND SAYING THE TIME IS FULFILLED AND THE KINGDOM OF GOD IS AT HAND REPENT AND BELIEVE IN THE GOSPEL PASSING ALONGSIDE THE SEA OF GALILEE HE SAW SIMON AND ANDREW THE BROTHER OF SIMON CASTING A NET INTO THE SEA FOR THEY WERE FISHERMEN AND JESUS SAID TO THEM FOLLOW ME AND I WILL MAKE YOU BECOME FISHERS OF MEN AND IMMEDIATELY THEY LEFT THEIR NETS AND FOLLOWED HIM AND GOING ON A LITTLE FARTHER HE SAW JAMES THE SON OF ZEBEDEE AND JOHN HIS BROTHER WHO WERE IN THEIR BOAT MENDING THE NETS AND IMMEDIATELY HE CALLED THEM AND THEY LEFT THEIR FATHER ZEBEDEE IN THE BOAT WITH THE HIRED SERVANTS AND FOLLOWED HIM"

We obtain

"WKH EHJLQQLQJ RI WKH JRVSHO RI MHVXV FKULVW WKH VRQ RI JRG DV LW LV ZULWWHQ LQ LVDLDK WKH

SURSKHW EHKROG L VHQG PB PHVVHQJHU EHIRUH BRXU
IDFH ZKR ZLOO SUHSDUH BRXU ZDB WKH YRLFH RI RQH
FUBLQJ LQ WKH ZLOGHUQHVV SUHSDUH WKH ZDB RI
WKH ORUG PDNH KLV SDWKV VWUDLJKW MRKQ
DSSHDUHG EDSWLCLQJ LQ WKH ZLOGHUQHVV DQG
SURFODLPLQJ D EDSWLVP RI UHSHQWDQFH IRU WKH
IRUJLYHQHVV RI VLQV DQG DOO WKH FRXQWUB RI
MXGHD DQG DOO MHUXVDOHP ZHUH JRLQJ RXW WR KLP
DQG ZHUH EHLQJ EDSWLCHG EB KLP LQ WKH ULYHU
MRUGDQ FRQIHVVLQJ WKHLU VLQV QRZ MRKQ ZDV
FORWKHG ZLWK FDPHOV KDLU DQG ZRUH D OHDWKHU
EHOW DURXQG KLV ZDLVW DQG DWH ORFXVWV DQG
ZLOG KRQHB DQG KH SUHDFKHG VDBLQJ DIWHU PH
FRPHV KH ZKR LV PLJKWLHU WKDQ L WKH VWUDS RI
ZKRVH VDQGDOV L DP QRW ZRUWKB WR VWRRS GRZQ
DQG XQWLH L KDYH EDSWLCHG BRX ZLWK ZDWHU EXW
KH ZLOO EDSWLCH BRX ZLWK WKH KROB VSLULW LQ
WKRVH GDBV MHVXV FDPH IURP QDCDUHWK RI
JDOLOHH DQG ZDV EDSWLCHG EB MRKQ LQ WKH
MRUGDQ DQG ZKHQ KH FDPH XS RXW RI WKH ZDWHU
LPPHGLDWHOB KH VDZ WKH KHDYHQV EHLQJ WRUQ
RSHQ DQG WKH VSLULW GHVFHQGLQJ RQ KLP OLNH D
GRYH DQG D YRLFH FDPH IURP KHDYHQ BRX DUH PB
EHORYHG VRQ ZLWK BRX L DP ZHOO SOHDVHG WKH
VSLULW LPPHGLDWHOB GURYH KLP RXW LQWR WKH
ZLOGHUQHVV DQG KH ZDV LQ WKH ZLOGHUQHVV IRUWB
GDBV EHLQJ WHPSWHG EB VDWDQ DQG KH ZDV ZLWK
WKH ZLOG DQLPDOV DQG WKH DQJHOV ZHUH
PLQLVWHULQJ WR KLP QRZ DIWHU MRKQ ZDV
DUUHVWHG MHVXV FDPH LQWR JDOLOHH SURFODLPLQJ
WKH JRVSHO RI JRG DQG VDBLQJ WKH WLPH LV
IXOILOOHG DQG WKH NLQJGRP RI JRG LV DW KDQG
UHSHQW DQG EHOLHYH LQ WKH JRVSHO SDVVLQJ
DORQJVLGH WKH VHD RI JDOLOHH KH VDZ VLPRQ DQG
DQGUHZ WKH EURWKHU RI VLPRQ FDVWLQJ D QHW
LQWR WKH VHD IRU WKHB ZHUH ILVKHUPHQ DQG
MHVXV VDLG WR WKHP IROORZ PH DQG L ZLOO PDNH
BRX EHFRPH ILVKHUV RI PHQ DQG LPPHGLDWHOB WKHB
OHIW WKHLU QHWV DQG IROORZHG

> *KLP DQG JRLQJ RQ D OLWWOH IDUWKHU KH VDZ MDPHV WKH VRQ RI CHEHGHH DQG MRKQ KLV EURWKHU ZKR ZHUH LQ WKHLU ERDW PHQGLQJ WKH QHWV DQG LPPHGLDWHOB KH FDOOHG WKHP DQG WKHB OHIW WKHLU IDWKHU CHEHGHH LQ WKH ERDW ZLWK WKH KLUHG VHUYDQWV DQG IROORZHG KLP"*

Alternatively, the term "cryptanalysis"[37] originally described the process of producing a readable text from encrypted texts without knowing the secret key. We assume that the enciphering class from which the text was created is known, but not the secret key.

Example 2.26 (Decryption of Caesar). In order to get a readable text from the encrypted Gospel passage in Example 2.25, we assume that a function with a letter shift was applied. There are 26 different possibilities of a letter shift that can be tested. With a sufficiently long text, it is easy to determine the right key. A further possibility for this kind of encryption is to obtain conclusions from the unreadable text on the basis of letter frequencies in a language.

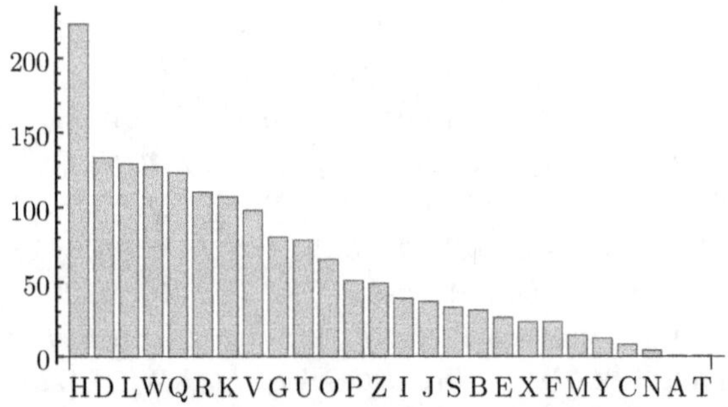

Figure 2.7 Bar chart of the letter frequencies of the encrypted Gospel passage.

Thus, the letter E occurs the most frequently in English texts, followed by T, A and O.[38] In the Gospel, which consists of 1623

[37] τὸ αναλύειν.

[38] For example, see a letter frequency table at https://en.wikipedia.org/wiki/Letter_frequency.

characters, H occurs 223 times, followed by D (133), L (129) and W (127), as shown in Figure 2.7. We assume that E has been transformed to H (a shift value of 3). Using a left shift by three letters (a shift value of -3),

$$d_3 : \Sigma_{\text{Lat}} \to \Sigma_{\text{Lat}},\ A \mapsto X, B \mapsto Y, C \mapsto Z, \ldots, X \mapsto U, \\ Y \mapsto V, Z \mapsto W,$$

we return the original text.

The two mappings of Examples 2.25 and 2.26 should ensure confidentiality by implementing the functionalities of encryption and decryption of data. There are mappings covering other security services. All such mappings are given a special designation.

Convention 2.27 (Cryptographical mapping). A *cryptographical mapping* is a mathematical mapping for implementing the cryptographical functionality affecting security services.

Thus, the focus of the tasks of cryptology has expanded significantly and we establish the terms in Section 2.5.

Convention 2.28 (Cryptology, cryptography, cryptanalysis). *Cryptology* is the science of designing (*cryptography*) and analyzing (*cryptanalysis*) cryptographical mappings.

After development, it has to be examined whether a cryptographical mapping fulfills its purpose of ensuring a security goal. Both subareas of cryptology belong together and cannot be viewed separately.

The problem of weak encryption in Example 2.25 can be addressed by adapting the frequencies of the letters. However, if we take the same alphabet for creating the ciphertext as for the plaintext, we cannot attain this goal. Thus, we have to make considerations. Let Σ be the alphabet for the plaintext, $p_s = \mathbb{P}(\{s\})$ the probability of occurrence of symbol $s \in \Sigma$ and $k \geq 1$ a fixed chosen real number. Furthermore, let M_s be a finite set that contains $\lceil p_s \cdot k \rceil$ different symbols, such that for any two different symbols $s, t \in \Sigma$, the sets M_s and M_t are disjoint, $M_s \cap M_t = \emptyset$ for $s \neq t$. Suppose that the probability of occurrence of every symbol in $m_s \in M_s$ follows a discrete uniform distribution, that is $\mathbb{P}(\{m_s\}) = \frac{1}{|M_s|}$. Then, the probability $\mathbb{P}(\{m\})$ for a symbol m in

$$M = \bigcup_{s \in \Sigma} M_s$$

is

$$\begin{aligned}
\mathbb{P}(\{m\}) &= \sum_{s\in\Sigma} \mathbb{P}(\{m\} \cap M_s) \\
&\overset{(1.8)}{=} \sum_{s\in\Sigma} \mathbb{P}(\{m\} \mid M_s) \cdot \mathbb{P}(M_s) \\
&= \sum_{s\in\Sigma} \mathbb{1}_{M_s}(m) \cdot \frac{1}{|M_s|} \cdot p_s \\
&\overset{m\in M_t}{=} \frac{p_t}{\lceil p_t \cdot k \rceil},
\end{aligned}$$

where $\mathbb{1}_{M_s}$ is the indicator function on M_s and $\mathbb{P}(\{m\} \mid M_s)$ is the conditional probability from Equation (1.8). Thus, it is possible to produce a nearly discrete uniform distribution over the symbols of M. This type of encryption is called *homophonic substitution*.

Example 2.29. Figure 2.8 shows the frequencies of 114 symbols enciphering the Gospel text from Example 2.25 using a homophonic substitution with parameter $k = 100$. The darker gray bars show the frequencies for the symbols representing the letter “E”. They are not distinctive. The horizontal line represents the expected frequency for each symbol. A more uniform distribution of the letters was obtained.

The cost of more security is dependent on two things. Firstly, the key size gets enlarged as more letters or symbols are needed. Secondly, the ciphertext gets expanded. To understand this, consider a binary representation of every single uppercase letter. We need $\lceil \log_2(26) \rceil = 5$ bits for the representation. Alternatively, we need $\lceil \log_2(114) \rceil = 7$ bits for representation in a homophonic substitution

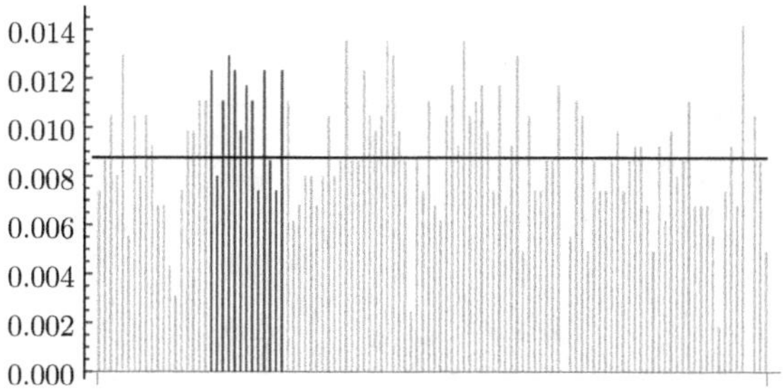

Figure 2.8 Bar chart of the letter frequencies of the homophone encrypted Gospel passage.

based on 114 symbols. This is called a *message expansion*. Thus, a homophonic substitution is not a powerful method for encryption. Unfortunately, cryptanalysts have already cracked the challenge: they examine combinations of symbols for statistical abnormalities.

2.5 Cryptographical Functionalities

We denote the functionalities of security services as *cryptographical functionalities*. Data processing is common to all of these functionalities. The data originates from a language $\mathcal{P} = \mathcal{P}_\Sigma$ based on an alphabet Σ. $\mathcal{P}$ is called the *plaintext space*. We distinguish between five cryptographical functionalities: ciphering, hash generation, signature generation, key management and random number generation, which we will examine in the following chapters. Some cryptographical functionalities can be made more defined. For example, ciphering consists of encryption and decryption of data, or key management that requires key generation and exchange. As shown in Table 2.2,[39] we can see which functionalities are necessary ($\checkmark$) or supportive ($\sim$) for the respective security services. Communication is for a specific purpose. Cryptographical functionalities are therefore, as a rule, embedded in a fixed process directed towards this purpose. The process of communication using cryptographical functionalities is subject to a specialized *communication protocol*.

[39]Done in the style of Picture 4.1 in (Sorge *et al.*, 2013).

Table 2.2 Cryptographical functionalities supporting security services.

	Ciphering	Hash generation	Signature generation	Key management	Random number generation
Confidentiality	✓			✓	~
Data integrity	~	✓	✓	~	~
Accessibility	~	~	~	✓	~
Accountability	✓	~	✓	✓	~
Privacy	✓			✓	~

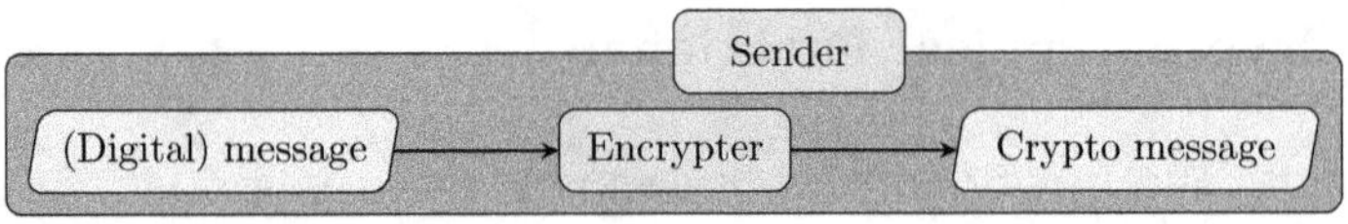

Figure 2.9 Encrypter in a communication system on the sender's side.

Convention 2.30 (Cryptographical protocol). A communication protocol whose execution is intended to ensure at least one security goal is called a *cryptographical protocol*.

When processing a cryptographical protocol, we need an additional component in a communication system to enable cryptographical functionalities that is called an *encrypter*, cf. Figure 2.9. Its main component is a cryptosystem.

2.5.1 *Ciphering*

If entity A wants to perform a secure message exchange with entity B, they have to encrypt their message. During this part of *ciphering* the aim of A is to transform a plaintext message m belonging to a plaintext space $\mathcal{P}$ using a *key* k_1 from a *key space* $\mathcal{K}$ into a ciphertext message c belonging to a *ciphertext space* $\mathcal{C}$. This process is called *encryption*, which we initially denote by a function

$$e : \mathcal{K} \times \mathcal{P} \to \mathcal{C}, \ (k_1, m) \mapsto c := e(k_1, m). \tag{2.4}$$

Next, B has to recycle the ciphertext message back into the plaintext message after the transmission. We denote this ciphering part, the *decryption* process, by a function

$$d : \mathcal{K} \times \mathcal{C} \to \mathcal{P}, \ (k_2, c) \mapsto \tilde{m} := d(k_2, c). \tag{2.5}$$

In fact, the recycling process is successful if and only if there is a corresponding key $k_2 \in \mathcal{K}$, such that

$$m = d(k_2, e(k_1, m)).$$

Plaintext-, key- and ciphertext spaces are each predefined sets of symbols. Every symbol is a concatenation of characters of an alphabet $(\Sigma, \preceq)$ formed from syntactic specifications. Usually, we write the key as a subscript for convenience, for instance

$$d_{k_2}(e_{k_1}(m)).$$

A and B should assume that everyone knows the used encryption method, i.e., the functions e and d. The only thing they should be aware of is to hide the key as it is the only protection mechanism. This approach is the most known and important premise of modern cryptography, and is called *Kerckhoffs' principle*.[40]

Definition 2.31 (Cipher system). Let $\mathcal{P}$ be a plaintext space, $\mathcal{K}$ be a key space and $\mathcal{C}$ be a ciphertext space. Along with a family

$$\mathcal{E} := \{e_k : \mathcal{P} \to \mathcal{C}; k \in \mathcal{K}\} \tag{2.6}$$

of encryption functions and a family

$$\mathcal{D} := \{d_k : \mathcal{C} \to \mathcal{P}; k \in \mathcal{K}\} \tag{2.7}$$

[40] Auguste Kerckhoffs (1835–1903).

of decryption functions, each indexed with all the keys from the key space $\mathcal{K}$, the tuple $(\mathcal{P}, \mathcal{C}, \mathcal{K}, \mathcal{E}, \mathcal{D})$ is called a *cipher system* if for all $m \in \mathcal{P}$ and for all $k_1 \in \mathcal{K}$ there exists a key $k_2 \in \mathcal{K}$ satisfying the equation

$$m = d_{k_2}(e_{k_1}(m)). \tag{2.8}$$

There are three different categories of cipher systems. A *private-key cipher system* reviewed in Chapters 4, 5, 6 and 9, requires the exact matching of the two keys, that is $k_1 = k_2$. k_1 is used in the same manner for encryption and decryption. If there are situations where usually k_1 and k_2 differ, $k_1 \neq k_2$, we will refer to a *public-key cipher system* reviewed in Chapters 5, 7, 8 and 10. A special cipher system arises from the combination of both forms, private-key and public-key, and is called a *hybrid cipher system*. For such a system, we need to work with both private-key and public-key cipher systems.

Simple cipher systems

We now consider two examples of cipher systems by applying Definition 2.31 and using the fact that computations can be outsourced from $\mathbb{Z}_n$ to $\mathbb{Z}$, that is, calculations can be performed in $\mathbb{Z}$, but they must be completed by a modulo operation. This work is shown in the context of Theorem 3.50, by applying the modulo operation at the end according to Theorem 1.2. The first example shows a private-key cipher system. We will investigate this kind of cipher system in Chapters 4 and 6.

Example 2.32 (Shift cipher). Let $\mathcal{P} = \mathcal{C} = \mathcal{K} := \mathbb{Z}_{26}$ and

$$e_k : \mathcal{P} \to \mathcal{C},\ m \mapsto e_k(m) := (m + k) \bmod 26,$$
$$d_k : \mathcal{C} \to \mathcal{P},\ c \mapsto d_k(c) := (c - k) \bmod 26.$$

Then $d_k(e_k(m)) = ((m + k) - k) \bmod 26 = m$ and thus we have a private-key cipher system. The same key, the *secret key*, is used for encryption and decryption. It generalizes the Caesar cipher known from Examples 2.25 and 2.26 by encoding the letters according to their order into increasing numbers starting from 0. By choosing $k = 3$ we obtain the Caesar cipher:

$$\mathrm{C} \xrightarrow{\text{code}} 2 \xrightarrow[\text{2+3 mod 26}]{\text{encrypt}} 5 \xrightarrow{\text{code}} \mathrm{F}.$$

Example 2.32 provides two aspects that must be mentioned. Firstly, the cipher system is a simple monoalphabetic substitution cipher, the shift cipher. Thus, the encryption process takes the symbols one by one for encrypting and decrypting. Such a process is called a *stream cipher*. If the same sequences of symbols occur, the resulting encrypted sequence is the same too. This is a vulnerability and we will look for mechanisms to overcome it in Section 4.2. Secondly, it raises the question whether the coding of symbols is itself a substitution cipher. The answer is "yes", but in the context of this book we will use the terms encoding and decoding in the manner of converting message sources to a format that can be used to encrypt and decrypt.[41]

The private-key cipher system in Example 2.32 uses a so-called mod-n-addition that will be formally introduced in Definition 3.47. The following example shows a public-key cipher system using the mod-n-multiplication, again defined in Definition 3.47. It is designed such that $n = 26$ is the product of two prime numbers 2 and 13.

Example 2.33 (RSA-light). For this cipher system, let $\mathcal{P} = \mathcal{C} := \mathbb{Z}_{26}$, $\mathcal{K} := \{26\} \times \{1, 5, 7, 11\}$ and with $(26, k_1), (26, k_2) \in \mathcal{K}$

$$e_{(26,k_1)} : \mathcal{P} \to \mathcal{C},\ m \mapsto e_{(26,k_1)}(m) := m^{k_1} \bmod 26,$$
$$d_{(26,k_2)} : \mathcal{C} \to \mathcal{P},\ c \mapsto d_{(26,k_2)}(c) := c^{k_2} \bmod 26.$$

We will show in Section 8.3 that in this situation

$$d_{(26,k_2)}\left(e_{(26,k_1)}(m)\right) = m^{k_1 \cdot k_2} \bmod 26 = m$$

[41]With the meaning of (Proakis, 2008, p. 80).

for some combinations of k_1 and k_2. Because of the different keys in the encryption and decryption process, we use a public-key cipher system. The key $(26, k_1)$ is called a *public key.* For decryption, the *private key* $(26, k_2)$ has to be used. This cipher system corresponds to the ideas to be discussed later in the RSA cipher system. By choosing $k = 7$, we obtain

$$\text{C} \xrightarrow{\text{code}} 2 \xrightarrow[2^7 \bmod 26]{\text{encrypt}} 24 \xrightarrow{\text{code}} \text{Y}.$$

We will examine public-key cipher systems in Chapters 7 and 8.

2.5.2 *Message digests*

Data integrity is about completeness and unalterability of data. Data should not be altered, deleted, be inadmissible or unauthorized. The integrity of an object can be verified using a so-called message digest. A given value is compared with the value generated by the object. If the values are equal, we assume data integrity.

Definition 2.34 (Message digest function, message digest). Let $\mathcal{P}$ be a language based on an alphabet Σ. A *message digest function* is a mapping $h : \mathcal{P} \to \Sigma^n$ assigning data to data with a fixed length. The resulting value is called a *message digest.*

The length of a message digest is usually shorter than the length of the data. Small changes in the data, like swapping two symbols or changing one symbol, should result in a completely different message digest.

ISBN-13-code

You can identify a book using a sequence

$$z_1 z_2 z_3 z_4 z_5 z_6 z_7 z_8 z_9 z_{10} z_{11} z_{12} - z_{13},$$

the International Standard Book Number (ISBN). In this case, all z_i for $i \in \{1, \ldots, 13\}$ belong to set $\mathbb{Z}_{10}$. The number consists of five parts: prefix, registration group, registrant, publication and check digit[42]:

$$\underbrace{978}_{\text{prefix}} - \underbrace{0}_{\text{group}} - \underbrace{387}_{\text{publisher}} - \underbrace{77993}_{\text{title}} - \underbrace{5}_{\text{check digit}}$$

For example, the group number 0 is used in countries where English is the first language. The check digit is defined by the message digest function $h : \mathbb{Z}_{10}^{12} \to \mathbb{Z}_{10}$,

$$(z_1, \ldots, z_{12}) \mapsto z_{13} := 10 - \left(\sum_{i=1}^{12} z_i \cdot 3^{(i+1) \bmod 2} \right) \bmod 10.$$

Referring to Definition 2.34, we use $\Sigma = \mathbb{Z}_{10}$, $\mathcal{P} = \mathbb{Z}_{10}^{12}$ and $n = 1$. An ISBN-13-code is defined by being a member of the set C of all 13-tuples $(z_1, \ldots, z_{13}) \in \mathbb{Z}_{10}^{13}$ applying $h(z_1, \ldots, z_{12}) = z_{13}$.

Example 2.35. The ISBN-13-code from (Li and Niederreiter, 2008) about coding and cryptology is 978-981-283-223-8. We calculate

$$10 - (9 + 8 + 8 + 2 + 3 + 2 + 3 \cdot (7 + 9 + 1 + 8 + 2 + 3)) \bmod 10 = 8$$

and confirm the correctness of the message digest $z_{13} = 8$.

Given an ISBN-13-code $c = (z_1, \ldots, z_{13}) \in C \subset \mathbb{Z}_{10}^{13}$ and the function

$$\begin{aligned} \tilde{h} : \mathbb{Z}_{10}^{13} \to \mathbb{Z}_{10}, \ (z_1, \ldots, z_{13}) &\mapsto \tilde{h}(z_1, \ldots, z_{13}) \\ &= \sum_{i=1}^{13} z_i \cdot 3^{(i+1) \bmod 2} \bmod 10, \end{aligned}$$

we obtain

$$\begin{aligned} \tilde{h}(c) &= \left(\sum_{i=1}^{12} z_i \cdot 3^{(i+1) \bmod 2} + z_{13} \right) \bmod 10 \\ &= \left(\sum_{i=1}^{12} z_i \cdot 3^{(i+1) \bmod 2} + 10 - \sum_{i=1}^{12} z_i \cdot 3^{(i+1) \bmod 2} \right) \bmod 10 \\ &= 10 \bmod 10 = 0. \end{aligned}$$

What happens if two digits swap or one digit changes?

[42]Here, the ISBN comes from (Hoffstein *et al.*, 2008).

Theorem 2.36. *Let C be the ISBN-13-code, $z \in C$ and $x, y \in \mathbb{Z}_{10}^{13}$ with $x \neq z$ and $y \neq z$. Suppose x arises from z by changing exactly one digit or y arises from z by swapping two directly adjacent, different digits on the condition that the difference is not equal to five. Then, x and y do not match the equation $\tilde{h}(x) = 0$ or $\tilde{h}(y) = 0$ and are not members of C.*

Proof. Let x and z be different at the ith position or otherwise be the same. Then

$$\tilde{h}(x) = (\tilde{h}(x) - \tilde{h}(z)) \bmod 10 = k \cdot (x_i - z_i) \bmod 10 \neq 0.$$

Depending on the index i, the value of k is either 1 or 3. Let $v = x_i - z_i \neq 0$. If $k = 1$, we get $1 \cdot v = v \neq 0$. Otherwise, $3 \cdot v \notin \{-20, -10, 0, 10, 20\}$. It follows that the product $k \cdot v \bmod 10$ is also different from zero (modulo 10). Thus, x is not an ISBN-13-code.

Now, let $y_i = z_{i+1}$ and $y_{i+1} = z_i$. Then

$$\tilde{h}(y) = (\tilde{h}(y) - \tilde{h}(z)) \bmod 10 = \pm 2 \cdot (y_i - z_i) \bmod 10.$$

Because of $y_i \neq z_i$, this product yields zero (modulo 10) iff the difference is equal to five. In all other cases, y is not an ISBN-13-code either. □

There are 10^{12} different ISBN-13 codes. The message digest function h is not an injective function. Many ISBN-13-codes collide with the check digit. For example, (Baigneres *et al.*, 2006) has the ISBN-13-code 978038727934-3, but the next edition of the same book has a different ISBN-13-code 978038750860-3. Both check digits are equal. This is not desirable with regard to the integrity of an ISBN-13-code, because it is very easy to create a wrong but nevertheless meaningful ISBN-13-code with a correct check digit.

MD5 message digest

The ISBN-13-code example shows the basic principle of message digest generation. While minor changes to an ISBN-13-code will not result in a valid ISBN-13-code, the generation has serious drawbacks. On one hand, a tuple of fixed length is provided for the generation of a check digit. On the other hand, since the length of the output is

Figure 2.10 Message digest of a downloadable file.

too small, many books have the same checksum. An example of the message digest of the freely available office package LibreOffice[43] is intended to show how these difficulties can be mitigated. A message digest, for example, the MD5 hash, is generated for the installer file (in the black frame of Figure 2.10). If a file is downloaded, the MD5 hash can be generated by its bytecode (see Figure 2.10, in the white frame) and compared with the MD5 hash on the website. If differences occur, there must be some difficulties with downloading, and the integrity of the file is violated. To generate the MD5 checksum, a bit string of any length is required as input. The output is a sequence of 128 bits.

$$\text{md5} : \mathbb{Z}_2^* \to \mathbb{Z}_2^{128}.$$

This message digest generation is not injective either, and there are files that have the same MD5 hash. Although the algorithm of generating the MD5 hash is open and known, it is much more difficult to generate a file that supplies a given hash. Nevertheless, it successfully demonstrated that MD5 hash generation is vulnerable and should not be used.[44] However, it is instructive to know the procedure.

Message digests, such as the MD5 hash, are called message detection codes (see Section 9.1). It is also possible to generate message digests based on private-key cipher systems. Such message digests

[43]Version 6.1.4 at this point in time, see https://www.libreoffice.org/.
[44]See http://www.mscs.dal.ca/~selinger/md5collision/.

are called message authentication codes (see Section 9.2). A combination of both message digest types leads to a hybrid form, the hash-based message authentication codes (see Section 9.3).

2.5.3 *Signature generation*

A (digital) signature is a key-based scheme for creating a test value whereby the authorship of data can be proven. The source of the data generates a signature using a key that is solely known to itself. A public key can then be used to confirm the authenticity of the signature. The data can be clearly assigned to the source. Conversely, the source cannot deny being the origin of the data and is accountable for them.

There are two different kinds of signature algorithms. Both transfer the data and the so-called signature. A digital signature can be as long as the original data. There has to be a recovery process in which data that is received can be compared with the original data directly (see Section 10.1). After proving conformity, originality is accepted. The second possibility is to generate a signed message detection code of the original message (see Section 10.1). This data is normally much shorter than the original message. A verification can be performed by recovering the message detection code and comparing it with the message detection code of the received message. Again, originality is accepted by proving conformity.

Example 2.37. By applying the public-key cipher system from Example 2.33, we can use the private key for "encryption", which is known by exactly one entity. This is be used instead of the public key. After the "decryption" process and after performing a check we can assume that the data is coming from the entity owning the private key. The data is allocated definitely.

2.5.4 *Key management and PRNGs*

Most of the named functionalities rely on keys that have to be generated, distributed, saved, sometimes recovered, invalidated and finally deleted. The generation process must not be deterministic or reproducible in a simple manner. It should seem to be random but it is typically not. Pseudorandom key generation is a deterministic generation process in which all keys have the same probability for being generated. Therefore, an initial value, called *seed*, is often used. A seed is frequently generated from the state of a computer system or by a hardware component. A generated key has to get distributed to all involved entities, which is done by an additional communication. Since keys are to be kept in confidence in a private-key cipher system, there often has to be a communication using an additional key. The latter key overrides the first key and a hierarchy is introduced. There is sometimes a master key deriving to subordinated keys. Public keys for public-key cipher systems are usually public domain. We investigate key management tasks in Section 7.1. A basis for key generation is generating truly random numbers, which is very difficult. An algorithm for generating a sequence of numbers, which seems to be random, is called a *pseudorandom number generator* (PRNG). Today's available algorithms imitate and make this task easier. Private-key cipher systems usually rely on such pseudorandom numbers. In contrast, public-key cipher systems have to do more, i.e., the pseudorandom number is a starting point for generating a big prime number. We discuss the generation of pseudorandom numbers in Section 11.4.

2.6 Cryptanalysis

The second part of cryptology affects cryptanalysis, which involves inventing new cryptographical mappings as test phases for attackers to prove them. Proving also means the analysis of reaching security goals. One of its main tasks is to recover the plaintext from a given ciphertext, if confidentiality is an underlying goal. Kerckhoffs' second principle[45] tells us

> "It should not require secrecy, and it should not be a problem if it falls into enemy hands."

[45] See (Kerckhoffs, 1883).

It is in the same logic as Shannon's maxim,

"The enemy knows the system."

Assuming that a cryptographical mapping is well-known, it depends on the quality of the key whether the plaintext can be recovered from the ciphertext. The easier this can be done, the weaker the cryptographical mapping. There are different levels of generic types of attacks against cryptosystems.

Brute-force attack

A first criterion of the quality of a cryptographical mapping is the cardinality of the key space. In a so-called *brute-force attack*, all of the possible keys are successively tested. Today's computational power allows one to break many cryptosystems, and the plaintext can be restored immediately. In reference to Example 2.32, by extending the Caesar cipher to the shift cipher, there would be more than one meaningful result found by a brute-force attack. For example, if we want to decrypt the ciphertext "YPCLY",[46] knowing that there is a shift cipher, we get the possible plaintexts

"YPCLY", "XOBKX", "WNAJW", "VMZIV", "ULYHU", "TKXGT", "SJWFS", "**RIVER**", "QHUDQ", "PGTCP", "OFSBO", "NERAN", "MDQZM", "LCPYL", "KBOXK", "JANWJ", "IZMVI", "HYLUH", "GXKTG", "FWJSF", "EVIRE", "DUHQD", "CTGPC", "BSFOB", "**ARENA**", "ZQDMZ".

Two are real candidates: "RIVER" and "ARENA". Although it delivers a meaningful result, one of the two keys is wrong. Such a key is called a *spurious key*.

Let $\mathcal{K}$ be a finite key space. First, we look at a random experiment modeling the mean number of trials. The term $\mathbb{P}(\{v\})$ refers to the probability of finding the right key exactly at step v after $v-1$ fails. There should be a discrete uniform distribution for all v's, which means that each value $v \in \{1, \ldots, |\mathcal{K}|\}$ is equally likely to be observed. To understand this, we depict the probability to get the

[46]In the style of (Stinson, 2005).

right key at step v after $v-1$ fails, if the probability of finding the right key at the first trial is

$$p_1 = \frac{1}{|\mathcal{K}|} = \frac{1}{|\mathcal{K}|+1-1} \tag{2.9}$$

and the fraction's denominator will be decreased at each step by one, which means finding the key within step v has a probability of

$$p_v = \frac{1}{|\mathcal{K}|+1-v}.$$

Next, we describe the situation of finding the right key at step v after $v-1$ fails. The probability of success after exactly v trials is

$$\begin{aligned}
\mathbb{P}(\{v\}) &= (1-p_1)\cdot(1-p_2)\cdot\ldots\cdot(1-p_{v-1})\cdot p_v \\
&= \left(1-\frac{1}{|\mathcal{K}|}\right)\cdot\left(1-\frac{1}{|\mathcal{K}|-1}\right)\cdot\ldots\cdot\left(1-\frac{1}{|\mathcal{K}|+1-(v-1)}\right) \\
&\quad \cdot\frac{1}{|\mathcal{K}|+1-v} \\
&= \left(\frac{|\mathcal{K}|-1}{|\mathcal{K}|}\right)\cdot\left(\frac{|\mathcal{K}|-2}{|\mathcal{K}|-1}\right)\cdot\ldots\cdot\left(\frac{|\mathcal{K}|+1-v}{|\mathcal{K}|+2-v}\right)\cdot\frac{1}{|\mathcal{K}|+1-v} \\
&= \frac{1}{|\mathcal{K}|}.
\end{aligned} \tag{2.10}$$

We determine the expectation $\mathbb{E}[V]$ of the associated random variable V with range $\{1,\ldots,|\mathcal{K}|\}$. How many trials are necessary on average? From Equations (2.9) and (2.10) it follows

$$\mathbb{P}(\{v\}) = \frac{1}{|\mathcal{K}|} \text{ for } v \in \{1,\ldots,|\mathcal{K}|\}.$$

Then, the expected number of trials is

$$\mathbb{E}[V] = \sum_{v=1}^{|\mathcal{K}|} v\cdot\mathbb{P}(\{v\}) = \frac{|\mathcal{K}|(|\mathcal{K}|+1)}{2|\mathcal{K}|} = \frac{|\mathcal{K}|+1}{2}. \tag{2.11}$$

Thus, a large cardinality of key space is very useful, but this unfortunately does not ensure security on its own.

Known-ciphertext attack

By smart trial and error of different keys the number of steps for searching plaintexts can be reduced. For example, the analysis of frequencies in Example 2.26 (Caesar cipher) enables us to find the right key after one step and we can recover the Gospel passage. It is assumed that different plaintexts $p_1, p_2, \ldots$ get encrypted with the same key k to ciphertexts $c_1 = e_k(p_1), c_2 = e_k(p_2), \ldots$. Additionally, it is assumed that some information about the plaintexts is included in the ciphertexts, i.e., the frequencies of the letters. If an opponent possesses some ciphertexts $c_1, c_2, \ldots$, then an attack is called a *known-ciphertext attack*. We will discuss the basic chances of success for such attacks in Section 5.2.3.

Known-plaintext attack

Sometimes, an opponent possesses ciphertexts: single and pairs of plain- and ciphertexts $(p_1, c_1),\ (p_2, c_2), \ldots, (p_n, c_n)$ that are generated by the same key, $c_i = e_k(p_i)$. An attack based on this knowledge is called a *known-plaintext attack*. The *linear cryptanalysis* where we will discuss the weakness of affin linear block ciphers in Section 4.2.3 is an example of this kind of attack.

Chosen-plaintext attack

When starting a *chosen-plaintext attack*, the opponent has provided pairs of plaintexts and ciphertexts, $(p_1, c_1),\ (p_2, c_2), \ldots, (p_n, c_n)$, similar to a known-plaintext attack. The difference between the two types of attacks is that they can choose a plaintext at will and encrypt these plaintexts with the key k that was identified. This allows one to look for patterns inside the cryptographical mapping and to transfer them to the plaintexts. This idea applies to *differential cryptanalysis*. There are successful attacks against the modification detection code generators MD4 and MD5, but also against private-key cipher systems like FEAL.[47]

Chosen-ciphertext attack

In contrast to a chosen plaintext attack, the class of *chosen-ciphertext*

[47] See (Stamp and Low, 2007, p. 170ff.).

attacks operates in the opposite manner. Some ciphertexts are chosen and the corresponding plaintexts get acquired by initiation of a decryption process. This results in more costs in the latter case. However, the idea of finding patterns is the same.

Related key attack

Another approach in attacking cipher systems is to utilize patterns in the choice of keys that are used to encrypt the plaintexts, called a *related key attack*. The keys are related in a special way and plaintexts have been encrypted by such different keys. The goal is to determine one of the keys. A common example of a related key attack concerns the WLAN standard protocol, Wired Equivalent Privacy (WEP), which was recently used. The cryptographical mapping RC4[48] was used inside and this function was successfully attacked.

Cryptanalysis of public-key ciphers

All mentioned attacks are concerned with breaking the cryptographical mappings of private-key cipher systems. Public-key intended cryptographical mappings can be attacked by discovering the mathematical methods based on a number theoretic considerations. While the named attacks look for one single key, the *public-key attack* concerns either the whole system or recovering the private key without breaking the situational cryptographical mapping. An example of such an attack is a *side channel attack*.[49] Here, the weakness of an implementation or the process itself is not affected, but the physical process on an executing computer is subject to eavesdropping. For example, timing information, while executing the square-and-multiply algorithm,[50] used in modular exponentiation depends linearly on the number of "1" bits in the key. If the algorithm is repeated many times with the same key and other input data, statistical information develops that could be used to determine the key.

---

[48]See (Stamp and Low, 2007, p. 103ff.).

[49]See (Martin, 2017, p. 43).

[50]See Algorithm 7.3.

Chapter 3

Basics of Algebra

Note 3.1. In this chapter, the requirements are:

- knowing the idea of an equivalence relation, and
- being able to calculate a remainder modulo n and handle prime numbers, see Section 1.1.

Selected literature: See (Buchmann, 2012; Durbin, 2009; Hardy *et al.*, 2008; Lang, 1984).

3.1 Algebraic Structures

Cryptology is based on number theory. Groups, fields, modular arithmetic, prime numbers (and generating them) are of chief importance.

We first have to investigate algebraic structures, as they are fundamental for all other results. Let us review well-known basic operations on real numbers as shown in Table 3.1. There are many calculating rules and properties concerning real numbers. Furthermore, numbers $0, 1 \in \mathbb{R}$ have special properties. The set of real numbers, together with addition and multiplication, forms an algebraic structure. Keeping these rules in mind, we can abstract the calculating rules and properties.

3.1.1 *Groups, rings and fields*

Addition and multiplication are both interior mappings *viz.* mappings concerning just one set. Every mapping takes one or more elements

Table 3.1 Basic arithmetic on $\mathbb{R}$.

	Example operation	Property
Addition	$3+4=7 \quad \in \mathbb{R}$	Closed under addition
	$(3+4)+5=12=3+(4+5)$	Associative law
	$3+0=3$	Identity element 0
	$3+4=7 \quad =4+3$	Commutation law
Multiplic.	$3\cdot 4=12 \quad \in \mathbb{R}$	Closed under multiplication
	$(3\cdot 4)\cdot 5=60=3\cdot(4\cdot 5)$	Associative law
	$3\cdot 1=3$	Identity element 1
	$3\cdot 4=12=4\cdot 3$	Commutation law
	$3\cdot(4+5)=27=3\cdot 4+3\cdot 5$	Distributive law

from this single set as input and also generates an output from this set. Binary mappings are very important in this regard.

Definition 3.2 (Interior binary mapping). An *interior binary mapping* on a set S is a mapping $* : S \times S \to S$, and is written using infix notation,

$$(x, y) \mapsto x * y.$$

Input		Output
x	y	$x * y$

Analogously, we can write other mappings:

$$x \circ y,\ x \cdot y,\ x + y,\ x \otimes y,\ x \oplus y,\ x +_n y,\ x \cdot_n y\ \ldots$$

Example 3.3 (XOR gate). *XOR* is a mapping on $\Sigma_{\text{bool}} = \{0, 1\}$, $\oplus : \Sigma_{\text{bool}} \times \Sigma_{\text{bool}} \to \Sigma_{\text{bool}}$.

Input		Output
x	y	$x \oplus y$
0	0	0
0	1	1
1	0	1
1	1	0

Remark 3.4. Looking at Σ_{bool} we can typically consider adding one number to another by $+$. But then, $1 + 1 \notin \Sigma_{\text{bool}}$ and this kind of addition is not an interior binary mapping on Σ_{bool}.

Example 3.5. With the sets

$$E = \{2 \cdot k;\ k \in \mathbb{Z}\}, \quad O = \{2 \cdot k + 1;\ k \in \mathbb{Z}\},\ E \cap O = \emptyset,$$

the mapping $+ : E \times E \to E$ is an interior binary mapping because $2 \cdot k_1 + 2 \cdot k_2 = 2 \cdot (k_1 + k_2) \in E$. However, the mapping $+ : O \times O \to O$ is not well-defined because $(2 \cdot k_1 + 1) + (2 \cdot k_2 + 1) = 2 \cdot (k_1 + k_2 + 1) \in E$.

We can then put together a set and $n > 0$ interior binary mappings on this set to a structure.

Definition 3.6 (Algebraic structure). Let S be a non-empty set. A structure $(S, *_1, \ldots, *_n)$ consisting of S and with $n > 0$ different interior binary mappings on S is called an *algebraic structure*.

Remark 3.7. If there are special elements of S requested for emphasis, they can be embedded into the structure's notation. For instance, $(S, *, e_*)$, $e_* \in S$, or more specifically, $(\Sigma_{\text{bool}}, \oplus, 0)$.

Example 3.8. Let $\mathbb{R}^{n \times n}$ be the set of any $n \times n$ real matrices and

$$S = \{M \in \mathbb{R}^{n \times n};\ \det(M) = 1\}$$

the subset of matrices with determinant 1. Typical operations on matrices, that is addition and multiplication, are denoted by $+$ and $\cdot$. The $n \times n$ identity matrix is denoted by I_n and the null matrix by O_n. Then $(\mathbb{R}^{n \times n}, +, O_n)$, $(\mathbb{R}^{n \times n}, \cdot, I_n)$ and $(S, \cdot, I_n)$ are algebraic structures. The last statement follows from the fact that the determinant of a matrix product of square matrices equals the product of their determinants.

In most cases, a mapping of an algebraic structure possesses some properties that are not only provided but necessary for further considerations. Firstly, it is sometimes possible to swap the inputs without changing the result. As shown in Example 3.3, there is no change by swapping the inputs x and y. As with the real numbers in Table 3.1, the XOR mapping fulfills the commutation law property. The commutation law applies to an interior binary mapping $* : S \times S \to S$ in the case of

$$\text{(A1),(M1)} \quad x * y = y * x \tag{3.1}$$

for all $x, y \in S$ and this mapping is then called *commutative*, or rather abelian.[1]

Remark 3.9. However, not all interior binary mappings have the commutation law property. From Example 3.8, $n = 2$ was chosen, then

$$\begin{pmatrix} 1 & 1 \\ 1 & 2 \end{pmatrix} \cdot \begin{pmatrix} 2 & 1 \\ 5 & 3 \end{pmatrix} = \begin{pmatrix} 7 & 4 \\ 12 & 7 \end{pmatrix} \neq \begin{pmatrix} 3 & 4 \\ 8 & 11 \end{pmatrix} = \begin{pmatrix} 2 & 1 \\ 5 & 3 \end{pmatrix} \cdot \begin{pmatrix} 1 & 1 \\ 1 & 2 \end{pmatrix}$$

Secondly, some interior binary mappings $* : S \times S \to S$ have to be serially performed more than once. If by fulfilling the associative law the order of execution does not matter, i.e.,

$$\text{(A2), (M2)} \quad (x * y) * z = x * (y * z), \tag{3.2}$$

for all $x, y, z \in S$, the interior binary mapping is called *associative*.

[1]Named after Niels H. Abel (1802–1829), a pioneer of modern algebra from Norway.

Example 3.10. XOR is associative, as shown in the following table.

			$(x \oplus y) \oplus z$		$x \oplus (y \oplus z)$	
x	y	z	$u = x \oplus y$	$u \oplus z$	$x \oplus v$	$v = y \oplus z$
0	0	0	0	**0**	**0**	0
0	0	1	0	**1**	**1**	1
0	1	0	1	**1**	**1**	1
0	1	1	1	**0**	**0**	0
1	0	0	1	**1**	**1**	0
1	0	1	1	**0**	**0**	1
1	1	0	0	**0**	**0**	1
1	1	1	0	**1**	**1**	0

Example 3.11. The multiplication of compatible matrices is associative. Let A, B and C be $m \times n$, $n \times l$ and $l \times r$ matrices. Looking at

$$\underbrace{(A \cdot B)}_{S} \cdot C \text{ and } A \cdot \underbrace{(B \cdot C)}_{T},$$

the following holds for the resulting element $d_{ik} = (A \cdot B \cdot C)_{ik}$ because of the calculation rules of the matrix' elements:

$$d_{\boldsymbol{ik}} = \underbrace{\sum_{j=1}^{l} \left(\sum_{v=1}^{n} a_{iv} \cdot b_{vj} \right)}_{s_{ij}} \cdot c_{j\boldsymbol{k}} = \sum_{v=1}^{n} a_{iv} \cdot \underbrace{\left(\sum_{j=1}^{l} b_{vj} \cdot c_{j\boldsymbol{k}} \right)}_{t_{v\boldsymbol{k}}}.$$

An algebraic structure with an associative interior binary mapping is called a *semi-group*. For example, $(\Sigma_{\text{bool}}, \oplus, 0)$ and $(S, \cdot, I_n)$ are semi-groups.

Sometimes, elements of a semi-group's set have a special property. They do not impact the execution of the interior binary mapping $* : S \times S \to S$, leaving all combined elements unchanged by applying $*$. Let $e_* \in S$ be an element of S. If

$$\text{(A3), (M3)} \quad e_* * x = x = x * e_* \tag{3.3}$$

applies for all $x \in S$, then e_* is called the *identity element* of S with respect to $*$. In this case, any other element $y \in S$ relating to an element $x \in S$ may exist, satisfying

$$\text{(A4), (M4)} \quad x * y = e_* = y * x. \tag{3.4}$$

Then, y is called the *inverse element* of x. Assuming that there is another inverse element $z \in S$ fulfilling $x*z = e_* = z*x$, we consider

$$y \overset{(3.3)}{=} e_* * y \overset{(3.4)}{=} (z * x) * y \overset{(3.2)}{=} z * (x * y) \overset{(3.4)}{=} z * e_* \overset{(3.3)}{=} z. \tag{3.5}$$

Thus, the inverse element is unique.

Example 3.12. Consider the set $\mathbb{Z}_3 = \{0, 1, 2\}$ and the following calculation rules for an additive mapping $+_3 : \mathbb{Z}_3 \times \mathbb{Z}_3 \to \mathbb{Z}_3$:

$$\begin{array}{c|ccc} +_3 & 0 & 1 & 2 \\ \hline 0 & 0 & 1 & 2 \\ 1 & 1 & 2 & 0 \\ 2 & 2 & 0 & 1 \end{array} \left.\vphantom{\begin{array}{c}0\\1\\2\end{array}}\right\} x +_3 y = x + y \bmod 3 \text{ cf. (1.1)}$$

This interior binary mapping $+_3$ is part of modular arithmetic. Imagine that we were on a train at 10 pm and embarking on a long trip that takes 6 hours. When do we arrive? We may count $(10 + 6) = 1 \cdot 12 + 4$ to determine the arrival time of 4 am. The mapping satisfies

$$x +_3 0 = 0 +_3 x = x$$

for each $x \in \mathbb{Z}_3$. Therefore, 0 is the identity element of $\mathbb{Z}_3$ with respect to $+_3$. Moreover, it is $1 +_3 2 = 2 +_3 1 = 0$ and $0 +_3 0 = 0$, such that 0 is its own inverse elements 1 and 2 are mutual inverse elements.

In the same way, we can look at a multiplication $\cdot_3 : \mathbb{Z}_3 \times \mathbb{Z}_3 \to \mathbb{Z}_3$:

$$\begin{array}{c|ccc} \cdot_3 & 0 & 1 & 2 \\ \hline 0 & 0 & 0 & 0 \\ 1 & 0 & 1 & 2 \\ 2 & 0 & 2 & 1. \end{array} \left.\vphantom{\begin{array}{c}0\\1\\2\end{array}}\right\} x \cdot_3 y = x \cdot y \bmod 3 \text{ cf. (1.1)}$$

Now, we obtain

$$x \cdot_3 1 = 1 \cdot_3 x = x$$

for each $x \in M$, and 1 is the identity element of $\mathbb{Z}_3$ with respect to $\cdot_3$. Because of $1 \cdot_3 1 = 1$ and $2 \cdot_3 2 = 1$, the elements 1 and 2 are their own inverse elements. However, 0 does not have any inverse element in $\mathbb{Z}_3$.

We can thus distinguish between semi-groups that have or do not have an identity element. The latter are called a *monoid.* Let $(S, *, e_*)$ be a monoid. Consider a second element $e \in S$ satisfying $e * x = x = x * e$ for all $x \in S$. Then it follows

$$e_* \overset{(A3)}{=} e_* * e \overset{(A3)}{=} e. \tag{3.6}$$

The identity element is unique; if each element of a monoid's set has an inverse element, a new structure is introduced that will be very important.

Definition 3.13 (Group). A *group* is a monoid $(S, *, e_*)$ with the extra property that each $x \in S$ has an inverse element $y \in S$. A group is commutative or abelian if the mapping $*$ is commutative.

Remark 3.14. (1) For the moment, the inverse element is denoted by x'. Because of $x * x' = e_*$, it follows that $(x')' = (x * x') * (x')' = x * (x' * (x')') = x$.

(2) An element $x \in S$ of a monoid $(S, *, e_*)$ is called a *unity element* if there is an inverse element $x' \in S$. We denote the set of unity elements by $S^\times$.

From the unity elements, we can build the so-called *unity group.*

Theorem 3.15 (Unity group). *Let $(S, *, e_*)$ be a monoid. The set of unity elements $S^\times$, together with the restricted interior binary mapping $*_{|S^\times} : S^\times \to S^\times$, $x *_{|S^\times} y = x * y$, yields the group $(S^\times, *, e_*)$.*

Proof. $e_* = e_* * e_*$ is its own inverse element, $e_* \in S^\times$. Hence, $S^\times$ can never be an empty set. Let $x \in S^\times$. Since $x * x' = e_* = x' * x$, the element x is the inverse element of x' and $x' \in S^\times$. Finally, the mapping is closed since for any $x, y \in S^\times$

$$(y' * x') * (x * y) = y' * (x' * x) * y = y' * e_* * y = y' * y = e_*.$$

Consequently, $x * y \in S^\times$ and $(S^\times, *, e_*)$ is a group. □

Example 3.16. $(\mathbb{Z}_3, \cdot_3, 1)$ is a monoid, $(\mathbb{Z}_3, +_3, 0)$ is a group. $(\mathbb{Z}_3^\times, \cdot_3, 1)$ is a group at which $\mathbb{Z}_3^\times = \{1, 2\}$ also.

Given $(\mathbb{Z}_6, \cdot_6, 1)$, we get just two unity elements 1 and 5 and thus $\mathbb{Z}_6^\times = \{1, 5\}$. This is based on the Cayley table (see Section 1.1.1)

$$\begin{array}{c|cccccc} \cdot_6 & 0 & 1 & 2 & 3 & 4 & 5 \\ \hline 0 & 0 & 0 & 0 & 0 & 0 & 0 \\ 1 & 0 & \mathbf{1} & 2 & 3 & 4 & 5 \\ 2 & 0 & 2 & 4 & 0 & 2 & 4 \\ 3 & 0 & 3 & 0 & 3 & 0 & 3 \\ 4 & 0 & 4 & 2 & 0 & 4 & 2 \\ 5 & 0 & 5 & 4 & 3 & 2 & \mathbf{1} \end{array} \left.\vphantom{\begin{array}{c}0\\0\\0\\0\\0\\0\end{array}}\right\} x \cdot_6 y = x \cdot y \bmod 6.$$

It yields $\mathbb{Z}_{26}^\times = \{1, 3, 5, 7, 9, 11, 15, 17, 19, 21, 23, 25\}$ through trial and error.

While finding the unity elements of $\mathbb{Z}_6$ is very simple, more issues are introduced by choosing the set $\mathbb{Z}_{26}$ in Example 3.16. We will have to determine a convenient way for doing this work. We proceed with some simple to understand examples of algebraic structures and more properties of groups.

Example 3.17. The additive structure $(\mathbb{N}, +)$ is a semi-group but not a monoid. The multiplicative structure $(\mathbb{Z}, \cdot, 1)$ is a monoid but is not a group. $(\mathbb{Z}, +, 0)$ is an abelian group.

Let $(S, *, e_*)$ be a group and $x, y, z \in S$. By application of the inverse element z' on the left side, it follows from $z * x = z * y$

$$x = (z' * z) * x = z' * (z * x) = z' * (z * y) = (z' * z) * y = y.$$

In the same way $x = y$ arises from $x * z = y * z$. Furthermore, if x and z are fixed, then

$$x * y = z \Leftrightarrow y = x' * z \text{ and } y * x = z \Leftrightarrow y = z * x'.$$

There is exactly one element $y \in S$ satisfying the particular equation.

Finite sets with a small number of elements can be checked up on forming a group. If S is a finite set, then a semi-group $(S, *)$ is a group iff[2] every element of S appears in each row and each column in a Cayley table of the mapping $*$.

Example 3.18. Let $\mathbb{Z}_5^\times = \{1, 2, 3, 4\}$. Based on the Cayley table

$\cdot_5$	1	2	3	4
1	1	2	3	4
2	2	4	1	3
3	3	1	4	2
4	4	3	2	1

the structure $(\mathbb{Z}_5^\times, \cdot_5, 1)$ is a group. Since the table is symmetric, the group is even abelian.

We combine $(\mathbb{Z}, +, 0)$ with $(\mathbb{Z}, \cdot, 1)$, producing the algebraic structure $(\mathbb{Z}, +, \cdot, 0, 1)$. Generally, algebraic structures occupy a special position fulfilling the requirements of an (additive) abelian group and a multiplicative semi-group if a new property combining the two interior mappings is introduced. We use the symbols $\oplus$ for addition and $\odot$ for multiplication.

(D1) $x \odot (y \oplus z) = (x \odot y) \oplus (x \odot z)$ and $(x \oplus y) \odot z = (x \odot z) \oplus (y \odot z)$

is called the distributive law of $\oplus$ and $\odot$. All common sets of numbers fulfill this property. This extension to two interior binary mappings yields a ring.

[2]cf. (Durbin, 2009).

Definition 3.19 (Ring). Let S be a set that contains a marked element $e_\oplus \in S$ and for which two interior binary mappings

$$\oplus : S \times S \to S \text{ (addition)},$$
$$\odot : S \times S \to S \text{ (multiplication)},$$

are defined. Then, $(S, \oplus, \odot, e_\oplus)$ is called a *ring* if for all $x, y, z \in S$ the following six properties are valid:

(A1) $x \oplus y = y \oplus x$ (commutation law),
(A2) $x \oplus (y \oplus z) = (x \oplus y) \oplus z$ (associative law),
(A3) there is an $e_\oplus \in S:\ e_\oplus \oplus x = x$ (identity element),
(A4) there is a $-x \in S : x \oplus (-x) = e_\oplus$ (inverse element),
(M2) $x \odot (y \odot z) = (x \odot y) \odot z$ (associative law),
(D1) $x \odot (y \oplus z) = (x \odot y) \oplus (x \odot z)$ and
$(x \oplus y) \odot z = (x \odot z) \oplus (y \odot z)$ (distributive laws).

Remark 3.20. (1) If there is an identity element $e_\odot$ of the multiplication $\odot$ (M3) that is different from the identity element $e_\oplus$ of the addition $\oplus$, we speak about a *ring with identity.*

(2) A ring is commutative if the multiplication $\odot$ is commutative (M1).

(3) Define $\ominus x := \oplus(-x)$.

Consider a ring and any two elements $x, y \in S$ with $x \odot y = e_\oplus$. If it always follows $a = e_\oplus$ or $b = e_\oplus$, then the ring is called a ring without zero divisors. Furthermore, if the ring without zero divisors is commutative and with identity, we have a *domain of integrity.*

The numbers -1 and 1 are unity elements of $\mathbb{Z}$ relating to the multiplication. However, they are the only one such element. In contrast, each real number (except for 0) has a multiplicative inverse element, which produces a new structure.

Definition 3.21 (Field). A commutative ring with identity is called a *field* if each non-zero element has a multiplicative inverse element (M4). A *finite field* is a field whose set has a finite number of elements.

A ring is more a general structure than a field. Therefore, every field is a ring and a commutative ring with identity is a field iff $S^\times = S\backslash\{0\}$, since $x \in S^\times$ iff there is a $x' \in S$ with $x \odot x' = e_\odot$ and $x' \in S^\times$. From Remark 3.20, it is clear that each field has at least two elements because the identity element of the multiplication has to differ from the identity element of the addition. However, these elements are unique as we have proven, cf. Equations (3.5) and (3.6).

Now, consider a domain of integrity based on the finite set S and any $a \in S$, $a \neq e_\oplus$. Define $f_a : S \to S$, $x \mapsto f(x) = a \odot x$. Then f_a is injective. Taking two elements $x, y \in S$ with $f_a(x) = f_a(y)$, i.e., $a \odot x = a \odot y$. This implies $a \odot (x \ominus y) = e_\oplus$. Since the ring is without zero divisors and $a \neq e_\oplus$, it follows $x \ominus y = e_\oplus$ and consequently, $x = y$. Since S is finite, f_a must be surjective too. Thus, f_a is bijective and there is a unique $b \in S$ with $f_a(b) = a \odot b = e_\odot$. Finally, $\odot$ is commutative and we get $a \odot b = b \odot a = e_\odot$. This means that $(S, \oplus, \odot, e_\oplus, e_\odot)$ is a field. Backward, each finite field is a commutative ring with identity. Any non-zero element has a unique inverse element. Consider $x, y \neq e_\oplus$ and $x \odot y = e_\oplus$. With the help of (A3) and (D1), it follows $e_\odot = (x' \odot x) \odot (y \odot y') = x' \odot (x \odot y) \odot y' = e_\oplus$. This is inconsistent with $e_\odot \neq e_\oplus$.

Corollary 3.22. *A ring element is a unity element iff it is not a zero divisor. Each finite domain of integrity is a finite field and vice versa.*

Instead of extending the structure, we now intend to apply one interior mapping repeatedly. Consider a semi-group $(S, *)$. For each $x_1, x_2, \ldots, x_n \in S$ $(n \geq 3)$, we define a mapping $S^n \to S$, $x := x_1 * x_2 * \ldots * x_n \in S$, by induction

$$x_1 * x_2 * \ldots * x_n := \mathop{\Huge *}_{i=1}^{n} x_i := \left(\mathop{\Huge *}_{i=1}^{n-1} x_i \right) * x_n. \tag{3.7}$$

From the associative law, it follows for any m satisfying $1 \leq m < n$ that

$$\mathop{\Huge *}_{i=1}^{n} x_i = \mathop{\Huge *}_{i=1}^{m} x_i * \mathop{\Huge *}_{i=m+1}^{n} x_i.$$

If all the inputs of the interior binary mapping are equal, for instance, $x \in S$, we get

$$\mathop{\Huge *}_{i=1}^{n} x = x * \ldots * x.$$

At this point n can be any positive integer. For abbreviation, we denote

$$\mathop{\Huge *}^{n} x = x * \ldots * x.$$

Therefore, the laws of exponentiation hold:

$$\mathop{\Huge *}^{m+n} x = \mathop{\Huge *}^{m} x * \mathop{\Huge *}^{n} x, \quad \mathop{\Huge *}^{m} \left(\mathop{\Huge *}^{n} x \right) = \mathop{\Huge *}^{m \cdot n} x. \tag{3.8}$$

If $(S, *, e_*)$ is a monoid, we allow the case $n = 0$ by defining $\mathop{\Huge *}^{0} x := e_*$. If $(S, *, e_*)$ is a group, we allow the case $n < 0$ by defining $\mathop{\Huge *}^{n} x := \mathop{\Huge *}^{|n|} x'$. Because of the uniqueness of the inverse element and

$$(x * \ldots * x) * (x' * \ldots * x') = x * \ldots * (x * x') * \ldots * x' = \ldots = e_*,$$

it applies

$$\left(\mathop{\Huge *}^{n} x \right)' = \mathop{\Huge *}^{n} x'. \tag{3.9}$$

Now, let $(S, \oplus, e_\oplus)$ be a group in an additive approach. Due to (A4) we denote the inverse element x' by $-x$ and

$$n \cdot x := \bigoplus^{n} x = \begin{cases} \underbrace{x \oplus \ldots \oplus x}_{n \text{ times}} & , \quad n > 0, \\ e_\oplus & , \quad n = 0, \\ \underbrace{(-x) \oplus \ldots \oplus (-x)}_{|n| \text{ times}}, & \quad n < 0. \end{cases}$$

Analogously, if $(S, \odot, e_\odot)$ is a group in a multiplicative approach we denote the inverse element x' by x^{-1} and

$$x^n := \bigodot^{n} x = \begin{cases} \underbrace{x \odot \ldots \odot x}_{n \text{ times}} & , \quad n > 0, \\ e_\odot & , \quad n = 0, \\ \underbrace{x^{-1} \odot \ldots \odot x^{-1}}_{|n| \text{ times}}, & \quad n < 0. \end{cases}$$

The set $\mathbb{Z}_5^*$ from the group in Example 3.18 contains four elements, which is called the order of the group.

Definition 3.23 (Order of a group or element). Let $(S, *, e_*)$ be a group.

(1) The number of elements in S is called the order of the group.
(2) The *order* of an element $x \in S$ is the smallest positive integer $n \in \mathbb{N}$ satisfying $\mathop{\ast}^{n} x = e_*$, i.e., the result is the identity element,

$$\mathrm{ord}_S(x) := \min\{n \in \mathbb{N};\ \mathop{\ast}^{n} x = e_*\}.$$

We set $\mathrm{ord}_S(x) = \infty$ if there is no such number n.

Remark 3.24. Assuming a multiplicative group $(S, \odot, e_\odot)$, we denote

$$\mathrm{ord}_S(x) = \min\{n \in \mathbb{N};\ x^n = e_\odot\},$$

in contrast, for an additive group $(S, \oplus, e_\oplus)$

$$\mathrm{ord}_S(x) = \min\{n \in \mathbb{N};\ n \cdot x = e_\oplus\}.$$

There are elements of a group that can reach each of the group elements by n-fold self-composition.

Definition 3.25 (Cyclic group, generator of a group). Let $(S, *, e_*)$ be a group and $x \in S$. Using the notation

$$\mathcal{L}(x) := \left\{\mathop{\ast}^{n} x;\ n \in \mathbb{Z}\right\}, \tag{3.10}$$

the group $(S, *, e_*)$ is called *cyclic* if an $x \in S$ exists satisfying $\mathcal{L}(x) = S$. Then x is called the *generator* of S and S is generated by x.

Remark 3.26. Using the notation for multiplicative or additive groups we write

$$\mathcal{L}(x) = \{x^n;\ n \in \mathbb{Z}\} \quad \text{(multiplicative spelling)},$$
$$\mathcal{L}(x) = \{n \cdot x;\ n \in \mathbb{Z}\} \quad \text{(additive spelling)}.$$

Any cyclic group is abelian,

$$\overset{m}{\ast} x * \overset{n}{\ast} x = \overset{m+n}{\ast} x = \overset{n+m}{\ast} x = \overset{n}{\ast} x * \overset{m}{\ast} x.$$

Any element of a cyclic group is a unity element,

$$\overset{m}{\ast} x * \overset{-m}{\ast} x = \overset{m-m}{\ast} x = \overset{0}{\ast} x = e_*.$$

A generator of a group is often not unique.

Example 3.27. (1) $(\mathbb{Z}, +, 0)$ is a cyclic group with generator 1. However, it is $\mathcal{L}(-1) = \mathbb{Z}$.

(2) Given $n\mathbb{Z} := \{z \cdot n;\ z \in \mathbb{Z}\} = \mathcal{L}(n)$, $n \in \mathbb{N}_0$, the structure $(n\mathbb{Z}, +, 0)$ is a cyclic group with generator n.

(3) $(\mathbb{Z}_5^\times, \cdot_5, 1)$ is a cyclic group with generators 2 and 3, $\mathcal{L}(2) = \mathcal{L}(3) = \mathbb{Z}_5^\times$. For example, $2^1 = 2$, $2^2 = 2 \cdot_5 2 = 4$, $2^3 = 4 \cdot_5 2 = 3$ and $2^4 = 3 \cdot_5 2 = 1$.

Remember the greatest common divisor $\mathrm{GCD}(x, y)$ and the least common multiple $\mathrm{LCM}(x, y)$ of two numbers $x, y \in \mathbb{Z}$ due to Definitions 1.7 and 1.12. For any $x \in S$ let $\mathrm{ord}_S(x) = u$ and $n \in \mathbb{N}$. Then,

$$\overset{u/\mathrm{GCD}(u,n)}{\ast} \left(\overset{n}{\ast} x \right) \overset{(3.8)}{=} \overset{n/\mathrm{GCD}(u,n)}{\ast} \left(\overset{u}{\ast} x \right) = e_*,$$

i.e., $u/\mathrm{GCD}(u,n)$ is a multiple of $\mathrm{ord}_S(\overset{n}{\ast} x)$. Let $e_* = \overset{k}{\ast} \left(\overset{n}{\ast} x \right) = \overset{n \cdot k}{\ast} x$ for any $k \in \mathbb{N}$. By setting $d = \mathrm{GCD}(n, u)$, there are relatively prime $v, w \in \mathbb{Z}$ with $u = d \cdot v$ and $n = d \cdot w$. It is $u | n \cdot k$ i.e., $n \cdot k = q \cdot u$ for any $q \in \mathbb{Z}$. Then, $d \cdot w \cdot k = q \cdot d \cdot v$. Consequently, v is a divisor of $k \cdot w$ and since v and w are relatively prime we obtain from Corollary 1.10 $v = {}^{u}/_{d} = {}^{u}/_{\mathrm{GCD}(n,u)}|k$. This is especially true for $k = \mathrm{ord}_S(\overset{n}{\ast}\, x)$. Thus, ${}^{u}/_{d}$ is a multiple and a divisor of k, i.e., $\mathrm{ord}_S(\overset{n}{\ast}\, x) = {}^{u}/_{\mathrm{GCD}(n,u)}$.

Corollary 3.28. *Let $(S, *, e_*)$ be a group, $n \in \mathbb{Z}$ and $ord_S(x) = u$ for any $x \in S$. Then*

$$ord_S\left(\overset{n}{\ast}\, x\right) = {}^{u}/_{GCD(n,u)}.$$

We can calculate the order of a composed element in an abelian group in some special case.

Lemma 3.29. *Let $(S, *, e_*)$ be an abelian group, $x, y \in S$, $m = ord_S(x)$ and $n = ord_S(y)$. If $GCD(m, n) = 1$, then $ord_S(x \cdot y) = LCM(m, n)$.*

Proof. Since the group is abelian, it applies

$$\overset{m\cdot n}{\ast}(x * y) = \overset{n}{\ast}\left(\overset{m}{\ast}\, x\right) * \overset{m}{\ast}\left(\overset{n}{\ast}\, y\right) = e_* * e_* = e_*.$$

For some d, it follows from $e_* = \overset{d}{\ast}(x * y)$ that

$$\overset{d}{\ast}\, x = \overset{-d}{\ast}\, y \Rightarrow \overset{n\cdot d}{\ast}\, x = \overset{-d}{\ast}\left(\overset{n}{\ast}\, y\right) = e_*,$$

or rather

$$\overset{-d}{\ast}\, x = \overset{d}{\ast}\, y \Rightarrow \overset{m\cdot d}{\ast}\, y = \overset{-d}{\ast}\left(\overset{m}{\ast}\, x\right) = e_*.$$

Assuming $\mathrm{GCD}(m, n) = 1$,

$$m|n \cdot d \overset{\text{Cor. 1.10}}{\Rightarrow} m|d \text{ and } n|m \cdot d \overset{\text{Cor. 1.10}}{\Rightarrow} n|d.$$

Hence, $\mathrm{LCM}(m, n)|d$. Furthermore, $\mathrm{ord}_S(x * y)|d$. Since the order is as small as possible, we obtain $\mathrm{ord}_S(x * y) = \mathrm{LCM}(m, n) \overset{\text{Cor. 1.15}}{=} m \cdot n$. □

3.1.2 *Subgroups*

A subset of a group's set can itself become a group.

Definition 3.30 (Subgroup). Let $(S, *, e_*)$ be a group and $U \subseteq S$ be a non-empty subset of S. Furthermore, let $*_{|U} : U \times U \to U$ be the induced restriction of $*$. Then, $(U, *_{|U}, e_*)$ is called a subgroup if

- $u *_{|U} v \in U$ for all $u, v \in U$ and $u' \in U$ for all $u \in U$,
- $(U, *_{|U}, e_*)$ is a group.

Remark 3.31. The restriction $*_{|U}$ is mostly abbreviated by $*$.

If $(U, *, e_*)$ is a subgroup, then $u * v' \in U$ for all $u, v \in U$. Conversely, let $u * v' \in U$ for all $u, v \in U$. Because of $U \neq \emptyset$, there must be any $u \in U$ resulting in $e_* = u * u' \in U$. For each $u \in U$, $u' = e_* * u' \in U$. Hence, containing u, v, the set U must also contain u, v'. Finally, $u * v = u * (v')' \in U$ for all $u, v \in U$.

Corollary 3.32. *Let $(S, *, e_*)$ be a group and U be a non-empty subset of S. Then $(U, *, e_*)$ is a subgroup iff $u * v' \in U$ for each $u, v \in U$.*

Each group has an order. Since a subgroup is itself a group, each of them also has an order. In consideration of the order of a subgroup based on the order of a group, we assume the group to be finite, i.e., the order of the group is finite.

Theorem 3.33 (Lagrange's[3] theorem). *Let $(S, *, e_*)$ be a finite group and $(U, *, e_*)$ be a subgroup. The number of elements of U divides the order of $(S, *, e_*)$.*

[3] J.-L. Lagrange (1736–1813).

Proof. Let $(U, *, e_*)$ be a subgroup of $(S, *, e_*)$ and $a, b \in S$. We define a as equivalent to b, $a \sim_U b$ if $a * b' \in U$. Consequently, the relation $\sim$ is an equivalence relation as $a \sim_U a$ because $a * a' = e_* \in U$ (reflexivity). Furthermore, let $a \sim_U b$, $a * b' \in U$. Thus, $(a * b')' = b * a' \in U$ and it follows $b \sim_U a$ (symmetry). Finally, assuming $c \in S$, $a \sim_U b$ and $b \sim_U c$, $a * b' \in U$ and $b * c' \in U$. Immediately, $c * b' \in U$ and $a * b' * b * c' = a * c' \in U$, $a \sim_U c$ (transitivity).

Let $[a] := \{b \in S;\ a \sim_U b\} = \{b \in S;\ a * b' \in U\}$ be the equivalence class of $a \in S$. Since a is not necessarily an element of U, the elements of $[a]$ can be represented by $b = h * a$, assuming $h \in U$, which is due to $a * b' = a * a' * h' = h' \in U$. Thus, we note $[a] = \{h * a;\ h \in U\}$.

Given $a, b \in S$, we define $f_{a,b} : [a] \to [b], h * a \mapsto h * b$. This mapping is bijective. Assuming $u \in [b]$, there is $h_1 \in U$ satisfying $u = h_1 * b$. Therefore, $w = h_1 * a \in [a]$ and $f_{a,b}(w) = u$, the mapping is surjective. Given $v \in [b]$, $h_2 \in U$ satisfying $v = h_2 * b$ and $x = h_2 * a$, such that $f_{a,b}(x) = v$. With $f_{a,b}(w) = f_{a,b}(x)$, we obtain $v = w$ and then $h_1 * b = h_2 * b$. It follows that $h_1 = h_2$, $w = h_1 * a = h_2 * a = x$ (injective).

Since $f_{a,b}$ is a bijective mapping, the sets $[a]$ and $[b]$ contain all the same number of elements. Since $[e_*] = \{h * e_*;\ h \in U\} = U$, the number of elements of the equivalence classes equals $|U|$. Since S is a disjoint union of equivalence classes based on $\sim_U$, $|S|$ has to be a multiple of $|U|$. □

Given $a \in S$, the structure $(\mathcal{L}(a), *, e_*)$ is a subgroup of $(S, *, e_*)$. Initially, $\mathop{\Huge *}^{0} a = e_* \in \mathcal{L}(a)$. Let $x = \mathop{\Huge *}^{m} a, y = \mathop{\Huge *}^{n} a \in \mathcal{L}(a)$. It follows

$$x * y' = \overset{m}{\mathop{\Huge *}} a * \left(\overset{n}{\mathop{\Huge *}} a \right)' \overset{(3.9)}{=} \overset{m}{\mathop{\Huge *}} a * \overset{n}{\mathop{\Huge *}} a'$$

$$= \overset{m}{\mathop{\Huge *}} a * \overset{-n}{\mathop{\Huge *}} a = \overset{\overbrace{m-n}^{\in \mathbb{Z}}}{\mathop{\Huge *}} a \in \mathcal{L}(a).$$

Thus, if $|S| < \infty$ is finite, the cardinality of $\mathcal{L}(a)$ is a divisor of S due to Theorem 3.33.

Corollary 3.34. *Let* $(S, *, e_*)$ *be a group and* $a \in S$. *Then,* $(\mathcal{L}(a), *, e_*)$ *is a subgroup. If* $|S| < \infty$, *it applies* $|\mathcal{L}(a)| \mid |S|$.

The order $n = \text{ord}_S(a)$ of one single element a of a finite group $(S, *, e_*)$ divides the order of the group, as the element generates a subgroup. All of the elements $\mathop{\ast}^{k} a$, $k = 1, \ldots, n$ are different. Any $m \in \mathbb{Z}$ can be written as $m = q \cdot n + r$ for some $0 \leq r < n$ and $q \in \mathbb{Z}$ due to Theorem 1.2. It follows $\mathop{\ast}^{m} a = \mathop{\ast}^{q \cdot n + r} a = \mathop{\ast}^{n \cdot q} a * \mathop{\ast}^{r} a = \mathop{\ast}^{r} a$. The order of a equals the order of the generated subgroup. Given $\mathop{\ast}^{n} a = e_*$ we can now compute $\mathop{\ast}^{|S|} a$ using the fact that $n \mid |S|$, i.e., $|S| = q \cdot n$ for some $q \in \mathbb{Z}$:

$$\mathop{\ast}^{|S|} a = \mathop{\ast}^{q \cdot n} a = \mathop{\ast}^{q} \left(\mathop{\ast}^{n} a \right) = \mathop{\ast}^{q} e_* = e_*.$$

Corollary 3.35. *Let* $(S, *, e_*)$ *be a finite group and* $a \in S$. *Then* $\mathop{\ast}^{|S|} a = e_*$ *applies.*

If $\mathcal{L}(a) = S$, we obtain $\text{ord}_S(a) = |S|$ and a is a generator of the group $(S, *, e_*)$.

Example 3.36. Let $S = \{1, 2\}$, $|S| = 2$. With the group $(S, \cdot_3, 1)$ we get

$\text{ord}_S(1) = 1$, since $1^1 = 1,\ 1^2 = 1 \cdot_3 1 = 1, \ldots$
$\text{ord}_S(2) = 2$, since $2^1 = 2,\ 2^2 = 2 \cdot_3 2 = 1,\ 2^3 = (2 \cdot_3 2) \cdot_3 2 = 2, \ldots$

as shown in the Cayley table in Example 3.12. The number 2 is a generator of the group.

The derivation of Corollary 3.35 again shows that there are integers that possess the same remainder after dividing by n. This relation between the integers provides

Definition 3.37 (Congruence modulo n). Let $a, b \in \mathbb{Z}$ and $n \in \mathbb{N}$ satisfying $a = q_1 n + r_1$ and $b = q_2 n + r_2$. Then, a is called *congruent* b modulo n,

$$a \equiv_n b \text{ or rather } a \equiv b \pmod{n},$$

if $r_1 = r_2$ applies.

The definition of the relation $\equiv_n$ is one possibility. There are other equivalents. Firstly,

$$a \equiv_n b \Leftrightarrow r_1 = r_2 \overset{(1.1)}{\Leftrightarrow} \rho_n(a) = \rho_n(b) \Leftrightarrow a \bmod n = b \bmod n.$$

Corollary 3.38. *Consider $a, b \in \mathbb{Z}$ with $a = q_1 n + r_1, b = q_2 n + r_2$. Then,*

$$a \equiv_n b \Leftrightarrow a \bmod n = b \bmod n.$$

Secondly, if n divides $a - b$, this produces the same relation.

$$\begin{aligned}
a \equiv_n b &\Rightarrow r_1 = r_2 \Rightarrow a = q_1 n + r,\ b = q_2 n + r \\
&\Rightarrow a - b = q_1 n + r - (q_2 n + r) = (q_1 - q_2)n \Rightarrow n \mid a - b. \\
n \mid a - b &\Rightarrow a - b = qn \text{ for any } q \in \mathbb{Z} \\
&\Rightarrow q_1 n + r_1 - (q_2 n + r_2) = (q_1 - q_2)n + (r_1 - r_2) \overset{!}{=} qn \\
&\Rightarrow r_1 - r_2 = q_3 n \text{ for any } q_3 \in \mathbb{Z}; \\
&\quad \text{since } -n < r_1 - r_2 < n \text{ we get } q_3 = 0 = r_1 - r_2. \\
&\Rightarrow r_1 = r_2 \Rightarrow a \equiv_n b.
\end{aligned}$$

Corollary 3.39. *Consider $a, b \in \mathbb{Z}$ with $a = q_1 n + r_1, b = q_2 n + r_2$. Then,*

$$a \equiv_n b \Leftrightarrow n \mid a - b.$$

Because of its properties, the relation $\equiv_n$ has a deep impact on further results, with the most important being an equivalence relation.

Theorem 3.40. *$\equiv_n$ is an equivalence relation on $\mathbb{Z}$.*

Proof. We have to show three properties.

Reflexivity: $a \equiv_n a$, because $a \bmod n = a \bmod n$.
Symmetry: $a \equiv_n b \Leftrightarrow a \bmod n = b \bmod n = a \bmod n \Leftrightarrow b \equiv_n a$.
Transitivity: $a \equiv_n b \wedge b \equiv_n c \Rightarrow a \bmod n = b \bmod n = c \bmod n \Rightarrow a \equiv_n c$. □

The sets $[r]_n := \{a \in \mathbb{Z} : a \equiv_n r\}$ are each called an *n-equivalence class*. Every r is the representative of $[r]_n$, but also each $a \in [r]_n$ that fulfills $a = q \cdot n + r$ for some $q \in \mathbb{Z}$.

Theorem 3.41. *There are exactly n different n-equivalence classes of $\mathbb{Z}$.*

Proof. For each $r \in \{0, \ldots, n-1\}$, the set $[r]_n$ is a n-equivalence class. To show this, let $r_1, r_2 \in \{0, \ldots, n-1\}$ with $r_1 \neq r_2$. Suppose $[r_1]_n = [r_2]_n$. Then $r_1 \equiv_n r_2$ and thus, $r_1 \bmod n = r_2 \bmod n$. However, this contradicts the assumption of $r_1 \neq r_2$. Consequently, there are at least n such n-equivalence classes. Furthermore, suppose there is any $b \in \mathbb{Z}$ with $b \notin [r]_n$ for all $r \in \{0, \ldots, n-1\}$. Then, $b = q_2 n + r_2 \Rightarrow r_2 \notin \{0, \ldots, n-1\}$. However, this contradicts the property that the remainder is a member of $\{0, \ldots, n-1\}$. □

Because of the unique representation $a = q_1 n + r_1$ for every $a \in \mathbb{Z}$, it follows from Theorem 3.41 that $\mathbb{Z}$ is a disjoint union of the n-equivalence classes.

$$\begin{aligned}\bigcup_{r=0}^{n-1} [r]_n = \bigcup_{r=0}^{n-1} \{a \in \mathbb{Z};\ a \equiv_n r\} &= \bigcup_{r=0}^{n-1} \{qn + r;\ q \in \mathbb{Z}\} \\ &= \{qn + r;\ q \in \mathbb{Z},\ r \in \{0, \ldots, n-1\}\} = \mathbb{Z}.\end{aligned}$$

We can think of this as n different number rays, cf. Figure 3.1 is illustrated for $n = 11$.

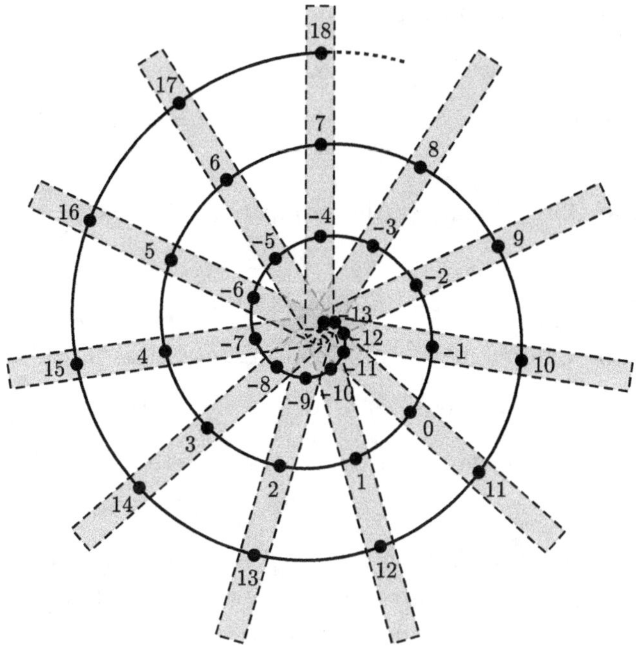

Figure 3.1 $\mathbb{Z}$ as a disjoint union of 11 equivalence classes.

3.2 Relatively Prime Residue Classes

3.2.1 *Group and ring homomorphisms*

It is often difficult or impossible to show a desired statement immediately. One idea is to reformulate the problem in a way that makes it easier to show the new statement. The original statement can be derived if there is a mapping between the two problems satisfying some properties.

Definition 3.42 (Group homomorphism). Let $(S, *, e_*)$ and $(T, \circ, e_\circ)$ be groups. A mapping $\psi : S \to T$ is called a *group homomorphism* from S to T if for all $a, b \in S$ it holds

$$\psi(a * b) = \psi(a) \circ \psi(b).$$

From Definition 3.42, it follows that

$$\psi(e_*) = \psi(e_* * e_*) = \psi(e_*) \circ \psi(e_*) \Rightarrow \psi(e_*) = e_\circ,$$
$$e_\circ = \psi(e_*) = \psi(a * a') = \psi(a) \circ \psi(a') \Rightarrow \psi(a') = \psi(a)'.$$

Example 3.43. Consider the group $(\mathbb{Z}, +, 0)$ and $n \in \mathbb{N}$. Then, the mapping

$$\psi_n : \mathbb{Z} \to \mathbb{Z},\ z \mapsto n \cdot z$$

is a group homomorphism from $\mathbb{Z}$ to $\mathbb{Z}$. For each $u, v \in \mathbb{Z}$,

$$\psi_n(u + v) = n \cdot (u + v) = n \cdot u + n \cdot v = \psi_n(u) + \psi_n(v).$$

Since the same group is used here twice, the homomorphism is called an *endomorphism*.

Two groups are called isomorphic if there is a bijective homomorphism between these groups. This mapping is then called *isomorphism*. The image of a homomorphism,

$$\text{Im}(\psi) := \psi(S) := \{t \in T;\ \text{there is an } s \in S \text{ satisfying } \psi(s) = t\} \subseteq T,$$

offers a special property. Consider $u, v \in S$ and $a = \psi(u), b = \psi(v) \in \psi(S)$. Then,

$$a \circ b' = \psi(u) \circ \psi(v)' = \psi(u) \circ \psi(v') = \psi(\underbrace{u * v'}_{\in S}) \in \psi(S). \tag{3.11}$$

Subsequently, it becomes apparent from Equation 3.11 that $(\psi(S), \circ, e_\circ)$ itself is a group.

Example 3.44. From Example 3.43, the image of the mapping $\psi_n : \mathbb{Z} \to \mathbb{Z},\ z \mapsto n \cdot z$ is given by

$$\begin{aligned}\text{Im}(\psi_n) &= \{n \cdot z;\ z \in \mathbb{Z}\} = \{a \in \mathbb{Z};\ n \mid a\} = \{a \in \mathbb{Z};\ a \equiv_n 0\} \\ &= [0]_n = n\mathbb{Z} \subset \mathbb{Z}.\end{aligned}$$

Thus, $(n\mathbb{Z}, +, 0)$ is a group.

The definition of a homomorphism between groups can be applied to rings immediately.

Definition 3.45 (Ring homomorphism). Let $(S, \oplus, \odot, 0_\oplus, 1_\odot)$ and $(T, +, \cdot, 0, 1)$ be rings. Then, a mapping $\psi : S \to T$ is called a *ring homomorphism* from S to T if for all $a, b \in S$ it holds

$$\psi(a \oplus b) = \psi(a) + \psi(b),$$
$$\psi(a \odot b) = \psi(a) \cdot \psi(b).$$

The equation

$$\psi(1_\odot) = \psi(1_\odot \odot 1_\odot) = \psi(1_\odot) \cdot \psi(1_\odot)$$

shows that $\psi(1_\odot) = 1$ is safe. Each ring homomorphism is a group homomorphism relating to the additive group of the ring. The set

$$\mathbb{Z}/\equiv_n := \{[r]_n;\ r \in \{0, \ldots, n-1\}\}$$

of all n-equivalence classes forms a ring. For this, we can equip the set with two interior binary mappings,

$$\oplus : \mathbb{Z}/\equiv_n \times \mathbb{Z}/\equiv_n \to \mathbb{Z}/\equiv_n,\quad [a]_n \oplus [b]_n := [a+b]_n, \text{ and}$$
$$\odot : \mathbb{Z}/\equiv_n \times \mathbb{Z}/\equiv_n \to \mathbb{Z}/\equiv_n,\quad [a]_n \odot [b]_n := [a \cdot b]_n.$$

Remember that $[a]_n = [r]_n$ if there is a number $q \in \mathbb{Z}$ satisfying $a = q \cdot n + r$.

Theorem 3.46. *$(\mathbb{Z}/\equiv_n, \oplus, \odot, [0]_n, [1]_n)$ is a commutative ring with identity.*

Proof. The two mappings are closed and well-defined. Given r_1, r_2, $s, t \in \{0, \ldots, n-1\}$ and $q_1, q_2, q_3, q_4 \in \mathbb{Z}$, we get four numbers by

$$\begin{aligned}
a &= q_1 \cdot n + r_1, \\
b &= q_2 \cdot n + r_2, \\
a + b &= (q_1 + q_2) \cdot n + \underbrace{(r_1 + r_2)}_{q_3 \cdot n + s} = (q_1 + q_2 + q_3) \cdot n + s, \text{ and} \\
a \cdot b &= (q_1 q_2 n + q_1 r_2 + q_2 r_1) \cdot n + \underbrace{(r_1 \cdot r_2)}_{q_4 \cdot n + t} \\
&= (q_1 q_2 n + q_1 r_2 + q_2 r_1 + q_4) \cdot n + t.
\end{aligned}$$

Hence, $[a]_n = [r_1]_n$, $[b]_n = [r_2]_n$, $[a+b]_n = [s]_n$ and $[a \cdot b]_n = [t]_n$ and therefore,

$$\begin{aligned}
[a]_n \oplus [b]_n &= [r_1]_n \oplus [r_2]_n = [r_1 + r_2]_n = [s]_n \in \mathbb{Z}/\equiv_n, \\
[a]_n \odot [b]_n &= [r_1]_n \odot [r_2]_n = [r_1 \cdot r_2]_n \\
&= [r_2 \cdot r_1]_n = [b]_n \odot [a]_n \text{ (commutative)} \\
&= [t]_n \in \mathbb{Z}/\equiv_n .
\end{aligned}$$

Associativity, (A2), (M2):

$$\begin{aligned}
([a]_n \oplus [b]_n) \oplus [c]_n &= [a+b]_n \oplus [c]_n = [(a+b)+c]_n \\
&= [a+(b+c)]_n = [a]_n \oplus [b+c]_n \\
&= [a]_n \oplus ([b]_n \oplus [c]_n), \\
([a]_n \odot [b]_n) \odot [c]_n &= [a \cdot b]_n \odot [c]_n = [(a \cdot b) \cdot c]_n \\
&= [a \cdot (b \cdot c)]_n = [a]_n \odot [b \cdot c]_n \\
&= [a]_n \odot ([b]_n \odot [c]_n).
\end{aligned}$$

Commutativity of addition, (A1):

$$[a]_n \oplus [b]_n = [a+b]_n = [b+a]_n = [b]_n + [a]_n.$$

Identity elements,(A3), (M3):

$$\begin{aligned}
[0]_n \oplus [a]_n &= [0+a]_n = [a]_n = [a+0]_n = [a]_n \oplus [0]_n, \\
[1]_n \odot [a]_n &= [1 \cdot a]_n = [a]_n = [a \cdot 1]_n = [a]_n \odot [1]_n.
\end{aligned}$$

Inverse element of addition, (A4): Let $-a := \tilde{q}n + \tilde{r}$. It is

$$[a]_n \oplus [\tilde{r}]_n = [a]_n \oplus [-a]_n = [a+(-a)]_n = [0]_n.$$

Distributivity, (D1):

$$\begin{aligned}
[a]_n \odot ([b]_n \oplus [c]_n) &= [a]_n \odot [b+c]_n = [a \cdot (b+c)]_n \\
&= [a \cdot b + a \cdot c]_n = ([a]_n \odot [b]_n) \oplus ([a]_n \odot [c]_n), \\
([a]_n \oplus [b]_n) \odot [c]_n &= [a+b]_n \odot [c]_n = [(a+b) \cdot c]_n \\
&= [a \cdot c + b \cdot c]_n = ([a]_n \odot [c]_n) \oplus ([b]_n \odot [c]_n).
\end{aligned}$$

□

Based on the set $\mathbb{Z}_n = \{0, \dots, n-1\}$ — cf. defined in (2.1), which is called the *set of remainder modulo n*, we can define operations for addition and multiplication. For this purpose, given any number $z \in \mathbb{Z}$, we are looking for such an $r \in \mathbb{Z}_n$ that $r = z \bmod n$.

Definition 3.47 (Mod-n-addition and mod-n-multiplication). For any $n \in \mathbb{N}$, let $\mathbb{Z}_n = \{0, \dots, n-1\}$ be the set of remainder modulo n. Define two binary operations on $\mathbb{Z}_n$, $+_n : \mathbb{Z}_n \times \mathbb{Z}_n \to \mathbb{Z}_n$ and $\cdot_n : \mathbb{Z}_n \times \mathbb{Z}_n \to \mathbb{Z}_n$, determined by

$$a +_n b := (a+b) \bmod n = \rho_n(a+b), \text{ (mod-}n\text{-addition)},$$
$$a \cdot_n b := (a \cdot b) \bmod n = \rho_n(a \cdot b), \text{ (mod-}n\text{-multiplication)}.$$

Remark 3.48.

(1) We denote $a^2 \bmod n := a \cdot_n a$ and similarly, cf. Formula (3.7)

$$a^k \bmod n := \underbrace{a \cdot_n \dots \cdot_n a}_{k-\text{times}}$$

for any $k \in \mathbb{N}$.

(2) The binary set $\mathbb{Z}_2 = \{0, 1\}$ is often written as $\mathbb{F}_2$ or Σ_{Bool}. $\Sigma^*_{\text{Bool}} = \mathbb{F}^*_2$ contains binary sequences of any length.

(3) Since $a + b = b + a$ and $a \cdot b = b \cdot a$, both the addition and multiplication modulo n are commutative.

Example 3.49. Look at the sequences

$$(a_n)_{n \in \mathbb{N}_0}, \quad a_n = 3^n \bmod 17,$$
$$(b_n)_{n \in \mathbb{N}_0}, \quad b_n = 4^n \bmod 17.$$

How many different numbers does each sequence have? Because of the multiplication modulo 17, the maximum number of different members is 16. The first 16 members of $(a_n)_{n \in \mathbb{N}_0}$ are

$$1, 3, 9, 10, 13, 5, 15, 11, 16, 14, 8, 7, 4, 12, 2, 6 \text{ (all different)}$$

Instead of 16 different members, the first 16 members of $(b_n)_{n\in\mathbb{N}_0}$ are

$$1, 4, 16, 13, 1, 4, 16, 13, 1, 4, 16, 13, 1, 4, 16, 13 \text{ (just four different)}$$

After fixing n, there is a different number of achieved remainder modulo n, depending on the choice of a.

Theorem 3.50. *If $n > 1$, then $(\mathbb{Z}_n, +_n, \cdot_n, 0, 1)$ is a commutative ring with identity.*

Proof. The mapping

$$f : \mathbb{Z}/\equiv_n \to \mathbb{Z}_n,\ [r]_n \mapsto f([r]_n) := r \bmod n$$

is bijective and a homomorphism relating to $+_n$ and $\cdot_n$. The ring structure is then transferred from $(\mathbb{Z}/\equiv_n, \oplus, \odot, [0]_n, [1]_n)$ to $(\mathbb{Z}_n, +_n, \cdot_n, 0, 1)$.

f is bijective: $|\mathbb{Z}/\equiv_n| = n = |\mathbb{Z}_n|$. Given $r \in \mathbb{Z}_n$, there is a $[r]_n$ fulfilling $f([r]_n) = r$ and $[r]_n \in \mathbb{Z}/\equiv_n$ (surjective). Given $[r_1]_n \neq [r_2]_n$ and $r_1, r_2 \in \mathbb{Z}_n$, look at $f([r_1]_n) = r_1$ and $f([r_2]_n) = r_2$. Since the n-equivalence classes are disjoint sets, we obtain $r_1 \neq r_2$ (injective).

Let $a = q_1 n + r_1$, $b = q_2 n + r_2$, $r := r_1 + r_2 \bmod n$ and $\tilde{r} := r_1 \cdot r_2 \bmod n$. Then, it follows

$$\begin{aligned}
f([a]_n \oplus [b]_n) &= f([a+b]_n) = f([r]_n) = r = r_1 + r_2 \bmod n \\
&= r_1 +_n r_2 = f([r_1]_n) +_n f([r_2]_n) \\
&= f([a]_n) +_n f([b]_n), \\
f([a]_n \odot [b]_n) &= f([a \cdot b]_n) = f([\tilde{r}]_n) = \tilde{r} = r_1 \cdot r_2 \bmod n \\
&= r_1 \cdot_n r_2 = f([r_1]_n) \cdot_n f([r_2]_n) \\
&= f([a]_n) \cdot_n f([b]_n), \\
f([0]_n) &= 0 \bmod n = 0, \\
f([1]_n) &= 1 \bmod n = 1.
\end{aligned}$$

From Remark 3.48 the multiplication is commutative and thus we have a commutative ring with identity. □

Example 3.51. $(\mathbb{Z}_5, +_5, \cdot_5, 0, 1)$ is a domain of integrity and from Corollary 3.22, a field. However, $(\mathbb{Z}_6, +_6, \cdot_6, 0, 1)$ is not a domain of integrity because there are zero divisors: $[2]_6 \odot [3]_6 = [0]_6$, specifically $2 \cdot_6 3 = 0$.

Remark 3.52. In the presence of an isomorphic mapping between two algebraic structures, we can identify one by another. We can identify $(\mathbb{Z}/\equiv_n, \oplus, \odot, [0]_n, [1]_n)$ by $(\mathbb{Z}_n, +_n, \cdot_n, 0, 1)$ and abbreviate this by $\mathbb{Z}/\equiv_n \cong \mathbb{Z}_n$. Since it applies that $(\mathbb{Z}_n, +_n, 0)$ is also an abelian group, identification can be transferred to a part of the structure. This means that $(\mathbb{Z}/\equiv_n, \oplus, [0]_n)$ gives the same structure as $(\mathbb{Z}_n, +_n, 0)$. We use the same abbreviation $\mathbb{Z}/\equiv_n \cong \mathbb{Z}_n$ as another meaning.

Given $a, b, c \in \mathbb{Z}$ and $r = a + b \bmod n$, the addition of the three numbers (in the same manner: multiplication) relating to $\mathbb{Z}_n$ is defined by

$$a +_n b +_n c := (a +_n b) +_n c.$$

Then,

$$\begin{aligned} a +_n b +_n c &= (a +_n b) +_n c = f([a + b]_n) +_n c \\ &= f([r]_n) +_n c = r +_n c \\ &= f([r + c]_n) = f([a + b + c]_n) \\ &= (a + b + c) \bmod n. \end{aligned}$$

Thus, computations can be "rolled out" from $\mathbb{Z}_n$ to $\mathbb{Z}$ and vice versa.

Example 3.53.

- $(17 + 16 + 10) \bmod 26 = (33 + 10) \bmod 26 = (7 + 10) \bmod 26 = 17$ or rather $(17 + 16 + 10) \bmod 26 = 43 \bmod 26 = 17$.
- $2^{10} \bmod 3 = (2^2 \bmod 3)^5 \bmod 3 = 1^5 \bmod 3 = 1$ or $2^{10} \bmod 3 = 1024 \bmod 3 = 1$.

$\mathbb{Z}_n$ possesses the structure of a commutative ring with identity. However, it does not necessarily form a field. For instance, $(\mathbb{Z}_4, +_4, \cdot_4, 0, 1)$ is no field because 2 has no multiplicative inverse element.

3.2.2 *Extended Euclidean algorithm*

The set $\mathbb{Z}_{26}^{\times}$ from Example 3.16 has 15 elements, which is not obvious at first. The cardinality of a group will now be determined.

Theorem 3.54. *Each subgroup of $(\mathbb{Z}, +, 0)$ is cyclic and takes the shape of $n\mathbb{Z}$.*

Proof. Assume a subgroup $(U, +, 0)$ of $(\mathbb{Z}, +, 0)$. If $U = \{0\}$, it applies $U = 0\mathbb{Z}$. If $U \neq \{0\}$, let n be the smallest positive element of U and $a \in U$ be any element. Then, it is $a = q \cdot n + r$ with some $q \in \mathbb{Z}$ and $r \in \mathbb{Z}_n$. Both $q \cdot n$ and $(-q \cdot n)$ are members of U. Thus, $r = a + (-q \cdot n)$ is a member of U. Since $0 \leq r < n$, r has to be zero and $n|a$, i.e., $a \in n\mathbb{Z}$. □

We keep the group $(\mathbb{Z}, +, 0)$ and use the fact that all the subgroups are known. A subgroup can be built upon more than one element. The notation is similar to Corollary 3.34 and is due to (1.2). For example, the multiplicative spelling $\mathcal{L}(a, b) := \{a^m \odot b^n;\ m, n \in \mathbb{Z}\}$ yields the subgroup $(\mathcal{L}(a, b), \odot, e_\odot)$, which is generated by $a, b \in S$. We prove this by assuming $c, d \in \mathcal{L}(a, b)$, $c = a^{m_1} \odot b^{n_1}$ and $d = a^{m_2} \odot b^{n_2}$. Then, $d^{-1} = (a^{m_2} \odot b^{n_2})^{-1} = b^{-n_2} \odot a^{-m_2}$ yields $c \odot d^{-1} = a^{m_1} \odot b^{n_1} \odot b^{-n_2} \odot a^{-m_2} = a^{m_1 - m_1} \odot b^{n_1 - n_2} \in \mathcal{L}(a, b)$.

Example 3.55. Let $(\mathbb{Z}, +, 0)$ and $a, b \in \mathbb{Z}$. Then, it is $\mathcal{L}(a, b) = \{m \cdot a + n \cdot b;\ m, n \in \mathbb{Z}\}$, and $(\mathcal{L}(a, b), +, 0)$ is a subgroup of $(\mathbb{Z}, +, 0)$ generated by a and b. Since the subgroups of $(\mathbb{Z}, +, 0)$ are known, we can find $d \in \mathbb{N}$ satisfying $\mathcal{L}(a, b) = d\mathbb{Z}$, which is $d|a, b$ because $a, b \in \mathcal{L}(a, b)$ and d is a common divisor of a and b. Consequently, each member is a multiple of d: given $a = z_1 \cdot d$ and $b = z_2 \cdot d$ for some $z_1, z_2 \in \mathbb{Z}$ and $m, n \in \mathbb{Z}:\ m \cdot a + n \cdot b = m \cdot z_1 \cdot d + n \cdot z_2 \cdot d = (m \cdot z_1 + n \cdot z_2) \cdot d \in d\mathbb{Z}$.

Assume $a \in \mathbb{Z}$, $b \in \mathbb{Z}\backslash\{0\}$ and $\mathcal{L}(a,b) = d\mathbb{Z}$. Due to Example 3.55 there are numbers $x, y \in \mathbb{Z}$ satisfying $d = x \cdot a + y \cdot b$. For any $t \in \mathbb{Z}$ and $t|a, b$, i.e., $a = v_1 \cdot t$ and $b = v_2 \cdot t$ for some $v_1, v_2 \in \mathbb{Z}$, it follows $t|d$ from

$$d = x \cdot a + y \cdot b = x \cdot v_1 \cdot t + y \cdot v_2 \cdot t = (x \cdot v_1 + y \cdot v_2) \cdot t.$$

The greatest common divisor of a and b is d,

$$d = \mathrm{GCD}(a,b).$$

Let $a = z_1 \cdot d$, $b = z_2 \cdot d$ for some $z_1, z_2 \in \mathbb{Z}$. Let $a = q \cdot b + r$ for some $q \in \mathbb{Z}$ and $r \in \mathbb{Z}_b$. Then it follows

$$r = a - q \cdot b = z_1 \cdot d - q \cdot z_2 \cdot d = (z_1 - q \cdot z_2) \cdot d,$$

i.e., $d \mid b, r$. For any common divisor t of r and b, i.e., $r = u_1 \cdot t$, $b = u_2 \cdot t$ for some $u_1, u_2 \in \mathbb{Z}$, $a = q \cdot b + r = q \cdot u_2 \cdot t + u_1 \cdot t = (q \cdot u_2 + u_1) \cdot t$, $t \mid a, b$. Since $d = \mathrm{GCD}(a,b)$, it is $t \leq d$. The greatest common divisor of a and b is also the greatest common divisor of b and r. The Euclidean algorithm[4] implements this and calculates the greatest common divisor of two given numbers.

Theorem 3.56 (Euclidean algorithm). *Let $a, b \in \mathbb{Z}$, $b \neq 0$ and $r_1 := a$, $r_2 := b$. The division with remainder*

$$r_i := q_i \cdot r_{i+1} + r_{i+2}$$

breaks after at most $n \leq |b|$ steps, assuming $|r_{i+2}| < |r_{i+1}|$, if $r_{i+2} \neq 0$. This means that there is an integer $n \leq |b|$ satisfying $r_{i+1} \neq 0$ supposing $i < n$ and $r_n = q_n \cdot r_{n+1} + 0$. Then $d := r_{n+1} =$ GCD(a,b) and we can compute numbers $x, y \in \mathbb{Z}$ possessing the property $d = x \cdot a + y \cdot b$.

Proof. We continue with the idea of iteration. The greatest common divisor of $r_1 := a$ and $r_2 := b$ is also the greatest common divisor of

[4]Euclid of Alexandria (circa 365–300 BC).

r_2 and r_3 defined by $r_1 = q_1 \cdot r_2 + r_3$ for $q_1 \in \mathbb{Z}$ and $r_3 \in \mathbb{Z}_{r_2}$. By defining

$$r_i := q_i \cdot r_{i+1} + r_{i+2}, \quad r_{i+2} \in \mathbb{Z}_{r_{i+1}}.$$

Consequently, there is an integer $n \leq |r_2|$ satisfying $r_n = q_n \cdot r_{n+1} + 0$. It follows

$$\left.\begin{array}{l} r_{n+1}|r_n \\ r_{n-1} = q_{n-1} \cdot r_n + r_{n+1} \end{array}\right\} \Rightarrow r_{n+1}|r_{n-1} \Rightarrow \ldots \Rightarrow r_{n+1}|r_2 \Rightarrow r_{n+1}|r_1.$$

Finally, $\mathrm{GCD}(q_n \cdot r_{n+1}, r_{n+1}) = r_{n+1}$, since r_{n+1} is a common divisor of the two integers and the largest element of $D_{r_{n+1}}$. □

The number of steps in this algorithm is a rough estimate.[5] We make this process clear with an example.

Example 3.57. Looking for $d = \mathrm{GCD}(36, 21)$, the Euclidean algorithm calculates

$$\begin{array}{rl} 36 = 1 \cdot 21 + 15, & 15 = 1 \cdot 36 + (-1) \cdot 21 \\ 21 = 1 \cdot 15 + 6, & 6 = (-1) \cdot 36 + 2 \cdot 21 \\ 15 = 2 \cdot 6 + 3, & 3 = 3 \cdot 36 + (-5) \cdot 21 \\ 6 = 2 \cdot 3 + 0. & \end{array}$$

Thus, $3 = \mathrm{GCD}(36, 21)$ and $3 = 3 \cdot 36 + (-5) \cdot 21$.

Example 3.57 shows the computing of the greatest common divisor and the processing of any representation

$$d = x \cdot a + y \cdot b.$$

In addition, it is necessary to extend the algorithm by carrying the coefficients along at each step. Algorithm 3.1 shows this process. Definition 1.7 enables computing of the greatest common divisor for more than two numbers, which is possible by a successive application of Algorithm 3.1.

[5] Given $a > b > 0$, the number of iterations increases at most to the number of digits, cf. (Hardy *et al.*, 2008).

Algorithm 3.1: Extended Euclidean algorithm

```
Require: a, b ∈ ℤ, b ≠ 0.
Ensure: d = GCD(a, b) with d = x[0] · a + y[0] · b.
x[0] := 1, x[1] := 0, y[0] := 0, y[1] := 1, vz := 1.
while b ≠ 0 do
    r := a%b.
    q := a/b.
    a := b.
    b := r.
    xt := x[1], yt := y[1].
    x[1] := q · x[1] + x[0], y[1] := q · y[1] + y[0].
    x[0] := xt, y[0] := yt.
    vz := −vz.
end while
x[0] := vz · x[0].
y[0] := −vz · y[0].
d := a.
return d, x[0], y[0].
```

Example 3.58.

$$\text{GCD}(36, 21, 15) = \text{GCD}(\text{GCD}(36, 21), 15) = \text{GCD}(3, 15) = 3.$$

Suppose that $1 = \text{GCD}(a, b)$. Then, there are numbers $x, y \in \mathbb{Z}$ satisfying $1 = x \cdot a + y \cdot b$. Let $x, y \in \mathbb{Z}$ numbers and $1 = x \cdot a + y \cdot b$ in reverse. If $t \in \mathbb{N}$ is a common divisor of a and b, i.e., $a = v_1 \cdot t$ and $b = v_2 \cdot t$, then it is $1 = x \cdot v_1 \cdot t + y \cdot v_2 \cdot t$. Consequently, d is a divisor of 1 and for that reason it follows $t = 1$: $1 = \text{GCD}(a, b)$.

Now, let us look at the set $\mathbb{Z}_n$. If a is a unity element of $\mathbb{Z}_n$, there is an element a' satisfying $1 = a \cdot_n a'$. However, this means that a and n have the greatest common divisor 1.

Theorem 3.59. *$(\mathbb{Z}_n, +_n, 0)$ is a cyclic group and each $a \in \mathbb{Z}_n$ is a generator of this group iff $GCD(a, n) = 1$.*

Proof. It is $\mathcal{L}(1) = \{z \cdot_n 1;\ z \in \mathbb{Z}\} = \{z \cdot_n 1;\ z \in \mathbb{Z}_n\} = \mathbb{Z}_n$. Thus, 1 is a generator of the group and it is a cyclic group.

"$\Rightarrow$": Let $a \in \mathbb{Z}_n$ be a generator, i.e., $\mathcal{L}(a) = \mathbb{Z}_n$. Then, there is a matching $a' \in \mathbb{Z}$ that fulfills $a' \cdot_n a = 1$. Since $a' \cdot a \equiv_n 1$, there is a $z' \in \mathbb{Z}$ satisfying $a' \cdot a = -z' \cdot n + 1$. We get $1 = a' \cdot a + z' \cdot n$ by reordering and thus $\text{GCD}(a, n) = 1$.

"$\Leftarrow$": Assuming $\text{GCD}(a, n) = 1$ for any $a \in \mathbb{Z}_n$, there is a number $a' \in \mathbb{Z}$ fulfilling $a' \cdot a \equiv_n 1$ and because of that $a' \cdot_n a = 1$. For each $z \in \mathbb{Z}_n$, it is $z = z \cdot_n 1 = z \cdot_n (a' \cdot_n a) = (z \cdot_n a') \cdot_n a$. Thus, for each $z \in \mathbb{Z}_n$, there is a number $u := z \cdot_n a' \in \mathbb{Z}$ satisfying $u \cdot_n a = z$. It follows that $\mathcal{L}(a) = \mathbb{Z}_n$. □

The set $\mathbb{Z}_n^\times$ of all unity elements of $\mathbb{Z}_n$ is a subset of $\mathbb{Z}_n$, which contains all relatively prime numbers with reference to n. We motivate this by a two-sided analysis. Firstly, from $\text{GCD}(a, n) = 1$, it follows

$$\begin{aligned}\text{GCD}(a, n) = 1 \Rightarrow 1 &= x \cdot a + y \cdot n \\ &\Rightarrow (1 - y \cdot n) \bmod n = x \cdot a \bmod n \\ &\Rightarrow x \cdot a \equiv_n 1 \Rightarrow x \cdot_n a = (q \cdot n + r) \cdot_n a \\ &= r \cdot_n a = 1,\ r \in \mathbb{Z}_n \\ &\Rightarrow a \in \mathbb{Z}_n^\times.\end{aligned}$$

Alternatively, if $a \in \mathbb{Z}_n^\times$, we obtain for some $x \in \mathbb{Z}_n$

$$\begin{aligned}x \cdot_n a = 1 &\overset{q \in \mathbb{Z}}{\Rightarrow} x \cdot a = q \cdot n + 1 \Rightarrow 1 = x \cdot a - q \cdot n \\ &\Rightarrow \text{GCD}(a, n) = 1.\end{aligned}$$

Corollary 3.60. *The equivalence $a \in \mathbb{Z}_n^\times \Leftrightarrow GCD(a, n) = 1$ applies.*

Corollary 3.60 shows a very important application of the extended Euclidean algorithm. If $a \in \mathbb{Z}_n^\times$ is a unity element, we can find its inverse element a^{-1}:

$$1 = x \cdot a + y \cdot n = (q \cdot n + r) \cdot a + y \cdot n \Rightarrow r \cdot_n a = 1 \Rightarrow a^{-1} = r \in \mathbb{Z}_n^\times.$$

Example 3.61. (1) We look for the inverse element of $a = 3$ in $(\mathbb{Z}_8^\times, \cdot_8, 1)$. It is $Z_8^\times = \{1, 3, 5, 7\}$, $1 = 3 \cdot 3 + (-1) \cdot 8$ and for that reason we have $a^{-1} = 3$. The element is self-inverse.

(2) The following table shows the inverse elements based on $(\mathbb{Z}_{26}^\times, \cdot_{26}, 1)$ in the second row corresponding to the given elements in the first row:

$x \in \mathbb{Z}_{26}^\times$	1	3	5	7	9	11	15	17	19	21	23	25
x^{-1} mod 26	1	9	21	15	3	19	7	23	11	5	17	25

Each element of the structure $(\mathbb{Z}_n^\times, \cdot_n, 1)$ has an inverse element that is an element of $\mathbb{Z}_n^\times$, which seems to be an existing group structure. We now prove this statement and will call it the *group of residue classes relatively prime to n*.

Theorem 3.62 (Group of residue classes relatively prime). *The set of relatively prime numbers with reference to $n \in \mathbb{N}$,*

$$\mathbb{Z}_n^\times = \{a \in \mathbb{Z}_n;\ GCD(a, n) = 1\},$$

together with the mod-n-multiplication and the identity element 1, $(\mathbb{Z}_n^\times, \cdot_n, 1)$, forms a group.

Proof. The associativity of the operation is assigned by the operation in $\mathbb{Z}_n$. From $\text{GCD}(1, n) = 1$, it follows $1 \in \mathbb{Z}_n^\times$. Given $a, b \in \mathbb{Z}_n^\times$ fulfilling $1 = x \cdot a + q \cdot n$ and $1 = y \cdot b + p \cdot n$, we obtain

$$\begin{aligned}
& x \cdot y \cdot a \cdot b = (1 - q \cdot n)(1 - p \cdot n) = 1 - (q \cdot p \cdot n - q - p) \cdot n \\
\Rightarrow \quad & 1 = x \cdot y \cdot a \cdot b + (q \cdot p \cdot n - q - p) \cdot n \Rightarrow \text{GCD}(a \cdot b, n) = 1 \\
\overset{a \cdot b = t \cdot n + r}{\Rightarrow} \quad & 1 = x \cdot y \cdot r + (x \cdot y \cdot t + q \cdot p \cdot n - q - p) \cdot n \\
\Rightarrow \quad & \text{GCD}(a \cdot_n b, n) = 1.
\end{aligned}$$

Since any element of $\mathbb{Z}_n^\times$ has an inverse element, the structure is a group. □

Since $(\mathbb{Z}_n, \cdot_n, 1)$ forms a monoid, Theorem 3.62 follows immediately from Theorem 3.15. If we look for a generator of the group $(\mathbb{Z}_8^\times, \cdot_8, 1)$, we cannot find any: $\mathcal{L}(1) = \{1\}$, $\mathcal{L}(3) = \{1, 3\}$, $\mathcal{L}(5) = \{1, 5\}$ and

$\mathcal{L}(7) = \{1, 7\}$. Thus, a group of residue classes relatively prime to n need not be a cyclic group. However, there are such cyclic groups.

Example 3.63. Given $\mathbb{Z}_5^\times = \{1, 2, 3, 4\}$, we get $\text{ord}_{\mathbb{Z}_5^\times}(2) = 4$. Each element of $\mathbb{Z}_5^\times$ is a power of 2. Thus $\mathcal{L}(2) = \mathbb{Z}_5^\times$.

A cyclic group $(S, *, e_*)$ possesses at least one generator $a \in S$. From Definition 3.23, $\text{ord}_S(a) = |S|$. Now, we look at the group of unity elements as a component of a field.

Theorem 3.64. *Let $(\mathbb{F}, +, \cdot, e_+, e.)$ be a field. If $(U, \cdot, e.)$ is a finite subgroup of the group $(\mathbb{F}^\times, \cdot, e.)$ of unity elements, then $(U, \cdot, e.)$ is cyclic.*

Proof. Assume that $(U, \cdot, e.)$ is not cyclic. Let $g \in U$ be an element with maximum order, i.e., $m = |\mathcal{L}(g)| = \text{ord}_U(g) = \max\{\text{ord}_U(x);\ x \in U\} < |U|$. Since $x^m = e.$ for $x \in \mathcal{L}(g)$, we have a closer look at the polynomial $x^m - e.$ in $\mathbb{F}$, which has m roots at most (see Corollary 6.24 for a proof). Since $m < |U|$, there is $h \in U$ satisfying $h^m \neq e.$. However, then $1 < n = \text{ord}_U(h) \leq m$ cannot be a divisor of m. If $\text{GCD}(m, n) = 1$, it follows from Lemma 3.29 that $\text{ord}_U(g \cdot h) = \text{LCM}(m, n) = m \cdot n > m$. Alternatively, if $\text{GCD}(m, n) > 1$, we use the prime factorizations

$$m = \prod_{j=1}^{k} p_j^{\alpha_j} \text{ and } n = \prod_{j=1}^{k} p_j^{\beta_j}.$$

Thus,

$$\underbrace{\prod_{j=1}^{k} p_j^{\min\{\alpha_j, \beta_j\}}}_{\text{GCD}(m,n)} \cdot \underbrace{\prod_{j=1}^{k} p_j^{\max\{\alpha_j, \beta_j\}}}_{\text{LCM}(m,n)} = m \cdot n$$

by Corollary 1.31. Let $\gamma_j = \max\{\alpha_j, \beta_j\}$ and define

$$a_{p_j} = \begin{cases} g^{m/p_j^{\gamma_j}}, & \alpha_j \geq \beta_j, \\ h^{n/p_j^{\gamma_j}}, & \alpha_j < \beta_j. \end{cases}$$

Consequently,

$$\operatorname{ord}_U(a_{p_j}) \overset{\text{Cor. 3.28}}{=} \left\{ \begin{array}{ll} \dfrac{m}{\operatorname{GCD}\left(m, p_j^{\gamma_j}\right)}, & \alpha_j \geq \beta_j, \\ \dfrac{n}{\operatorname{GCD}\left(n, p_j^{\gamma_j}\right)}, & \alpha_j < \beta_j. \end{array} \right\} = p_j^{\gamma_j}.$$

Since the $p_j^{\gamma_j}$ are pairwise relatively prime, we can calculate the order of $a_{p_1} \cdot \ldots \cdot a_{p_k} = g^u \cdot h^v \in U$ for some $u, v \in \mathbb{N}$ using Lemma 3.29 again, obtaining

$$\operatorname{ord}_U\left(\prod_{j=1}^{k} a_{p_j}\right) = \prod_{j=1}^{k} p_j^{\gamma_j} = \operatorname{LCM}(m, n) > m.$$

However, both cases contradict the assumption of the maximum order of g, and $(U, \cdot, e.)$ is definitely cyclic. □

From a finite field, the group of unity elements is also finite and is a cyclic self-subgroup.

Corollary 3.65. *If the field* $(\mathbb{F}, +, \cdot, e_+, e.)$ *is finite, then* $(\mathbb{F}^\times, \cdot, e.)$ *is cyclic. Particularly,* $(\mathbb{Z}_p^\times, \cdot_p, 1)$ *is cyclic.*

Example 3.66. Given a finite field $(\mathbb{F}, +, \cdot, e_+, e.)$, $a \in \mathbb{F}^\times$ and $n = \operatorname{ord}_{\mathbb{F}^\times}(a)$. Consider the two cyclic groups $(\mathbb{F}^\times, \cdot, e.)$ and $(\mathbb{Z}_n, +_n, 0)$ and define the mapping

$$\psi_a : \mathbb{Z}_n \to \mathbb{F}^\times, \quad x \mapsto \psi_a(x) = a^x.$$

Then, $\psi_a(\mathbb{Z}_n) = \mathcal{L}(a)$ and since $(\mathbb{F}^\times, \cdot, e.)$ is cyclic

$$\psi_a(x +_n y) = a^{x +_n y} \overset{\text{cycl.}}{=} a^x \cdot a^y = \psi_a(x) \cdot \psi_a(y).$$

Thus, ψ is a group homomorphism and $(\mathcal{L}(a), \cdot_{|\mathcal{L}(a)}, e.)$ is a cyclic subgroup of $(\mathbb{F}^\times, \cdot, e.)$, according to Theorem 3.64.

Although the statement is very general, we can now classify each cyclic group after a short investigation. We want to identify a cyclic group by the well-known group $(\mathbb{Z}_n, +_n, 0)$.

Theorem 3.67. *Given a cyclic group $(S, *, e_*)$, let $a \in S$ be a generator of the group and $n = |S|$. Then, there is an isomorphic mapping between $\mathbb{Z}/\equiv_n$ and S,*

$$\psi : \mathbb{Z}/\equiv_n \to S,\ [r]_n \mapsto \overset{r}{\ast}\, a.$$

Proof. Firstly, we have $|\mathbb{Z}/\equiv_n| = n = |S|$. It applies

$$\psi([r]_n \oplus [s]_n) = \overset{r+s}{\ast}\, a = \overset{r}{\ast}\, a * \overset{s}{\ast}\, a = \psi([r]_n) * \psi([s]_n).$$

Thus, ψ is a homomorphism. Because of

$$\{[r]_n;\ \overset{r}{\ast}\, a = e_*\} \overset{0 \le r < n}{=} \{[0]_n\},$$

the mapping is injective. An injective mapping between two sets of the same length is also surjective. Hence, ψ is bijective and

$$(S, *, e_*) \cong (\mathbb{Z}/\equiv_n, \oplus, [0]_n) \cong (\mathbb{Z}_n, +_n, 0). \qquad \square$$

Remembering Theorem 3.59, we know that $(\mathbb{Z}_n, +_n, 0)$ has $|\mathbb{Z}_n^\times|$ generators. Accordingly, any cyclic group with $n = |S|$ has $|\mathbb{Z}_n^\times|$ generators.

Example 3.68. $\mathbb{Z}_6^\times = \{1, 5\}$, $(\mathbb{Z}_6^\times, \cdot_6, 1) \cong (\mathbb{Z}_2, +_2, 0)$ and $(\mathbb{Z}_6^\times, \cdot_6, 1)$ has one generator: $|\mathbb{Z}_2^\times| = |\{1\}| = 1 \Rightarrow \mathcal{L}(5) = \mathbb{Z}_6^\times$.

One possibility to decide whether a group $(\mathbb{Z}_n^\times, \cdot_n, 1)$ is cyclic or not is to determine an element $a \in \mathbb{Z}_n^\times$ possessing full order, $\mathrm{ord}_{\mathbb{Z}_n^\times}(a) = |\mathbb{Z}_n^\times|$. If n is very huge this is hard to do. Firstly, it is hard to find all the elements of the group of residue classes relatively prime to n. This number can be written as a mapping depending on n. The mapping is named after Euler.[6]

[6]Leonhard Euler (1707–1783).

Definition 3.69 (Euler's ϕ-function). The number of elements of $\mathbb{Z}_n^\times$ is denoted by

$$\phi(n) := |\mathbb{Z}_n^\times| = |\{a \in \mathbb{Z}_n;\ \ \mathrm{ggT}(a,n) = 1\}|.$$

In doing so, $\phi : \mathbb{N} \to \mathbb{N}$, $n \mapsto \phi(n)$ is called *Euler's ϕ-function.*

The first 150 values of Euler's ϕ-function is shown in Figure 3.2.

Let $(S, *, e_*)$ be a group and $a \in S$ with $\mathrm{ord}_S(a) = n < \infty$, i.e., $\overset{n}{\ast}\, a = e_*$. We look at the set

$$\mathcal{L}_n(a) := \left\{ \overset{k}{\ast}\, a;\ k \in \mathbb{Z}_n \right\}.$$

For any $x \in \mathcal{L}_n(a)$, it applies $x = \ast^k\, a \in \mathcal{L}(a)$ for some $k \in \mathbb{Z}_n \subset \mathbb{Z}$. Alternatively, for any $x \in \mathcal{L}(a)$, i.e., $x = \ast^m\, a$, $m = q \cdot n + r \in \mathbb{Z}$, $r \in \mathbb{Z}_n$, we obtain

$$x = \overset{m}{\ast}\, a = \overset{q \cdot n + r}{\ast}\, a = \overset{n \cdot q}{\ast}\, a * \overset{r}{\ast}\, a = \overset{r}{\ast}\, a \in \mathcal{L}_n(a).$$

Together, $\mathcal{L}(a) = \mathcal{L}_n(a)$.

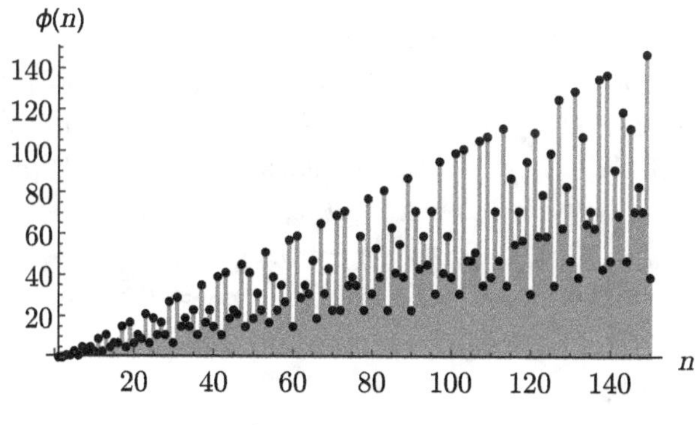

Figure 3.2 The first 150 values of Euler's ϕ-function.

Corollary 3.70. *Let $(S, *, e_*)$ be a group and $a \in S$ with $ord_S(a) = n < \infty$. It follows $\mathcal{L}(a) = \mathcal{L}_n(a)$, and $(\mathcal{L}(a), *, e_*)$ has $\phi(n)$ generators.*

The computation of $\phi(n)$ is the next task. We know from the Fundamental Theorem of Arithmetic 1.29 n decomposes into prime factors, $n = p_1^{\alpha_1} \cdot \ldots \cdot p_k^{\alpha_k}$. This is a rather complex task, which is why this is used in cryptology. For determining the number of elements of the group of residue classes relatively prime to n, $(\mathbb{Z}_n^\times, \cdot_n, 1)$, we use the following result.

Theorem 3.71. *Given a prime power p^r with p prime and $r \in \mathbb{N}$,*

$$\phi(p^r) = p^{r-1} \cdot (p-1).$$

Proof. There are p^r candidates for members of the set of unity elements. One such candidate may be $a \in \{0, \ldots, p^r - 1\}$. This number a can be written as a p-adic number due to (2.2) by

$$a = a_0 + a_1 p + \cdots + a_{r-1} p^{r-1}, \quad a_i \in \{0, \ldots, p-1\},$$
$$i = 0, \ldots, r-1.$$

According to Corollary 3.60, it holds $\text{GCD}(a, p^r) = 1$. However, we also have $\text{GCD}(a, p^r) = 1$ iff $a_0 \neq 0$. If $\text{GCD}(a, p^r) = 1$, it follows $1 = a \cdot x + p^r \cdot y = a_0 \cdot x + a_1 \cdot x \cdot p + a_2 \cdot x \cdot p^2 + \cdots + a_{r-1} \cdot x \cdot p^{r-1} + y \cdot p^r$ for $x, y \in \mathbb{Z}$. If $a_0 = 0$ is valid, $p \mid 1$ and p would not be prime. This would contradict the assumption and implies $a_0 \neq 0$. Conversely, if $\text{GCD}(a, p^r) = b > 1$ in which b is a multiple of p, i.e., $b = z \cdot p$, $b = z \cdot p \mid a$ and thus $p \mid a$, $a = k \cdot z \cdot p = a_0 + a_1 p + \cdots + a_{r-1} p^{r-1}$ for $k, z \in \mathbb{Z}$. It follows $a_0 = 0$.

Thus, all of the candidates satisfying $a_0 = 0$ must be excluded. Specifically, p^{r-1} pieces for each power of p at the p-adic representation of a. Finally,

$$\phi(p^r) = p^r - p^{r-1} = p^{r-1} \cdot (p-1). \qquad \square$$

For a decomposed number n, there is a simple way to determine $\phi(n)$. However, the formula's validity is based on the Chinese remainder theorem.

3.2.3 *Chinese remainder theorem*

Definition 3.72 (Direct product of rings). For all $i = 1, \ldots, k$, let $(R_i, +_{R_i}, \cdot_{R_i}, 0_{R_i}, 1_{R_i})$ be rings. Then, we define a sum and a product on the Cartesian product $R := R_1 \times \cdots \times R_k$ by

$$+_R : R^2 \to R,$$
$$(u_1, \ldots, u_k) +_R (v_1, \ldots, v_k) := (u_1 +_{R_1} v_1, \ldots, u_k +_{R_k} v_k), \text{ and}$$
$$\cdot_R : R^2 \to R,$$
$$(u_1, \ldots, u_k) \cdot_R (v_1, \ldots, v_k) := (u_1 \cdot_{R_1} v_1, \ldots, u_k \cdot_{R_k} v_k).$$

This is called the *direct product* of the rings $R_1, \ldots, R_k$.

The direct product of rings forms a ring. However, we still have to calculate the properties of this ring, but this can easily be done since all of the properties transfer component-wise.

Theorem 3.73. *Let $(R_i, +_{R_i}, \cdot_{R_i}, 0_{R_i}, 1_{R_i})$ be rings for all $i = 1, \ldots, k$, and $R = R_1 \times \cdots \times R_k$, $+_R, \cdot_R$, as defined in Definition 3.72. Let $1_R := (1_{R_1}, \ldots, 1_{R_k})$ and $0_R := (0_{R_1}, \ldots, 0_{R_k})$. Then $(R, +_r, \cdot_r, 0_R, 1_R)$ is a ring with identity. If all rings are commutative, then their direct product is also commutative.*

Proof. Let $a, b, c \in R$.

(A1)
$$a +_R b = (\ldots, a_i +_{R_i} b_i, \ldots) = (\ldots, b_i +_{R_i} a_i, \ldots) = b +_R a$$

(A2)
$$a +_R (b +_R c) = (\ldots, a_i +_{R_i} (b_i +_{R_i} c_i), \ldots) = (\ldots, (a_i +_{R_i} b_i) +_{R_i} c_i, \ldots) = (a +_R b) +_R c$$

(A3)
$$0_R +_R a = (\ldots, 0_{R_i} +_{R_i} a_i, \ldots) = (\ldots, a_i, \ldots) = a$$

$$
\begin{aligned}
&\text{(A4)} & -a &:= (-a_1, \ldots, -a_k)\\
&& a +_R (-a) &= (\ldots, a_i +_{R_i} (-a_i), \ldots) = (\ldots, 0_{R_i}, \ldots) = 0\\
&\text{(M2)} & a \cdot_R (b \cdot_R c) &= (\ldots, a_i \cdot_{R_i} (b_i \cdot_{R_i} c_i), \ldots)\\
&& &= (\ldots, (a_i \cdot_{R_i} b_i) \cdot_{R_i} c_i, \ldots) = (a \cdot_R b) \cdot_R c\\
&\text{(M3)} & 1_R \cdot_R a &= (\ldots, 1_{R_i} \cdot_{R_i} a_i, \ldots) = (\ldots, a_i, \ldots) = a\\
&\text{(D1)} & a \cdot_R (b +_R c) &= (\ldots, a_i \cdot_{R_i} (b_i +_{R_i} c_i), \ldots)\\
&& &= (\ldots, (a_i \cdot_{R_i} b_i) +_{R_i} (a_i \cdot_{R_i} c_i), \ldots)\\
&& &= (\ldots, a_i \cdot_{R_i} b_i, \ldots) +_R (\ldots, a_i \cdot_{R_i} c_i, \ldots)\\
&& &= (a \cdot_R b) +_R (a \cdot_R c)\\
&& (a +_R b) \cdot_R c &= (\ldots, (a_i +_{R_i} b_i) \cdot_{R_i} c_i, \ldots)\\
&& &= (\ldots, a_i \cdot_{R_i} c_i, \ldots) +_R (\ldots, b_i \cdot_{R_i} c_i, \ldots)\\
&& &= (a \cdot_R c) +_R (b \cdot_R c)\\
&\text{(M1)} & a \cdot_R b &= (\ldots, a_i \cdot_{R_i} b_i, \ldots) = (\ldots, b_i \cdot_{R_i} a_i, \ldots)\\
&& &= b \cdot_R a
\end{aligned}
$$

□

Example 3.74. Consider the set

$$R := \mathbb{Z}_2 \times \mathbb{Z}_3 = \{(0,0), (1,0), (0,1), (1,1), (0,2), (1,2)\}, \ |R| = 6.$$

Using the operations from Definition 3.72, we get a ring structure.

$+_R/\cdot_R$	$(0,0)$	$(1,0)$	$(0,1)$	$(1,1)$	$(0,2)$	$(1,2)$
$(0,0)$	(0,0)/(0,0)	(1,0)/(0,0)	(0,1)/(0,0)	(1,1)/(0,0)	(0,2)/(0,0)	(1,2)/(0,0)
$(1,0)$	(1,0)/(0,0)	(0,0)/(1,0)	(1,1)/(0,0)	(0,1)/(1,0)	(1,2)/(0,0)	(0,2)/(1,0)
$(0,1)$	(0,1)/(0,0)	(1,1)/(0,0)	(0,2)/(0,1)	(1,2)/(0,1)	(0,0)/(0,2)	(1,0)/(0,2)
$(1,1)$	(1,1)/(0,0)	(0,1)/(1,0)	(1,2)/(0,1)	(0,2)/(1,1)	(1,0)/(0,2)	(0,0)/(1,2)
$(0,2)$	(0,2)/(0,0)	(1,2)/(0,0)	(0,0)/(0,2)	(1,0)/(0,2)	(0,1)/(0,1)	(1,1)/(0,1)
$(1,2)$	(1,2)/(0,0)	(0,2)/(1,0)	(1,0)/(0,2)	(0,0)/(1,2)	(1,1)/(0,1)	(0,1)/(1,1).

Comparing $\mathbb{Z}_2 \times \mathbb{Z}_3$ from Example 3.74 with the ring structure of $\mathbb{Z}_6$, because of the six elements, shows some parallels. We can identify each element of $\mathbb{Z}_2 \times \mathbb{Z}_3$ by a bijective mapping

$$
\begin{aligned}
\mathbb{Z}_6 \to \mathbb{Z}_2 \times \mathbb{Z}_3,\ & z \mapsto (z \bmod 2, z \bmod 3)\\
& 0 \mapsto (0,0), 1 \mapsto (1,1), 2 \mapsto (0,2),\\
& 3 \mapsto (1,0), 4 \mapsto (0,1), 5 \mapsto (1,2).
\end{aligned}
$$

Thus, even the operations make sense. For example, $(1,0) +_{\mathbb{Z}_2\times\mathbb{Z}_3} (1,2) = (0,2)$ corresponds to $3 +_6 5 = 2$. The two rings seem to be isomorphic (and they are),

$$(\mathbb{Z}_2 \times \mathbb{Z}_3, +_{\mathbb{Z}_2\times\mathbb{Z}_3}, \cdot_{\mathbb{Z}_2\times\mathbb{Z}_3}, (0,0), (1,1)) \cong (\mathbb{Z}_6, +_6, \cdot_6, 0, 1).$$

Theorem 3.75. *Let $n_1, \ldots, n_k \in \mathbb{N}$ be mutually relatively prime numbers and $n = n_1 \cdot \ldots \cdot n_k$. Then, there is an isomorphism*

$$f : \mathbb{Z}_n \to \mathbb{Z}_{n_1} \times \cdots \times \mathbb{Z}_{n_k},\ z \mapsto (z \textit{ mod } n_1, \ldots, z \textit{ mod } n_k).$$

Proof. Firstly, $|\mathbb{Z}_n| = n = n_1 \cdot \ldots \cdot n_k = |\mathbb{Z}_{n_1}| \cdot \ldots \cdot |\mathbb{Z}_{n_k}|$. Next, we show that f is a ring homomorphism. Consider

$$n = n_i \cdot \underbrace{n_1 \cdot \ldots \cdot n_{i-1} \cdot n_{i+1} \cdot \ldots \cdot n_k}_{M_i} =: n_i \cdot M_i,$$

$$\begin{aligned}
(a+b) \bmod n_i &= (q \cdot n + r) \bmod n_i, \quad q \in \mathbb{Z}, r \in \mathbb{Z}_n,\\
&= ((q_i \cdot M_i) \cdot n_i + r) \bmod n_i\\
&= r \bmod n_i\\
&= (a +_n b) \bmod n_i\\
(a \cdot b) \bmod n_i &= (q_a \cdot n + r_a)(q_b \cdot n + r_b) \bmod n_i,\\
&\quad q_a, q_b \in \mathbb{Z}, r_a, r_b \in \mathbb{Z}_n,\\
&= ((q_a M_i) \cdot n_i + r_a)((q_b M_i) \cdot n_i + r_b) \bmod n_i\\
&= \underbrace{r_a \cdot r_b}_{q_{ab} M_i \cdot n_i + r_{ab},\ r_{ab} = a \cdot_n b} \bmod n_i\\
&= (a \cdot_n b) \bmod n_i.
\end{aligned}$$

It follows

$$\begin{aligned}
f(a +_n b) &= ((a +_n b) \bmod n_1, \ldots, (a +_n b) \bmod n_k)\\
&= ((a+b) \bmod n_1, \ldots, (a+b) \bmod n_k)\\
&= (a \bmod n_1 +_{n_1} b \bmod n_1, \ldots, a \bmod n_k +_{n_k} b \bmod n_k)\\
&= (a \bmod n_1, \ldots, a \bmod n_k)\\
&\quad +_{\mathbb{Z}_1\times\cdots\times\mathbb{Z}_k} (b \bmod n_1, \ldots, b \bmod n_k)\\
&= f(a) +_{\mathbb{Z}_1\times\cdots\times\mathbb{Z}_k} f(b).
\end{aligned}$$

and

$$\begin{aligned} f(a \cdot_n b) &= ((a \cdot_n b) \bmod n_1, \ldots, (a \cdot_n b) \bmod n_k) \\ &= ((a \cdot b) \bmod n_1, \ldots, (a \cdot b) \bmod n_k) \\ &= (a \bmod n_1 \cdot_{n_1} b \bmod n_1, \ldots, a \bmod n_k \cdot_{n_k} b \bmod n_k) \\ &= (a \bmod n_1, \ldots, a \bmod n_k) \cdot_{\mathbb{Z}_1 \times \cdots \times \mathbb{Z}_k} \\ &\quad \times (b \bmod n_1, \ldots, b \bmod n_k) \\ &= f(a) \cdot_{\mathbb{Z}_1 \times \cdots \times \mathbb{Z}_k} f(b). \\ f(0) &= (0, \ldots, 0), \\ f(1) &= (1, \ldots, 1). \end{aligned}$$

If the mapping is injective, then it is surjective and bijective overall. The homomorphism f is injective iff $f^{-1}(\{(0, \ldots, 0)\}) = \{0\}$. Let $a \in \{z \in \mathbb{Z}_n;\ f(z) = (0, \ldots, 0)\}$. Then, $x \bmod n_i = 0$ for all $i = 1, \ldots, n$, i.e., a is a multiple of all n_i. Thus, a is a multiple of $\text{LCM}(n_1, \ldots, n_k)$ and since all the n_i's are mutually relatively prime numbers, $n = \text{LCM}(n_1, \ldots, n_k)$. This implies $a \bmod n = 0$, i.e., $a = 0$. □

The reversal situation of the mapping f is not very hard to compute. Therefore, we wish to solve a system of congruences,

$$x \equiv_{n_1} a_1, \quad x \equiv_{n_2} a_2, \quad \ldots, \quad x \equiv_{n_k} a_k, \tag{3.12}$$

in which all n_i are mutually relatively prime numbers.

Theorem 3.76. *Let $n_1, \ldots, n_k \in \mathbb{N}$ be mutually relatively prime numbers, $n := n_1 \cdot \ldots \cdot n_k$ and $M_i := \prod_{j \neq i} n_j = n/n_i$. Then, we have GCD$(n_i, M_i) = 1$.*

Proof. Since $n_1, \ldots, n_k$ are mutually relatively prime numbers, there are numbers $x_j, y_j \in \mathbb{Z}$, $j \neq i$, with

$$1 = x_j \cdot n_i + y_j \cdot n_j \Leftrightarrow y_j \cdot n_j = 1 - x_j \cdot n_i.$$

It follows

$$\prod_{j\neq i} y_j \cdot n_j = M_i \cdot \prod_{j\neq i} y_j = \prod_{j\neq i} (1 - x_j \cdot n_i)$$
$$= 1 + n_i \cdot f(n_i, x_1, \ldots, x_{i-1}, x_{i+1}, \ldots, x_k),$$

in which f is an unspecified mapping. By rearranging the equation, we get

$$1 = \underbrace{-f(n_i, x_1, \ldots, x_{i-1}, x_{i+1}, \ldots, x_k)}_{\tilde{x}_i} \cdot n_i + \underbrace{\prod_{j\neq i} y_j}_{\tilde{y}_i} \cdot M_i$$

and thus $\mathrm{GCD}(n_i, M_i) = 1$. □

Theorem 3.77 (Chinese remainder theorem). *Let $n_1, \ldots, n_k \in \mathbb{N}$ be mutually relatively prime numbers, $n := n_1 \cdot \ldots \cdot n_k$ and $a_1, \ldots, a_k \in \mathbb{Z}$. Then, the system of congruences* (3.12) *has a unique solution $x \in \mathbb{Z}_n$.*

Proof. Existence: Let $M_i := n/n_i$ for all $i = 1, \ldots, k$. Firstly, $\mathrm{GCD}(n_i, M_i) = 1$ follows from Theorem 3.76. By using the extended Euclidean algorithm, we can compute numbers $\tilde{y}_i$ satisfying

$$\tilde{y}_i \cdot M_i \equiv_{n_i} 1, \quad \text{for all } i = 1, \ldots, k.$$

By setting

$$x := \left(\sum_{i=1}^{k} a_i \cdot \tilde{y}_i \cdot M_i \right) \bmod n, \tag{3.13}$$

we obtain

$$a_i \cdot \tilde{y}_i \cdot M_i = a_i \cdot (1 - \tilde{x}_i \cdot n_i) = a_i - a_i \cdot \tilde{x}_i \cdot n_i \equiv_{n_i} a_i, \quad \forall i = 1, \ldots, k.$$

Any n_i, $i \neq j$, is a divisor of M_j and thus,

$$a_j \cdot \tilde{y}_j \cdot M_j \equiv_{n_i} 0, \quad \text{for all } i \neq j.$$

Together, it follows

$$x \equiv_{n_i} a_i \cdot \tilde{y}_i \cdot M_i + \sum_{j \neq i} a_j \cdot \tilde{y}_j \cdot M_j \equiv_{n_i} a_i, \quad \text{for all } i = 1, \dots, k.$$

Uniqueness: Let x and $\hat{x}$ be two different solutions. Then, by setting $x = q \cdot n_i \cdot M_i + r$ and $\hat{x} = \hat{q} \cdot n_i \cdot M_i + \hat{r}$, we get

$$x - \hat{x} = (q - \hat{q}) \cdot n_i \cdot M_i + (r - \hat{r}).$$

Alternatively, it is $x - \hat{x} = t \cdot n_i$, and consequently, $r - \hat{r} = u_i \cdot n_i$ for every $i = 1, \dots, k$. Since n_i are mutually relatively prime numbers, $\text{LCM}(n_1, \dots, n_k) = n$ and $r - \hat{r}$ has to be a multiple of n. Since they are remainders modulo n, we obtain $r - \hat{r} = 0 \bmod n$. Finally, $x - \hat{x} = 0 \bmod n$. □

Remark 3.78. The statements in this section will apply, especially if the primes n_i are prime powers $p_i^{\alpha_i}$. Furthermore, iff $\text{GCD}(a, n) = 1$ we can solve

$$a \cdot x \bmod n = b, \quad n = p_1^{\alpha_1} \cdot \ldots \cdot p_k^{\alpha_k},$$

by solving the congruences

$$x \equiv_{p_j^{\alpha_j}} b \cdot (a^{-1} \bmod p_j^{\alpha_j}). \tag{3.14}$$

This is because $a \cdot x - b \bmod n = 0 \Leftrightarrow a \cdot x - b \bmod p_j^{\alpha_j} = 0$ for all j.

Example 3.79. Look at the following congruences:

$$x \equiv_{11} 5, \quad x \equiv_{13} 7.$$

$\text{GCD}(11, 13) = 1$ and we obtain a unique x (mod $11 \cdot 13$) fulfilling the two equations. We calculate

$$1 = 6 \cdot 13 - 7 \cdot 11$$

and finally, $x = 5 \cdot 6 \cdot 13 - 7 \cdot 7 \cdot 11 \bmod 143 = 137$, which is equal to the problem of solving

$$47 \cdot x \bmod 143 = 4.$$

Finally, we write an algorithm for solving congruences according to Theorem 3.77 by Algorithm 3.2.

Algorithm 3.2: Chinese remainder algorithm

Require: $n = p_1^{\alpha_1} \cdot \ldots \cdot p_k^{\alpha_k}$, $p_i \neq p_j$, $i \neq j$ and $a_1, \ldots, a_k \in \mathbb{Z}$.
Ensure: $x \in \mathbb{Z}_n$ with $x \equiv_{p_i^{\alpha_i}} a_i$, $i = 1, \ldots, k$.

for $i = 1$ **to** k **do**
  $M_i := {}^{n}/_{p_i^{\alpha_i}}$.
  $\tilde{y}_i := M_i^{-1} \bmod p_i^{\alpha_i}$.
end for
$x := 0$.
for $i = 1$ **to** k **do**
  $x := x + a_i \cdot \tilde{y}_i \cdot M_i \bmod n$.
end for
return x.

If $a \in \mathbb{Z}_n^{\times}$, i.e., $\mathrm{GCD}(a, n) = 1$, $\mathrm{GCD}(a, n_i) = 1$ is applied from $1 = x \cdot a + y \cdot n = x \cdot a + y \cdot M_i \cdot n_i$ and $a \bmod n_i \in \mathbb{Z}_{n_i}^{\times}$. Alternatively, if $(a_1, \ldots, a_k) \in \bigtimes_{i=1}^{k} \mathbb{Z}_{n_i}^{\times}$, there is a unique $x \in \mathbb{Z}_n$ with $x \equiv_{n_i} a_i$ for all $i = 1, \ldots, k$, referring to Theorem 3.77. Thus, $x - a_i = q_i \cdot n_i$ or $a_i = x - q_i \cdot n_i$. Since $\mathrm{GCD}(a_i, n_i) = 1$, there are numbers u_i, v_i satisfying $1 = u_i \cdot a_i + v_i \cdot n_i = u_i \cdot (x - q_i \cdot n_i) + v_i \cdot n_i = u_i \cdot x + (v_i - u_i \cdot q_i) \cdot n_i$. By setting $w_i = v_i - u_i \cdot q_i$, it follows

$$\prod_{i=1}^{n} v_i \cdot n_i = \prod_{i=1}^{k} (1 - u_i \cdot x) \Leftrightarrow \quad n \cdot \prod_{i=1}^{k} v_i = 1 - x \cdot g(u_1, \ldots, u_k, x),$$

in which g is an unspecified mapping. Thus, $\mathrm{GCD}(x, m) = 1$, $x \in \mathbb{Z}_n^{\times}$. With reference to Theorem 3.75, we get a group isomorphism by

$$f_{|\mathbb{Z}_n^{\times}} : \mathbb{Z}_n^{\times} \to \bigtimes_{i=1}^{k} \mathbb{Z}_{n_i}^{\times}, \quad a \mapsto f_{|\mathbb{Z}_n^{\times}}(a) := (a \bmod n_1, \ldots, a \bmod n_k), \tag{3.15}$$

i.e., $\left(\bigtimes_{i=1}^{k} \mathbb{Z}_{n_i}^{\times}, \odot, (1, \ldots, 1) \right)$ is a group.

Corollary 3.80.

$$|\mathbb{Z}_n^\times| = \left|\bigtimes_{i=1}^{k} \mathbb{Z}_{n_i}^\times\right| = |\mathbb{Z}_{n_1}^\times| \cdot \ldots \cdot |\mathbb{Z}_{n_k}^\times|.$$

Theorem 3.81. *Let $n = n_1 \cdot \ldots \cdot n_k$ with $GCD(n_i, n_j) = 1$ for $i \neq j$. Then, $\phi(n) = \phi(n_1) \cdot \ldots \cdot \phi(n_k)$ applies.*

Proof. With reference to Corollary 3.80, the number of elements of $\mathbb{Z}_n^\times$ is equal to the number of elements of $\bigtimes_{i=1}^{n} \mathbb{Z}_{m_i}^\times$. □

Corollary 3.82. *If $n = p_1^{\alpha_1} \cdot \ldots \cdot p_k^{\alpha_k}$ is the decomposing of n into prime factors,*

$$\phi(n) = \prod_{i=1}^{k} \phi(p_i^{\alpha_i}) = \prod_{i=1}^{k} p_i^{\alpha_i - 1}(p_i - 1).$$

By assuming $n = p_1 \cdot p_2$ with p_1, p_2 prime,

$$\phi(n) = (p_1 - 1) \cdot (p_2 - 1).$$

Example 3.83.

- $\mathbb{Z}_{23}^\times = \{1, 2, \ldots, 22\}$: $\phi(23) = 23 - 1 = 22$.
- $n = 21 = 3 \cdot 7$: $\phi(21) = (3 - 1) \cdot (7 - 1) = 12$. It is $\mathbb{Z}_{21}^\times = \{1, 2, 4, 5, 8, 10, 11, 13, 16, 17, 19, 20\}$.
- $n = 9 = 3 \cdot 3$: $\phi(9) = 3^1 \cdot (3 - 1) = 6 \neq 4 = (3 - 1) \cdot (3 - 1)$ and $\mathbb{Z}_9^\times = \{1, 2, 4, 5, 7, 8\}$.

Raising to the power of $\phi(n)$ in the group $(\mathbb{Z}_n^\times, \cdot_n, 1)$ of residue classes, relatively prime to n is a special case of Corollary 3.35.

Theorem 3.84 (Euler's theorem). *Let $n \in \mathbb{N}$, $n > 1$, and $a \in \mathbb{Z}$ satisfying GCD$(a, n) = 1$. Then, $a^{\phi(n)} \equiv_n 1$.*

Proof. We know that $|\mathbb{Z}_n^\times| = \phi(n)$ and use $r = a \bmod n$ as an element of $\mathbb{Z}_n^\times$. It follows from Corollary 3.35 that

$$a^{|\mathbb{Z}_n^\times|} = a^{\phi(n)} = r^{\phi(n)} \equiv_n 1. \qquad \square$$

Example 3.85. Consider $n = 21$, $k = 11$ and $x = 5$. Since $5^5 \bmod 21 = 17$ and $5^6 \bmod 21 = 1$, we obtain $x^k \bmod n = 5^{11} \bmod 21 = 17$. We need to compute the inverse element of $k \bmod \phi(n)$ to recover 5 from 17. Therefore, $\phi(21) = 2 \cdot 6 = 12$ and GCD$(11, 12) = 1$, and thus, $k' = 11$ since $11 \cdot 11 - 12 \cdot 10 = 1$ using the extended Euclidean algorithm. Last step: $17^{11} \bmod 21 = 5^{11 \cdot 11} \bmod 21 = 5^{12 \cdot 10 + 1} \bmod 21 = 5$.

If p is a prime number, then $\phi(p) = p - 1$. Hence, Theorem 3.84 applies to Fermat's[7] little theorem.

Corollary 3.86 (Fermat's little theorem). *Let $p \in \mathbb{N}$ be a prime number and $a \in \mathbb{Z}$ satisfying GCD$(a, p) = 1$. Then, it follows $a^{p-1} \equiv_p 1$.*

After calculating all the elements of a group, we have to check the order of each element in a second step. From Example 3.51, there is a dependency on n on whether $\mathbb{Z}_n$ forms a field. This relates to the existence of an inverse element for each member of $\mathbb{Z}_n$. However, this can be achieved by choosing a prime number. Now, let p be a prime number that yields $\phi(p) = p - 1$. Every member of $\mathbb{Z}_p^\times$ has a unique inverse element. This fulfills Definition 3.21, i.e., $(\mathbb{Z}_p, +_p, \cdot_p, 0, 1)$ is a field. Alternatively, if p is not a prime number, then there are numbers $a, b \in \mathbb{Z}_p \backslash \{0\}$ with $a \cdot b = p$. However, then $a \cdot b \equiv_p 0$ and

[7]Pierre de Fermat (1607–1665).

$a, b \not\equiv_p 0$. $(\mathbb{Z}_p, +_p, \cdot_p, 0, 1)$ is a ring with zero divisors and it cannot be a field.

Corollary 3.87. $(\mathbb{Z}_p, +_p, \cdot_p, 0, 1)$ *is a field iff* p *is a prime number.*

The set $\mathbb{Z}_p$ for p prime is often denoted by $GF(p)$ at which GF is the abbreviation for Galois[8] field. From Theorem 3.65, it follows that the structure $(\mathbb{Z}_p^\times, \cdot_p, 1)$ is a cyclic group. This group can be identified by $(\mathbb{Z}_{p-1}, +_{p-1}, 0)$ and possesses $\phi(p-1)$ generators, following Theorem 3.67.

Corollary 3.88. *Let* p *be a prime number. Then,* $(\mathbb{Z}_p^\times, \cdot_p, 1)$ *is cyclic and has* $\phi(p-1)$ *generators.*

From Corollary 3.87, there is no field based on the set $\mathbb{Z}_8$. However, there are fields containing eight elements. To see this, we firstly define the characteristic of a field. Let $(\mathbb{F}, +, \cdot, 0, 1)$ be a field. Then, the *characteristic* of this field is the smallest number $n \in \mathbb{N}$ satisfying

$$\overset{n}{+}1 = 1 + \cdots + 1 = 0,$$

i.e., n is the additive order of 1 in $\mathbb{F}$, $n = \mathrm{ord}_{\mathbb{F}}(1)$. If no such number exists, then n is set to zero. This means that there is no number $n \in \mathbb{N}$, such that $\overset{n}{+}1 = 0$. Consider that there are any two numbers $m, n \in \mathbb{N}$, such that

$$\overset{m}{+}1 = \overset{n}{+}1.$$

Since $(\mathbb{F}, +, \cdot, 0, 1)$ is a field,

$$\overset{m-n}{+}1 = \overset{m}{+}1 + \overset{-n}{+}1 = \overset{n}{+}1 + \overset{n}{+}(-1) = 0 \Rightarrow m = n.$$

All of the values $\overset{n}{+}1$ are distinct and we obtain $|\mathbb{F}| = \infty$. Alternatively, if $n < \infty$, consider $n = p \cdot q$ to be composed for any

[8]Évariste Galois (1811–1832).

$n > p, q > 1$. It follows

$$0 = \overset{n}{+}1 = \overset{p\cdot q}{+}1 = \overset{p}{+}\left(\overset{q}{+}1\right) = \overset{p}{+}\left(1 \cdot \overset{q}{+}1\right) = \overset{p}{+}1 \cdot \overset{q}{+}1.$$

Since $(\mathbb{F}, +, \cdot, 0, 1)$ is a field, $\overset{p}{+}1 = 0$ or $\overset{q}{+}1 = 0$. However, this is contradictory to n being a characteristic of the field. Therefore, n has to be a prime number. For example, the characteristic of $(\mathbb{Z}_p, +_p, \cdot_p, 0, 1)$ is p. If $(\mathbb{F}, +, \cdot, 0, 1)$ has characteristic $p < \infty$, define the mapping

$$\psi : \mathbb{Z}_p \to \mathbb{F},\ r \mapsto r \cdot 1 := \overset{r}{+}1.$$

The mapping ψ is a homomorphism since

$$\begin{aligned}\psi(r+s) &= \overset{r+s}{+}1 = \overset{r}{+}1 + \overset{s}{+}1 = \psi(r) + \psi(s), \text{ and}\\ \psi(r \cdot s) &= (r \cdot s) \cdot 1 = \overset{r\cdot s}{+}1 = \overset{r}{+}\left(\overset{s}{+}1\right) \cdot 1 = \overset{r}{+}1 \cdot \overset{s}{+}1\\ &= \psi(r) \cdot \psi(s).\end{aligned}$$

Furthermore, ψ is injective since

$$\psi(r) = 0 \Leftrightarrow \overset{r}{+}1 = 0 \Leftrightarrow r = k \cdot p \Leftrightarrow r = 0.$$

An injective homomorphism between finite sets of the same length is bijective and thus ψ is an isomorphism between $\mathbb{Z}_p$ and $\psi(\mathbb{Z}_p)$. This implies that $U = \psi(\mathbb{Z}_p)$ gets a field, too. We just have to restrict the mappings on U: $(U, +_U, \cdot_U, 0, 1)$ is a field containing $|U| = p$ elements. Generally, a *subfield* of a field $(\mathbb{F}, +, \cdot, 0, 1)$ is a field based on a subset $F \subseteq \mathbb{F}$ with respect to the field operations inherited from $\mathbb{F}$. $\mathbb{F}$ is then called *extension*. Since each subfield contains 1, it contains $r \cdot 1$, $r \in \mathbb{Z}_n$, too. Thus, $U = \psi(\mathbb{Z}_p)$ is part of each subfield of $(\mathbb{F}, +, \cdot, 0, 1)$, and $(U, +_U, \cdot_U, 0, 1)$ is the smallest subfield of $(\mathbb{F}, +, \cdot, 0, 1)$,

$$U = \bigcap F,\ F \subseteq \mathbb{F} \text{ and } (F, +_U, \cdot_U, 0, 1) \text{ is a subfield},$$

and is called a *prime field*. The mapping ψ is unique since if there is another such mapping ψ' we get $\psi'(1) = 1$ and

$$\begin{aligned}\psi'(r) &= \psi'(1 + \cdots + 1) = \psi'(1) + \cdots + \psi'(1)\\ &= 1 + \cdots + 1 = r \cdot 1 = \psi(r).\end{aligned}$$

Thus, the prime field of a finite field always contains the p elements $r \cdot 1$, $r \in \mathbb{Z}_p$, and it applies

$$(U, +_U, \cdot_U, 0, 1) \cong (\mathbb{Z}_p, +_p, \cdot_p, 0, 1).$$

But what is the cardinality of $\mathbb{F}$? We have to recall another structure type from linear algebra called vector space to answer this question. The following results from linear algebra are abbreviated.[9]

Definition 3.89 (Vector space over $\mathbb{F}$). A *vector space* over a field $(\mathbb{F}, +, \cdot, 0, 1)$ is a set V together with two operations

$$\begin{aligned}\oplus &: V \times V \to V,\ (x, y) \mapsto x \oplus y, \text{ and}\\ \star &: \mathbb{F} \times V \to V,\ (\lambda, x) \mapsto \lambda \star x,\end{aligned}$$

satisfying the following properties for all $x, y \in V$ and for all $\lambda, \mu \in \mathbb{F}$:

(V1-4) There is a vector $\vec{0}$ called zero vector, such that $(V, \oplus, \vec{0})$ is an abelian group,

(V5) $\lambda \star (\mu \star x) = (\lambda \cdot \mu) \star x$,

(V6) $1 \star x = x$,

(V7) $\lambda \star (x \oplus y) = (\lambda \star x) \oplus (\lambda \star y)$, and

(V8) $(\lambda + \mu) \star x = \lambda \star x \oplus \mu \star x$.

Each element of V is called a *vector* of the vector space $(V, \oplus, \star, \vec{0})$. A subset $U \subseteq V$ together with the restricted mappings $\oplus_{|U}$ and $\star_{|U}$ is a *vector subspace* $(U, \oplus_{|U}, \star_{|U}, 0)$ if for all $x, y \in V$ and for all $\lambda \in \mathbb{F}$, it applies $x \oplus_{|U} y = x \oplus y \in U$ and $\lambda \star_{|U} x = \lambda \star x \in U$.

---

[9] For detailed information, see (Lang, 1987).

Remark 3.90. Every algebraic structure that fulfills the properties (V1) to (V8) is called a *module* if the underlying structure is a commutative ring with identity. Every vector space is a module. Every vector subspace is itself a vector space.

A collection of linear independent vectors that spans V is called a basis of the vector space and is often denoted by $\mathcal{B}$. Each vector $v \in V$ can be represented by a linear combination of the basis' elements. In the finite case, the basis could be $\mathcal{B} = \{b_1, \ldots, b_n\}$ and we obtain a unique representation

$$v = \lambda_1 \star b_1 \oplus \ldots \oplus \lambda_n \star b_n \text{ for some } \lambda_1, \ldots, \lambda_n \in \mathbb{F}. \tag{3.16}$$

The dimension of a vector space is the cardinality of a basis of the vector space, $\dim(V) = |\mathcal{B}|$. Although a basis is not unique, the dimension remains the same always. A simple example of a vector space is the one based on the set U^n: U^n, which generates the so-called *canonical vector space* over the field $(U, +_U, \cdot_U, 0, 1)$.

Theorem 3.91. *Let* $(\mathbb{F}, +, \cdot, 0, 1)$ *be a finite field and* $(U, +_U, \cdot_U, 0, 1)$ *be its prime field with characteristic* p. *Define*

$$\oplus : \mathbb{F} \times \mathbb{F} \to \mathbb{F},\ (x, y) \mapsto x \oplus y := x + y, \text{ and}$$
$$\star : U \times \mathbb{F} \to \mathbb{F},\ (u, x) \mapsto u \star x := u \cdot x.$$

Then, $(\mathbb{F}, \oplus, \star, 0) = (\mathbb{F}, +, \cdot, 0)$ *is a vector space over* $(U, +_U, \cdot_U, 0, 1)$.

Proof. (V1-4) Since $(\mathbb{F}, +, \cdot, 0, 1)$ is a field, $(\mathbb{F}, \oplus, 0)$ is an abelian group.

(V5) $\lambda \star (\mu \star x) = \lambda \cdot (\mu \cdot x) = (\lambda \cdot \mu) \cdot x = (\lambda \cdot_U \mu) \star x$,

(V6) $1 \star x = 1 \cdot x = x$,

(V7) $\lambda \star (x \oplus y) = \lambda \cdot (x + y) = \lambda \cdot x + \lambda \cdot y = \lambda \star x \oplus \lambda \star y$, and

(V8) $(\lambda +_U \mu) \star x = (\lambda + \mu) \cdot x = \lambda \cdot x + \mu \cdot x = \lambda \star x \oplus \mu \star x$.

□

The dimension of the vector space $(\mathbb{F}, +, \cdot, 0)$ is called the *degree of a field extension* and is denoted by $[\mathbb{F} : U] = \dim(\mathbb{F})$. If $|\mathbb{F}| < \infty$, there must be a finite number of linear independent vectors of $\mathbb{F}$. Consider $[\mathbb{F} : U] = n$. Then, there is a basis $\mathcal{B} = \{b_1, \ldots, b_n\}$ of $(\mathbb{F}, +, \cdot, 0)$. Since we have a unique representation according to (3.16), we can use the mapping

$$\psi_{\mathcal{B}} : U^n \to \mathbb{F}, \; (\lambda_1, \ldots, \lambda_n) \mapsto \bigoplus_{i=1}^{n} \lambda_i \star b_i, \tag{3.17}$$

which is an isomorphism. It follows

$$|\mathbb{F}| = |U^n| = |U|^n = p^n.$$

Corollary 3.92. *A finite vector space $(\mathbb{F}, +, \cdot, 0)$ over the prime field $(U, +_U, \cdot_U, 0, 1)$ with characteristic p has p^n elements if the degree of a field extension is $[\mathbb{F} : U] = n$.*

We denote such a finite field by $\mathrm{GF}(p^n)$.

Chapter 4

Classical Private-Key Ciphering

Note 4.1. In this chapter, the requirements are:

- being able to calculate a remainder modulo n, see Section 1.1,
- being able to apply the XOR gate and knowing the basics about groups and rings, see Section 3.1,
- knowing linear structures and mappings, see Section 3.2, and
- knowing the structure of cipher systems, see Section 2.5.

Selected literature: See (Dworkin, 2016b; Hoffstein *et al.*, 2008; Martin, 2017; Stinson, 2005).

Private-key cipher systems are widely used because they are fast and powerful. The typical flow of a private-key cipher system,

$$(\mathcal{P}, \mathcal{C}, \mathcal{K}_S, \mathcal{E}_S, \mathcal{D}_S),$$

is shown in Figure 4.1. A plaintext $m \in \mathcal{P}$ together with a private key $k \in \mathcal{K}_S$ of entity A is transferred to an encryption function $e_k \in \mathcal{E}_S$. There is a ciphertext $c \in \mathcal{C}$ after the encryption process. It is possible for entity B to decrypt the transferred ciphertext c using a decryption function $d_k \in \mathcal{D}_S$ after a completed key exchange via a secure channel. Since the same key is used symmetrically on both sides, the sets concerned are given the index S. If no mistake was made during decryption, the resulting text is the plaintext m again. A plaintext is not encrypted in one pass, but is divided into blocks of equal length that are separately encrypted. It is possible in this way

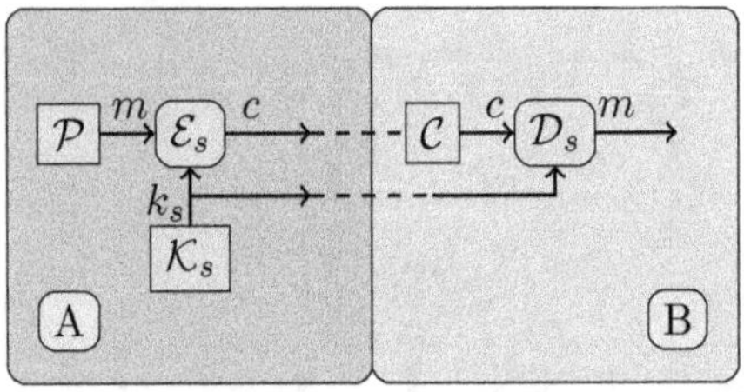

Figure 4.1 Scheme of private-key cipher systems.

to force a single key of certain length and to automate the encryption of a multitude of different plaintexts. Otherwise, we might have to repeatedly create encryption functions, depending on the length of the plaintext.

4.1 Permutations

Let X be a finite set. If a mapping $f : X \to X$ is bijective, it is called a *permutation* on X. All of the permutations on X are collected into a set $S(X)$,

$$S(X) = \{f : X \to X;\ f \text{ bijective}\}.$$

Since a finite set X containing $n = |X|$ elements is equipotent with the set $\{1, \ldots, n\}$, we look at the permutations

$$\pi : \{1, 2, \ldots, n\} \to \{1, 2, \ldots, n\},\ i \mapsto \pi(i).$$

We can note such a permutation by writing i and $\pi(i)$ among each other and framing it with round brackets, as well as the Caesar cipher in (2.3).

Example 4.2. Let $n = 3$. Then, these six permutations

$$\begin{pmatrix} 1 & 2 & 3 \\ 1 & 2 & 3 \end{pmatrix}, \begin{pmatrix} 1 & 2 & 3 \\ 1 & 3 & 2 \end{pmatrix}, \begin{pmatrix} 1 & 2 & 3 \\ 2 & 1 & 3 \end{pmatrix}, \begin{pmatrix} 1 & 2 & 3 \\ 2 & 3 & 1 \end{pmatrix},$$
$$\begin{pmatrix} 1 & 2 & 3 \\ 3 & 1 & 2 \end{pmatrix}, \begin{pmatrix} 1 & 2 & 3 \\ 3 & 2 & 1 \end{pmatrix}$$

are possible on $\{1, 2, 3\}$.

Let $\circ$ be the successive application of two permutations on X,

$$\circ : S(X) \times S(X) \to S(X),\ (f, g) \mapsto f \circ g.$$

The permutation $\mathrm{id}_X : X \to X,\ x \mapsto x$ on X acts as an identity element for the successive application, since for all $f \in S(X)$ and $x \in X$ we have

$$(f \circ \mathrm{id}_X)(x) = f(\mathrm{id}_X(x)) = f(x) = \mathrm{id}_X(f(x)) = (\mathrm{id}_X \circ f)(x).$$

Since f is bijective, there is always an inverse bijective mapping $f^{-1} : X \to X$. Thus, $(S(X), \circ, \mathrm{id}_X)$ forms a group. But this group is usually not commutative.

Example 4.3. Let $n = 3$. Then, the following computation shows that the mapping $\circ$ is usually not commutative:

$$\begin{pmatrix} 1 & 2 & 3 \\ 1 & 3 & 2 \end{pmatrix} \circ \begin{pmatrix} 1 & 2 & 3 \\ 3 & 1 & 2 \end{pmatrix} = \begin{pmatrix} 1 & 2 & 3 \\ 2 & 1 & 3 \end{pmatrix}$$
$$\begin{pmatrix} 1 & 2 & 3 \\ 3 & 1 & 2 \end{pmatrix} \circ \begin{pmatrix} 1 & 2 & 3 \\ 1 & 3 & 2 \end{pmatrix} = \begin{pmatrix} 1 & 2 & 3 \\ 3 & 2 & 1 \end{pmatrix}.$$

We denote the permutations of {1,2,. . . .n} by $S_n = S(\{1, 2, \ldots, n\})$. When creating any $\pi \in S_n$, we have n possibilities to assign a number to 1 first. Then, there are $n - 1$ possibilities for 2 left, and so on. We estimate there will overall be $n!$ possibilities.

Theorem 4.4. *The set S_n of all permutations of $\{1, 2, \ldots, n\}$ has $n!$ elements, $|S_n| = n!$.*

Proof. We prove this by induction on n:

Basis: $|S_1| = 1 \quad \checkmark$.
Induction hypothesis: $|S_n| = n!$ is right.
Induction step: we choose any $x \in \{1, 2, \ldots, n + 1\}$. Without loss of generality, let us assume $x = 1$. Now, we fix the mapping $1 \mapsto y$ for any $y \in \{1, 2, \ldots, n + 1\}$, which yields $n + 1$ possibilities. Afterwards, we have to map the rest. We need a bijective mapping from the set $\{2, 3, \ldots, n + 1\}$ to the set $\{1, 2, \ldots, y - 1, y + 1, \ldots, n + 1\}$.

Based on the induction hypothesis, we have $n!$ possibilities. There are $(n+1) \cdot n! = (n+1)!$ possibilities altogether. □

Example 4.5.

- $|S(\Sigma_{\text{Lat}})| = 26! = 403291461126605635584000000 \approx 2^{89}$,
- $|S(\Sigma_{\text{Lat}}^3)| = (26^3)! = 17576! = 1.2 \cdot 10^{66979} \approx 2^{222497}$,
- $|S(\Sigma_{\text{Bool}}^3)| = (2^3)! = 40320 \approx 2^{16}$, and
- $|S(\mathbb{Z}_n^t)| = (n^t)!$.

There are a large number of permutations on sets with few elements. A string Σ^t of length t consisting of symbols of an alphabet of length n has $(n^t)!$ different permutations. A subset of such large numbers of permutations arises from changing just the positions of the symbols in the string. Let $\pi \in S_t$. A *symbol permutation* is the mapping

$$\Sigma^t \to \Sigma^t,\ (m_1, \ldots, m_t) \mapsto (m_{\pi(1)}, \ldots, m_{\pi(t)}).$$

If Σ_{Bool} is the underlying alphabet, then the symbol permutation is called *bit permutation*. The set of all symbol permutations has $m!$ elements.

Example 4.6. Consider

$$\pi = \begin{pmatrix} 1 & 2 & 3 \\ 3 & 1 & 2 \end{pmatrix}.$$

Then, $(S, E, C) \in \Sigma_{\text{Lat}}^3$ maps to (C, S, E) and $(0, 0, 1) \in \Sigma_{\text{Bool}}^3$ maps to $(1, 0, 0)$.

Two special symbol permutations are the circular left shift about k positions,

$$\pi(i) = ((i - 1 + k) \bmod t) + 1,$$

and the circular right shift about k positions,

$$\pi(i) = ((i - 1 - k) \bmod t) + 1.$$

Let π be a permutation of S_t. Then a non-empty subset $C = \{c_0, \ldots, c_{k-1}\}$ of S_t is called an orbit of length k if $c_{(i+1) \bmod k} = \pi(c_i)$ for all $i = 0, \ldots, k-1$. An orbit of length 1 is a fixpoint. It immediately follows that $c_{i \bmod k} = \pi^i(c_0)$ for all $i \in \mathbb{N}_0$. Since $c_0 = \pi^k(c_0)$, we obtain $c_i = \pi^k(c_i)$ for $i = 0, \ldots, k-1$.

A permutation with at most one orbit of length $k > 1$ is called a *cyclic permutation*. Circular left or right shifts are special cyclic permutations, each with an orbit of length t. We declare a cyclic permutation by indexing the corresponding permutation in ascending order: $\pi_{c_0,\ldots,c_{k-1}}$. The indices not appearing here are intended to be unchanged by $\pi_{c_0,\ldots,c_{k-1}}$. Another usual notation is the cycle notation: $(c_0\, c_1 \ldots c_{k-1})$.

Example 4.7. Let us assume

$$\pi = \begin{pmatrix} 1 & 2 & 3 \\ 3 & 1 & 2 \end{pmatrix}, \psi = \begin{pmatrix} 1 & 2 & 3 & 4 \\ 3 & 4 & 1 & 2 \end{pmatrix}.$$

Here, we have a cyclic permutation $\pi_{1,3,2}$, and two such $\psi_{1,3}$ and $\psi_{2,4}$. It is also possible to write $\pi_{3,2,1}$ or $\pi_{2,1,3}$ instead of $\pi_{1,2,3}$. $\psi_{2,4}$ means the permutation

$$\psi_{2,4} = \begin{pmatrix} 1 & 2 & 3 & 4 \\ 1 & 4 & 3 & 2 \end{pmatrix}.$$

The cycle notation can be $(1\,3\,2)$ for the permutation π.

Any permutation may be written as successive applications of cyclic permutations and is unique except for the order of the disjoint cyclic permutations and the choice of the first element of each cyclic permutation.

Example 4.8.

$$\pi = \begin{pmatrix} 1 & 2 & 3 & 4 \\ 3 & 4 & 1 & 2 \end{pmatrix} = \pi_{1,3} \circ \pi_{2,4} = \pi_{2,4} \circ \pi_{1,3}.$$

Because of the disjoint index sets $\{1, 3\}$ and $\{2, 4\}$, the order of execution is arbitrarily. The cyclic notation is combined: $\pi = (1\,3)$ $(2\,4)$.

From alphabet Σ_{Lat}, we can create the following permutation:

$$(AELTPHQXRU)(BKNW)(CMOY)(DFG)(IV)(JZ)(S).$$

This permutation was used as a part—a "rotor" from 1930—of the Enigma transformations for each letter, which can be specified mathematically as a product of permutations.[1]

The number of permutations $\pi_n \in S_n$ generated by exactly k disjoint cyclic permutations is given by the Stirling numbers of the first kind, $s_{n,k}$. We use these results and the following recursion formula from (Mariconda, 2016).

$$s_{n,k} = \begin{cases} 1, & n = k = 0, \\ 0, & n \in \mathbb{N}, k = 0 \text{ or } n = 0, k \in \mathbb{N}, \\ s_{n-1,k-1} + (n-1)s_{n-1,k}, & n, k \in \mathbb{N}. \end{cases}$$

Example 4.9. $s_{2,0} = 0$, $s_{2,1} = s_{2,2} = 1$,
$s_{4,2} = s_{3,1} + 3 \cdot s_{3,2} = s_{2,0} + 2 \cdot s_{2,1} + 3 \cdot s_{2,1} + 6 \cdot s_{2,2} = 0 + 5 + 6 = 11$,
$s_{8,4} = 6769$, and
$s_{26,7} = 137464682179679269786800000$.

4.2 Block Ciphers

A string of length t is also called a *block*. A block cipher encrypts any block of fixed length t and creates an output of the same length.

Definition 4.10 (Block cipher). Let $t \in \mathbb{N}$ be fixed and Σ be an alphabet. Then, a cipher system

$$(\mathcal{P}, \mathcal{C}, \mathcal{K}_s, \mathcal{E}_s, \mathcal{D}_s)$$

satisfying $\mathcal{P} = \mathcal{C} = \Sigma^t$ is called a *block cipher* of *block size* t.

Let any $m \in \Sigma^q$, $t \cdot (l-1) < q \leq t \cdot l$ for some $l \in \mathbb{N}$ be divided into l blocks of length t,

$$m = m_1 || m_2 || \ldots || m_l.$$

[1]See (Rejewski, 1981).

Then, there is a $c \in \Sigma^{t \cdot l}$,

$$c = c_1 || c_2 || \dots || c_l,$$

satisfying $c_i = e_{k_i}(m_i)\ \forall i \in \{1, \dots, l\}$. If $q < t \cdot l$, the last block has to be padded to the right length to get the block size, i.e., a multiple of the block size. An example of a possible padding method is the 1-0 padding.[2] The idea is to append a "1" to the end of m_l and then to add as many "0"s necessary to complete this block. This method guarantees complete reconstruction of the underlying plaintext.

Theorem 4.11. *Any encryption function of a block cipher is a permutation.*

Proof. There is a decryption function consistent with an encryption function: $d_k(e_k(m)) = m$. Thus, an encryption function is injective. However, an injective encryption function $e_k : \Sigma^t \to \Sigma^t$ is also surjective. It follows that e_k is a permutation. □

In this way, we can note down the most general block cipher

$$\mathcal{P} = \mathcal{C} = \Sigma^t,\ \mathcal{K}_s = S(\Sigma^t),$$

and

$$\mathcal{E}_s = \mathcal{D}_s = \mathcal{K}_s,\ d_k(e_k(m)) = k^{-1}(k(m)) = m.$$

Assuming $|\Sigma| = n$, we have $|\mathcal{K}_s| = (n^t)!$ different keys. By choosing this cipher system, we have to consider saving n^t values for any key.

Example 4.12. Look at the UTF-8 alphabet and let $t = 4$. Then, there are $1114112^4 = 1.5 \cdot 10^{24}$ different values to note down based on one chosen key. Another example is Σ_{Bool} and $t = 128$ that yields $2^{128} = 3.4 \cdot 10^{38}$ values.

[2]ISO/IEC 9797-1, padding method 2.

4.2.1 *Linear mappings and matrices*

Given the ring $(\mathbb{Z}_n, +_n, \cdot_n, 0, 1)$, define $\mathbb{Z}_n^k$ by

$$\mathbb{Z}_n^k := \{\underbrace{(z_1, \ldots, z_k)}_{\vec{z}},\ z_i \in \mathbb{Z}_n\}.$$

Two elements of $\mathbb{Z}_n^k$ can be added using component-by-component addition

$$\begin{aligned}\oplus_n^k : \mathbb{Z}_n^k \times \mathbb{Z}_n^k \to \mathbb{Z}_n^k,\ (u_1, \ldots, u_k) \oplus_n^k (v_1, \ldots, v_k) \\ := (u_1 +_n v_1, \ldots, u_k +_n v_k)\end{aligned}$$

and multiplied using component-by-component multiplication

$$\begin{aligned}\odot_n^k : \mathbb{Z}_n^k \times \mathbb{Z}_n^k \to \mathbb{Z}_n^k,\ (u_1, \ldots, u_k) \odot_n^k (v_1, \ldots, v_k) \\ := (u_1 \cdot_n v_1, \ldots, u_k \cdot_n v_k).\end{aligned}$$

The tuples $\vec{0} = (0, \ldots, 0)$ and $\vec{1} = (1, \ldots, 1)$ are identity elements concerning addition and multiplication. The structure $(\mathbb{Z}_n^k, \oplus_n, \odot_n, \vec{0}, \vec{1})$ is a ring. The reason is that all the properties of a ring can be shown by tracing back the operations to the component-by-component computation, each with the ring $\mathbb{Z}_n$. For instance, we look at the commutative property of addition:

$$\begin{aligned}(u_1, \ldots, u_k) \oplus_n^k (v_1, \ldots, v_k) &= (u_1 +_n v_1, \ldots, u_k +_n v_k) \\ &= (v_1 +_n u_1, \ldots, v_k +_n u_k) \\ &= (v_1, \ldots, v_k) \oplus_n^k (u_1, \ldots, u_k).\end{aligned}$$

We now introduce a scalar multiplication by

$$\star_n^k : \mathbb{Z}_n \times \mathbb{Z}_n^k \to \mathbb{Z}_n^k,\ \lambda \star_n^k (u_1, \ldots, u_k) := (\lambda \cdot_n u_1, \ldots, \lambda \cdot_n u_k).$$

The tuples $\vec{e}_i \in \mathbb{Z}_n^k$, which are one in the ith component and zero otherwise, have the property that each element of $\mathbb{Z}_n^k$ can be written as a linear combination,

$$(z_1, \ldots, z_k) = z_1 \star_n^k \vec{e}_1 + \ldots + z_k \star_n^k \vec{e}_k.$$

Given any $u, v \in \mathbb{Z}_n^l$ and $\lambda \in \mathbb{Z}_n$ a mapping $f : \mathbb{Z}_n^l \to \mathbb{Z}_n^k$ concerning two canonical modules due to Remark 3.90 is called $\mathbb{Z}_n$-*linear* if the following properties are met:

$$f(\vec{u} \oplus_n^l \vec{v}) = f(\vec{u}) \oplus_n^k f(\vec{v}) \text{ and}$$
$$f(\lambda \star_n^l \vec{u}) = \lambda \star_n^k f(\vec{u}).$$

Example 4.13. The mapping

$$f : \mathbb{Z}_5^3 \to \mathbb{Z}_5^2,\ f(z_1, z_2, z_3) = (2 \cdot_5 z_1 +_5 z_2, 4 \cdot_5 z_3 +_5 z_1)$$

is $\mathbb{Z}_5$-linear. By writing $f = (f_1, f_2)$ as a composition of two scalar functions

$$f_1(z_1, z_2, z_3) = 2 \cdot_5 z_1 +_5 1 \cdot_5 z_2 +_5 0 \cdot_5 z_3, \text{ and}$$
$$f_2(z_1, z_2, z_3) = 1 \cdot_5 z_1 +_5 0 \cdot_5 z_2 +_5 4 \cdot_5 z_3,$$

there is a scheme visible. Again, we check the first property component-by-component.

$$\begin{aligned}
f_1(\vec{u} \oplus_n^l \vec{v}) &= 2 \cdot_5 (u_1 +_5 v_1) +_5 1 \cdot_5 (u_2 +_5 v_2) +_5 0 \cdot_5 (u_3 +_5 v_3) \\
&= 2 \cdot_5 u_1 +_5 2 \cdot_5 v_1 +_5 1 \cdot_5 u_2 +_5 1 \cdot_5 v_2 \\
&\quad +_5 0 \cdot_5 u_3 +_5 0 \cdot_5 v_3 \\
&= (2 \cdot_5 u_1 +_5 1 \cdot_5 u_2 +_5 0 \cdot_5 u_3) \\
&\quad +_5 (2 \cdot_5 v_1 +_5 1 \cdot_5 v_2 +_5 0 \cdot_5 v_3) \\
&= f_1(\vec{u}) +_5 f_1(\vec{v}), \text{ and} \\
f_2(\vec{u} \oplus_n^l \vec{v}) &= 1 \cdot_5 (u_1 +_5 v_1) +_5 0 \cdot_5 (u_2 +_5 v_2) +_5 4 \cdot_5 (u_3 +_5 v_3) \\
&= 1 \cdot_5 u_1 +_5 1 \cdot_5 v_1 +_5 0 \cdot_5 u_2 +_5 0 \cdot_5 v_2 \\
&\quad +_5 4 \cdot_5 u_3 +_5 4 \cdot_5 v_3 \\
&= (1 \cdot_5 u_1 +_5 0 \cdot_5 u_2 +_5 4 \cdot_5 u_3) \\
&\quad +_5 (1 \cdot_5 v_1 +_5 0 \cdot_5 v_2 +_5 4 \cdot_5 v_3) \\
&= f_2(\vec{u}) +_5 f_2(\vec{v}).
\end{aligned}$$

In the same way, the second property can be proven.

Example 4.13 shows that the coefficients of a $\mathbb{Z}_n$-linear mapping are essential. The six coefficients from there should be put together.

Definition 4.14 (Matrix on $\mathbb{Z}_n$). A (k,l)-matrix or short form matrix A on $\mathbb{Z}_n$ is a mapping

$$A : \{1,\ldots,k\} \times \{1,\ldots,l\} \to \mathbb{Z}_n,\ a_{ij} := A(i,j).$$

We denote a matrix by $A = (a_{ij}) \in \mathbb{Z}_n^{k,l}$.

We note a matrix by a rectangular scheme that features k rows and l columns,

$$A = (a_{ij}) = \begin{pmatrix} a_{11} & \ldots & a_{1l} \\ \vdots & & \vdots \\ a_{k1} & \ldots & a_{kl} \end{pmatrix} \in \mathbb{Z}_n^{k,l}.$$

A matrix $A \in \mathbb{Z}_n^{k,1}$ is called a column vector while $A \in \mathbb{Z}_n^{1,l}$ is called a row vector. Similarly, each element $\vec{z} \in \mathbb{Z}_n^k$ can be considered both a row vector and a column vector. For instance,

$$(1,4,3) \cong \begin{pmatrix} 1 & 4 & 3 \end{pmatrix} \cong \begin{pmatrix} 1 \\ 4 \\ 3 \end{pmatrix}.$$

This is because of an isomorphism between $\mathbb{Z}_n^k$ and $\mathbb{Z}_n^{k,1}$ or $\mathbb{Z}_n^{1,k}$. Thus, we have to introduce an addition and scalar multiplication for matrices on $\mathbb{Z}_n$. This happens in the same way as for matrices on $\mathbb{R}$. Let $A = (a_{ij})$ and $B = (b_{ij})$ (k,l)-matrices on $\mathbb{Z}_n$ and $\lambda \in \mathbb{Z}_n$. We define

$$A +_n B := (a_{ij} +_n b_{ij}) \text{ and}$$
$$\lambda \cdot_n A := (\lambda \cdot_n a_{ij}).$$

The addition is commutative and associative. Furthermore, we can define a multiplication of compatible matrices $A \in \mathbb{Z}_n^{k,l}$ and $B \in \mathbb{Z}_n^{l,m}$,

$$\mathbb{Z}_n^{k,m} \ni C = (c_{ij}) = A \cdot_n B \Leftrightarrow c_{ij} = \left(\sum_{q=1}^{l} a_{iq} \cdot b_{qj} \right) \bmod n.$$

The number of columns of A has to match the number of rows of B. This operation is associative. To do so, we have to look at the products $F = A \cdot_n B$, $G = B \cdot_n C$ and $D = A \cdot_n (B \cdot_n C)$. Then, we get

$$\begin{aligned}
d_{ij} &= \left(\sum_{q=1}^{l} a_{iq} \cdot g_{qj}\right) \bmod n = \left(\sum_{q=1}^{l} a_{iq} \cdot \left(\sum_{r=1}^{m} b_{qr} \cdot c_{rj}\right)\right) \bmod n \\
&= \left(\sum_{q=1}^{l}\sum_{r=1}^{m} a_{iq} \cdot b_{qr} \cdot c_{rj}\right) \bmod n = \left(\sum_{r=1}^{m}\sum_{q=1}^{l} a_{iq} \cdot b_{qr} \cdot c_{rj}\right) \bmod n \\
&= \left(\sum_{r=1}^{m} \left(\sum_{q=1}^{l} a_{iq} \cdot b_{qr}\right) \cdot c_{rj}\right) \bmod n = \left(\sum_{r=1}^{m} f_{ir} \cdot c_{rj}\right) \bmod n.
\end{aligned}$$

Thus, $D = (A \cdot_n B) \cdot_n C$.

Example 4.15.

$$A = \begin{pmatrix} 2 & 1 & 0 \\ 1 & 0 & 4 \end{pmatrix},\ B = \begin{pmatrix} 4 & 3 & 3 \\ 0 & 1 & 2 \end{pmatrix},\ \vec{z} = (1,4,2) \cong \begin{pmatrix} 1 \\ 4 \\ 2 \end{pmatrix} \text{ and } \lambda = 2.$$

$$A +_5 B = \begin{pmatrix} 1 & 4 & 3 \\ 1 & 1 & 1 \end{pmatrix},\ \lambda \cdot_5 A = \begin{pmatrix} 4 & 2 & 0 \\ 2 & 0 & 3 \end{pmatrix} \text{ and } A \cdot_5 \vec{z} = \begin{pmatrix} 1 \\ 4 \end{pmatrix}.$$

Example 4.15 indicates that by comparing with

$$f(1,4,2) = (1,4)$$

a $\mathbb{Z}_n$-linear mapping can be represented by a matrix like in the $\mathbb{R}$-linear case. The simplest $\mathbb{Z}_n$-linear mapping is given by the zero matrix $Z = (z_{ij}) \in \mathbb{Z}_n^{k,l}$, $z_{ij} = 0$. It is an identity element relating to the addition of matrices. In this context the matrix $-A = (-a_{ij})$ is the inverse element of a matrix A relating to addition because $(a_{ij} - a_{ij}) \bmod n = 0$. $(\mathbb{Z}_n^{k,l}, +_n, Z)$ is an abelian group. The multiplication is more difficult. This operation is closed only if $k = l$. Then, we get the special class of square matrices $A \in \mathbb{Z}_n^{k,k}$. In the set of square matrices, the matrix

$$E_k = (e_{ij}),\ e_{ij} = \begin{cases} 1, & i = j, \\ 0, & i \neq j, \end{cases}$$

is an identity element relating to the multiplication because

$$c_{ij} = \left(\sum_{q=1}^{l} a_{iq} \cdot e_{qj} \right) \bmod n = a_{ij}.$$

$(\mathbb{Z}_n^{k,k}, \cdot_n, E_k)$ is a monoid with identity. The distributive laws can be shown just as with the associativity. Together, $(\mathbb{Z}_n^{k,k}, +_n, \cdot_n, Z, E_k)$ is a ring with identity, however, the multiplication is not generally commutative. A very simple counterexample is

$$\begin{pmatrix} 1 & 0 \\ 0 & 0 \end{pmatrix} \cdot_n \begin{pmatrix} 0 & 1 \\ 0 & 0 \end{pmatrix} = \begin{pmatrix} 0 & 1 \\ 0 & 0 \end{pmatrix} \neq \begin{pmatrix} 0 & 0 \\ 0 & 0 \end{pmatrix} = \begin{pmatrix} 0 & 1 \\ 0 & 0 \end{pmatrix} \cdot_n \begin{pmatrix} 1 & 0 \\ 0 & 0 \end{pmatrix}.$$

In any case, a matrix does not always have an inverse element. For instance,

$$\begin{pmatrix} 0 & 1 \\ 0 & 0 \end{pmatrix} \cdot_n \begin{pmatrix} a_{11} & a_{12} \\ a_{21} & a_{22} \end{pmatrix} = \begin{pmatrix} a_{21} & a_{22} \\ 0 & 0 \end{pmatrix}$$

can never be the identity matrix. Let

$$\mathrm{GL}(k, \mathbb{Z}_n) := (\mathbb{Z}_n^{k,k})^{\times} = \{A \in \mathbb{Z}_n^{k,k};\ A \text{ invertible}\},$$

be the set of all invertible (k, k)-matrices on $\mathbb{Z}_n$. Then, $(\mathrm{GL}(k, \mathbb{Z}_n), \cdot_n, E_k)$ is a group (cf. Theorem 3.15), the *general linear group*. Each matrix A in $\mathrm{GL}(k, \mathbb{Z}_n)$ is a unity element. To identify whether a matrix is invertible, we use the determinant. Let $A_{i,j}$ be the matrix that arises by eliminating the ith row and jth column of a matrix $A = (a_{ij}) \in \mathbb{Z}_n^{k,k}$ and let $i \in \{1, \ldots, k\}$ be invariant. Then, the determinant of A is the value of the mapping

$$\det : \mathbb{Z}_n^{k,k} \to \mathbb{Z},\ \det(A) = \begin{cases} \sum_{j=1}^{k} (-1)^{i+j} a_{ij} \det(A_{i,j}), & k > 1, \\ a_{11}, & k = 1. \end{cases}$$

In the same way, this value can be computed using the columns (the summation over i and j being invariant). Referring to (Lang, 1984), $A \in \mathrm{GL}(k, \mathbb{Z}_n)$ iff $\det(A)$ and n are relatively prime numbers, $\det(A) \in \mathbb{Z}_n^\times$. The matrix

$$\mathrm{adj}(A) = \begin{cases} (\tilde{a}_{ij}) \text{ and } \tilde{a}_{ij} = ((-1)^{i+j} \det(A_{j,i})) \bmod n, & k > 1, \\ 1, & k = 1, \end{cases}$$

is the adjoint of A while i and j are running through $1, \ldots, k$. The inverse matrix can be computed by

$$A^{-1} = (\det(A))^{-1} \cdot \mathrm{adj}(A) \bmod n,$$

in which each component of the matrix has to be taken modulo n at the end.

Example 4.16. Let $A \in \mathbb{Z}_{13}^{3,3}$ with

$$A := \begin{pmatrix} 1 & 2 & 3 \\ 2 & 3 & 1 \\ 3 & 2 & 1 \end{pmatrix}.$$

Then, the determinant is $\det(A) = -12 \equiv_{13} 1$, and the adjoint gets

$$\mathrm{adj}(A) = \begin{pmatrix} 1 & 4 & 6 \\ 1 & 5 & 5 \\ 8 & 4 & 12 \end{pmatrix}.$$

The inverse matrix is the adjoint here: $A^{-1} = 1 \cdot \mathrm{adj}(A)$.

Finally, we define an affine transformation. Therefore, we abbreviate the notation using z without an arrow, $z = \vec{z} \in \mathbb{Z}_n^l$, and omit the symbol of multiplication if the last operation is modulo n.

Definition 4.17 (Affine transformation modulo n). Let $A \in \mathbb{Z}_n^{k,l}$ and $b \in \mathbb{Z}_n^l$. Any mapping $f : \mathbb{Z}_n^l \to \mathbb{Z}_n^k$,

$$z \mapsto f(z) := (Az + b) \bmod n$$

is called an *affine transformation* modulo n.

Since $f(0) = b$, the mapping $f(z) - f(0) = (Az + b - b) \bmod n = Az \bmod n$ is $\mathbb{Z}_n$-linear.

4.2.2 *Affine block ciphers*

Any block cipher is a permutation. A special kind of permutation is a bijective affine transformation. Many classical cipher systems use affine transformations modulo n for encryption or decryption.

Definition 4.18 (Affine block cipher). Given $\mathcal{P} = \mathcal{C} = \mathbb{Z}_n^t$, let $\mathcal{K}_s \subseteq \mathbb{Z}_n^{t,t} \times \mathbb{Z}_n^t$ be chosen in such a way that there is an inverse matrix $A^{-1} \in \mathbb{Z}_n^{t,t}$ for each $A \in \mathbb{Z}_n^{t,t}$ satisfying $(A, b) \in \mathcal{K}_s$ and $(A^{-1}, b) \in \mathcal{K}_s$. Then, $(\mathcal{P}, \mathcal{C}, \mathcal{K}_s, \mathcal{E}_s, \mathcal{D}_s)$ providing

$$\begin{aligned} e_{(A,b)} &: \mathbb{Z}_n^t \to \mathbb{Z}_n^t, \quad m \mapsto (Am + b) \bmod n, \text{ and} \\ d_{(A,b)} &: \mathbb{Z}_n^t \to \mathbb{Z}_n^t, \quad c \mapsto A^{-1}(c - b) \bmod n. \end{aligned}$$

is called an *affine block cipher* with block size $t \in \mathbb{N}$.

Remark 4.19. The case $t = 1$ is a special monoalphabetic cipher and it can be written as a permutation.

Example 4.20. Given $n = 26$, $t = 1$, $a = 3$ and $b = 7$. According to Example 4.8, the encryption function $e_{(3,7)}(m) = 3m+7 \bmod 26$ can be written as

$$(AHCNUP)(BKLOXY)(DQ)(ETMRGZ)(FWVSJI)$$

in the cyclic notation. To determine the decryption function, we have to compute $a^{-1} = 9$ and $b' = 15 \equiv_{26} -9 \cdot 7$. Figure 4.2 shows the linear structure of the encryption function.

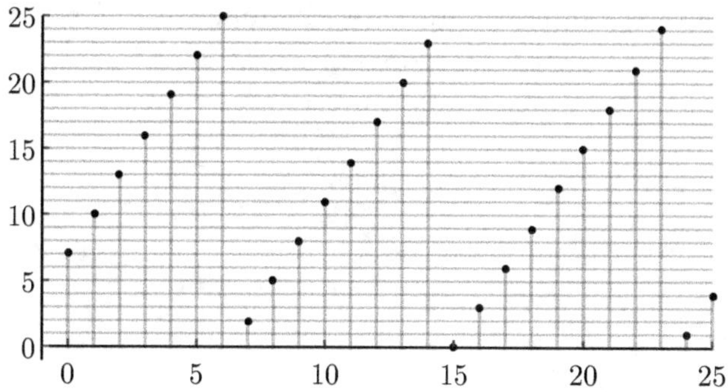

Figure 4.2 Linear structure in the affine linear encryption.

Example 4.21 (ATBASH). The *ATBASH* cipher is a block cipher with block size $t = 1$ and $\mathcal{P} = \mathcal{C} = \mathbb{Z}_{26}$. The encryption function uses $a = b = 25$,

$$m \mapsto e_{(25,25)}(m) = (25m + 25) \bmod 26.$$

This matches the letter's permutation

$$\begin{pmatrix} ABCDEFGHIJKLMNOPQRSTUVWXYZ \\ ZYXWVUTSRQPONMLKJIHGFEDCBA \end{pmatrix}.$$

The letters are reverse ordered. The plaintext

SECURITYISTHEMAINGOALOFCRYPTOGRAPHY

gets encrypted to

HVXFIRGBRHGSVNZRMTLZOLUXIBKGLTIZKSB.

By execution of the same function, the original text is recovered. Since $-1 \equiv_{26} 25$ and $-25 \equiv_{26} 1$, we get

$$25(25m + 25) + 25 \bmod 26 = (-1)(-1)m - 25 + 25 \bmod 26 = m.$$

Thus, the ATBASH cipher is a so-called *involution*.

Furthermore, examples of affine block ciphers are depending on the choice of t and on suitable possibilities of a and A. The following ciphers based on Σ_{Lat} are well known.

- Block size $t = 1$ (monoalphabetic):
  - *Shift cipher*, key $(1, b)$,
  - *Multiplication cipher*, key $(a, 0)$,
  - *Monoalphabetic substitution cipher*, key (a, b).
- Block size $t > 1$ (polyalphabetic):
  - *Vigenère cipher*,[3] key $(E_t, \vec{b})$,
  - *Hill cipher*[4] (linear), key $(A, \vec{0})$,
  - *Transposition cipher*, key $(\tilde{E}_t, \vec{0})$ and $\tilde{E}_t \in \mathbb{Z}_2^{t,t}$, where there is just once 1, and otherwise 0, in each row and column. This is a special case of the Hill cipher.

Example 4.22. An example of an invalid monoalphabetic substitution cipher is the choice of $a = 4$. If $t = 1$ and $b = 1$, then the encryption function

$$e_{(4,1)} : \mathbb{Z}_{26} \to \mathbb{Z}_{26},\ m \mapsto e_{(4,1)}(m) = (4m + 1) \bmod 26$$

encrypts the letters E and R to the same letter R,

$$4 \cdot 4 + 1 = 17 \equiv_{26} 69 = 4 \cdot 17 + 1.$$

The plaintext

SECURITYISTHEMAINGOALOFCRYPTOGRAPHY

gets encrypted to

VRJDRHZTHVZDRXBHBZFBTFVJRTJZFZRBJDT.

Since $GCD(4, 26) = 2 \neq 1$, the original plaintext cannot be recovered.

---

[3]Blaise de Vigenère (1523–1596).
[4]Lester S. Hill (1890–1961).

Example 4.23 (ROT13 and substitution). Let $m = 1$, the plaintext is

SECURITYISTHEMAINGOALOFCRYPTOGRAPHY

as usual.

- $a = 1$ and $b = 13$ (ROT13):

  FRPHEVGLVFGURZNVATBNYBSPELCGBTENCUL,

- $a = 3$ and $b = 7$ (cf. Example 4.20):

  JTNPGFMBFJMCTRHFUZXHOXWNGBAMXZGHACB.

Example 4.24 (Vigenère and Hill). Let $t = 5$, the plaintext is

SECURITYISTHEMAINGOALOFCRYPTOGRAPHY

again.

- Vigenère key: MATHS.

  EEVBJUTRPKFHXTSUNZVSXOYJJKPMVYDAIOQ.

  Therefore, we calculate $18 +_{26} 12 = 4$, $4 +_{26} 0 = 4$, $2 +_{26} 19 = 21$, $20 +_{26} 7 = 1$, and so on.
- Hill key: AFFINEBLOCKCIPHERSCANDOIT, line by line,

$$A = \begin{pmatrix} 0 & 5 & 5 & 8 & 13 \\ 4 & 1 & 11 & 14 & 2 \\ 10 & 2 & 8 & 15 & 7 \\ 4 & 17 & 18 & 2 & 0 \\ 13 & 3 & 14 & 8 & 19 \end{pmatrix}$$

  VWZIDTVKXTVJAFEZVAZBUTPMWWIYTRBPROH.

  For instance, the first letter of the cipher text is computed by $18 \cdot 0 + 4 \cdot 5 + 2 \cdot 5 + 20 \cdot 8 + 17 \cdot 13 = 411 \equiv_{26} 21$, which is decoded to V. To get back the plaintext, we have to invert matrix A

resulting in

$$A^{-1} = \begin{pmatrix} 25 & 5 & 16 & 17 & 23 \\ 4 & 14 & 16 & 11 & 20 \\ 18 & 13 & 18 & 7 & 18 \\ 1 & 1 & 21 & 18 & 12 \\ 11 & 9 & 0 & 4 & 8 \end{pmatrix}.$$

We obtain a particular case of the Hill cipher if the columns are permutations of the unit vector. To understand this we look at any symbol permutation $f : \Sigma^t \to \Sigma^t$. Since the alphabet of length n is equivalent to $\mathbb{Z}_n$, we say $\Sigma = \mathbb{Z}_n$. With

$$f(s_1, \ldots, s_t) = (s_{\pi(1)}, \ldots, s_{\pi(t)}),$$

there is a $\mathbb{Z}_n$-linear function because

$$\begin{aligned} f(s) \oplus_n^t f(u) &= f(s_1, \ldots, s_t) \oplus_n^t f(u_1, \ldots, u_t) \\ &= (s_{\pi(1)}, \ldots, s_{\pi(t)}) \oplus_n^t (u_{\pi(1)}, \ldots, u_{\pi(t)}) \\ &= (s_{\pi(1)} +_n u_{\pi(1)}, \ldots, s_{\pi(t)} +_n u_{\pi(t)}) \\ &= ((s \oplus_n^t u)_{\pi(1)}, \ldots, (s \oplus_n^t u)_{\pi(t)}) \\ &= f(s \oplus_n^t u), \text{ and} \\ \lambda \star_n^t f(s) &= \lambda \star_n^t (s_{\pi(1)}, \ldots, s_{\pi(t)}) \\ &= (\lambda \star_n^t s_{\pi(1)}, \ldots, \lambda \star_n^t s_{\pi(t)}) \\ &= ((\lambda \star_n^t s)_{\pi(1)}, \ldots (\lambda \star_n^t s)_{\pi(t)}) \\ &= f(\lambda \star_n^t s_1, \ldots, \lambda \star_n^t s_t) = f(\lambda \star_n^t s). \end{aligned}$$

Thus, we look for a matrix A_f representing f. In particular, if $s = e_i$ is a unit vector, then

$$As = Ae_i = a_{\cdot i}.$$

Additionally, the ith unit vector is mapped to a unit vector again. Under the permutation π we have to find the index that is mapped to i. Thus,

$$f(e_i) = e_{\pi^{-1}(i)},$$

and the ith column of A_f is $a_{\cdot i} = e_{\pi^{-1}(i)}$. We denote this permutation matrix of the identity matrix by E_π.

Example 4.25 (Transposition). Let $t > 1$, the plaintext is

SECURITYISTHEMAINGOALOFCRYPTOGRAPHY

again.

$$\pi = \begin{pmatrix} 1 & 2 & 3 & 4 & 5 \\ 2 & 4 & 3 & 5 & 1 \end{pmatrix} = (3)(1245), \quad \pi^{-1} = \begin{pmatrix} 1 & 2 & 3 & 4 & 5 \\ 5 & 1 & 3 & 2 & 4 \end{pmatrix}.$$

The permutation can be written by the encryption matrix

$$E_\pi = \begin{pmatrix} 0 & 1 & 0 & 0 & 0 \\ 0 & 0 & 0 & 1 & 0 \\ 0 & 0 & 1 & 0 & 0 \\ 0 & 0 & 0 & 0 & 1 \\ 1 & 0 & 0 & 0 & 0 \end{pmatrix}.$$

The plaintext gets encrypted to

EUCRSTIYSIHMEATNOGAIOCFRLPOTGYAHPYR.

To decrypt the ciphertext, we have to transpose E_π.

A historical example of a transposition cipher is the use of a scytale consisting of a wooden cylinder with a strip of parchment wound around it, on which a message is written. In our notation, the block size matches the size of the plaintext. For instance, the word "SECURITY" could be encrypted by use of the arrangement

$$\begin{matrix} S & E & C \\ U & R & I \\ T & Y & \end{matrix}.$$

The result is "SUTERYCI". The corresponding permutation is

$$\pi = \begin{pmatrix} 1 & 2 & 3 & 4 & 5 & 6 & 7 & 8 \\ 1 & 4 & 7 & 2 & 5 & 8 & 3 & 6 \end{pmatrix} = (1)(5)(24)(37)(68).$$

4.2.3 *Cryptanalysis of affine block ciphers*

The monoalphabetic substitution cipher based on the uppercase Latin alphabet offers a choice of $\phi(26) \cdot 26 = 312$ different keys, which is insufficient to avoid a brute-force search. Another approach is to use the Bayes' theorem (1.10). A known-plaintext attack yields the most probable combination for the key.[5] Commonly, there are $26! \approx 2^{88}$ different keys that will make such a search impossible. However, it is not difficult to decrypt the ciphertext. As shown in Example 2.25, only a search for frequencies of letters or letter combinations is necessary.

Using a *polyalphabetic cipher* ($t > 1$), the block size has to be found first. For instance, the block size of the Vigenère cipher in Example 4.24 is $t = 5$. However, the plaintext is too short. Let us perform it again with "MATHS" and use the beginning of the Gospel passage like in Example 2.25.

"FHXIW SIGUA ZGHML TEZVK BEEVX VELBK OHKPK F**TAL**K ANHMY ADTZA FILDJ UTMLF UNBZS UAAAZ QP-KVH TEMIW TOEKA EEGKE KMXZK QNZLJ NEYVJ QY-HBJ RAVLO TOPPD XPKLH MRXFG GRPHQ FHXCG UCXVX ANXJJ KIGNA Z**TAL**O ULWLJ ZELZH DEIHJ Q**TAL**O MYHML TEEVJ PMTRW TILWS FHLZL DABNZ FJHOF MPILS DEWIS BTBGA ZGBUL TEPPD PEKUW ESTUV BRHJD MIFPF SAUHH FILTG RRXWW ZTTUU QFHYL TEYVJ SIOLF QS-LVX EIGZS ZDTSD FHXJG GNMYQ AFCBV QATUV MLEQW DULHD QMPLJ QGHPF SONAL AHBTS ZDPLJ QBXPF SBTWL UZXKT KHBTA Z**TAL**J UVXYB ARWHF OOGMW ES-BUY FHXPJ EIGZF AWCVZ ZWTZU XOMOW PWBAZ OAFLD EHTPJ MNWDG DETSW M**TAL**J NEEAS DONUV TILDS USMHF PAMLD ACNZL EAGKO ULWOG ZERHF PHXWJ QAVOW PSTFA ZGTML QRFLU AMXZZ QWAVA EMBNZ FIXYL TAGPL TELAJ MPHMO TOLLK MNWHD EITTF ATPVJ FHRAG ETHVH POPUS ZDNUL UEBOS HEUHH FISLV KONDA FHPHL QRUBL TEPPD XBTWL UZXFG GWBAZ FHXOG XYLWA DIMPF FHHZW PARZB QSNZU MMXMJ AMGHR MRXAZ AFZHD ULXLS ZDPHK NAIAA LEWIQ VOAUA **ZTAL**B ARWHF MNWDZ QNALU MMXBH AUMVX FHXDS

[5]The image on the cover of this book shows the result of such an attack.

FEKPE YEWPS FEEFZ QSTDL TEALS HEGZT QIGNL ARGVH QNTUV FHXZH URBAV QSVLF PIGNG ZHBTD UKXHV AVXHF PAOVA OEVHE QFKVE TETCW ZYHBS DEFFT QL-HCW PSHUO UTAFG GITTO QLEWD QALLV FHXZH UR-BAA YMXKA MTXSQ PRHCW TIFVM FIGAG FHXDA XDXYF QSLHF PHXDS EIGAZ QWBSV QRGLK EFHYL KDTFK NEBUY FEFWL QDUFK MTTUS ZDALO MSPPL T**TAL**O UL-WHF UMTSK MNWAZ QAGNW XSPLJ QMBUA ETXYA ZG-MVZ UMGVO MFMLJ VOAUO MSTYJ QSMLV VELBK OAFLA ZTHNS XIELW BRHJD MIFPF S**TAL**Y ASILD AFZVV MN-WZS KIGNL TEMPE QILMM XFBSD QDTUV FHXRA ZG-WVE AFZVV USTAZ MNWYW BEGAS ZDULD UEOLA Z**TAL**Y ASILD BALZA ZGTSG ZGLPV Q**TAL**K QAHMY MLBSW QHXZS ISBTG ZAGKS ZDKLO FHXIJ A**TAL**J AFLPE AN-VHK FIGNS ZEMPF FOMOW EETMG D**TAL**Q IEKLX US-ALJ YEGHF PJXZM ESTPV FOMOW YFHSD AWFLS ZDBDA XLFHC QYHBT QCHTW RILOW DSHME QNTUV UMFLV UAMLD K**TAL**Q XEYAL TEBYF QTLHF PFHSD AWXKZ UM-TUV SOBUY ANTSA FTELX MRMOW DHXZS IJTTW E**TAL**K ANHMR QBXKW QAGKB AHGOA EBKVL TEKDZ AWXYW UNMOW URUVS FMXUV UNZAZ QNXAK MNWPE YEWPS FEEFZ QCTSD QDMOW YAGKL TERSW RTMOW URYHL TEKGW NEWLW UNMOW NOTAO UTAAZ QHBYW PSXYN MNMZS ZDYVD XOPLV"

If the block size is unknown, the *Kasiski test*[6] can help. For this purpose, we consider that the same plaintext sequence on the same block position is encrypted to the same ciphertext. Thus, if we find a coinciding sequence of letters, their distance in the text can be a multiple of the block size. The more such distances are found the better the true block size can be localized. In the last ciphertext, the mode of the three-letter sequences is "**TAL**" (14 occurrences). The distances between the consecutive occurrences are very interesting:

[6] Friedrich Wilhelm Kasiski (1805–1881).

120, 20, 210, 75, 275, 285, 100, 85, 25, 40, 35, 90 and 65. The greatest common divisor of these numbers is 5. This is a candidate for the block size, and we know it is the block size. Next, we can make a frequency analysis for each of the five parts of the text, just as in Example 2.26. Since the letter Q is the mode of the first group of letters (46 times) and there is a distance of 12 letters from E to Q, the first letter of the key is almost certainly M.

Another approach utilizes the features of the language to find the period. In a language, a text $w = (w_1, \ldots, w_n)$ is characterized by some periodicity, which means that syllables in this context may have a similar length, and letter sequences are repeated very often. This can be investigated by testing the mean total number of matchings between the letter sequence and the letter sequence that was shifted by exactly d letters,

$$\kappa(d, w) = \frac{1}{n-d} \left|\{0 < i < n-d;\ w_i = w_{i+d}\}\right|.$$

Figure 4.3 shows the results for κ indicating that the period may consist of five letters.

There is another safe method to find the key of an affine block cipher. After a possibly successful Kasiski test, an attack model can be attempted. For this purpose, we start a known-plaintext attack. We need $t+1$ different plaintexts $m_0, \ldots, m_t$ and corresponding

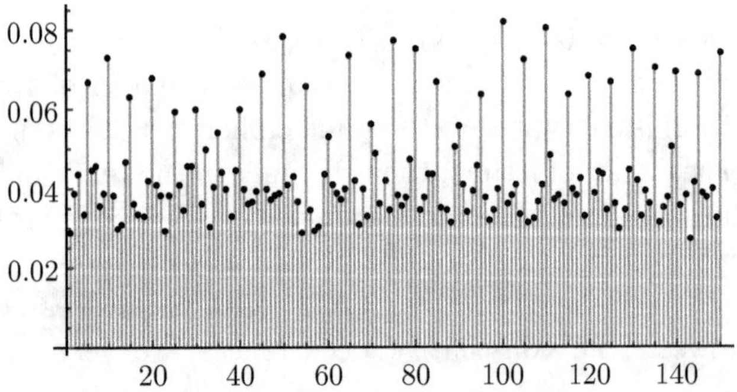

Figure 4.3 $\kappa(d, w)$ indicating the period of five letters.

ciphertexts $c_0, \ldots, c_t$ encrypted by the same key. Then, we obtain

$$\begin{aligned}(c_j - c_i) \bmod 26 &= ((Am_j + b) - (Am_i + b)) \bmod 26 \\ &= A(m_j - m_i) \bmod 26,\end{aligned}$$

and summarizing

$$\underbrace{\begin{pmatrix} c_1 - c_0 & \ldots & c_t - c_{t-1} \end{pmatrix}}_{C} = A \cdot \underbrace{\begin{pmatrix} m_1 - m_0 & \ldots & m_t - m_{t-1} \end{pmatrix}}_{P}.$$

If P is invertible in $\mathbb{Z}_{26}$, then it is $A = C \cdot P^{-1} \bmod 26$. We can find such a matrix P based on an appropriate choice of plaintexts. Finally, the shift b can be found by

$$b = (c_0 - Am_0) \bmod 26.$$

Example 4.26. If the plaintext is the beginning of the Gospel passage and the ciphertext is as above, we try to set the block size to $t = 5$ after the Kasiski test. Then, the first two blocks produce

m_1	m_0	c_1	c_0
GINNI	THEBE	SIGUA	FHXIW
$(6, 8, 13, 13, 8)$	$(19, 7, 4, 1, 4)$	$(18, 8, 6, 20, 0)$	$(5, 7, 23, 8, 22)$
$(13, 1, 9, 12, 4)$		$(13, 1, 9, 12, 4)$	

Altogether,

$$\begin{pmatrix} 13 & 7 & 20 & 8 & 20 \\ 1 & 24 & 24 & 0 & 0 \\ 9 & 1 & 18 & 5 & 7 \\ 12 & 18 & 9 & 0 & 6 \\ 4 & 11 & 25 & 13 & 13 \end{pmatrix} = A \cdot \begin{pmatrix} 13 & 7 & 20 & 8 & 20 \\ 1 & 24 & 24 & 0 & 0 \\ 9 & 1 & 18 & 5 & 7 \\ 12 & 18 & 9 & 0 & 6 \\ 4 & 11 & 25 & 13 & 13 \end{pmatrix} \bmod 26.$$

This can be satisfied by choosing $A = E_5$. Since we have a Vigenère cipher, this comes as little surprise. At last, we compute

$$b = (c_0 - Am_0) \bmod 26 = (12, 0, 19, 7, 18)$$

meeting the key “MATHS”.

4.3 Block Cipher Modes of Operation

A block cipher is context-insensitive if the encryption process of a block is not dependent on the encryption of earlier blocks. So far, this is our approach. The next step is to generate dependencies between a block and its predecessors. This is called a *context-sensitive block cipher*.

The National Institute of Standards and Technology (NIST) recommends one of the following five standards for providing data confidentiality.

ECB mode of operation
Until now, we have encrypted blocks m_i of plaintexts into ciphertexts c_i in sequence. For this reason, the simplest case arises if

$$c_i = e_k(m_i)$$

applies and therefore any block is encrypted separately. This mode is called the *electronic codebook mode* (ECB). Equal plaintexts are mapped to equal ciphertexts when using the same key. This leads to insecure messages because information in the plaintext can be preserved in the ciphertext. Figure 4.4 shows such a case. On the left, there is a monitor test image that has been encrypted using the ECB mode and an encryption function called DES (cf. Section 6.2), resulting in the black and white image on the right. Many structural information and patterns of the left image are recognized in the right image. Thus, we can deduce the original picture.

It is very unsatisfying that any given plaintext block gets encrypted to the same ciphertext block if the key is the same. The next example substantiates the encryption. We now focus on bitwise encryption techniques and consider solutions for this problem. The solutions here can also be found in (Martin, 2017). To overcome the named problem, we choose the permutation $\pi : \Sigma_{\text{Bool}}^5 \to \Sigma_{\text{Bool}}^5$,

$$\pi = \begin{pmatrix} 1 & 2 & 3 & 4 & 5 \\ 3 & 5 & 2 & 4 & 1 \end{pmatrix} = (1325)(4). \tag{4.1}$$

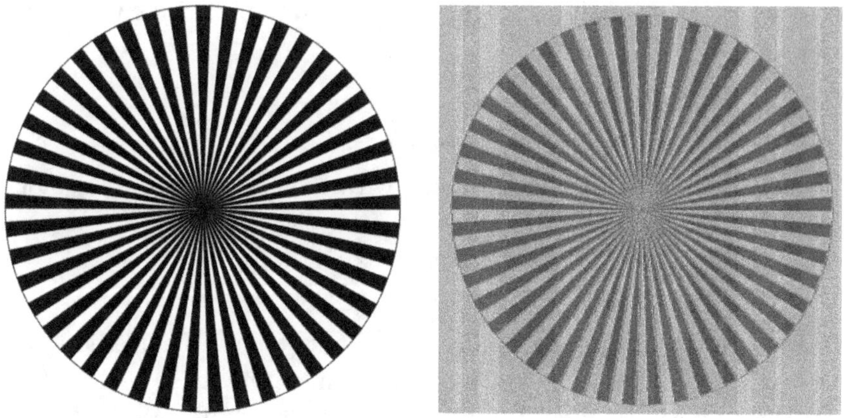

Figure 4.4 ECB mode. Patterns of the original picture are recognizable.

Example 4.27 (ECB). The string "SCIENCE" that comes from Σ^7_{Latext} is represented by a five-bit code. In ECB mode, we get

$$c_i = e_\pi(b_1, b_2, b_3, b_4, b_5) = (b_{\pi(1)}, b_{\pi(2)}, b_{\pi(3)}, b_{\pi(4)}, b_{\pi(5)})$$
$$= (b_3, b_5, b_2, b_4, b_1).$$

The plaintext is encrypted to "DCEQ?CQ":

i	Symbol	Bit code, m_i	Integer value	$c_i = e_\pi(m_i)$	Symbol	Integer value
1	S	10010	18	00011	D	3
2	C	00010	2	00010	C	2
3	I	01000	8	00100	E	4
4	E	00100	4	10000	Q	16
5	N	01101	13	11100	?	28
6	C	00010	2	00010	C	2
7	E	00100	4	10000	Q	16

For decryption, we have to use the inverse permutation

$$\pi^{-1} = \begin{pmatrix} 1 & 2 & 3 & 4 & 5 \\ 5 & 3 & 1 & 4 & 2 \end{pmatrix} = (1523)(4). \tag{4.2}$$

CBC mode of operation

By using the ciphertext created at the last block encryption step, we can solve the problem of information preservation. The ciphertext is used as an additional input and is linked by the bitwise XOR gate.

$$\oplus : \Sigma_{\text{Bool}} \times \Sigma_{\text{Bool}} \to \Sigma_{\text{Bool}},\ (u, v) \mapsto u \oplus v := u +_2 v,$$

$$\oplus : \Sigma^n_{\text{Bool}} \times \Sigma^n_{\text{Bool}} \to \Sigma^n_{\text{Bool}},$$
$$(u_{n-1} \dots u_0, v_{n-1} \dots v_0) \mapsto u \oplus v := (u_{n-1} \oplus v_{n-1}, \dots, u_0 \oplus v_0).$$

If the last ciphertext block is linked with the current plaintext block by XOR for encryption purpose, we use the *cipher block chaining mode* (CBC). The encryption step is as follows:

$$c_i = e_k(m_i \oplus c_{i-1}).$$

In the first step, there is no last ciphertext block. Thus, there has to be an initial block c_0, which is called an *initialization vector* (IV). An IV is an arbitrary and public domain. The XOR gate is its own inverse element. For the decryption process, we therefore use the XOR and the last ciphertext block again,

$$m_i = d_k(c_i) \oplus c_{i-1}.$$

Looking at the resulting monitor test image in Figure 4.5, we cannot recognize any pattern.

Let us go through such an encryption process under the same conditions as in the Example 4.27.

Figure 4.5 CBC mode. There is no structural information preserved in the image.

Example 4.28 (CBC). We choose the string "SCIENCE" from Σ^7_{Latext} again. Assuming

$$m_i = (u_1, u_2, u_3, u_4, u_5), c_{i-1} = (v_1, v_2, v_3, v_4, v_5)$$
$$(b_1, b_2, b_3, b_4, b_5) = (u_1 \oplus v_1, u_2 \oplus v_2, u_3 \oplus v_3, u_4 \oplus v_4, u_5 \oplus v_5),$$

we obtain

$$\begin{aligned} c_i &= e_\pi(b_1, b_2, b_3, b_4, b_5) = (b_{\pi(1)}, b_{\pi(2)}, b_{\pi(3)}, b_{\pi(4)}, b_{\pi(5)}) \\ &= (b_3, b_5, b_2, b_4, b_1) \end{aligned}$$

in CBC mode. By using the initial value IV = 11001, the plaintext is encrypted to "OUVJQD":

i	Symbol	Bit code, m_i	$m_i \oplus c_{i-1}$	$c_i = e_\pi(m_i \oplus c_{i-1})$	Symbol	Integer value
0				11001		
1	S	10010	01011	01110	*O*	14
2	C	00010	01100	10100	*U*	20
3	I	01000	11100	10101	*V*	21
4	E	00100	10001	01001	*J*	9
5	N	01101	00100	10000	*Q*	16
6	C	00010	10010	00011	*D*	3
7	E	00100	00111	11010	.	26

For decryption, we use the inverse permutation again.

CFB mode of operation

The block sizes of plaintext and ciphertext conform with the block size that has to be encrypted. Let the block size that has to be encrypted be fixed to m and the block size of the plain- and ciphertext be $1 \leq j \leq t$. Now, we will use another block cipher mode of operation. A first possibility is to use the *cipher feedback mode* (CFB). We need a *register* $r_i \in \Sigma^t_{\text{Bool}}$. An initial r_1 is given and made public (IV). The block size of plain- and ciphertexts is given by j satisfying $1 \leq j \leq t$, $m_i, c_i \in \Sigma^j_{\text{Bool}}$. Let $e_k : \Sigma^t_{\text{Bool}} \to \Sigma^t_{\text{Bool}}$ be an encryption function (any block cipher) of block size t. We first encrypt the register by $e_k(r_i)$ and then take the j highest valued bits from the result,

$$s_{j,t} : \Sigma^t_{\text{Bool}} \to \Sigma^j_{\text{Bool}}, \; x \mapsto s_{j,t}(x) = x \cdot 2^{-(t-j)}.$$

In the next step, we link the result by XOR with the plaintext to get the ciphertext,

$$c_i = m_i \oplus s_{j,t}(e_k(r_i)).$$

Lastly, we must update the register by

$$r_i = (r_{i-1} \cdot 2^j \bmod 2^t) + c_{i-1},\ i > 1.$$

After the left shift about j bits, the register is leveled at t bits by the modulo operation. The last j bits are 0. These bits are filled with the last ciphertext block. Because of the XOR gate, the decryption process runs due to the same rules. The only modification is to switch the roles of p_i and c_i,

$$m_i = c_i \oplus s_{j,t}(e_k(r_i)).$$

Example 4.29 (CFB). We encrypt the string "SCIENCE" from Σ^7_{Latext} again. By assuming $j = 5$ and $t = 8$, we need a new encryption function, for instance,

$$\pi = \begin{pmatrix} 1 & 2 & 3 & 4 & 5 & 6 & 7 & 8 \\ 3 & 5 & 2 & 7 & 1 & 4 & 8 & 6 \end{pmatrix} = (1325)(4786), \tag{4.3}$$

and an initial register,

$$\text{IV} = r_1 = 00101101. \tag{4.4}$$

Finally, we get the ciphertext "KZEUMLP". We look at this process using three tables: one for encrypting the register, one for creating the ciphertext and one for updating the register. We have to read all in parallel.

i	r_i	$e_\pi(r_i)$	$s_{5,8}(e_\pi(r_i))$
1	00101101	11000|011	11000
2	10101010	11011|000	11011
3	01011001	01100|110	01100
4	00100100	10000|001	10000
5	10010100	00001|101	00001
6	10001100	01001|001	01001
7	10001011	01011|010	01011

i	Symbol	Bit code, m_i	$s_{5,8}(e_\pi(r_i))$	$c_i = m_i \oplus s_{5,8}(e_\pi(r_i))$	Symbol	Integer value
1	S	10010	11000	01010	K	10
2	C	00010	11011	11001	Z	25
3	I	01000	01100	00100	E	4
4	E	00100	10000	10100	U	20
5	N	01101	00001	01100	M	12
6	C	00010	01001	01011	L	11
7	E	00100	01011	01111	P	15

i	r_{i-1}	$r_{i-1} \cdot 2^5 \bmod 2^8$	c_{i-1}	$r_i = (r_{i-1} \cdot 2^5 \bmod 2^8) + c_{i-1}$
1				00101101
2	00101|101	101|00000	01010	10101010
3	10101|010	010|00000	11001	01011001
4	01011|001	001|00000	00100	00100100
5	00100|100	100|00000	10100	10010100
6	10010|100	100|00000	01100	10001100
7	10001|100	011|00000	01011	10001011

For decryption, we use the inverse permutation

$$\pi = \begin{pmatrix} 1 & 2 & 3 & 4 & 5 & 6 & 7 & 8 \\ 5 & 3 & 1 & 6 & 2 & 8 & 4 & 7 \end{pmatrix} = (1523)(4687). \tag{4.5}$$

OFB mode of operation

The *Output Feedback Mode* (OFB) depicts a little variation of the CFB. Instead of using c_{i-1} in the register updating process, the highest valued bits of the encrypted register from the last block are used, i.e.,

$$r_i = (r_{i-1} \cdot 2^j \bmod 2^t) + s_{j,t}(e_k(r_{i-1})),\ i > 1.$$

The rest remains unchanged. One advantage is that we can prepare the register in advance without waiting for the actual encryption.

Example 4.30 (OFB). We encrypt the string "SCIENCE" from Σ^7_{Latext} again. By assuming $j = 5$ and $t = 8$, we need an encryption function, for instance, the same as for the CFB mode,

$$\pi = \begin{pmatrix} 1 & 2 & 3 & 4 & 5 & 6 & 7 & 8 \\ 3 & 5 & 2 & 7 & 1 & 4 & 8 & 6 \end{pmatrix} = (1325)(4786), \tag{4.6}$$

and an initial register is the same as for the CFB mode

$$\mathrm{IV} = r_1 = 00101101. \tag{4.7}$$

Finally, we get the ciphertext "KCAQFKM". We look at this process using three tables again: one for encrypting the register, one for creating the ciphertext and one for updating the register. We have to read all in parallel.

i	r_{i-1}	$r_{i-1} \cdot 2^5 \bmod 2^8$	$e_\pi(r_{i-1})$	$s_{5,8}(e_\pi(r_{i-1}))$	$r_i = (r_{i-1} \cdot 2^5 \bmod 2^8) + s_{5,8}(e_\pi(r_{i-1}))$
1					00101101
2	00101|101	10100000	11000|011	11000	10111000
3	10111|000	00000000	11001|100	11001	00011001
4	00011|001	00100000	01000|110	01000	00101000
5	00101|000	00000000	11000|000	11000	00011000
6	00011|000	00000000	01000|100	01000	00001000
7	00001|000	00000000	01000|000	01000	00001000
8	00001|000	00000000	01000|000	01000	00001000

i	Symbol	Bit code, m_i	$s_{5,8}(e_\pi(r_i))$	$c_i = m_i \oplus s_{5,8}(e_\pi(r_i))$	Symbol	Integer value
1	S	10010	11000	01010	K	10
2	C	00010	11001	00010	C	2
3	I	01000	01000	00000	A	0
4	E	00100	11000	10000	Q	16
5	N	01101	01000	00101	F	5
6	C	00010	01000	01010	K	10
7	E	00100	01000	01100	M	12

The decryption process can be done in the same way again.

CTR mode of operation

There is another variation of the CFB and OFB. The *Counter Mode* (CTR) adds neither c_{i-1} (CFB) nor $s_{j,t}(e_k(r_{i-1}))$ (OFB) to the register in the register updating process, but a counter value that has to be updated after each step. This can be done by increasing the last value starting at 0. Preparing the register is also possible.

Example 4.31 (CTR). We encrypt the string "SCIENCE" from $\Sigma^7_{\mathrm{Latext}}$ by assuming the same parameters $j = 5$ and $t = 8$ and the same permutation as for the CFB mode again. The initial register is the same as for the CFB mode,

$$\mathrm{IV} = r_1 = 00101101. \tag{4.8}$$

The result is a ciphertext “KTIWLWF”. The register can be computed separately from the ciphertext creating process.

i	r_{i-1}	$r_{i-1} \cdot 2^5 \bmod 2^8$	$e_\pi(r_{i-1})$	$s_{5,8}(e_\pi(r_{i-1}))$	z_i	$r_i = (r_{i-1} \cdot 2^5 \bmod 2^8) + z_i$
1						00101101
2	$00101 \mid 101$	10100000	$11000 \mid 011$	11000	000	10100000
3	$10100 \mid 000$	00000000	$10001 \mid 000$	10001	001	00000001
4	$00000 \mid 001$	00100000	$00000 \mid 010$	00000	010	00100010
5	$00100 \mid 010$	01000000	$10010 \mid 000$	10010	011	01000011
6	$01000 \mid 011$	01100000	$00110 \mid 010$	00110	100	01100100
7	$01100 \mid 100$	10000000	$10100 \mid 001$	10100	101	10000101
8	$10000 \mid 101$	10100000	$00001 \mid 011$	00001	110	10100110

i	Symbol	Bit code, m_i	$s_{5,8}(e_\pi(r_i))$	$c_i = m_i \oplus s_{5,8}(e_\pi(r_i))$	Symbol	Integer value
1	S	10010	11000	01010	K	10
2	C	00010	10001	10011	T	19
3	I	01000	00000	01000	I	8
4	E	00100	10010	10110	W	22
5	N	01101	00110	01011	L	11
6	C	00010	10100	10110	W	22
7	E	00100	00001	00101	F	5

The decryption process can be done the same way by switching the roles of plain- and ciphertext.

In (Dworkin, 2001), the OFB and CTR modes are declared while assuming $j = t$. There are other block cipher modes of operation. For instance, the modes FF1 and FF3 are depicted in (Dworkin, 2016b). There, it is possible to process number-based strings in addition to the bitwise strings. Furthermore, FF1 and FF3 are based on a Feistel cipher that will be discussed in detail in Section 6.1.

All modes of operation except the ECB mode blur resulting information that is created by encrypting the same blocks. This increases security.

Chapter 5

Theoretical Bounds for Secure Ciphering

Note 5.1. In this chapter, the requirements are:

- being familiar with the basics of probability theory, see Section 1.2, and
- knowing affine block ciphers, see Section 4.2.

Selected literature: See (Cover and Thomas, 2006; Massey, 1988; Shannon, 1949; Webster and Tavares, 1986).

Consider an experiment where the result is not clear. For example, we are waiting for three consecutive binary messages X, Y and Z, each with a block size of 2. We also know the joint probabilities for each combination.

Since $p_{Y|X}(00|10) = \frac{10/861}{335/861} = \frac{2}{67} = 0.03$ is very small, we should be very surprised if the sequence 1000 is produced. Alternatively, it would be of little surprise if the first bit of X was 1, because $p_X(10) + p_X(11) = \frac{5}{7} = 0.714$. The higher the probability of one result, the smaller the uncertainty. In particular, if the probability of one result is equal to 1, the result is clear and there is no surprise. We want to measure this level of uncertainty that is called the *amount of uncertainty* in (Shannon, 1949). The two events $A = \{10, 11\}$ and $B = \{01, 11\}$ from the power set $\mathcal{P}(X)$ are independent, since $\mathbb{P}_X(A \cap B) = \mathbb{P}_X(\{11\}) = \frac{40}{123} = \frac{5}{7} \cdot \frac{56}{123} = \mathbb{P}_X(A) \cdot \mathbb{P}_X(B)$. Each event yields an amount of uncertainty. From the independency, the amount

Table 5.1 Joint probabilities for three two-bit messages.

X		00				01				10				11				
Z		00	01	10	11	00	01	10	11	00	01	10	11	00	01	10	11	$\mathbb{P}_Y$
Y	00	$\frac{10}{861}$	$\frac{11}{861}$	$\frac{4}{861}$	$\frac{1}{861}$	$\frac{4}{861}$	$\frac{2}{861}$	$\frac{1}{287}$	$\frac{1}{287}$	$\frac{1}{287}$	$\frac{1}{287}$	$\frac{1}{287}$	$\frac{1}{861}$	$\frac{1}{287}$	$\frac{4}{123}$	$\frac{20}{861}$	$\frac{10}{861}$	$\frac{109}{861}$
	01	$\frac{2}{287}$	$\frac{10}{861}$	$\frac{1}{123}$	$\frac{1}{123}$	$\frac{10}{861}$	$\frac{1}{123}$	$\frac{2}{123}$	$\frac{1}{123}$	$\frac{6}{287}$	$\frac{29}{861}$	$\frac{22}{861}$	$\frac{26}{861}$	$\frac{16}{861}$	$\frac{1}{41}$	$\frac{8}{287}$	$\frac{19}{861}$	$\frac{81}{287}$
	10	$\frac{2}{123}$	$\frac{3}{287}$	$\frac{13}{861}$	$\frac{3}{287}$	$\frac{4}{861}$	$\frac{1}{287}$	$\frac{4}{287}$	$\frac{8}{861}$	$\frac{9}{287}$	$\frac{19}{861}$	$\frac{26}{861}$	$\frac{32}{861}$	$\frac{2}{123}$	$\frac{5}{287}$	$\frac{19}{861}$	$\frac{6}{287}$	$\frac{242}{861}$
	11	$\frac{5}{861}$	$\frac{2}{123}$	$\frac{2}{287}$	$\frac{8}{861}$	$\frac{4}{287}$	$\frac{4}{287}$	$\frac{4}{861}$	$\frac{1}{123}$	$\frac{31}{861}$	$\frac{4}{123}$	$\frac{4}{123}$	$\frac{13}{287}$	$\frac{6}{287}$	$\frac{29}{861}$	$\frac{4}{287}$	$\frac{2}{123}$	$\frac{89}{287}$
$\mathbb{P}_Z$		$\frac{65}{287}$					$\frac{80}{287}$					$\frac{31}{123}$					$\frac{209}{861}$	1
$\mathbb{P}_X$			$\frac{134}{861}$				$\frac{16}{123}$				$\frac{335}{861}$				$\frac{40}{123}$			

of uncertainty of the intersection should be the sum of the single uncertainties. These considerations suggest measuring the amount of uncertainty by a mapping based on the probabilities, regardless of the actual outcomes. Such a reasonably continuous mapping

$$U : [0,1] \to [0,\infty],\ U(1) = 0,\ \lim_{p\to 0} U(p) = \infty,\ U(p\cdot q) = U(p) + U(q)$$

is given by the negative logarithm. By introducing[1] the normalization condition $U(\frac{1}{2}) = 1$, we obtain $U(p) = -\log_2(p)$. Before we proceed to rate the whole distribution with regard to the amount of uncertainty, we have to present additional results from probability theory.

5.1 Conditional Expectation

Let $(\Omega, \mathcal{F}, \mathbb{P})$ be a probability space, $A \in \mathcal{F}$ be an event and $\mathbb{P}(A) > 0$. The random variable

$$X \cdot \mathbb{1}_A : \Omega \to X(A) \cup \{0\},$$

$$X \cdot \mathbb{1}_A(\omega) := X(\omega) \cdot \mathbb{1}_A(\omega) := \begin{cases} X(\omega), & \omega \in A, \\ 0, & \omega \notin A, \end{cases}$$

has the probability mass function (for $x \neq 0$)

$$\begin{aligned} p_{X\cdot\mathbb{1}_A}(x) &= \mathbb{P}((X\cdot\mathbb{1}_A)^{-1}(\{x\})) \\ &= \mathbb{P}(\{\omega \in \Omega;\ \omega \in A \wedge X(\omega) = x\}) \\ &= \mathbb{P}(\{\omega \in A;\ X(\omega) = x\}). \end{aligned} \tag{5.1}$$

[1] Binary calculation due to (Shannon, 1949, p. 42). The unit of information is called a *bit* (binary digit), as recommended by John W. Tukey (1915–2000).

The *conditional expectation* of X given the occurrence of event A is defined as

$$\begin{aligned}\mathbb{E}[X|A] &:= \frac{\mathbb{E}[X \cdot \mathbb{1}_A]}{\mathbb{P}(A)} \\ &= \frac{1}{\mathbb{P}(A)} \cdot \sum_{x \in X(A)} x \cdot p_{X \cdot \mathbb{1}_A}(x) \\ &= \frac{1}{\mathbb{P}(A)} \cdot \sum_{\omega \in A} X(\omega) \cdot \mathbb{P}(\{\omega\}). \end{aligned} \tag{5.2}$$

Let $Y : \Omega \to \Phi \subseteq \mathbb{R}$ be another discrete random variable. In the special case of $A = \{Y = y_0\} := \{\omega \in \Omega;\ Y(\omega) = y_0\}$, we obtain

$$\begin{aligned} p_{X \cdot \mathbb{1}_{\{Y=y_0\}}}(x) &= \mathbb{P}(\{\omega \in \Omega;\ Y(\omega) = y_0 \wedge X(\omega) = x\}) \\ &= p_{X,Y}(x, y_0), \end{aligned} \tag{5.3}$$

the joint probability distribution of X and Y at (x, y_0) and it follows

$$\begin{aligned}\mathbb{E}[X|\{Y = y_0\}] &= \frac{\mathbb{E}[X \cdot \mathbb{1}_{\{Y=y_0\}}]}{\mathbb{P}(\{Y = y_0\})} \\ &= \frac{1}{p_Y(y_0)} \cdot \sum_{x \in X(A)} x \cdot p_{X \cdot \mathbb{1}_{\{Y=y_0\}}}(x) \\ &= \frac{1}{p_Y(y_0)} \cdot \sum_{x \in X(A)} x \cdot p_{X,Y}(x, y_0) \\ &= \sum_{x \in X(A)} x \cdot p_{X|Y}(x|y_0). \end{aligned} \tag{5.4}$$

Again, consider a real-valued function $f : X(\Omega) \to \mathbb{R}$. The conditional expectation of the corresponding random variable $F : \Omega \to \mathbb{R}$, $F = f(X)$, given event A is

$$\mathbb{E}[F|A] = \mathbb{E}[f(X)|A] = \frac{1}{\mathbb{P}(A)} \cdot \sum_{x \in X(A)} f(x) \cdot p_{X \cdot \mathbb{1}_A}(x).$$

By setting $A = \{Y = y_0\}$

$$\mathbb{E}[f(X)|\{Y = y_0\}] = \sum_{x \in X(A)} f(x) \cdot p_{X|Y}(x|y_0). \tag{5.5}$$

Applying a real-valued function $f : X(\Omega) \times Y(\Omega) \to \mathbb{R}$ with corresponding $F = f(X,Y)$ yields

$$\mathbb{E}[f(X,Y)|A] = \frac{1}{\mathbb{P}(A)} \cdot \sum_{x\in X(A)} \sum_{y\in Y(A)} f(x,y) \cdot p_{(X,Y)\cdot \mathbb{1}_A}(x,y)$$

and

$$\begin{aligned}
&\mathbb{E}[f(X,Y)|\{Y = y_0\}] \\
&\quad = \frac{1}{p_Y(y_0)} \cdot \sum_{x\in X(A)} \sum_{y\in Y(A)} f(x,y) \cdot p_{(X,Y)\cdot \mathbb{1}_{\{Y=y_0\}}}(x,y) \\
&\quad = \frac{1}{p_Y(y_0)} \cdot \sum_{x\in X(A)} f(x,y_0) \cdot p_{X,Y}(x,y_0) && (5.6) \\
&\quad = \sum_{x\in X(A)} f(x,y_0) \cdot p_{X|Y}(x|y_0). && (5.7)
\end{aligned}$$

Equation (5.6) can be multiplied by $p_Y(y_0)$ and then summed over all y_0, resulting in

$$\begin{aligned}
&\sum_{y_0\in Y(\Omega)} p_Y(y_0) \cdot \mathbb{E}[f(X,Y)|\{Y = y_0\}] \\
&\quad = \sum_{y_0\in Y(\Omega)} \sum_{x\in X(A)} f(x,y_0) \cdot p_{X,Y}(x,y_0) \\
&\quad = \mathbb{E}[f(X,Y)]. && (5.8)
\end{aligned}$$

Consider an event $B = \{Y = y_0\} \cap A$ with $\mathbb{P}(B) = p_Y(y_0|A) \cdot \mathbb{P}(A)$. Hence, it is traceable in the same way to

$$\begin{aligned}
&\mathbb{E}[f(X,Y)|\{Y = y_0\} \cap A] \\
&\quad = \frac{1}{p_Y(y_0|A) \cdot \mathbb{P}(A)} \cdot \sum_{x\in X(B)} f(x,y_0) \cdot p_{(X,Y)\cdot \mathbb{1}_A}(x,y_0) && (5.9) \\
&\Rightarrow \mathbb{E}[f(X,Y)|A] = \sum_{y_0\in Y(\Omega)} p_Y(y_0|A) \cdot \mathbb{E}[f(X,Y)|\{Y = y_0\} \cap A]. && (5.10)
\end{aligned}$$

Equations (5.8) and (5.7) are referred to as *statements of the theorem on total expectation*.[2] Three discrete random variables X, Y and Z and event $B = \{Y = y_0\} \cap \{Z = z_0\}$ yield

$$\begin{aligned}&\mathbb{E}[f(X,Y,Z)|\{Y = y_0\} \cap \{Z = z_0\}]\\&= \frac{1}{p_Z(z_0) \cdot p_{Y|Z}(y_0|z_0)} \cdot \sum_{x \in X(B)} f(x, y_0, z_0) \cdot p_{X,Y,Z}(x, y_0, z_0)\end{aligned} \tag{5.11}$$

$$\Rightarrow \mathbb{E}[f(X,Y,Z)|\{Z = z_0\}]$$

$$= \sum_{x \in X(B)} \sum_{y_0 \in Y(\Omega)} f(x, y_0, z_0) \cdot p_{X,Y|Z}(x, y_0|z_0) \tag{5.12}$$

$$= \sum_{y_0 \in Y(\Omega)} p_{Y|Z}(y_0|z_0) \cdot \mathbb{E}[f(X,Y,Z)|\{Y = y_0\} \cap \{Z = z_0\}]. \tag{5.13}$$

5.2 Information Theory

Based on a discrete random variable $X : \Omega \to \Psi$, the mapping U measuring the amount of uncertainty of one certain result, which is called self-information by Fano,[3] can be interpreted as a random variable $U : \Psi \to [0, \infty]$, $U(x) = -\log_2(\mathbb{P}_X(\{x\}))$. Any occurring uncertainty emerges with a probability of $\mathbb{P}_X(\{x\})$. To measure the uncertainty of the whole experiment, we build the expectation value of U. For convenience, we drop the zero probabilities. To achieve this, we use the support of a function $f : D \to \mathbb{R}$, $\text{supp}(f) := \{x \in D;\ f(x) \neq 0\}$. Here, we look at $\text{supp}(\mathbb{P}_X) := \text{supp}(p_X)$ and make use of

$$\lim_{p \to 0} p \log(p) \overset{\text{L'Hospital}}{=} 0.$$

[2] James Lee Massey (1934–2013), cf. (Massey, 1988), and http://www.isiweb.ee.ethz.ch/archive/massey_scr/.

[3] Robert M. Fano (1917–2016), see (Fano, 1961).

Definition 5.2 (Shannon entropy). The *uncertainty* (or Shannon entropy) of a discrete random variable $X : \Omega \to \Psi$ is the quantity

$$H(X) := \mathbb{E}[-\log_2(\mathbb{P}_X(X))] = -\sum_{x \in \text{supp}(\mathbb{P}_X)} \mathbb{P}_X(\{x\}) \cdot \log_2(\mathbb{P}_X(\{x\})). \tag{5.14}$$

For each $x \in \text{supp}(\mathbb{P}_X)$, $0 < \mathbb{P}_X \leq 1$ and therefore,

$$-\mathbb{P}_X(\{x\}) \cdot \log_2(\mathbb{P}_X(\{x\})) \begin{cases} = 0, & \mathbb{P}_X(\{x\}) = 1, \\ > 0, & \mathbb{P}_X(\{x\}) < 1. \end{cases} \tag{5.15}$$

The example from Table 5.1 yields $H(X) = 1.857$.

Example 5.3. Let $X : \Omega \to \{0,1\}$ be a binary random variable and $\mathbb{P}_X(\{1\}) = p \in (0,1]$.

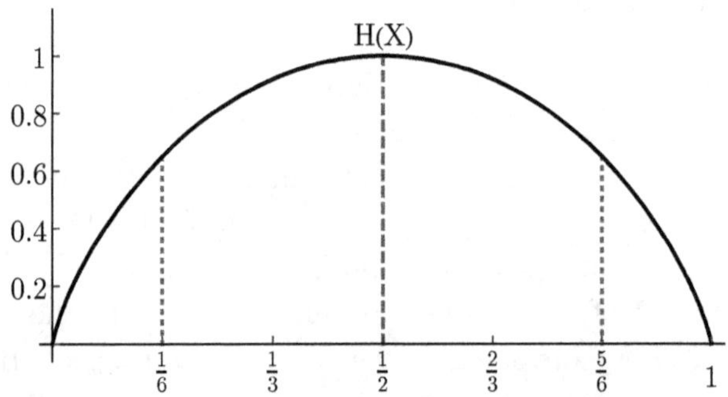

Figure 5.1 Entropy of a binary random variable.

The Shannon entropy is

$$H(X) = -p \cdot \log_2(p) - (1-p)\log_2(1-p),$$

$$p = \frac{1}{2} \Rightarrow H(X) = 1, \text{ and}$$

$$p = \frac{5}{6} \text{ or } p = \frac{1}{6} \Rightarrow H(X) = 0.65.$$

A useful result that can help prove some of the following results is the *IT-inequality.*[4]

Theorem 5.4 (IT-inequality). *For a positive number $a \in \mathbb{R}^+$, it applies*

$$\log(a) \leq (a-1)\log(e) \tag{5.16}$$

with equality iff $a = 1$.

Proof. Consider $a \in \mathbb{R}^+$. If $a = 1$, then it is $\ln(a) = 0 = a - 1$. Otherwise,

$$\frac{d\ln(a)}{da} = \frac{1}{a}\begin{cases} > 1, & a < 1, \\ < 1, & a > 1. \end{cases}$$

However,

$$\frac{d(a-1)\ln(e)}{da} = 1.$$

Therefore, there is no other point of intersection between the two functions. Hence, $\ln(a) \leq (a-1)$ with equality iff $a = 1$, which can be multiplied by $\log(e)$ and it follows (5.16). □

A lower bound of $H(X)$ is given by Equation (5.15). However, there is also an upper bound of $H(X)$.

Theorem 5.5. *If $X : \Omega \to \Psi$ is a discrete random variable and the image of X has l elements, i.e., $l = |X(\Omega)|$, then*

$$0 \leq H(X) \leq \log_2(l) \tag{5.17}$$

with equality on the right iff $\mathbb{P}_X(\{x\}) = \frac{1}{l}$ for all $x \in supp(\mathbb{P}_X)$, and equality on the left iff $\mathbb{P}_X(\{x\}) = 1$ for exactly one $x \in supp(\mathbb{P}_X)$, i.e., $|supp(\mathbb{P}_X)| = 1$.

[4] Named by Massey, see (Massey, 1988).

Proof. Equation (5.15) provides $H(X) = 0$ iff $\mathbb{P}_X(\{x\}) = 1$ for every $x \in \text{supp}(\mathbb{P}_X)$, which can be true for exactly one such x.

$$\begin{aligned}
H(X) - \log_2(l) &= - \sum_{x \in \text{supp}(\mathbb{P}_X)} \mathbb{P}_X(\{x\}) \cdot \log_2(\mathbb{P}_X(\{x\})) - \log_2(l) \\
&= \sum_{x \in \text{supp}(\mathbb{P}_X)} \mathbb{P}_X(\{x\}) \left(\log_2 \left(\frac{1}{\mathbb{P}_X(\{x\})} \right) - \log_2(l) \right) \\
&= \sum_{x \in \text{supp}(\mathbb{P}_X)} \mathbb{P}_X(\{x\}) \cdot \log_2 \left(\frac{1}{l \cdot \mathbb{P}_X(\{x\})} \right) \\
&\overset{(5.16)}{\leq} \sum_{x \in \text{supp}(\mathbb{P}_X)} \mathbb{P}_X(\{x\}) \left(\frac{1}{l \cdot \mathbb{P}_X(\{x\})} - 1 \right) \cdot \log_2(e) \\
&= \left(\sum_{x \in \text{supp}(\mathbb{P}_X)} \frac{1}{l} - \sum_{x \in \text{supp}(\mathbb{P}_X)} \mathbb{P}_X(\{x\}) \right) \cdot \log_2(e) \\
&\leq (1 - 1) \cdot \log_2(e) \\
&= 0.
\end{aligned}$$

There is equality at the point when using the IT-Inequality iff $l \cdot \mathbb{P}_X(\{x\}) = 1$ for all $x \in \text{supp}(\mathbb{P}_X)$. However, there are l such values. In this case, the second inequality is also an equality. □

We defined the conditional expectation of a random variable in Equation (5.2). Similarly, it is useful to define the conditional uncertainty. Thinking about a ciphertext as a random variable that depends on the source, i.e., the plaintext and key, we have to consider the impact on the ciphertext if any of the source is known.

Definition 5.6. Let X, Y and Z be discrete random variables. If the event $\{Y = y_0\}$ or the event $\{Y = y_0\} \cap \{Z = z_0\}$ appears, the *conditional uncertainty* of X is

$$H(X|\{Y = y_0\}) = - \sum_{x \in \text{supp}(\mathbb{P}_{X|Y}(\cdot|y_0))} p_{X|Y}(x|y_0) \cdot \log_2(p_{X|Y}(x|y_0)), \text{ and} \tag{5.18}$$

$$H(X|\{Y = y_0\} \cap \{Z = z_0\}) = -\sum_{x \in \mathrm{supp}(\mathbb{P}_{X|Y,Z}(\cdot|y_0,z_0))} p_{X|Y,Z}(x|y_0, z_0) \cdot \log_2(p_{X|Y,Z}(x|y_0, z_0)). \tag{5.19}$$

By considering the uncertainty as an expectation and by setting $F(X, Y) = -\log_2(p_{X|Y}(X|Y))$,

$$\begin{aligned} H(X|\{Y = y_0\}) &\overset{(5.18)}{=} - \sum_{x \in \mathrm{supp}(\mathbb{P}_{X|Y}(\cdot|y_0))} \log_2(p_{X|Y}(x|y_0)) \cdot p_{X|Y}(x|y_0) \\ &= \sum_{x \in \mathrm{supp}(\mathbb{P}_{X|Y}(\cdot|y_0))} F(x, y_0) \cdot p_{X|Y}(x|y_0) \\ &\overset{(5.7)}{=} \mathbb{E}[F(X, Y)|\{Y = y_0\}] \\ &= \mathbb{E}[-\log_2(p_{X|Y}(X|Y))|\{Y = y_0\}]. \end{aligned}$$

As in the succeeding considerations after Equation (5.6), we can take the sum over all y_0, resulting in

$$\begin{aligned} &\sum_{y_0 \in \mathrm{supp}(\mathbb{P}_Y)} p_Y(y_0) H(X|\{Y = y_0\}) = \sum_{y_0 \in \mathrm{supp}(\mathbb{P}_Y)} p_Y(y_0) \mathbb{E}[F(X, Y)|\{Y = y_0\}] \\ &\overset{(5.8)}{=} \mathbb{E}[F(X, Y)] = \mathbb{E}[-\log_2(p_{X|Y}(X|Y))] \\ &= - \sum_{(x,y) \in \mathrm{supp}(\mathbb{P}_{X,Y})} p_{X,Y}(x, y) \cdot \log_2(p_{X|Y}(x|y)) \\ &\overset{(5.14)}{=:} H(X|Y). \end{aligned}$$

Definition 5.7. Let X and Y be discrete random variables. The conditional uncertainty (*equivocation*) of X given Y is

$$H(X|Y) = \sum_{y_0 \in \mathrm{supp}(\mathbb{P}_Y)} p_Y(y_0) H(X|\{Y = y_0\}). \tag{5.20}$$

Remark 5.8. Applying Theorem 5.5 to the definitions of $H(X|\{Y = y_0\})$ and $H(X|Y)$ yields (with equality analogously)

$$0 \leq H(X|\{Y = y_0\}), H(X|Y) \leq \log_2(l).$$

By applying the idea of summing over all y_0 in $\text{supp}(\mathbb{P}_{Y|Z}(.,z_0))$ in Equation (5.19),

$$H(X|Y,\{Z=z_0\}) = \mathbb{E}[-\log_2(p_{X|Y,Z}(X|Y,Z))|\{Z=z_0\}]$$
$$\overset{(5.11)}{=} \sum_{y_0\in\text{supp}(\mathbb{P}_{Y|Z}(.,z_0))} p_{Y|Z}(y_0|z_0)\cdot \underbrace{\mathbb{E}[-\log_2(p_{X|Y,Z}(X|Y,Z))|\{Y=y_0\}\cap\{Z=z_0\}]}_{H(X|\{Y=y_0\}\cap\{Z=z_0\})}.$$

Example 5.9 (Data from Table 5.1).

$$H(X)=1.857,\ H(Y)=1.931,\ H(Z)=1.996,$$

$$\left.\begin{aligned}H(X|\{Y=00\})&=1.629\\ H(X|\{Y=01\})&=1.849\\ H(X|\{Y=10\})&=1.839\\ H(X|\{Y=11\})&=1.780\end{aligned}\right\}\Rightarrow H(X|Y)=1.797\le H(X),\ \text{and}$$

$$\left.\begin{aligned}H(X|Y\cap\{Z=00\})&=1.794\\ H(X|Y\cap\{Z=01\})&=1.750\\ H(X|Y\cap\{Z=10\})&=1.773\\ H(X|Y\cap\{Z=11\})&=1.706\end{aligned}\right\}\Rightarrow H(X|Y,Z)=1.755.$$

5.2.1 *Kullback–Leibler divergence*

We can measure the directed difference between two probability distributions[5] for the purpose of calculating how much information is lost if we replace one distribution with another.

Definition 5.10 (Kullback–Leibler divergence). Let X and Y be discrete random variables with $X(\Omega) = Y(\Omega)$. The Kullback–Leibler divergence is defined by

$$D(\mathbb{P}_X||\mathbb{P}_Y) = \begin{cases}\sum\limits_{x\in\text{supp}(\mathbb{P}_X)} p_X(x)\log_2\left(\frac{p_X(x)}{p_Y(x)}\right), & p_Y(x)>0 \text{ for all } x,\\ \infty, & p_Y(x)=0 \text{ for any } x.\end{cases}$$

[5]cf. (Kullback, 1997).

Example 5.11 (Data from Table 5.1).

$$\begin{array}{ll} D(\mathbb{P}_X||\mathbb{P}_Y) = 0.106, & D(\mathbb{P}_Y||\mathbb{P}_X) = 0.124, \\ D(\mathbb{P}_X||\mathbb{P}_Z) = 0.154, & D(\mathbb{P}_Z||\mathbb{P}_X) = 0.169, \text{ and} \\ D(\mathbb{P}_Y||\mathbb{P}_Z) = 0.053, & D(\mathbb{P}_Z||\mathbb{P}_Y) = 0.060. \end{array}$$

Example 5.11 shows that the Kullback–Leibler divergence is not symmetric. If all $p_Y(x) > 0$, we can transform the term into

$$\begin{aligned} D(\mathbb{P}_X||\mathbb{P}_Y) &= \sum_{x\in\text{supp}(\mathbb{P}_X)} p_X(x)\log_2\left(\frac{p_X(x)}{p_Y(x)}\right) \\ &= \sum_{x\in\text{supp}(\mathbb{P}_X)} p_X(x)\cdot\log_2(p_X(x)) - \sum_{x\in\text{supp}(\mathbb{P}_X)} p_X(x)\cdot\log_2(p_Y(x)) \\ &= \mathbb{E}[\log_2(p_X(X))] - \mathbb{E}[\log_2(p_Y(X))], \end{aligned}$$

regarding the expectation difference based on the probability distribution of X.

Theorem 5.12. *The following inequation is valid:*

$$D(\mathbb{P}_X||\mathbb{P}_Y) \geq 0, \tag{5.21}$$

with equality iff $p_X(x) = p_Y(y)$ *for all* $x \in$ *supp*$(\mathbb{P}_X)$.

Proof. If $p_Y(x) = 0$ for any $x \in \text{supp}(\mathbb{P}_X)$, then $D(\mathbb{P}_X||\mathbb{P}_Y) = \infty$. Let $p_Y(x) > 0$ for all x.

$$\begin{aligned} -D(\mathbb{P}_X||\mathbb{P}_Y) &= \sum_{x\in\text{supp}(\mathbb{P}_X)} p_X(x)\log_2\left(\frac{p_Y(x)}{p_X(x)}\right) \\ &\overset{(5.16)}{\leq} \sum_{x\in\text{supp}(\mathbb{P}_X)} p_X(x)\left(\frac{p_Y(x)}{p_X(x)} - 1\right)\cdot\log_2(e) \\ &= \left(\sum_{x\in\text{supp}(\mathbb{P}_X)} p_Y(x) - \sum_{x\in\text{supp}(\mathbb{P}_X)} p_X(x)\right)\log_2(e) \\ &\leq (1-1)\log_2(e) = 0. \end{aligned}$$

The two inequalities get equalities iff (from Theorem 5.4) $\frac{p_Y(x)}{p_X(y)} = 1$, i.e., $p_Y(x) = p_X(x)$ for all x. □

If X and Y are discrete random variables and the images of X and Y have the same l elements, and Y has the uniform probability distribution $p_Y(x) = \frac{1}{l}$ for all x, then

$$\begin{aligned} 0 &\leq D(\mathbb{P}_X||\mathbb{P}_Y) = \mathbb{E}[\log_2(p_X(X))] - \mathbb{E}[\log_2(p_Y(X))] \\ &= \mathbb{E}[\log_2(p_X(X))] - \mathbb{E}[\log_2\left(l^{-1}\right)] = \mathbb{E}[\log_2(l)] - \mathbb{E}[-\log_2(p_X(X))] \\ &= \log_2(l) - H(X), \end{aligned}$$

which confirms the right side of the estimation (5.17). One essential application of Theorem 5.12 concerns an estimation between uncertainty and conditional uncertainty that states that uncertainty never increases by conditioning.

Theorem 5.13. *For any two discrete random variables X and Y, it applies*

$$H(X|Y) \leq H(X) \tag{5.22}$$

with equality iff X and Y are independent random variables.

Proof.

$$\begin{aligned} H(X) - H(X|Y) &= \mathbb{E}[-\log_2(\mathbb{P}_X(X))] - \mathbb{E}[-\log_2(\mathbb{P}_{X|Y}(X|Y))] \\ &= \mathbb{E}\left[\log_2\left(\frac{\mathbb{P}_{X|Y}(X|Y)}{\mathbb{P}_X(X)}\right)\right] \\ &= \mathbb{E}\left[\log_2\left(\frac{\mathbb{P}_{X|Y}(X|Y)\mathbb{P}_Y(Y)}{\mathbb{P}_X(X)\mathbb{P}_Y(Y)}\right)\right] \\ &= \mathbb{E}\left[\log_2\left(\frac{\mathbb{P}_{X,Y}(X,Y)}{\mathbb{P}_X(X)\mathbb{P}_Y(Y)}\right)\right] \\ &= D(\mathbb{P}_{X,Y}||\mathbb{P}_X\mathbb{P}_Y) \\ &\geq 0. \end{aligned}$$

Iff $p_{X,Y}(x,y) = p_X(x) \cdot p_Y(y)$ for all x, y (the random variables X and Y are independent according to (1.7)), we have $H(X) = H(X|Y)$. □

Since

$$\frac{p_{X|Y,Z}(x|y,z)}{p_{X|Z}(x|z)} = \frac{p_{X,Y|Z}(x,y|z)}{p_{Y|Z}(y|z) \cdot p_{X|Z}(x|z)},$$

we obtain from Equation (5.22)

$$\begin{aligned}
&H(X|\{Z=z_0\}) - H(X|Y,\{Z=z_0\}) \\
&= \mathbb{E}\left[\log_2\left(\frac{p_{X|Y,Z}(X|Y,Z)}{p_{X|Z}(X|Z)}\right)|\{Z=z_0\}\right] \\
&= \mathbb{E}\left[\log_2\left(\frac{p_{X|Y,Z}(X|Y,\{Z=z_0\})}{p_{X|Z}(X|\{Z=z_0\})}\right)\right] \\
&= \mathbb{E}\left[\log_2\left(\frac{p_{X,Y|Z}(X,Y|\{Z=z_0\})}{p_{X|Z}(X|\{Z=z_0\}) \cdot p_{Y|Z}(Y|\{Z=z_0\})}\right)\right] \\
&= D\left(\mathbb{P}_{X,Y|\{Z=z_0\}}||\mathbb{P}_{X|\{Z=z_0\}} \cdot \mathbb{P}_{Y|\{Z=z_0\}}\right) \geq 0,
\end{aligned}$$

which equals iff $p_{X,Y|Z}(x,y|z_0) = p_{X|Z}(x|z_0) \cdot p_{Y|Z}(y|z_0)$ for all x, y. Thus,

$$H(X|Y,\{Z=z_0\}) \leq H(X|\{Z=z_0\}). \tag{5.23}$$

Similar to Equation (5.23) and using Equation (5.6), we can calculate

$$H(X|Y,Z) \leq H(X|Z)$$

with equality iff $p_{X,Y|Z}(x,y|z) = p_{X|Z}(x|z) \cdot p_{Y|Z}(y|z)$ for all x, y, z.

Since the joint probability distribution of discrete random variables X, Y and Z is denoted by

$$\begin{aligned}
\mathbb{P}_{X,Y,Z}(\{x,y,z\}) &= \mathbb{P}(\{X=x\} \cap \{Y=y\} \cap \{Z=z\}) \\
&\overset{(1.11)}{=} p_{Z|X,Y}(z|x,y) \cdot \ldots p_{Y|X}(y|x) \cdot p_X(x),
\end{aligned}$$

we can write

$$\begin{aligned}
H(X,Y,Z) &= \mathbb{E}[-\log_2(\mathbb{P}_{X,Y,Z}(X,Y,Z))] \\
&= \mathbb{E}[-\log_2(\mathbb{P}_{Z|X,Y}(Z|X,Y) \cdot \mathbb{P}_{Y|X}(Y|X) \cdot \mathbb{P}_X(X))] \\
&= \mathbb{E}[-\log_2(\mathbb{P}_{Z|X,Y}(Z|X,Y))] \\
&\quad + \mathbb{E}[-\log_2(\mathbb{P}_{Y|X}(Y|X))] + \mathbb{E}[-\log_2(\mathbb{P}_X(X))] \\
&= H(X) + H(Y|X) + H(Z|X,Y).
\end{aligned} \tag{5.24}$$

In doing so, the order of the random variables is arbitrary. Equation (5.24) is called the *chain rule for uncertainty.* A conditioned version of the chain rule can be obtained by treating one more line in the following way.

$$\begin{aligned} H(X,Y|\{Z=z_0\}) &= \mathbb{E}[-\log_2(p_{X,Y|Z})(X,Y|Z)|\{Z=z_0\}] \\ &= -\frac{1}{p_Z(z_0)} \sum_{(x,y)\in \mathrm{supp}(\mathbb{P}_{X,Y|Z}(.,.|z_0))} \log_2(p_{X,Y|Z})(x,y|z_0)) \\ &\quad \cdot p_{X,Y,Z}(x,y,z_0) \\ &= - \sum_{(x,y)\in \mathrm{supp}(\mathbb{P}_{X,Y|Z}(.,.|z_0))} \log_2(p_{X,Y|Z})(x,y|z_0)) \cdot p_{X,Y|Z}(x,y|z_0), \end{aligned}$$

and

$$\begin{aligned} &H(X,Y|Z) \\ &= \mathbb{E}[-\log_2(\mathbb{P}_{X,Y|Z}(X,Y|Z))] \\ &= \mathbb{E}\left[-\log_2\left(\frac{1}{\mathbb{P}_Z(Z)}\mathbb{P}_{X,Y,Z}(X,Y,Z)\right)\right] \\ &= \mathbb{E}\left[-\log_2\left(\frac{1}{\mathbb{P}_Z(Z)}\cdot \mathbb{P}_Z(Z)\cdot \mathbb{P}_{X|Z}(X|Z)\cdot \mathbb{P}_{Y|X,Z}(Y|X,Z)\right)\right] \\ &= H(X|Z)+H(Y|X,Z). \end{aligned}$$

5.2.2 *Transinformation*

Shannon[6] denotes information as a difference of uncertainties, addressing the amount of information that is transferred by random variable Y to random variable X. Fano[7] calls this mutual information.

Definition 5.14 (Transinformation). The *transinformation* (*mutual information*) between two discrete random variables X and Y is

$$I(X;Y) := H(X) - H(X|Y). \tag{5.25}$$

[6]cf. (Shannon, 1949).
[7]See (Fano, 1961).

Since the chain rule (5.24) yields

$$H(X,Y) = H(X) + H(Y|X) = H(Y) + H(X|Y),$$

then

$$\begin{aligned} I(X;Y) &= H(X) - H(X|Y) = H(Y) - H(Y|X) = I(Y;X) \\ &= H(X) + H(Y) - H(X,Y). \end{aligned} \tag{5.26}$$

The mutual information is symmetric and $I(X;Y) \overset{(5.22)}{\geq} 0$. We get

$$H(X,Y) \leq H(X) + H(Y).$$

X gives the same amount to Y and backwards. Similarly, we can define the conditional mutual information by

$$I(X;Y|Z) = H(X|Z) - H(X|Y,Z) = H(Y|Z) - H(Y|X,Z). \tag{5.27}$$

Example 5.15 (Data from Table 5.1).

$$\begin{aligned} H(X,Y) &= H(Y) + H(X|Y) = 3.728, \\ I(X;Y) &= H(X) + H(Y) - H(X,Y) = 0.061. \end{aligned}$$

5.2.3 *Perfect secrecy and unicity distance*

A non-probabilistic cryptosystem has at least one of the following types of information:

- (Plaintext) messages $m = (m_1, \ldots, m_n) \in \mathcal{P}^n$,
- Ciphertext messages $c = (c_1, \ldots, c_n) \in \mathcal{C}^n$,
- A key $k \in \mathcal{K}$ used to encrypt, hash or sign the messages.

Let $M^n : \Omega \to \mathcal{P}^n$, $C^n : \Omega \to \mathcal{C}^n$ and $K : \Omega \to \mathcal{K}$ be corresponding random variables. We can then interpret the term $\text{supp}(\mathbb{P}_{M^n})$. For example, $n = 5$. There are meaningful strings of this length, i.e., "ARENA" from Σ_{Lat}^5 and there are meaningless strings like "FQLKD" because the letter "U" typically appears after "Q". The probability of the latter string should be zero while the probability of the first string should be greater than zero. In the same way, other supports are interpretable. Before any additional information arises, the key uncertainty is given by

$$H(K) = -\sum_{k\in\mathcal{K}} \log_2(p_K(k)) \cdot p_K(k) \overset{(5.17)}{\leq} \log_2|\mathcal{K}|,$$

and the message uncertainty is given in the same way by

$$H(M^n) = -\sum_{m\in\mathcal{P}^n} \log_2(p_{M^n}(m)) \cdot p_{M^n}(m) \overset{(5.17)}{\leq} n \cdot \log_2|\mathcal{P}|.$$

Consider a known ciphertext attack by observing the transmitted message. The key equivocation then is

$$H(K|C^n) = -\sum_{c\in \operatorname{supp}(\mathbb{P}_{C^n})} p_{C^n}(c) H(K|\{C^n = c\}) \overset{(5.22)}{\leq} H(K), \tag{5.28}$$

and the message equivocation gets

$$H(M^n|C^n) = -\sum_{c\in \operatorname{supp}(\mathbb{P}_{C^n})} p_{C^n}(c) H(M^n|\{C^n = c\}) \overset{(5.22)}{\leq} H(M^n).$$

Since the plaintext can undoubtedly be recovered if the ciphertext and the key are known, the uncertainty becomes zero,

$$H(M^n|C^n, K) = 0. \tag{5.29}$$

Alternatively, the ciphertext can be computed uniquely if the plaintext and key are known, i.e.,

$$H(C^n|M^n, K) = 0. \tag{5.30}$$

The uncertainty of the plaintext and key, given the ciphertext, can be written either way as

$$\begin{aligned} H(K, M^n|C^n) &= H(K|C^n) + H(M^n|K, C^n) \overset{(5.29)}{=} H(K|C^n) \\ &= H(M^n|C^n) + H(K|M^n, C^n). \end{aligned}$$

Because $H(K|M^n, C^n) \geq 0$, we obtain an important estimation for $H(M^n|C^n)$.

Proposition 5.16.

$$H(M^n|C^n) \leq H(K|C^n). \tag{5.31}$$

A cipher system is commonly accepted if knowledge of the ciphertext gives no additional information about the original plaintext. In terms of Shannon, we use transinformation to define this idea.

Definition 5.17. A cipher system is said to have *perfect secrecy* if

$$I(M^n; C^n) = 0. \tag{5.32}$$

The definition means that

$$\begin{aligned} & H(M^n) - H(M^n|C^n) = H(C^n) - H(C^n|M^n) = 0 \\ \Leftrightarrow\ & H(M^n) = H(M^n|C^n) \text{ and } H(C^n) = H(C^n|M^n). \end{aligned} \tag{5.33}$$

However, this is equivalent to the independence of M^n and C^n referred to in Theorem 5.13. A really interesting consequence of perfect secrecy persists in the estimation of the number of necessary keys to get perfect secrecy.

Theorem 5.18. *A cipher system with perfect secrecy must satisfy the inequality*

$$H(M^n) \leq H(K). \tag{5.34}$$

Proof.

$$H(M^n) \overset{(5.33)}{=} H(M^n|C^n) \overset{(5.31)}{\leq} H(K|C^n) \overset{(5.22)}{\leq} H(K). \qquad \square$$

Assuming equiprobable keys, perfect secrecy satisfies $H(M^n) \leq H(K) = \log_2(|\mathcal{K}|)$. Since

$$\begin{aligned} I(M^n; C^n) &= H(M^n) - H(M^n|C^n) \geq H(M^n) - H(K|C^n) \\ &\geq H(M^n) - H(K) = H(M^n) - \log_2(|\mathcal{K}|), \end{aligned}$$

a small number of keys enhances the mutual information between M^n and C^n. That is, more information about the plaintext is available.

Example 5.19. Let $(G, \star, e_\star)$ be a finite group of order $l = |G|$ and $M^n, C^n, K : \Omega \to G^n$ be random variables. The components K_i are considered to be independent and likely to be equally distributed. A cipher system satisfying

$$C_i = M_i \star K_i \quad \text{for all } i = 1, \ldots, n$$

is called a *group-operation cipher* following Massey (1988). Furthermore, the key should be independent from the choice of the plaintext, that is

$$p_K(k) = p_{K|M}(k|m).$$

Because $(G, \star, e_\star)$ is a group, each element has a unique inverse element. Firstly, let us look at the probability of outcome c,

$$\begin{aligned} p_{C^n}(c) = p_{M^n \star K}(c) &= \sum_{m \star k = c} p_{M^n, K}(m, k) \\ &= \sum_{m \star k = c} p_{K|M^n}(k|m) \cdot p_{M^n}(m) \\ &= \sum_{m \star k = c} p_K(k) \cdot p_{M^n}(m) = \frac{1}{l^n} \sum_k \sum_{m = c \star k^{-1}} p_{M^n}(m) \\ &= \frac{1}{l^n} \sum_m p_{M^n}(m) = \frac{1}{l^n}. \end{aligned}$$

Alternatively,

$$\begin{aligned} p_{C^n|M^n}(c|m) = p_{M^n \star K|M^n}(c|m) &= \sum_{m \star k = c} p_K(k) = \sum_{k = m^{-1} \star c} p_K(k) \\ &= p_K(m^{-1} \star c) = \frac{1}{l^n}. \end{aligned}$$

Together, $p_{C^n|M^n}(c|m) = p_{C^n}(c)$ and C^n and M^n are independent. Using Theorem 5.13, it follows $H(M^n) = H(M^n|C^n)$ and finally, $I(M^n; C^n) = 0$. A group-operation cipher generates perfect secrecy.

A cipher system possessing perfect secrecy is called a *one-time pad.* The first such system was introduced by Miller[8] in 1882 and rediscovered by Vernam[9] in 1917.

Perfect secrecy is a property of a ciphertext-only environment. A known-plaintext attack cancels this term of secrecy. Another point is that reusing a key is not advisable. Given the cipher system of Example 5.19, consider the use of a key k twice:

$$c_1 = m_1 \star k \text{ and } c_2 = m_2 \star k.$$

Now, we can compute

$$c_2 \star c_1^{-1} = (m_2 \star k) \star (m_1 \star k)^{-1} = (m_2 \star k) \star (k^{-1} \star m_1^{-1}) = m_2 \star m_1^{-1}.$$

By knowing the ciphertexts, there is some information about the plaintexts that thwarts the motto of no information referred to in Definition 5.17. This idea will be reintroduced in Section 8.4 when examining the public-key El-Gamal cipher system.

We should have a closer look at the key equivocation from (5.28). Remembering the chain rule (5.24), we can observe that

$$\begin{aligned} H(K, M^n, C^n) &\overset{(5.24)}{=} H(K) + H(M^n|K) + H(C^n|K, M^n) \\ &\overset{(5.24)}{=} H(K, M^n) + H(C^n|K, M^n). \end{aligned}$$

Using Equation (5.30), $H(C^n|K, M^n) = 0$, and assuming the independence of the key and plaintext, it follows

$$H(K, M^n, C^n) \overset{(5.30)}{=} H(K, M^n) = H(K) + H(M^n). \tag{5.35}$$

Exchanging the parts of C^n and M^n, we determine

$$H(K, M^n, C^n) \overset{(5.24)}{=} H(K, C^n) + H(M^n|K, C^n) \overset{(5.29)}{=} H(K, C^n). \tag{5.36}$$

Together, the rule for the key equivocation is

$$\begin{aligned} H(K|C^n) &\overset{(5.24)}{=} H(K, C^n) - H(C^n) \\ &\overset{(5.36)}{=} H(K, M^n, C^n) - H(C^n) \\ &\overset{(5.35)}{=} H(K) + H(M^n) - H(C^n). \end{aligned}$$

[8]Frank Miller (1842–1925).
[9]Gilbert S. Vernam (1890–1960).

Proposition 5.20. *A cipher system ensuring independency of the key and plaintext fulfills the equality*

$$H(K|C^n) = H(K) + H(M^n) - H(C^n). \tag{5.37}$$

By exploiting a brute-force attack in Section 2.6, we introduced a spurious key, which means that there is at least one key besides the sought key yielding a meaningful decryption of a ciphertext. Let c be a string of length n, i.e., $c \in \mathcal{C}^n$. The set

$$K(c) := \{k \in \mathcal{K};\text{ there is an } x \in \operatorname{supp}(\mathbb{P}_{P^n}) : e_k(x) = c\}$$

is the set of all possible keys for c mapping a meaningful plaintext to c. It contains at least one key, namely the correct key. All other $|K(c)| - 1$ keys of $K(c)$ are spurious keys. Thus, we can interpret $K(c)$ as being the support of the conditional probability of K, given $C^n = c$,

$$K(c) = \operatorname{supp}(\mathbb{P}_{K|C^n}(\cdot|c)). \tag{5.38}$$

Consider the random variable $S : \mathcal{C}^n \to \mathbb{N}$, $S(c) = |K(c)| - 1$. We can compute the average number of spurious keys as

$$\begin{aligned}
\bar{s}_n := \mathbb{E}[S] &= \sum_{y\in\mathcal{C}^n} p_{C^n}(c)\cdot(|K(c)| - 1)\\
&= \sum_{c\in\mathcal{C}^n} p_{C^n}(c)\cdot|K(c)| - \sum_{c\in\mathcal{C}^n} p_{C^n}(c) &(5.39)\\
&= \sum_{c\in\mathcal{C}^n} p_{C^n}(c)\cdot|K(c)| - 1. &(5.40)
\end{aligned}$$

Using the IT-inequality from Theorem 5.4, we can majorize the key equivocation by

$$\begin{aligned}
H(K|C^n) &\overset{(5.20)}{=} \sum_{c\in\operatorname{supp}(\mathbb{P}_{C^n})} p_{C^n}(c) H(K|\{C^n = c\})\\
&\leq \sum_{c\in\operatorname{supp}(\mathbb{P}_{C^n})} p_{C^n}(c)\cdot\log_2(|\operatorname{supp}(\mathbb{P}_{K|C^n}(\cdot|c))|)\\
&\overset{(5.38)}{=} \sum_{c\in\operatorname{supp}(\mathbb{P}_{C^n})} p_{C^n}(c)\cdot\log_2(|K(c)|)
\end{aligned}$$

$$\overset{(5.16)}{\leq} \sum_{c \in \text{supp}(\mathbb{P}_{C^n})} p_{C^n}(c)(|K(c)| - 1) \cdot \log_2(e)$$

$$\overset{(5.40)}{=} \bar{s}_n \cdot \log_2(e). \tag{5.41}$$

Next, consider a language $\mathcal{L}$ over an alphabet $\mathcal{P}$. Following (Hellman, 1977) and (Stinson, 2005) the information rate of strings from $\mathcal{P}^n$ is an n-average entropy per symbol,

$$H_{\mathcal{L},n} := \frac{H(M^n)}{n}.$$

If n increases, the entropy per character decreases, since the count of meaningful messages of length n divided by length decreases. The entropy of $\mathcal{L}$ per symbol is the amount of information per element for data of infinite length defined by Cover.[10] Due to Takahira,[11] we can estimate this rate using an encoding rate. A sequence of size n can be compressed by a universal compressor like the PPM (Prediction by Partial Match[12]). Such a compression divided by n never reaches the information rate, but it is an upper limit. By considering a large text corpus (we took different samples from subsequent linked Wikipedia texts, starting at a single article each with different text orders), we can estimate the entropy rate in bits per symbol. Figure 5.2 shows estimations for two different corpora from Wikipedia.

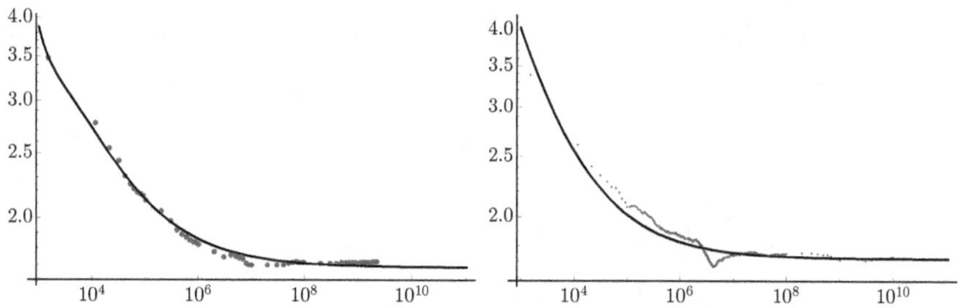

Figure 5.2 Extrapolation for the entropy of spoken English in bits per symbol with added raw data of one single run.

[10]See (Cover and Thomas, 2006).
[11]See (Takahira *et al.*, 2016).
[12]See (Cleary and Witten, 1984).

Thus, the estimation for spoken English is approximately

$$H_{\mathcal{L}} := \lim_{n\to\infty} H_{\mathcal{L},n} = 1.7 \in (1,2).$$

If all characters are equally likely, then the maximum amount of information bits is called the absolute information rate and is given by the maximum entropy of the alphabet,

$$G := \log_2(|\mathcal{P}|), i.e. \log_2(|\Sigma_{\text{Lat}}|) = 4.7.$$

There are $2^{G\cdot n}$ possible strings. The redundancy of a language is defined by

$$R := G - H_{\mathcal{L}}.$$

If $H_{\mathcal{L}} = 1.5$ and $\mathcal{P} = \Sigma_{\text{Lat}}$, we obtain $R = 4.7 - 1.7 = 3.0$. Consequently, the relative redundancy

$$R_{\mathcal{L}} := \frac{R}{G} = 1 - \frac{H_{\mathcal{L}}}{\log_2(|\mathcal{P}|)}$$

here is about 0.64. Theoretically, we want to consider how many ciphertexts it takes to recover the key. For a large n we estimate

$$H(M^n) \approx n \cdot H_{\mathcal{L}} = n(1 - R_{\mathcal{L}}) \log_2(|\mathcal{P}|).$$

In our approach, we assume a string length of n for both plaintexts and ciphertexts. In extension, we adopt $|\mathcal{P}^n| = |\mathcal{C}^n|$. Thus,

$$H(C^n) \leq n \cdot \log_2(|\mathcal{C}|) = n \cdot \log_2(|\mathcal{P}|). \tag{5.42}$$

Next, we minorize the key equivocation by

$$\begin{aligned} H(K|C^n) &\overset{(5.37)}{=} H(K) + H(M^n) - H(C^n) \\ &\overset{(5.42)}{\geq} H(K) + n(1 - R_{\mathcal{L}}) \log_2(|\mathcal{P}|) - n \log_2(|\mathcal{P}|) \\ &= H(K) - n \cdot R_{\mathcal{L}} \log_2(|\mathcal{P}|). \end{aligned} \tag{5.43}$$

Equations (5.41) and (5.43), together with $H(K) = \log_2(|K|)$, enable the estimation

$$\begin{aligned} \bar{s}_n \cdot \log_2(e) &\overset{(5.41)}{\geq} H(K|\mathcal{C}^n) \overset{(5.43)}{\geq} \log_2(|K|) - n \cdot R_{\mathcal{L}} \log_2(|\mathcal{P}|) \\ \Leftrightarrow \bar{s}_n &\geq \log_2(|K|) - n \cdot R_{\mathcal{L}} \log_2(|\mathcal{P}|). \end{aligned} \tag{5.44}$$

If the average number of spurious keys is zero, we can determine the used key uniquely. However, this does not mean that we have any algorithm to break the cipher system. It merely is an indication of how many symbols of ciphertext are needed to break the system. Therefore, we solve the last equation for n, assuming $\bar{s}_n = 0$, $|\mathcal{P}| > 1$ and $R_{\mathcal{L}} \neq 0$:

$$n \geq \frac{\log_2(|K|)}{R_{\mathcal{L}} \log_2(|\mathcal{P}|)} = \frac{\log_2(|K|)}{R}.$$

Example 5.21. Let $\mathcal{P} = \Sigma_{\text{Lat}}$. A permutation cipher with block size $t = 1$ has $|S(\Sigma_{\text{Lat}})| = 26!$ different keys. Therefore, we have to capture at least

$$n_0 = \left\lceil \frac{\log(26!)}{0.64 \cdot \log(26)} \right\rceil = 30$$

letters of ciphertext. If the block size is $t = 2$, the number of ciphertexts increases to

$$n_0 = \left\lceil \frac{\log((26^2)!)}{0.64 \cdot \log(26)} \right\rceil = 1791.$$

We get a linear decrease of the average number of spurious keys as a function of n relating to Equation (5.44).

5.3 Strict Avalanche Criteria

Diffusion means that the statistical structure of the plaintext is scattered into long-range statistics of the ciphertext. This is achieved by each plaintext digit affecting the value of as many ciphertext digits as possible; generally, this is equivalent to each ciphertext digit being affected by many plaintext digits.

Example 5.22 (Vigenère and Hill). Let us view Example 4.24 again. The plaintext

SECURITYISTHEMAINGOALOFCRYPTOGRAPHY

gets encrypted by the Vigenère cipher to

EEVBJUTRPKFHXTSUNZVSXOYJJKPMVYDAIOQ

using the key MATHS. If we change some character in the plaintext, i.e., U→I, we obtain

EEV[P]JUTRPKFHXTSUNZVSXOYJJKPMVYDAIOQ.

This is just a single change in the ciphertext and provides no diffusion. The Hill cipher can do it a bit more. The key AFFINEBLOCKCIPHERSCANDOIT used here will transform the plaintext into

VWZIDTVKXTVJAFEZVAZBUTPMWWIYTRBPROH.

The same change in the plaintext results in

[DKBKL]TVKXTVJAFEZVAZBUTPMWWIYTRBPROH,

and the whole first block has been changed.

Confusion seeks to make the relationship between the statistics of the ciphertext and the value of the encryption key as complex as possible, to counteract attempts to discover the key. This means that each character of the ciphertext should depend on as many possible characters of the key.

Example 5.23. Example 5.22 shows the impact of a letter change using the Vigenère and Hill cipher. We look at a change of one key letter. Again,

SECURITYISTHEMAINGOALOFCRYPTOGRAPHY

is encrypted to

EEVBJUTRPKFHXTSUNZVSXOYJJKPMVYDAIOQ

using the key MATHS. If we change some character in the key, i.e., A→O, we get

E[S]VBJU[H]RPKF[V]XTSU[B]ZVSX[C]YJJK[D]MVYD[O]IOQ.

This is a single change in each block of the ciphertext and provides some weak confusion. The Hill cipher instead transforms the plaintext into

VWZIDTVKXTVJAFEZVAZBUTPMWWIYTRBPROH.

Changing the key to AFFINEBL**A**CKCIPHERSCANDOIT (O→A) results in

V[C]ZIDT[N]KXTV[X]AFEZ[H]AZBU[R]PMWW[U]YTRB[V]ROH

and a very similar effect, according to the Vigenère cipher, can be observed.

Since a character of the ciphertext in a Hill cipher depends on m key characters and a whole block depends on a single plaintext character, it is interesting to try to spread the block characters on the whole ciphertext. This can be done by a subsequent transposition over the total block size. Each character of one block gets spread over all the other blocks. Afterwards, a reapplication of the Hill cipher can be done, and so on.

Example 5.24. The following transposition of block size $t = 35$,

$$\pi = (1\ 34\ 15\ 24\ 27\ 3\ 18\ 33\ 23\ 35\ 7\ 20\ 17\ 8\ 12\ 14\ 32\ 31\ 5\ 2\ 26\ 11\ 22)$$
$$(4\ 10\ 30\ 13\ 6\ 28\ 29\ 21\ 9)(19\ 25),$$

works as follows: inside each bracket, the position of the letters are changed to the successor position, i.e., a "V" at position 1 is moved to position 34. An "O" at position 34 is moved to position 15 and so on until there is a cyclic ending. This transposition is applied to the ciphertext and then to the changed ciphertext,

VWZID TVKXTVJAFEZVAZBUTPMWWIYTRBPROH, and
DKBKL TVKXTVJAFEZVAZBUTPMWWIYTRBPROH,

from Example 5.22, resulting in

TDIXBAHVUIWKRJOZBZWVTVREZWMTYTPFAVP, and
TLIXBAHVUKWKRJOZBBWVTVREZKMTYTPFADP.

Reapplication of the Hill cipher yields

SXOFZOOSRDZXLKIHYTNFBAFTPWHFGXYZIFN, and
GFELXOSGRPZXLKIRUJXHBAFTPWLPKXKHYVZ.

Nearly the whole ciphertext gets affected.

Such a proceeding was recommended by Shannon[13] who called it a *product cipher*. A *substitution-permutation network* is a product cipher composed over several rounds, each involving substitutions and permutations. Since affine block ciphers are weak (as shown in Section 4.2.3), a substitution is a non-linear transformation today. If an internal invariant function is used at each round, this function is called a *round function*.

Based on binary alphabets, a cryptographical mapping f can be assessed to yield diffusion or confusion according to Webster and Tavares (1986). Let $m_r \in \mathbb{Z}_2^n$ be any message and $k \in \mathbb{Z}_2^u$ be any key. Define $q_i = m_r \oplus 2^i$, $i = 1, \ldots, n$, the message based on m_r, which is changed at exactly one bit position. Next, we look at $d_i^r = f(m_r, k) \oplus f(q_i, k) \in \mathbb{Z}_2^v$, which indicates the bitwise differences of the two outputs of f. Let d_{ij}^r be the jth bit of d_i^r, $j = 1, \ldots, v$, and $i = 1, \ldots, n$. The number $v_j^r = \frac{1}{n} \sum_{i=1}^{n} d_{ij}^r$ yields the mean changes of the jth bit upon the flipped bits. By repeating this with changing input messages up to R times, we can calculate an overall mean change of the jth bit upon the flipped bits, $v_j = \frac{1}{R} \sum_{r=1}^{R} v_j^r$. In the

[13]See (Shannon, 1949).

same way, we can fix the input message and run through different keys and their bitwise disturbance.

Definition 5.25 (SMAC and SKAC). Let $f : \mathbb{Z}_2^n \times \mathbb{Z}_2^u \to \mathbb{Z}_2^v$ be a cryptographical mapping. f is said to be message-complete if $d_{ij}^r \neq 0$ for all message bit flips of index $i = 1, \ldots, n$ and all bits of index $j = 1, \ldots, v$, and fulfills the *strict message avalanche criterion* (SMAC) if $v_j = \frac{1}{2}$ for all bits of index $j = 1, \ldots, v$. Similarly, f is said to be key-complete if $d_{ij}^r \neq 0$ for all key bit flips of index $i = 1, \ldots, u$ and all bits of index $j = 1, \ldots, v$, and fulfills the *strict key avalanche criterion* (SKAC) if $v_j = \frac{1}{2}$ for all bits of index $j = 1, \ldots, v$.

In the following chapters, we investigate the criteria of Definition 5.25.

Chapter 6

Modern Private-Key Ciphering

Note 6.1. In this chapter, the requirements are:

- knowing the idea of perfect secrecy, see Section 5.2,
- being familiar with basics of number theory, see Section 1.1, and
- being familiar with extended basics of algebra, see Sections 3.1 and 3.2.

Selected literature: See (Dworkin *et al.*, 2001; Hoffstein *et al.*, 2008; Holden, 2017; Lidl and Niederreiter, 1996).

Modern digital cryptography seeks to obscure relationships between the input block and output block. Otherwise, a decryption without circumstance will appear, as shown in Example 2.26. Thus, we need to formalize the term of security. A cipher system $(\mathcal{P}, \mathcal{C}, \mathcal{K}, \mathcal{E}, \mathcal{D})$ is to be broken if everything is known about the used cipher system except the encryption key $k \in \mathcal{K}$ and if there exists the possibility of reconstructing the corresponding plaintext from any ciphertext. If the cipher systems' keyspace $\mathcal{K}$ is not large enough, an exhaustive search for the key can be performed. In fact, a brute-force attack (cf. page 62) against modern cipher systems is possible, but the costs are too high, even if an attacker has an unbounded amount of computation. We want to discuss secure cipher systems as a matter of confidentiality, as one of the listed security goals of a communication system within the scope of Convention 2.15. In a private-key system, any plaintext $m \in \mathcal{P}$ gets transmitted from a sender over a

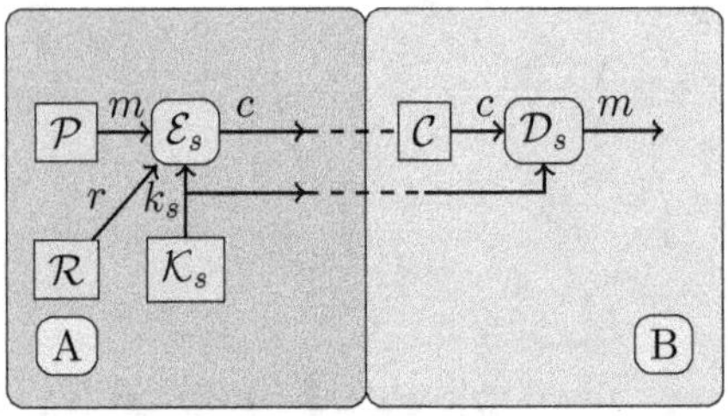

Figure 6.1 Private-key cipher system with randomizer.

possibly insecure channel after an encrypting process supported by a secret key $k_s \in \mathcal{K}_s$. The key itself has to be carried over a secure channel protected from an eavesdropper. In extension to Figure 4.1 and by using the fact that homophonic substitution is complicating the attack on the cipher, we introduce an extra module to the scheme of private-key cipher systems. A randomizer as suggested in (Massey, 1988) can generate a randomizing sequence to disguise statistical properties like those in the homophonic substitution in Section 2.4, as shown in Example 2.29. Figure 6.1 shows this context. The randomizer can also be integrated into the encryption part of the communication system directly. The encryption function maps the plaintext to the ciphertext using the key and randomizing sequence,

$$c = e_{k,r}(m).$$

Instead, the decryption should not require the randomizer and should only depend on the key,

$$m = d_k(c).$$

We note a randomized cipher system by $(\mathcal{P}, \mathcal{C}, \mathcal{K}, \mathcal{R}, \mathcal{E}, \mathcal{D})$. In 1949, Shannon published "Communication Theory of Secrecy Systems"[1] to answer the question of how much information of the plaintext is preserved in the ciphertext, which we examined in Chapter 5. For that purpose, he used concepts of probability to formalize the question. From now on, we regard p, r, k_s and c as realizations of

[1]See (Shannon, 1949).

stochastic independent random variables P, C, K and R due to the letters in Figure 6.1.

Example 6.2 (One-time-pad). Consider the randomized cipher system $(\mathbb{Z}_n, \mathbb{Z}_n, \mathbb{Z}_n, \mathbb{Z}_n, \mathcal{E}_s, \mathcal{D}_s)$ in which

$$\mathcal{E}_s = \{e_{k,r} : \mathbb{Z}_n \to \mathbb{Z}_n;\ e_{k,r}(m) = m +_n (k +_n r)\}, \text{ and}$$
$$\mathcal{D}_s = \{d_{k,r} : \mathbb{Z}_n \to \mathbb{Z}_n;\ d_{k,r}(c) = c +_n ((-k) +_n (-r))\}.$$

We assume r to be chosen due to uniform distribution on $\mathbb{Z}_n$ and $k \in \mathbb{Z}_n$ can be a fixed secret key. We have a cipher system because

$$d_{k,r}(e_{k,r}(m)) = m +_n (k +_n r) +_n ((-k) +_n (-r)) = m.$$

This system operates on the finite group $(\mathbb{Z}_n, +_n, 0)$ and enables perfect secrecy, according to Example 5.19.

6.1 Feistel Ciphers

A *Feistel cipher*, developed by Horst Feistel[2] at IBM, is a very common class of symmetric block ciphers that satisfies the ciphering functionality. The encryption and decryption processes are nearly the same. It works with *rounds*, as suggested by Shannon, at a product cipher, cf. Section 5.3, meaning that an internal function called a *round function* is used more than once, like an iterative cycle. In doing so, an even-numbered bitstream m of length $2q$ is mapped to a bitstream c of the same length within n rounds. m is first divided into two parts, $m = L_0||R_0$, of the same length. During the ith round, a bitstream $L_i||R_i$ is composed of $L_{i-1}||R_{i-1}$ by

$$\begin{aligned} L_i &= R_{i-1}, \text{ and} \\ R_i &= f_{k_i}(R_{i-1}) \oplus L_{i-1}, \end{aligned} \tag{6.1}$$

in which the round function f_{k_i} is a mapping $f_{k_i} : \mathbb{F}_2^q \to \mathbb{F}_2^q$. The key normally changes in each round. With it, we get a *keystream*. We obtain another round key with each round. To get back c from m,

[2]Horst Feistel (1915–1990).

the rounds have to be reversed. This means

$$\begin{aligned} R_{i-1} &= L_i, \text{ and} \\ L_{i-1} &= f_{k_i}(R_{i-1}) \oplus R_i = f_{k_i}(L_i) \oplus R_i. \end{aligned} \tag{6.2}$$

The encryption and decryption processes use the same function. No inversion has to be done. Hence, the round function needs not be injective. The round function can itself consist of a substitution-permutation component.

Example 6.3. Consider the bitstream 1010011||1001001. We want to execute a Feistel cipher. To this end, we determine the block size $t = 2q = 14$ and the number of rounds $n = 6$. Let the round function be $f_{k_i}(x) := x \oplus k_i$ and $k_{i+1} := k_i \oplus (k_i + 1_2)$, $k_0 = 0$ be the keystream.

i	k_i	L_i	R_i
0	$0000000_{(2)}$	$1010011_{(2)}$	$1001001_{(2)}$
1	$0000001_{(2)}$	$1001001_{(2)}$	$0011011_{(2)}$
2	$0000011_{(2)}$	$0011011_{(2)}$	$1010001_{(2)}$
3	$0000111_{(2)}$	$1010001_{(2)}$	$1001101_{(2)}$
4	$0001111_{(2)}$	$1001101_{(2)}$	$0010011_{(2)}$
5	$0011111_{(2)}$	$0010011_{(2)}$	$1000001_{(2)}$
6	$0111111_{(2)}$	$1000001_{(2)}$	$1101101_{(2)}$

6.2 Data Encrypton Standard

Since 1977, the *Data Encrypton Standard* (DES) is one of the most known and used ciphers. A key bitstream of 56 bits is used, $\mathcal{K} = \mathbb{F}_2^{56}$, and a block size of 64 bits. Such a 64 bitstream

$$m = b_1 b_2 b_3 b_4 b_5 \cdots b_{63} b_{64}$$

gets encrypted to a bitstream of 64 bits, $\mathcal{P} = \mathcal{C} = \mathbb{F}_2^{64}$. The following lines show the algorithm of DES. The DES starts with an initial permutation of the input block.

$$\begin{aligned} &\mathrm{IP} : \mathbb{F}_2^{64} \to \mathbb{F}_2^{64}, \\ &\mathrm{IP}(b_1 b_2 b_3 b_4 b_5 \cdots b_{63} b_{64}) = b_{58} b_{50} b_{42} b_{34} b_{26} \cdots b_{15} b_7 =: \tilde{m}. \end{aligned}$$

We depict this permutation by a table with 4 rows and 16 columns, like a box.

Table 6.1 IP.

58	50	42	34	26	18	10	2	60	52	44	36	28	20	12	4
62	54	46	38	30	22	14	6	64	56	48	40	32	24	16	8
57	49	41	33	25	17	9	1	59	51	43	35	27	19	11	3
61	53	45	37	29	21	13	5	63	55	47	39	31	23	15	7

Table 6.2 IP^{-1}.

40	8	48	16	56	24	64	32	39	7	47	15	55	23	63	31
38	6	46	14	54	22	62	30	37	5	45	13	53	21	61	29
36	4	44	12	52	20	60	28	35	3	43	11	51	19	59	27
34	2	42	10	50	18	58	26	33	1	41	9	49	17	57	25

Next, it follows a Feistel cipher according to (6.1) with 16 rounds. The bitstream $\tilde{m}$ is divided into two bitstreams, $\tilde{m} = L_0||R_0$, $L_0, R_0 \in \mathbb{F}_2^{32}$ of 32 bits each. A round key $k_i \in \mathbb{F}_2^{48}$, $i = 1, \ldots, 16$, is necessary for each round, which is scheduled successively starting at $k \in \mathbb{F}_2^{56}$. During the term, the key k is enlarged by *parity bits*,

$$\text{Par} : \mathbb{F}_2^{56} \to \mathbb{F}_2^{64},$$

where a single bit is included after every seventh bit. This can be done by the even parity mode. If the number of the 1 bits is even, the parity bit gets zero, otherwise, it is one. However, this is just for controlling and does not impact the further encryption process. After that, a mapping

$$\text{PC}_1 : \mathbb{F}_2^{64} \to \mathbb{F}_2^{56}$$

is executed, which represents a change in bit positions.

Table 6.3 PC_1.

57	49	41	33	25	17	9	1	58	50	42	34	26	18
10	2	59	51	43	35	27	19	11	3	60	52	44	36
63	55	47	39	31	23	15	7	62	54	46	38	30	22
14	6	61	53	45	37	29	21	13	5	28	20	12	4

Table 6.4 PC_2.

14	17	11	24	1	5	3	28	15	6	21	10
23	19	12	4	26	8	16	7	27	20	13	2
41	52	31	37	47	55	30	40	51	45	33	48
44	49	39	56	34	53	46	42	50	36	29	32

Table 6.5 LS_i.

1	1	2	2	2	2	2	2	1	2	2	2	2	2	2	1

This is a permutation of the 56 key bits. The eight parity bits are discarded. The 56 bits are divided into two parts of 28 bits. Each of them gets mapped by a circular left shift

$$\text{LS}_i : \mathbb{F}_2^{28} \to \mathbb{F}_2^{28}, \ i = 1, \ldots, 16.$$

The shift size depends on the number of passed rounds. In the first two rounds, a 1-bit circular left shift is used, then six times a 2-bit circular left shift, and so on. After the circular left shift in the ith round, the round key k_i is generated by concatenating the two parts and executing the mapping

$$\mathrm{PC}_2 : \mathbb{F}_2^{56} \to \mathbb{F}_2^{48},$$

consisting of position changes. The bit numbers 9, 18, 22, 25, 35, 38, 43 and 54 are omitted. Together, the key k_i is generated by the mapping in Algorithm 6.1. The main items of the DES are the round functions $f_{k_i} : \mathbb{F}_2^{32} \to \mathbb{F}_2^{32}$. Firstly, the input bitstream R_{i-1} consisting of 32 bits is expanded to 48 bits by

$$E : \mathbb{F}_2^{32} \to \mathbb{F}_2^{48}$$

referred to in Table 6.6.

Algorithm 6.1: Key generation for the DES

Require: $k \in \mathbb{Z}_2^{56}$.
Ensure: Round key $k_i \in \mathbb{Z}_2^{48}$.
1: $k_i :=$
$$\left(\mathrm{PC}_2 \circ \begin{pmatrix}\mathrm{LS}_i \\ \mathrm{LS}_i\end{pmatrix} \circ \begin{pmatrix}\mathrm{LS}_{i-1} \\ \mathrm{LS}_{i-1}\end{pmatrix} \circ \cdots \circ \begin{pmatrix}\mathrm{LS}_1 \\ \mathrm{LS}_1\end{pmatrix} \circ \mathrm{PC}_1 \circ \mathrm{Par}\right)(k)$$
2: **return** k_i.

Table 6.6 E.

32	1	2	3	4	5	4	5	6	7	8	9
8	9	10	11	12	13	12	13	14	15	16	17
16	17	18	19	20	21	20	21	22	23	24	25
24	25	26	27	28	29	28	29	30	31	32	1

Table 6.7 P.

16	7	20	21	29	12	28	17	1	15	23	26	5	18	31	10
2	8	24	14	32	27	3	9	19	13	30	6	22	11	4	25

This is not a permutation because some bit numbers in the first and last columns are doubled. The bits of position $4k$ are mapped to the positions $6k - 1 \bmod 32$ and $6k + 1 \bmod 32$. Similarly, the bits of position $4k+1$ are mapped to the positions $6k \bmod 32$ and $6k+2 \bmod 32$. The result is linked with the round key by XOR

$$\oplus_{f_{k_i}} : \mathbb{F}_2^{48} \times \mathbb{F}_2^{48} \to \mathbb{F}_2^{48},\ (a, k_i) \mapsto u = a \oplus k_i.$$

The bitstream is then divided into eight parts, $u = u_1||u_2||\cdots||u_8$, each of them containing six bits. A substitution box is executed on each part. The boxes $S_i : \mathbb{F}_2^6 \to \mathbb{F}_2^4$, $i = 1, \ldots, 8$,

Table 6.8 S_1.

14	4	13	1	2	15	11	8	3	10	6	12	5	9	0	7
0	15	7	4	14	2	13	1	10	6	12	11	9	5	3	8
4	1	14	8	13	6	2	11	15	12	9	7	3	10	5	0
15	12	8	2	4	9	1	7	5	11	3	14	10	0	6	13

Table 6.9 S_2.

15	1	8	14	6	11	3	4	9	7	2	13	12	0	5	10
3	13	4	7	15	2	8	14	12	0	1	10	6	9	11	5
0	14	7	11	10	4	13	1	5	8	12	6	9	3	2	15
13	8	10	1	3	15	4	2	11	6	7	12	0	5	14	9

Table 6.10 S_3.

10	0	9	14	6	3	15	5	1	13	12	7	11	4	2	8
13	7	0	9	3	4	6	10	2	8	5	14	12	11	15	1
13	6	4	9	8	15	3	0	11	1	2	12	5	10	14	7
1	10	13	0	6	9	8	7	4	15	14	3	11	5	2	12

Table 6.11 S_4.

7	13	14	3	0	6	9	10	1	2	8	5	11	12	4	15
13	8	11	5	6	15	0	3	4	7	2	12	1	10	14	9
10	6	9	0	12	11	7	13	15	1	3	14	5	2	8	4
3	15	0	6	10	1	13	8	9	4	5	11	12	7	2	14

Table 6.12 S_5.

2	12	4	1	7	10	11	6	8	5	3	15	13	0	14	9
14	11	2	12	4	7	13	1	5	0	15	10	3	9	8	6
4	2	1	11	10	13	7	8	15	9	12	5	6	3	0	14
11	8	12	7	1	14	2	13	6	15	0	9	10	4	5	3

Table 6.13 S_6.

12	1	10	15	9	2	6	8	0	13	3	4	14	7	5	11
10	15	4	2	7	12	9	5	6	1	13	14	0	11	3	8
9	14	15	5	2	8	12	3	7	0	4	10	1	13	11	6
4	3	2	12	9	5	15	10	11	14	1	7	6	0	8	13

Table 6.14 S_7.

4	11	2	14	15	0	8	13	3	12	9	7	5	10	6	1
13	0	11	7	4	9	1	10	14	3	5	12	2	15	8	6
1	4	11	13	12	3	7	14	10	15	6	8	0	5	9	2
6	11	13	8	1	4	10	7	9	5	0	15	14	2	3	12

Table 6.15 S_8.

13	2	8	4	6	15	11	1	10	9	3	14	5	0	12	7
1	15	13	8	10	3	7	4	12	5	6	11	0	14	9	2
7	11	4	1	9	12	14	2	0	6	10	13	15	3	5	8
2	1	14	7	4	10	8	13	15	12	9	0	3	5	6	11

have to be read in the following way: $S_i(b_1b_2b_3b_4b_5b_6)$ is the binary string that arises from the boxes' row $b_1b_6 \in \{0,1,2,3\}$ and column $b_2b_3b_4b_5 \in \{0,1,\ldots,15\}$. We have to start counting at zero. For instance, the bitstream $u_7 = 110010$ gets $S_7(u_7) = 1111$, since there is the number 15 in the third row $(10_{(2)} = 2)$ and tenth column

$(1001_{(2)} = 9)$ of S_7. Together, the mapping is

$$S : \mathbb{F}_2^{48} \to \mathbb{F}_2^{32},\ u \mapsto S(u) = \begin{pmatrix} S_1(u_1) \\ S_2(u_2) \\ S_3(u_3) \\ S_4(u_4) \\ S_5(u_5) \\ S_6(u_6) \\ S_7(u_7) \\ S_8(u_8) \end{pmatrix}.$$

A permutation

$$P : \mathbb{F}_2^{32} \to \mathbb{F}_2^{32},$$

consisting of the position changes referring to Table 6.7 follows. Overall, we have the Feistel scheme

$$L_i = R_{i-1} \text{ and } R_i = (P \circ S \circ \oplus_{f_{k_i}} \circ E)(R_{i-1}) \oplus L_{i-1}.$$

After 16 rounds, the two parts L_{16} and R_{16} are concatenated and swapped by the permutation $T : F_2^{64} \to \mathbb{F}_2^{64}$.

Table 6.16 T.

33	34	35	36	37	38	39	40	41	42	43	44	45	46	47	48
49	50	51	52	53	54	55	56	57	58	59	60	61	62	63	64
1	2	3	4	5	6	7	8	9	10	11	12	13	14	15	16
17	18	19	20	21	22	23	24	25	26	27	28	29	30	31	32

The operation ends by the permutation IP^{-1} referring to Table 6.2, which is the inverse permutation of IP.

Algorithm 6.2: Feistel rounds of the DES

Require: Key $k \in \mathbb{Z}_2^{56}$, plaintext $m \in \mathbb{Z}_2^{64}$.
Ensure: Encrypted plaintext, $c = e_k(m)$.

$L_0||R_0 := \text{IP}(m)$.

16 Feistel rounds:

$L_i := R_{i-1},\ R_i := L_{i-1} \oplus \big((\text{P} \circ \text{S} \circ \oplus_{f_{k_i}} \circ \text{E})(R_{i-1})\big)$

$c := \left(\text{IP}^{-1} \circ \text{T}\right)(L_{16}||R_{16})$

return c.

Security of the DES

The DES fulfills both the strict message avalanche criterion and the strict key avalanche criterion from Definition 5.25.

Example 6.4. Based on a 64-bit block size, the resulting binary sequences show a 50% change probability. This happens in both situations: a fixed key with bit flips in the message, and a fixed message with bit flips in the key. The data shown here is won empirically based on 2^{15} randomly chosen messages and keys.

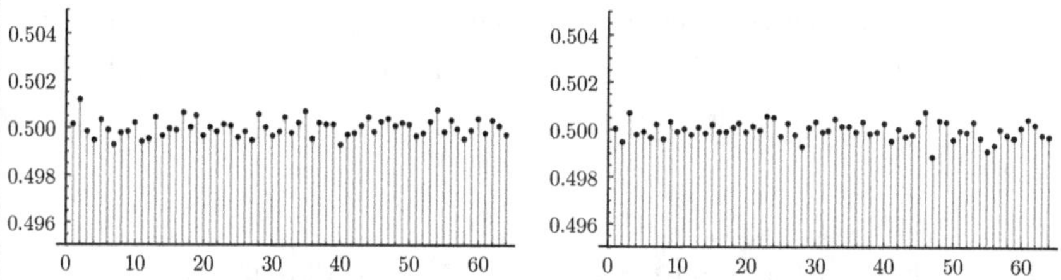

Figure 6.2 Strict avalanche criterion for the DES: empirical probabilities of bit changes of the 64 output bits resulting from bit flips in the message (left) with a fixed key or in the key (right) with a fixed message.

According to Holden,[3] a group has built a scalable machine in the late 90s that takes about 56 hours to crack a 56-bit key of the DES. Scalable means that u such machines reduce the time to crack by the factor $\frac{1}{u}$. The author states that the DES is no longer secure after this time. However, there is a possibility to preserve its concept, which can be done using the DES more than once. The key changes with each use. Two serial executions of the DES are not suitable. If an attacker starts a known-plaintext attack knowing a pair (m, c), the encryption

$$c = e_{k_2}(e_{k_1}(m))$$

can be broken by a *meet in the middle attack*. Firstly, it is

$$e_{k_1}(m) = x := d_{k_2}(c).$$

[3]See (Holden, 2017).

Next, a table has to be established for that purpose, which contains all the possible combinations of the keys k_1 and k_2. A candidate for the key pair of length 112 bits is found if the values $e_{k_1}(p)$ and $d_{k_2}(c)$ agree. Because of the block size, there are 2^{64} different keys and 2^{64} different possible results x. This causes an average of 2^{48} hits. A second pair $(\tilde{m}, \tilde{c})$ then almost certainly finds the sought after key. Another version of a practical DES is the *Triple-DES*

$$c = e_{k3}(d_{k2}(e_{k1}(m))).$$

After encrypting m, the result is "decrypted" by the second key. The step finishes by encrypting again. A disadvantage of this kind of encryption is the triple amount effort of computation. However, this version is still deemed to be secure, as asserted in (Hoffstein *et al.*, 2008).

6.3 AES: Substitution–Permutation Networks

Since the DES is no longer considered safe, the National Institute of Standards and Technology (NIST) called for a competition for a successor in 1997. A special case of the Rijndal-cipher by Rijmen and Daemen[4] won and became the *Advanced Encryption Standard* (AES).[5] The key concept is based on the basic concepts of substitution and permutation running over certain rounds. Its mathematics is based on special finite fields.

6.3.1 *Construction of finite fields*

The elements of a finite field can be perceived as polynomials over the field $(\mathbb{Z}_p, +_p, \cdot_p, 0, 1)$ at which p has to be prime due to Corollary 3.87. The proof of this result goes beyond the scope of this book. However, we will explore the basic ideas. First of all, we define a polynomial.

[4]Vincent Rijmen, born 1970, and Joan Daemen, born 1965.

[5]The original specification can be found in (Dworkin *et al.*, 2001).

Definition 6.5. Let $(\mathbb{F}, +, \cdot, 0, 1)$ be a field. A *polynomial* in X with coefficients $a_i \in \mathbb{F}$, $i = 1, \ldots, n$ and $n < \infty$, is denoted by

$$P(X) = a_0 + a_1 \cdot X + \cdots + a_{n-1} \cdot X^{n-1} + a_n \cdot X^n.$$

The *degree* of a non-zero polynomial is the exponent of the highest power of X that appears. The corresponding coefficient is called the *leading coefficient.* If $a_i = 0$ for all $i \in \mathbb{N}$, the degree is set to $-\infty$. The set of all polynomials in X over $\mathbb{F}$ is denoted by $\mathbb{F}[X]$.

X can be substituted by any $x \in \mathbb{F}$. We then evaluate the polynomial and $P(x) \in \mathbb{F}$ is the value of $P(X)$ at x:

$$\begin{aligned}\psi_x : \mathbb{F}[X] \to \mathbb{F},\ P(x) := \psi_x(P(X)) &:= a_0 + a_1 \cdot x \\ &+ \cdots + a_{n-1} \cdot x^{n-1} + a_n \cdot x^n.\end{aligned}$$

If $P(x) = 0$, then x is a *zero* of $P(X)$.

Example 6.6.

- $\mathbb{F} = \mathbb{R}$, $P(X) = X^8 + X^4 + X - 1 \in \mathbb{R}(X)$, $x = -1$. We abbreviate the degree of $P(X)$ by $\deg(P) = 8$ and evaluate $P(x) = 1 + 1 - 1 - 1 = 0$, $x = -1$ is a zero.
- Let p be prime. From Theorem 3.50, $(\mathbb{Z}_p, +_p, \cdot_p, 0, 1)$ is a field. $P(X) = X^8 + X^4 + X^3 + X + 1 \bmod p \in \mathbb{Z}_p[X]$, $P(1) = 5 \bmod p$.
- $x^{\mathbb{F}} := x + 0 \cdot X + 0 \cdot X^2 + \cdots \in \mathbb{F}$ for all $x \in \mathbb{F}$ is a constant polynomial, $x^{\mathbb{F}} \in \mathbb{F}[X]$.

Given $n \geq m$ and two polynomials P and Q over $\mathbb{F}$, we can define an addition, a scalar multiplication and a multiplication on $\mathbb{F}[X]$. It is necessary to fill up the missing coefficients of Q with zeros,

$$P(X) = a_n \cdot X^n + \cdots + a_1 \cdot X + a_0, \text{ and}$$

$$Q(X) = b_n \cdot X^n + \cdots + b_1 \cdot X + b_0,\ b_{m+1} = \cdots = b_n = 0.$$

Then, we define

$$+^{\mathbb{F}} : \mathbb{F}[X] \times \mathbb{F}[X] \to \mathbb{F}[X],$$

$$(P +^{\mathbb{F}} Q)(X) := (a_n + b_n) \cdot X^n + \cdots + (a_1 + b_1) \cdot X + (a_0 + b_0), \quad (6.3)$$

$$\star^{\mathbb{F}} : \mathbb{F} \times \mathbb{F}[X] \to \mathbb{F}[X],$$

$$(\lambda \star^{\mathbb{F}} P)(X) := (\lambda \cdot a_n) \cdot X^n + \cdots + (\lambda \cdot a_1) \cdot X + (\lambda \cdot a_0), \text{ and} \quad (6.4)$$

$$\cdot^{\mathbb{F}} : \mathbb{F}[X] \times \mathbb{F}[X] \to \mathbb{F}[X],$$

$$P(X) \cdot^{\mathbb{F}} Q(X) := (P \cdot^{\mathbb{F}} Q)(X) := c_{n+m} \cdot x^{n+m} + \cdots + c_1 \cdot x + c_0, \quad (6.5)$$

in which

$$c_k := \sum_{i=0}^{k} a_i \cdot b_{k-i} = \sum_{i+j=k} a_i \cdot b_j,\ 0 \leq k \leq n+m.$$

Example 6.7. It applies $X^m \cdot^{\mathbb{F}} X^n = X^{m+n}$ since

$$c_k = \sum_{i+j=k} a_i \cdot b_j = \begin{cases} 1, & k = m+n, i = m, j = n, \\ 0, & \text{all other cases.} \end{cases}$$

Let $P(X) = X^3 + X^2 + 1,\ Q(X) = 2X^2 + 1 \in \mathbb{R}[X]$.

$$\begin{aligned} (P +^{\mathbb{R}} Q)(X) &= X^3 + (1+2)X^2 + (1+1) = X^3 + 3X^2 + 2, \text{ and} \\ (P \cdot^{\mathbb{R}} Q)(X) &= 2X^5 + 2X^4 + 2X^2 + X^3 + X^2 + 1 \\ &= 2X^5 + 2X^4 + X^3 + 3X^2 + 1. \end{aligned}$$

$c_2 = \sum_{i=0}^{2} a_i b_{k-i} = a_0 b_2 + a_1 b_1 + a_2 b_0 = 1 \cdot 2 + 0 \cdot 0 + 1 \cdot 1 = 3.$

Remember the evaluation function ψ_x. It applies

$$\psi_x(P(X) +^{\mathbb{F}} Q(X)) \overset{(6.3)}{=} \psi_x(P(X)) + \psi_x(Q(X)), \text{ and}$$

$$\begin{aligned} \psi_x(P(X) \cdot^{\mathbb{F}} Q(X)) &\overset{(6.5)}{=} \sum_{k=0}^{n+m} c_k \cdot x^k = \sum_{k=0}^{n+m} \left(\sum_{i+j=k} a_i \cdot b_j \right) \cdot x^k \\ &= \sum_{k=0}^{n+m} \sum_{i+j=k} a_i \cdot x^i \cdot b_j \cdot x^j \end{aligned}$$

$$= \sum_{i=0}^{n} a_i \cdot x^i \cdot \sum_{j=0}^{m} b_j \cdot x^j$$
$$= \psi_x(P(X)) \cdot \psi_x(Q(X)).$$

Corollary 6.8. *The evaluation function ψ_x is a homomorphism.*

We briefly examine the degree of a polynomial in some situations. For scalar multiplication the degree does not change if $\lambda \neq 0$,

$$\deg(P) = n, \lambda \neq 0 \Rightarrow \deg(\lambda \star^{\mathbb{F}} P) = n. \tag{6.6}$$

Similarly, the degree remains unchanged for addition if the leading coefficient a_n is not equal to $-b_n$,

$$\deg(P) = n = \deg(Q),\ a_n \neq -b_n \Rightarrow \deg(P +^{\mathbb{F}} Q) = n. \tag{6.7}$$

Remark 6.9. So far, it is possible to define polynomials based on commutative rings with identity without limitation. However, the following results depend on the field structure in particular.

If $P(X) \neq 0^{\mathbb{F}} \neq Q(X)$, $\deg(P) = m$ and $\deg(Q) = n$, the degree of $(P \cdot^{\mathbb{F}} Q)(X)$ is given by

$$m, n \geq 0 \Rightarrow \deg(P \cdot^{\mathbb{F}} Q) = \deg(P) + \deg(Q) = m + n, \tag{6.8}$$

because

$$c_{m+n} = a_0 \cdot \underbrace{b_{m+n}}_{0} + \cdots + a_{m-1} \cdot \underbrace{b_{n+1}}_{0} + \underbrace{a_m \cdot b_n}_{\neq 0} + \underbrace{a_{m+1}}_{0}$$
$$\cdot b_{n-1} + \cdots + \underbrace{a_{m+n}}_{0} \cdot b_0.$$

Since $P(X) \neq 0^{\mathbb{F}} \Leftrightarrow \deg(P) \geq 0$, it follows

$$(P \cdot^{\mathbb{F}} Q)(X) = 0^{\mathbb{F}} \overset{(6.8)}{\Rightarrow} \deg(P) = -\infty \text{ or } \deg(Q) = -\infty$$
$$\Rightarrow P(X) = 0^{\mathbb{F}} \text{ or } Q(X) = 0^{\mathbb{F}}.$$

Hence, there are no zero divisors. If $Q(X) = 0^{\mathbb{F}}$, then $(P +^{\mathbb{F}} Q)(X) = P(X)$, because $a_k + b_k = a_k$. In the same way, if $Q(X) = 1^{\mathbb{F}}$, we get $(P \cdot^{\mathbb{F}} Q)(X) = P(X)$ because $c_k = 1^{\mathbb{F}} \cdot b_k = b_k$. Both polynomials are identity elements with respect to each of their operations. By defining

$$-P(X) := \sum_{i=1}^{n}(-a_i)X^i = ((-1)^{\mathbb{F}} \cdot^{\mathbb{F}} P)(X),$$

we note the following results that can be shown through laborious recalculation[6]:

- $(\mathbb{F}[X], +^{\mathbb{F}}, \star^{\mathbb{F}}, 0^{\mathbb{F}})$ is a vector space over $\mathbb{F}$,
- $(\mathbb{F}[X], +^{\mathbb{F}}, \cdot^{\mathbb{F}}, 0^{\mathbb{F}}, 1^{\mathbb{F}})$ is a domain of integrity,
- Field elements can be identified by constant polynomials, cf. Example 6.6.

Remark 6.10.

- Some of the elements of $\mathbb{F}[X]$ are unity elements, for example, $P(X), Q(X)$. Say, $P(X) \cdot^{\mathbb{F}} Q(X) = 1^{\mathbb{F}}$. We obtain

$$\begin{aligned} 0 &= \deg(1^{\mathbb{F}}) = \deg(P(X) \cdot^{\mathbb{F}} Q(X)) \\ &\overset{(6.8)}{=} \deg(P(X)) + \deg(Q(X)) \\ &\Rightarrow \deg(P(X)) = \deg(Q(X)) = 0 \Rightarrow P(X), Q(X) \in \mathbb{F}. \end{aligned} \tag{6.9}$$

- Since $(\mathbb{F}[X], +^{\mathbb{F}}, \cdot^{\mathbb{F}}, 0^{\mathbb{F}}, 1^{\mathbb{F}})$ is a domain of integrity, we can reduce by a polynomial:

$$\begin{aligned} &U(X) \cdot^{\mathbb{F}} P(X) = V(X) \cdot^{\mathbb{F}} P(X) \\ &\overset{(D1)}{\Rightarrow} (U(X) -^{\mathbb{F}} V(X)) \cdot^{\mathbb{F}} P(X) = 0^{\mathbb{F}} \Rightarrow U(X) = V(X). \end{aligned} \tag{6.10}$$

- Since $(\mathbb{F}[X], +^{\mathbb{F}}, \star^{\mathbb{F}}, 0^{\mathbb{F}})$ is a vector space over $\mathbb{F}$, there must be a basis $\mathcal{B}$. However, each polynomial is a linear combination of the polynomials X^i. Thus,

$$\mathcal{B} = \{1, X, X^2, \ldots\}.$$

[6]See (Lidl and Niederreiter, 1996) or (Buchmann, 2004).

Let $\mathbb{F}[X]_n$ be the set of all polynomials with degree smaller than n,

$$\begin{aligned}\mathbb{F}[X]_n &:= \{P(X);\ \deg(P) < n\} \\ &= \{a_0 + a_1 \cdot X + \cdots + a_{n-1} \cdot X^{n-1};\ a_i \in \mathbb{F}\}.\end{aligned}$$

Consider $(\mathbb{F}, +, \cdot, 0, 1)$ is finite, $|\mathbb{F}| = p < \infty$. Any coefficient can take p different values. Since there are n coefficients, there are p^n different polynomials, $|\mathbb{F}[X]_n| = p^n$.

Corollary 6.11. *If* $(\mathbb{F}, +, \cdot, 0, 1)$ *is a finite field,* $|\mathbb{F}| = p < \infty$, *it applies* $|\mathbb{F}[X]_n| = p^n$.

Example 6.12. $\mathbb{Z}_3[X]_3 = \{0, 1, 2, X, X +_3 1, X +_3 2, 2 \cdot_3 X, 2 \cdot_3 X +_3 1, 2 \cdot_3 X +_3 2, X^2, X^2 +_3 1, X^2 +_3 2, X^2 +_3 X, X^2 +_3 X +_3 1, X^2 +_3 X +_3 2, X^2 +_3 2 \cdot_3 X, X^2 +_3 2 \cdot_3 X +_3 1, X^2 +_3 2 \cdot X +_3 2, 2 \cdot_3 X^2, 2 \cdot_3 X^2 +_3 1, 2 \cdot_3 X^2 +_3 2, 2 \cdot_3 X^2 +_3 X, 2 \cdot_3 X^2 +_3 X +_3 1, 2 \cdot_3 X^2 +_3 X +_3 2, 2 \cdot_3 X^2 +_3 2 \cdot_3 X, 2 \cdot_3 X^2 +_3 2 \cdot_3 X +_3 1, 2 \cdot_3 X^2 +_3 2 \cdot_3 X +_3 2\}$.

The degree rules (6.6) and (6.7) show that the restricted mappings $\star^{\mathbb{F}}_{|\mathbb{F}[X]_n}$ and $+^{\mathbb{F}}_{|\mathbb{F}[X]_n}$ are closed. It follows that $(\mathbb{F}[X]_n, +^{\mathbb{F}}_{|\mathbb{F}[X]_n}, \star^{\mathbb{F}}_{|\mathbb{F}[X]_n}, 0^{\mathbb{F}})$ is a vector subspace of $(\mathbb{F}[X], +^{\mathbb{F}}, \star^{\mathbb{F}}, 0^{\mathbb{F}})$. This vector space has a basis $\mathcal{B}_{\mathbb{F}[X]_n} = \{1, X, \ldots, X^{n-1}\}$. Define the mapping

$$\psi : \mathbb{F}[X]_n \to \mathbb{F}^n,\ a_0 + a_1 \cdot X + \cdots a_{n-1} \cdot X^{n-1} \mapsto (a_0, a_1, \ldots, a_{n-1}).$$

This mapping is bijective, which is clear from the mapping rule and from $|\mathbb{F}[X]_n| = p^n = |\mathbb{F}^n|$, and a homomorphism. To see the latter, we calculate

$$\begin{aligned}\psi(P(X) +^{\mathbb{F}} Q(X)) &= \psi((a_0 + b_0) + \cdots + (a_{n-1} + b_{n-1}) \cdot X^{n-1}) \\ &= (a_0 + b_0, a_1 + b_1, \ldots, a_{n-1} + b_{n-1}) \\ &= (a_0, a_1, \ldots, a_{n-1}) + (b_0, b_1, \ldots, b_{n-1}) \\ &= \psi(P(X)) + \psi(Q(X)) \\ \psi(\lambda \star^{\mathbb{F}} P(X)) &= \psi((\lambda \cdot a_0) + (\lambda \cdot a_1) \cdot X + \cdots (\lambda \cdot a_{n-1}) \cdot X^{n-1}) \\ &= (\lambda \cdot a_0, \lambda \cdot a_1, \ldots, \lambda \cdot a_{n-1}) \\ &= \lambda \cdot (a_0, a_1, \ldots, a_{n-1}) \\ &= \lambda \cdot \psi(P(X)).\end{aligned}$$

ψ is a vector space isomorphism since $\mathbb{F}^n$ generates the canonical vector space over $\mathbb{F}$. We know from the mapping in (3.17) that $\mathbb{F}^n$ can be identified by a vector space up to isomorphism, which is an extension of $\mathbb{F}$ containing p^n elements. We can identify $\mathbb{F}[X]_n$ and $\mathbb{F}^n$ by a field isomorphism. However, at this point, $\mathbb{F}[X]_n$ is not a field, as $\cdot^{\mathbb{F}}_{|\mathbb{F}[X]_n}$ is not closed yet because of the statement in (6.8).

This situation is comparable to the sets $\mathbb{Z}$ and $\mathbb{Z}_n$. $\mathbb{Z}$ does not generate a field; only the modulo operation restricts the multiplication and addition, resulting in a field structure. However, remember that a field structure for $\mathbb{Z}_n$ does not occur for every $n \in \mathbb{N}$. We guess that n has to be a prime power for obtaining a field structure. Incidentally, the polynomial addition does not matter. As a starting point, a division with remainder is appropriated.

Theorem 6.13. *Let $N(X), P(X) \in \mathbb{F}[X]$ and $n = deg(N) \geq 0$. Then, there exist unique polynomials $Q(X) \in \mathbb{F}[X]$ and $R(X) \in \mathbb{F}[X]_n$ satisfying*

$$P(X) = Q(X) \cdot^{\mathbb{F}} N(X) +^{\mathbb{F}} R(X).$$

Proof. Existence: If $P(X) = 0^{\mathbb{F}}$, take $Q(X) = R(X) = 0^{\mathbb{F}}$.
Let $k = \deg(P) - \deg(N)$.
If $k < 0$, take $Q(X) = 0^{\mathbb{F}}$ and $R(X) = P(X)$.
If $k \geq 0$, we show it by induction on k.

Basis: $k = 0$ and $n = \deg(P) = \deg(N)$. Given $P(X) = \sum_{i=0}^{n} a_i \cdot X^i$, $a_n \neq 0$, and $N(X) = \sum_{i=0}^{n} b_i \cdot X^i$, $b_n \neq 0$, take $Q(X) = a_n \cdot b_n^{-1}$. It follows

$$\begin{aligned} R(X) = P(X) -^{\mathbb{F}} Q(X) \cdot^{\mathbb{F}} N(X) &= \sum_{i=0}^{n} \left(a_i - a_n \cdot b_n^{-1} \cdot b_i\right) \cdot X^i \\ &= \sum_{i=0}^{n-1} \left(a_i - a_n \cdot b_n^{-1} \cdot b_i\right) \cdot X^i. \end{aligned}$$

Hence, $\deg(R) \leq n - 1 < \deg(N)$.

Induction hypothesis: $k-1 \to k$.
Induction step: Consider $n = \deg(N)$, $P(X) = \sum_{i=0}^{n+k} a_i \cdot X^i$, $a_{n+k} \neq 0$ and $N(X) = \sum_{i=0}^{n} b_i \cdot X^i$, $b_n \neq 0$. Now, choose $\tilde{S}(X) = a_{n+k} \cdot b_n^{-1} \cdot X^k$, and we obtain

$$\begin{aligned}
\tilde{R}(X) &= P(X) -^{\mathbb{F}} Q(X) \cdot^{\mathbb{F}} N(X) \\
&= \sum_{i=0}^{n+k} a_i \cdot X^i -^{\mathbb{F}} \sum_{i=0}^{n} a_{n+k} \cdot b_n^{-1} \cdot b_i \cdot X^i \cdot X^k \\
&= \sum_{i=0}^{n+k} a_i \cdot X^i -^{\mathbb{F}} \sum_{i=k}^{n+k} a_{n+k} \cdot b_n^{-1} \cdot b_{i-k} \cdot X^i \\
&= \sum_{i=k}^{n+k} \left(a_i - a_{n+k} \cdot b_n^{-1} \cdot b_{i-k}\right) \cdot X^i +^{\mathbb{F}} \sum_{i=0}^{k-1} a_i \cdot X^i.
\end{aligned}$$

Hence, $\deg(\tilde{R}) \leq n+k-1$. Using the induction hypothesis, there are polynomials $\hat{Q}(X)$ and $\hat{R}(X)$, such that $\deg(R) < \deg(N)$ and

$$\tilde{R}(X) = \hat{Q}(X) \cdot^{\mathbb{F}} N(X) +^{\mathbb{F}} \hat{R}(X).$$

Together, that yields

$$\begin{aligned}
P(X) &= \tilde{Q}(X) \cdot^{\mathbb{F}} N(X) + \tilde{R}(X) \\
&= \tilde{Q}(X) \cdot^{\mathbb{F}} N(X) +^{\mathbb{F}} \hat{Q}(X) \cdot^{\mathbb{F}} N(X) +^{\mathbb{F}} \hat{R}(X) \\
&= \underbrace{(\tilde{Q}(X) +^{\mathbb{F}} \hat{Q}(X))}_{Q(X)} \cdot^{\mathbb{F}} N(X) +^{\mathbb{F}} \underbrace{\hat{R}(X)}_{R(X)}, \ \deg(\hat{R}) < n.
\end{aligned}$$

Uniqueness: Suppose there is another representation $P(X) = Q'(X) \cdot^{\mathbb{F}} N(X) +^{\mathbb{F}} R'(X)$, $\deg(R') < n$. Then, it applies

$$\begin{aligned}
0^{\mathbb{F}} &= P(X) -^{\mathbb{F}} P(X) \\
&= (Q(X) \cdot N(X) +^{\mathbb{F}} R(X)) -^{\mathbb{F}} (Q'(X) \cdot^{\mathbb{F}} N(X) +^{\mathbb{F}} R'(X)) \\
&= (Q(X) -^{\mathbb{F}} Q'(X)) \cdot^{\mathbb{F}} N(X) +^{\mathbb{F}} (R(X) -^{\mathbb{F}} R'(X)).
\end{aligned}$$

Consequently, $(Q(X) -^{\mathbb{F}} Q'(X)) \cdot^{\mathbb{F}} N(X) = -(R(X) -^{\mathbb{F}} R'(X)) \in \mathbb{F}[X]_n$. If $Q(X) -^{\mathbb{F}} Q'(X) \neq 0^{\mathbb{F}}$, there is a contradiction to $\deg((Q(X) -^{\mathbb{F}} Q'(X)) \cdot N(X)) \geq n$. Thus, $Q(X) = Q'(X)$. It follows that $R(X) = R'(X)$ immediately. □

Example 6.14.

- $\mathbb{R}[X]: \ X^3 + X^2 + 1 = (\frac{1}{2} \cdot X + \frac{1}{2}) \cdot (2 \cdot X^2 + 1) + (-\frac{1}{2} \cdot X + \frac{1}{2}),$
- $\mathbb{Z}_3[X]: \ X^3 +_3 X^2 +_3 1 = (2 \cdot_3 X +_3 2) \cdot_3 (2 \cdot_3 X^2 +_3 1) +_3 (X +_3 2),$
- $\mathbb{Z}_3[X]: \ 2 \cdot_3 X^6 +_3 X^4 +_3 2 \cdot X^3 +_3 2 \cdot X +_3 2$
  $= (X^4 +_3 X) \cdot_3 (2 \cdot_3 X^2 +_3 1) +_3 (X +_3 2),$
- $\mathbb{Z}_3[X]: \ 2 \cdot_3 X^3 +_3 2 \cdot X^2 +_3 X +_3 1 = (X +_3 1) \cdot_3 (2 \cdot_3 X^2 +_3 1),$
- $\mathbb{Z}_2[X]: \ X^2 +_2 1 = (X +_2 1) \cdot_2 (X +_2 1).$

Define the mapping

$$\rho_{N(X)} : \mathbb{F}[X] \to \mathbb{F}[X]_n, \ P(X) = Q(X) \cdot^{\mathbb{F}} N(X) +^{\mathbb{F}} R(X) \mapsto R(X)$$

in the same way as in (1.1). Then, we get an equivalence relation denoted by

$$\begin{aligned} P(X) \equiv_{N(X)} Q(X) &\Leftrightarrow \rho_{N(X)}(P(X)) = \rho_{N(X)}(Q(X)) \\ &\Leftrightarrow P(X) = Q(X) \pmod{N(X)}. \end{aligned}$$

The representatives of the $N(X)$-equivalence classes $[R(X)]_{N(X)}$ are the polynomials of $\mathbb{F}[X]_n$. Using the addition $+^{\mathbb{F}}_{|\mathbb{F}[X]_n}$ and defining a multiplication

$$\begin{aligned} \cdot^{\mathbb{F}}_{N(X)} : \mathbb{F}[X]_n \times \mathbb{F}[X]_n \to \mathbb{F}[X]_n, \ P(X) \cdot^{\mathbb{F}}_{N(X)} Q(X) \\ := \rho_{N(X)}(P(X) \cdot^{\mathbb{F}} Q(X)), \end{aligned}$$

we get a ring structure. $(\mathbb{F}[X]_n, +^{\mathbb{F}}_{|\mathbb{F}[X]_n}, 0^{\mathbb{F}})$ is an abelian group and for each $P(X), Q(X), T(X) \in \mathbb{F}[X]_n$ and $1^{\mathbb{F}} \in \mathbb{F}[X]_n$, (M2), (D1) and (M1) follow from

$$\begin{aligned} P(X) \cdot^{\mathbb{F}}_{N(X)} (Q(X) \cdot^{\mathbb{F}}_{N(X)} T(X)) &= \rho_{N(X)}(P(X) \cdot^{\mathbb{F}} (Q(X) \cdot^{\mathbb{F}} T(X))) \\ &= \rho_{N(X)}((P(X) \cdot^{\mathbb{F}} Q(X)) \cdot^{\mathbb{F}} T(X)) \\ &= (P(X) \cdot^{\mathbb{F}}_{N(X)} Q(X)) \cdot^{\mathbb{F}}_{N(X)} T(X), \end{aligned}$$

$$\begin{aligned} P(X) \cdot^{\mathbb{F}}_{|\mathbb{F}[X]_n} & (Q(X) +^{\mathbb{F}}_{N(X)} T(X)) \\ &= \rho_{N(X)}(P(X) \cdot^{\mathbb{F}} (Q(X) +^{\mathbb{F}} T(X)) \\ &= \rho_{N(X)}(P(X) \cdot^{\mathbb{F}} Q(X) +^{\mathbb{F}} P(X) \cdot^{\mathbb{F}} T(X)) \\ &= P(X) \cdot^{\mathbb{F}}_{|\mathbb{F}[X]_n} Q(X) +^{\mathbb{F}}_{N(X)} P(X) \cdot^{\mathbb{F}}_{|\mathbb{F}[X]_n} T(X)), \end{aligned}$$

$$
\begin{aligned}
(P(X)+^{\mathbb{F}}_{|\mathbb{F}[X]_n}Q(X)) \cdot^{\mathbb{F}}_{N(X)} T(X) &= \rho_{N(X)}((P(X) +^{\mathbb{F}} Q(X)) \cdot^{\mathbb{F}} T(X)) \\
&= \rho_{N(X)}(P(X) \cdot^{\mathbb{F}} T(X) +^{\mathbb{F}} Q(X) \cdot^{\mathbb{F}} T(X)) \\
&= P(X) \cdot^{\mathbb{F}}_{|\mathbb{F}[X]_n} T(X) +^{\mathbb{F}}_{N(X)} Q(X) \cdot^{\mathbb{F}}_{|\mathbb{F}[X]_n} T(X), \\
P(X) \cdot^{\mathbb{F}}_{N(X)} Q(X) &= \rho_{N(X)}(P(X) \cdot^{\mathbb{F}} Q(X)) \\
&= \rho_{N(X)}(Q(X) \cdot^{\mathbb{F}} R(X)) \\
&= Q(X) \cdot^{\mathbb{F}}_{N(X)} P(X), \text{ and} \\
1^{\mathbb{F}} \cdot^{\mathbb{F}}_{N(X)} P(X) &= \rho_{N(X)}(1^{\mathbb{F}} \cdot^{\mathbb{F}} P(X)) \\
&= \rho_{N(X)}(P(X)), \quad 1^{\mathbb{F}} \neq 0^{\mathbb{F}}.
\end{aligned}
$$

Corollary 6.15. $(\mathbb{F}[X]_n, +^{\mathbb{F}}_{|\mathbb{F}[X]_n}, \cdot^{\mathbb{F}}_{N(X)}, 0^{\mathbb{F}}, 1^{\mathbb{F}})$ *is a commutative ring with identity.*

Example 6.16. Look at the ring $(\mathbb{Z}_3[X]_3, +^{\mathbb{Z}_3}_{|\mathbb{Z}_3[X]_3}, \cdot^{\mathbb{Z}_3}_{X^3+_3X^2+_31}, 0^{\mathbb{F}}, 1^{\mathbb{F}})$.

- $(X^2 +_3 2) +^{\mathbb{Z}_3}_{|\mathbb{Z}_3[X]} (2 \cdot_3 X^2 +_3 1) = 0^{\mathbb{Z}_3} \in \mathbb{Z}_3[X]_3$,
- $(2 \cdot_3 X +_3 2) +^{\mathbb{Z}_3}_{|\mathbb{Z}_3[X]} (2 \cdot_3 X^2 +_3 1) = 2 \cdot_3 X^2 +_3 2 \cdot_3 X +_3 3 = 2 \cdot_3 X^2 + 2 \cdot_3 X \in \mathbb{Z}_3[X]_3$,
- $(2 \cdot_3 X +_3 2) \cdot^{\mathbb{Z}_3}_{X^3+_3X^2+_31} (2 \cdot X^2 + 1) = 4 \cdot_3 X^3 +_3 4 \cdot X^2 +_3 2 \cdot X +_3 2 \pmod{X^3 +_3 X^2 +_3 1} = X^3 +_3 X^2 +_3 2 \cdot_3 X +_3 2 \pmod{X^3 +_3 X^2 +_3 1} = 2 \cdot_3 X +_3 1 \in \mathbb{Z}_3[X]_3$.

$(\mathbb{F}[X]_n, +^{\mathbb{F}}_{|\mathbb{F}[X]_n}, \cdot^{\mathbb{F}}_{N(X)}, 0^{\mathbb{F}}, 1^{\mathbb{F}})$ is a field if all elements of $\mathbb{F}[X]_n$ are unity elements modulo $N(X)$. However, from Example 6.14, we see that $(X +_2 1) \in \mathbb{Z}_2[X]$ is no unity element modulo $X^2 +_2 1$, because $(X +_2 1) \cdot^{\mathbb{Z}_2} (X +_2 1) (\text{mod } X^2 + 1) = 0^{\mathbb{Z}_2}$. $X +_2 1$ is a zero divisor. Hence, we have to consider a rule that makes such a finite ring into a finite field. From Corollary 3.22, we have to ensure that the ring is a domain of integrity. This can be done by showing that some $P(X) \in \mathbb{F}[X]_n$ are "relatively prime" to $N(X)$. We have to translate this term to the context of polynomials.

A polynomial $P(X) \in \mathbb{F}[X]$ is called a *divisor* of $N(X) \in \mathbb{F}[X]$ if there is another polynomial $Q(X) \in \mathbb{F}[X]$ satisfying $N(X) = Q(X) \cdot^{\mathbb{F}} P(X)$. $N(X)$ is called a *multiple* of $P(X)$. In Example 6.14, $X +_2 1 \in \mathbb{Z}_2[X]$ is a divisor of $X^2 +_2 1 \in \mathbb{Z}_2[X]$. An *improper divisor* $P(X)$ is a divisor applying $\deg(P) = 0$ or $\deg(P) = \deg(N)$. If $N(X)$ has only improper divisors, $N(X)$ is called *irreducible.*

Example 6.17. $\mathbb{Z}_2[X]_3 = \{0, 1, X, X +_2 1, X^2, X^2 +_2 1, X^2 +_2 X, X^2 +_2 X +_2 1\}$.

- $N(X) = X^3 +_2 1$: $N(X)$ is not irreducible since $(X^2 +_2 X +_2 1) \cdot^{\mathbb{Z}_2} (X +_2 1) = X^3 +_2 2 \cdot_2 X^2 +_2 2 \cdot_2 X +_2 1 = X^3 +_2 1$.
- $N(X) = X^3 +_2 X +_2 1$ is irreducible.

Henceforth, the term "relatively prime" means two polynomials having no common divisor featuring a degree greater than zero. For example, the polynomials $X^3 +_2 1$ and $X^2 +_2 1$ have the common divisor $X +_2 1$, and they are not relatively prime. Now, choose $P(X), N(X) \in \mathbb{F}[X] \setminus \{0^{\mathbb{F}}\}$. Let

$$\mathcal{S}_{P,N} = \{Q(X);\ Q(X) \text{ is a multiple of both } P(X) \text{ and } N(X)\}$$

be the set of polynomials that has the common divisors $P(X)$ and $N(X)$. It applies $\deg(S) \geq \max\{\deg(P), \deg(N)\}$ for all $S(X) \in \mathcal{S}_{P,N}$. $\mathcal{S}_{P,N} \neq \emptyset$ since $P(X) \cdot^{\mathbb{F}} N(X) \in \mathcal{S}$. There is a polynomial $A(X) \in \mathcal{S}_{P,N}$ with the smallest degree greater or equal to zero, $\deg(A) \leq \deg(S)$ for all $S(X) \in \mathcal{S}_{P,N}$. Such a polynomial is called the *least common multiple* of $P(X)$ and $N(X)$, denoted by $A(X) = \mathrm{LCM}(P, N)$. For any $S(X) \in \mathcal{S}_{P,N}$, we can write

$$S(X) = Q(X) \cdot^{\mathbb{F}} A(X) +^{\mathbb{F}} R(X)$$

for some $Q(X), R(X) \in \mathbb{F}[X]$ and $\deg(R) < \deg(A)$. Since $P(X)$ and $N(X)$ are divisors of both, $A(X)$ and $S(X)$, they must be divisors of $R(X)$, too. However, $\deg(R) < \deg(A)$. Thus, $R(X) = 0^{\mathbb{F}}$. If $A(X)$ and $B(X)$ are two different least common multiples, they are divisors of each other.

$$\begin{aligned} A(X) &= U(X) \cdot^{\mathbb{F}} B(X) = U(X) \cdot^{\mathbb{F}} V(X) \cdot^{\mathbb{F}} A(X) \\ &\Rightarrow U(X) \cdot^{\mathbb{F}} V(X) = 1^{\mathbb{F}} \overset{(6.9)}{\Rightarrow} U(X), V(X) \in \mathbb{F}. \end{aligned}$$

Corollary 6.18. *A least common multiple $LCM(P, N)$ is a divisor of any other multiple of $P(X)$ and $N(X)$, and it is determined except for a scalar factor.*

Let $A(X) = \mathrm{LCM}(P, N)$ and $A(X)/P(X) := Q(X)$ for $A(X) = Q(X) \cdot^{\mathbb{F}} P(X)$. If there is a common divisor $T(X)$ of $A(X)/P(X)$ and $A(X)/N(X)$, i.e.,

$$A(X)/P(X) = T(X) \cdot^{\mathbb{F}} V(X) \text{ and } A(X)/N(X) = T(X) \cdot^{\mathbb{F}} W(X),$$

then we obtain a common multiple of $P(X)$ and $N(X)$,

$$\begin{aligned} P(X) \cdot^{\mathbb{F}} T(X) \cdot^{\mathbb{F}} V(X) &= N(X) \cdot^{\mathbb{F}} T(X) \cdot^{\mathbb{F}} W(X) \\ &\Rightarrow P(X) \cdot^{\mathbb{F}} V(X) = N(X) \cdot^{\mathbb{F}} W(X). \end{aligned}$$

Since $T(X) \cdot^{\mathbb{F}} P(X) \cdot^{\mathbb{F}} V(X) = A(X) = \mathrm{LCM}(P, N)$, the polynomial $T(X)$ is constant according to Corollary 6.18. It follows that $A(X)/P(X)$ and $A(X)/N(X)$ are relatively prime. Alternatively, if $V(X)/P(X)$ and $V(X)/N(X)$ are relatively prime, then there is just a constant polynomial $F(X)$ applying $V(X)/P(X) = F(X) \cdot^{\mathbb{F}} Q_1(X)$ and $V(X)/N(X) = F(X) \cdot^{\mathbb{F}} Q_2(X)$. However, there is a polynomial $U(X)$ satisfying

$$\begin{aligned} V(X) &= U(X) \cdot^{\mathbb{F}} A(X) = U(X) \cdot^{\mathbb{F}} A(X)/P(X) \cdot^{\mathbb{F}} P(X) \\ &= U(X) \cdot^{\mathbb{F}} A(X) = U(X) \cdot^{\mathbb{F}} A(X)/N(X) \cdot^{\mathbb{F}} N(X) \end{aligned}$$

Reducing by $P(X)$ or $N(X)$ yields

$$V(X)/P(X) = U(X) \cdot^{\mathbb{F}} A(X)/P(X), \; V(X)/N(X) = U(X) \cdot^{\mathbb{F}} A(X)/N(X).$$

Hence, $U(X)$ is a common divisor and is a constant polynomial. It follows $V(X) = \mathrm{LCM}(P, N)$. If $P(X)$ and $N(X)$ are relatively prime, then $V(X) = P(X) \cdot^{\mathbb{F}} N(X)$ is their least common multiple because $V(X)/P(X) = N(X)$ and $V(X)/N(X) = P(X)$.

Corollary 6.19. *Let $A(X)$ be a multiple of $P(X)$ and $N(X)$. $A(X) = LCM(P, N)$ iff $A(X)/P(X)$ and $A(X)/N(X)$ are relatively prime. If $P(X)$ and $N(X)$ are relatively prime, then $P(X) \cdot^{\mathbb{F}} N(X) = LCM(P, N)$.*

Let $V(X) = F(X) \cdot^{\mathbb{F}} N(X) = Q(X) \cdot^{\mathbb{F}} P(X)$ be a multiple of $P(X)$ and $N(X)$. If $P(X)$ and $N(X)$ are relatively prime it follows

$$\begin{aligned} Q(X) \cdot^{\mathbb{F}} P(X) &= V(X) = U(X) \cdot^{\mathbb{F}} \mathrm{LCM}(P, N) \\ &= U(X) \cdot^{\mathbb{F}} P(X) \cdot^{\mathbb{F}} N(X) \\ &\Rightarrow Q(X) = U(X) \cdot^{\mathbb{F}} N(X) \\ &\Rightarrow N(X) \text{ is a divisor of } Q(X). \end{aligned}$$

Corollary 6.20. *If $P(X)$ and $N(X)$ are relatively prime and $N(X)$ is a divisor of $P(X) \cdot^{\mathbb{F}} Q(X)$, then $N(X)$ is a divisor of $Q(X)$.*

Now, all of the preliminaries are given to prove an important statement.

Theorem 6.21. $(\mathbb{F}[X]_n, +^{\mathbb{F}}_{|\mathbb{F}[X]_n}, \cdot^{\mathbb{F}}_{N(X)}, 0^{\mathbb{F}}, 1^{\mathbb{F}})$ *is a field iff every polynomial $P(X) \in \mathbb{F}[X]_n$ with degree $0 < deg(P) < deg(N)$ is no divisor of $N(X)$.*

Proof. "$\Rightarrow$": Let $(\mathbb{F}[X]_n, +^{\mathbb{F}}_{|\mathbb{F}[X]_n}, \cdot^{\mathbb{F}}_{N(X)}, 0^{\mathbb{F}}, 1^{\mathbb{F}})$ be a field and there are no zero divisors. Let $P(X) \in \mathbb{F}[X]_n$ with degree $0 < \deg(P) < \deg(N)$ and $F(X) \in \mathbb{F}[X]_n$ be a common divisor of $N(X)$ and $P(X)$, i.e., $N(X) = Q(X) \cdot^{\mathbb{F}} F(X)$ and $P(X) = T(X) \cdot^{\mathbb{F}} F(X)$. It follows

$$\begin{aligned} N(X) \cdot^{\mathbb{F}} T(X) &= Q(X) \cdot^{\mathbb{F}} F(X) \cdot^{\mathbb{F}} T(X) \\ &= Q(X) \cdot^{\mathbb{F}} T(X) \cdot^{\mathbb{F}} F(X) = Q(X) \cdot^{\mathbb{F}} P(X). \end{aligned}$$

This implies $Q(X) \cdot^{\mathbb{F}}_{N(X)} P(X) = 0^{\mathbb{F}}$ and $P(X)$ is a zero divisor of $N(X)$. However, this contradicts the assumption that there are no zero divisors.

"$\Leftarrow$": Let $P(X) \in \mathbb{F}[X]_n$ with degree $0 < \deg(P) < \deg(N)$ be a zero divisor of $N(X)$. Then, there is a $Q(X) \in \mathbb{F}[X]_n$, $Q(X) \neq 0^{\mathbb{F}}$, satisfying $Q(X) \cdot^{\mathbb{F}}_{N(X)} P(X) = 0^{\mathbb{F}}$. It follows $Q(X) \cdot^{\mathbb{F}} P(X) = F(X) \cdot^{\mathbb{F}} N(X)$ for some $F(X) \in \mathbb{F}[X]$. That means that $N(X)$ is a divisor of $Q(X) \cdot^{\mathbb{F}} P(X)$. Assuming that $P(X)$ and $N(X)$ are relatively prime polynomials, it follows from Corollary 6.20 that $N(X)$ is a divisor of $Q(X)$, i.e., $Q(X) = U(X) \cdot^{\mathbb{F}} N(X)$ and $\deg(Q) = \deg(U \cdot^{\mathbb{F}} N) = \deg(U) + \deg(N) \geq \deg(N)$. However, this contradicts $Q(X) \in \mathbb{F}[X]_n$. $P(X)$ and $N(X)$ cannot be relatively prime. $\square$

Remark 6.22.

- $N[X]$ has to be irreducible to create a field.
- It can be shown that each finite field is representable by an appropriate $(\mathbb{F}[X]_n, +^{\mathbb{F}}_{|\mathbb{F}[X]_n}, \cdot^{\mathbb{F}}_{N(X)}, 0^{\mathbb{F}}, 1^{\mathbb{F}})$, except for isomorphism.[7]
- We denote such a field by $\mathbb{F}[X]/N(X)$.

We want to clarify when a polynomial is irreducible and how many zeros it can have.

Theorem 6.23. *Let $P(X) \in \mathbb{F}[X]$ be a polynomial and $z \in \mathbb{F}$ satisfying $\psi_z(P(X)) = P(z) = 0^{\mathbb{F}}$ (z is a zero). Then, there exists a $Q(X) \in \mathbb{F}[X]$, such that $P(X) = Q(X) \cdot^{\mathbb{F}} (X - z)$.*

Proof. If $\deg(P) \leq 0$, i.e., $P(X) = x^{\mathbb{F}}$, then $P(X) = 0^{\mathbb{F}}$. For example, $\deg(P) \geq 1$. Then there are polynomials $Q(X)$ and $R(X)$, according to Theorem 6.13 applying

$$P(X) = Q(X) \cdot^{\mathbb{F}} (X -^{\mathbb{F}} z) +^{\mathbb{F}} R(X), \ \deg(R) < 1.$$

Using the evaluation homomorphism ψ_z, we obtain

$$\begin{aligned} 0^{\mathbb{F}} = \psi_z(P(X)) &= \psi_z(Q(X)) \cdot \psi_z(X -^{\mathbb{F}} z) + \psi_z(R(X)) = \psi_z(R(X)) \\ &\Rightarrow R(X) = 0^{\mathbb{F}}. \end{aligned}$$

$\square$

We now deal with the number of zeros a polynomial can at most possess. Suppose $P(X) \in \mathbb{F}[X]$, $P(X) \neq 0^{\mathbb{F}}$, and $n = \deg(P)$. If $n = 0$, there is no zero since $P(X) \neq 0^{\mathbb{F}}$. Considering $n > 0$, we make the statement that $P(X)$ has at most $\deg(P)$ zeros and posesses an induction scheme. Now, let the induction hypothesis be true., i.e., if

[7] See (Lidl and Niederreiter, 1996). However, this is beyond the scope of this book.

$\deg(P) = n - 1$, then $P(X)$ will have $n - 1$ zeros at most. Induction step: if $P(X)$ does not have a zero, the assertion is true. In contrast, if $P(X)$ has a zero z, we use Theorem 6.23, writing

$$P(X) = Q(X) \cdot^{\mathbb{F}} (X - z),$$

and $\deg(Q) = n - 1$. However, based on the induction hypothesis, $Q(X)$ has at most $n - 1$ zeros. Thus, $P(X)$ has at most $n = \deg(P)$ zeros.

Corollary 6.24. *Let $P(X) \in \mathbb{F}[X]$ be a polynomial, $P(X) \neq 0^{\mathbb{F}}$, and $n = \deg(P)$. Then, $P(X)$ has n zeros at most.*

Furthermore, it follows immediately from Theorem 6.23 that a polynomial with degree ≥ 2 is not irreducible if there is a zero. The converse applies for degrees 2 and 3. To see this, consider that $P(X)$ is not irreducible. Then, there is a divisor $Q(X)$ of $P(X)$ and $Q(X)$, or $P(X)/Q(X)$ has degree 1. Consequently, there is a zero. However, $X^4 +_2 1 = (X^2 +_2 1) \cdot^{\mathbb{Z}_2} (X^2 +_2 1)$ is not irreducible in $\mathbb{Z}_2[X]$.

Example 6.25. Let us consider a finite field $\mathrm{GF}(2^3) := \mathbb{Z}_2[X]/(X^3 +_2 X^2 +_2 1)$. The corresponding prime field should be $(\mathbb{Z}_2, +_2, \cdot_2, 0, 1)$. We compare the sets $\mathbb{Z}_2^3$ and $\mathbb{Z}_2[X]_3$ and identify the elements by elements from $\mathbb{Z}_{2^3}$.

Table 6.17 Basic arithmetic on $\mathbb{Z}_2^3$.

$\mathbb{Z}_2^3$	$\mathbb{Z}_2[X]_3$	$\mathbb{Z}_{2^3}$
$(0,0,0)$	0	0
$(0,0,1)$	1	1
$(0,1,0)$	X	2
$(0,1,1)$	$X +_2 1$	3
$(1,0,0)$	X^2	4
$(1,0,1)$	$X^2 +_2 1$	5
$(1,1,0)$	$X^2 +_2 X$	6
$(1,1,1)$	$X^2 +_2 X +_2 1$	7
$\mathcal{B}_{\mathbb{Z}_2^3} = \{(0,0,1),(0,1,0),(1,0,0)\}$	$\mathcal{B}_{\mathbb{Z}_2[X]_3} = \{1, X, X^2\}$	$\mathcal{B}_{\mathbb{Z}_8} = \{1,2,4\}$

Addition is a component-wise calculation modulo 2. For example:

$$(0,1,0) +_2 (0,1,1) = (0,0,1),$$
$$X +^{\mathbb{Z}_2} X +_2 1 = 1, \text{ and}$$
$$2 \oplus 3 = 1 \text{ (XOR)}.$$

Since $\psi_0(X^3 +_2 X^2 +_2 1) = \psi_1(X^3 +_2 X^2 +_2 1) = 1 \neq 0$ and $\psi_0(X^3 +_2 X +_2 1) = \psi_1(X^3 +_2 X +_2 1) = 1 \neq 0$, both polynomials are irreducible.

Let $N(X) = X^3 +_2 X^2 +_2 1$. We want to compute $(X^2 +_2 X +_2 1) \cdot^{\mathbb{Z}_2} X^2 +_2 1 \pmod{X^3 +_2 X^2 +_2 1}$:

$$(X^2 +_2 X +_2 1) \cdot^{\mathbb{Z}_2} (X^2 +_2 1) = X^4 +_2 X^3 +_2 X +_2 1.$$

Afterwards, we get

$$X^4 +_2 X^3 +_2 X +_2 1 = X \cdot^{\mathbb{Z}_2} (X^3 +_2 X^2 +_2 1) + 1$$

by polynomial division. Together, the multiplication yields

$$(X^2 +_2 X +_2 1) \cdot^{\mathbb{Z}_2} (X^2 +_2 1) \pmod{X^3 +_2 X^2 +_2 1} = 1.$$

This means $7 \odot 5 = 1$.

We can note the Cayley tables for the field $(\mathbb{Z}_8, \oplus, \odot, 0, 1)$ based on the field $\mathbb{Z}_2[X]/(X^3 +_2 X^2 +_2 1)$. Remember that each number has to appear in each row and column of the addition table, and the numbers 1 to 7 should appear in each row and column of the multiplication table, except for the first ones.

$\oplus$	0	1	2	3	4	5	6	7
0	0	1	2	3	4	5	6	7
1	1	0	3	2	5	4	7	6
2	2	3	0	1	6	7	4	5
3	3	2	1	0	7	6	5	4
4	4	5	6	7	0	1	2	3
5	5	4	7	6	1	0	3	2
6	6	7	4	5	2	3	0	1
7	7	6	5	4	3	2	1	0

$\odot$	0	1	2	3	4	5	6	7
0	0	0	0	0	0	0	0	0
1	0	1	2	3	4	5	6	7
2	0	2	4	6	5	7	1	3
3	0	3	6	5	1	2	7	4
4	0	4	5	1	7	3	2	6
5	0	5	7	2	3	6	4	1
6	0	6	1	7	2	4	3	5
7	0	7	3	4	6	1	5	2

However, there is another irreducible polynomial with degree 3: $X^3 +_2 X +_2 1$. The addition remains unchanged. Instead, the multiplication changes in $\mathbb{Z}_2[X]/(X^3 +_2 X +_2 1)$ to

$\odot$	0	1	2	3	4	5	6	7
0	0	0	0	0	0	0	0	0
1	0	1	2	3	4	5	6	7
2	0	2	4	6	3	1	7	5
3	0	3	6	5	7	4	1	2
4	0	4	3	7	6	2	5	1
5	0	5	1	4	2	7	3	6
6	0	6	7	1	5	3	2	4
7	0	7	5	2	1	6	4	3

If $(\mathbb{F}[X]_n, +^{\mathbb{F}}_{|\mathbb{F}[X]_n}, \cdot^{\mathbb{F}}_{N(X)}, 0^{\mathbb{F}}, 1^{\mathbb{F}})$ is a field, each $0^{\mathbb{F}} \neq P(X) \in \mathbb{F}[X]_n$ has an inverse element. We can find such an inverse element using the extended Euclidean algorithm 3.1 applied to polynomials. To see this, consider a domain of integrity $(\mathbb{F}[X], +^{\mathbb{F}}, \cdot^{\mathbb{F}}, 0^{\mathbb{F}}, 1^{\mathbb{F}})$ and two polynomials $P(X), S(X) \in \mathbb{F}[X]$ for investigation. Firstly, there is a representation

$$\begin{aligned} P(X) &= Q(X) \cdot^{\mathbb{F}} S(X) +^{\mathbb{F}} R(X), \\ &\deg(R) < \deg(S) =: n. \end{aligned}$$

Now, if $T(X)$ is a common divisor of $P(X)$ and $S(X)$, i.e.,

$$P(X) = Q_1(X) \cdot^{\mathbb{F}} T(X),\ S(X) = Q_2(X) \cdot^{\mathbb{F}} T(X)$$

we get

$$\begin{aligned} R(X) &= P(X) -^{\mathbb{F}} Q(X) \cdot^{\mathbb{F}} S(X) \\ &= (Q_1(X) -^{\mathbb{F}} Q(X) \cdot^{\mathbb{F}} Q_2(X)) \cdot^{\mathbb{F}} T(X), \end{aligned}$$

and $T(X)$ is a divisor of $R(X)$, too. Alternatively, if $T(X)$ is a common divisor of $S(X)$ and $R(X)$,

$$S(X) = Q_1(X) \cdot^{\mathbb{F}} T(X),\ R(X) = Q_2(X) \cdot^{\mathbb{F}} T(X),$$

we obtain

$$\begin{aligned} P(X) &= Q(X) \cdot^{\mathbb{F}} S(X) +^{\mathbb{F}} R(X) \\ &= (Q(X) \cdot^{\mathbb{F}} Q_1(X) +^{\mathbb{F}} Q_2(X)) \cdot^{\mathbb{F}} T(X). \end{aligned}$$

$T(X)$ is also a divisor of $P(X)$.

Corollary 6.26. *Let $P(X) = Q(X) \cdot^{\mathbb{F}} S(X) +^{\mathbb{F}} R(X)$. Then, $T(X)$ is a common divisor of $P(X)$ and $S(X)$ iff $T(X)$ is a common divisor of $S(X)$ and $R(X)$.*

After at most $n-1$ steps, the process stops. If at any step $R(X) = 0^{\mathbb{F}}$, there is a common divisor of $P(X)$ and $S(X)$ with degree greater than 0. Otherwise, there is a remainder $R(X) = 1^{\mathbb{F}}$. Then, there is no divisor with degree greater than 0 and the polynomials are relatively prime.

Example 6.27. Let $\mathbb{F} = \mathbb{Z}_3[X]$, $P(X) = X^3 +_3 X^2 +_3 1$, $S_1(X) = 2 \cdot_3 X^2 +_3 1$ and $S_2(X) = X^2 +_3 1$.

$$\begin{aligned} X^3 +_3 X^2 +_3 1 &= (2 \cdot_3 X +_3 2) \cdot^{\mathbb{Z}_3} (2 \cdot_3 X^2 +_3 1) +^{\mathbb{Z}_3} (X +_3 2), \\ 2 \cdot_3 X^2 +_3 1 &= (2 \cdot_3 X +_3 2) \cdot^{\mathbb{Z}_3} (X +_3 2) \\ &\Rightarrow X +_3 2 \text{ is a common divisor of } P(X) \\ &\quad \text{and } S_1(X), \\ X^3 +_3 X^2 +_3 1 &= (X +_3 1) \cdot^{\mathbb{Z}_3} (X^2 +_3 1) +^{\mathbb{Z}_3} 2 \cdot_3 X, \\ X^2 +_3 1 &= 2 \cdot_3 X \cdot^{\mathbb{Z}_3} 2 \cdot_3 X +^{\mathbb{Z}_3} 1^{\mathbb{Z}_3} \\ &\Rightarrow \text{only } 1^{\mathbb{Z}_3} \text{ is a common divisor of } P(X) \\ &\quad \text{and } S_2(X), \\ 1^{\mathbb{Z}_3} &= (X^2 +_3 1) -^{\mathbb{Z}_3} 2 \cdot_3 X \cdot^{\mathbb{Z}_3} 2 \cdot_3 X \\ &= (X^2 +_3 1) -^{\mathbb{Z}_3} 2 \cdot_3 X \cdot^{\mathbb{Z}_3} ((X^3 +_3 X^2 +_3 1) \\ &\quad -^{\mathbb{Z}_3} (X +_3 1) \cdot^{\mathbb{Z}_3} (X^2 +_3 1)) \\ &= X \cdot^{\mathbb{Z}_3} (X^3 +_3 X^2 +_3 1) \\ &\quad +(2 \cdot_3 X^2 +_3 2 \cdot_3 X +_3 1) \cdot^{\mathbb{Z}_3} (X^2 +_3 1). \end{aligned}$$

6.3.2 *Components of the AES*

The AES works on bytes. Each byte can be represented as a sequence of eight bits or as a sequence of two hexadecimal numbers, i.e.,

$$45_{(10)} = \underbrace{0010}_{2_{(10)}}\underbrace{1101}_{13_{(10)}}{}_{(2)} = 2d_{(16)}.$$

A byte is an element of the field GF(2^8). The multiplication of two bytes is done according to the multiplication of polynomials modulo the irreducible polynomial

$$N(X) = X^8 +_2 X^4 +_2 X^3 +_2 X +_2 1 \in \mathbb{Z}_2[X].$$

Example 6.28.

$$\begin{aligned}45 \odot 45 &\cong (X^5 +_2 X^3 +_2 X^2 +_2 1) \cdot^{\mathbb{Z}_2} (X^5 +_2 X^3 +_2 X^2 +_2 1)\\ &\quad (\text{mod } X^8 +_2 X^4 +_2 X^3 +_2 X +_2 1)\\ &= X^{10} +_2 X^6 +_2 X^4 +_2 1\\ &\quad (\text{mod } X^8 +_2 X^4 +_2 X^3 +_2 X +_2 1)\\ &= X^5 +_2 X^4 +_2 X^3 +_2 X^2 +_2 1\\ &\cong 61.\end{aligned}$$

The *Rijndael field* is based on the set $\mathbb{Z}_2[X]/(X^8 +_2 X^4 +_2 X^3 +_2 X +_2 1)$ of polynomials with degree less than 8. We have the cardinality $|\mathbb{Z}_2[X]/(X^8 +_2 X^4 +_2 X^3 +_2 X +_2 1)| = 2^8 = 256$. Given a polynomial $P(X) \in \mathbb{Z}_2[X]/(X^8 +_2 X^4 +_2 X^3 +_2 X +_2 1)$, we will find its inverse polynomial $P^{-1}(X) \in \mathbb{Z}_2[X]/(X^8 +_2 X^4 +_2 X^3 +_2 X +_2 1)$, such that

$$P(X) \cdot^{\mathbb{F}}_{N(X)} P^{-1}(X) = 1^{\mathbb{F}}.$$

Corollary 6.26 is used as a guide and Example 6.27 is used to solve this problem. We have to find the representation of $1^{\mathbb{F}}$ by inverse calculation using the extended Euclidean algorithm.

Example 6.29. $P(X) = X^5 +_2 X^3 +_2 X^2 +_2 1$.

$$\begin{aligned} N(X) &= P(X) \cdot^{\mathbb{Z}_2} (X^3 +_2 X +_2 1) +^{\mathbb{Z}_2} X^2, \\ P(X) &= X^2 \cdot^{\mathbb{Z}_2} (X^3 +_2 X +_2 1) +^{\mathbb{Z}_2} 1^{\mathbb{Z}_2}, \\ 1^{\mathbb{Z}_2} &= P(X) -^{\mathbb{Z}_2} X^2 \cdot^{\mathbb{Z}_2} (X^3 +_2 X +_2 1) \\ &= P(X) -^{\mathbb{Z}_2} (N(X) -^{\mathbb{Z}_2} P(X) \cdot^{\mathbb{Z}_2} (X^3 +_2 X +_2 1) \\ &\quad \cdot^{\mathbb{Z}_2} (X^3 +_2 X +_2 1) \\ &= P(X) \cdot^{\mathbb{Z}_2} \underbrace{(X^6 +_2 X^2)}_{P^{-1}(X)} +^{\mathbb{Z}_2} N(X) \cdot^{\mathbb{Z}_2} (X^3 +_2 X +_2 1). \end{aligned}$$

We obtain $45 \odot 68 = 1$ expressed by decimal numbers. All pairs of mutual inverse elements are given in the following list:

1↔1	2↔141	3↔246	4↔203	5↔82	6↔123
7↔209	8↔232	9↔79	10↔41	11↔192	12↔176
13↔225	14↔229	15↔199	16↔116	17↔180	18↔170
19↔75	20↔153	21↔43	22↔96	23↔95	24↔88
25↔63	26↔253	27↔204	28↔255	29↔64	30↔238
31↔178	32↔58	33↔110	34↔90	35↔241	36↔85
37↔77	38↔168	39↔201	40↔193	42↔152	44↔48
45↔68	46↔162	47↔194	49↔69	50↔146	51↔108
52↔243	53↔57	54↔102	55↔66	56↔242	59↔111
60↔119	61↔187	62↔89	65↔254	67↔103	70↔245
71↔105	72↔167	73↔100	74↔171	76↔84	78↔233
80↔237	81↔92	83↔202	86↔135	87↔191	91↔240
93↔236	94↔97	98↔175	99↔211	101↔166	104↔244
106↔145	107↔223	109↔147	112↔121	113↔183	114↔151
115↔133	117↔181	118↔186	120↔182	122↔208	124↔161
125↔250	126↔129	127↔130	128↔131	132↔150	134↔190
136↔155	137↔158	138↔149	139↔217	140↔247	142↔185
143↔164	144↔222	148↔216	154↔159	156↔249	157↔220
160↔251	163↔195	165↔184	169↔200	172↔206	173↔231
174↔210	177↔224	179↔239	188↔189	196↔218	197↔212
198↔228	205↔252	207↔230	213↔219	214↔226	215↔234
221↔248	227↔235				

A general investigation of the multiplication yields an easy to implement procedure. Consider any polynomial in $\mathbb{Z}_2[X]_8$,

$$P(X) = a_7 \cdot_2 X^7 +_2 \cdots +_2 a_1 \cdot_2 X +_2 a_0.$$

If we multiply $P(X)$ by X, we get

$$a_7 \cdot_2 X^8 +_2 \cdots +_2 a_1 \cdot_2 X^2 +_2 a_0 \cdot_2 X.$$

We compute the result modulo $N(X)$. If $a_7 = 0$, nothing changes and the result is $a_6 \cdot_2 X^7 +_2 \cdots +_2 a_1 \cdot_2 X^2 +_2 a_0 \cdot_2 X$. However, if $a_7 = 1$, we have to execute a polynomial division.

$$a_7 \cdot_2 X^8 +_2 \cdots +_2 a_1 \cdot_2 X^2 +_2 a_0 \cdot_2 X = a_7 \cdot^{\mathbb{Z}_2} N(X) +^{\mathbb{Z}_2} R(X)$$

with the remainder

$$\begin{aligned} R(X) = a_6 \cdot_2 X^7 +_2 a_5 \cdot_2 X^6 +_2 a_4 \cdot_2 X^5 + (a_3 +_2 a_7) \cdot_2 X^4 \\ +_2 (a_2 +_2 a_7) \cdot_2 X^3 +_2 a_1 \cdot_2 X^2 \\ +_2 (a_0 +_2 a_7) \cdot_2 X +_2 (0 +_2 a_7). \end{aligned}$$

This marks a left shift ($\ll$) by one bit, and if $a_7 = 1$, this is followed by a subsequent XOR operation with the bit sequence $00011011_{(2)}$.

Example 6.30. We calculate $45 \odot 68$ again. Since

$$45 \cong X^5 +_2 X^3 +_2 X^2 +_2 1 \text{ and } 68 \cong X^6 +_2 X^2,$$

we get

a_7	Operation	Sequence	Progress
		$00101101_{(2)}$	$\cong 45$
0	$\ll$	$01011010_{(2)}$	$\cdot_2 X$
0	$\ll$	$10110100_{(2)}$	$\cdot_2 X^2$
1	$\ll$	$01101000_{(2)}$	
	$\oplus$	$01110011_{(2)}$	$\cdot_2 X^3$
0	$\ll$	$11100110_{(2)}$	$\cdot_2 X^4$
1	$\ll$	$11001100_{(2)}$	
	$\oplus$	$11010111_{(2)}$	$\cdot_2 X^5$
1	$\ll$	$10101110_{(2)}$	
	$\oplus$	$10110101_{(2)}$	$\cdot_2 X^6$

Together, we can calculate

$$\begin{aligned}45 \odot 68 &= 45 \odot (4 \oplus 64) = 45 \odot 4 \oplus 45 \odot 64\\ &\cong 10110100_{(2)} +_2 10110101_{(2)} = 1_{(2)}\\ &\cong 1.\end{aligned}$$

Since

$$(\mathbb{Z}_2[X]/(X^8 +_2 X^4 +_2 X^3 +_2 X +_2 1),$$
$$+^{\mathbb{Z}_2}_{|\mathbb{Z}_2[X]_8}, \cdot^{\mathbb{Z}_2}_{X^8+_2X^4+_2X^3+_2X+_21}, 0, 1)$$

is a field (the Rijndael field), we can generate a polynomial ring based on the set $\mathbb{G}[Y] := \mathbb{Z}_2[X]/(X^8 +_2 X^4 +_2 X^3 +_2 X +_2 1)[Y]_4$ of polynomials on $\mathbb{Z}_2[X]/(X^8 +_2 X^4 +_2 X^3 +_2 X +_2 1)$. Any polynomial

$$\begin{aligned}P(Y) = a_3 \cdot^{\mathbb{Z}_2}_{X^8+_2X^4+_2X^3+_2X+_21} Y^3\\ +^{\mathbb{Z}_2}_{|\mathbb{Z}_2[X]_8} a_2 \cdot^{\mathbb{Z}_2}_{X^8+_2X^4+_2X^3+_2X+_21} Y^2\\ +^{\mathbb{Z}_2}_{|\mathbb{Z}_2[X]_8} a_1 \cdot^{\mathbb{Z}_2}_{X^8+_2X^4+_2X^3+_2X+_21} Y +^{\mathbb{Z}_2}_{|\mathbb{Z}_2[X]_8} a_0, \ a_i \in \mathbb{Z}_2[X]_8,\end{aligned}$$

is very difficult to use. Thus, we abbreviate the notation at this point. The coefficients are the essential points. Since all a_i are polynomials that can be represented by values in $\mathbb{Z}_{256}$, we shortly denote

$$P(Y) = [a_3, a_2, a_1, a_0], \ a_i \in \mathbb{Z}_{256}.$$

For example, we get a special polynomial

$$A(Y) = [03_{(16)}, 01_{(16)}, 01_{(16)}, 02_{(16)}], \tag{6.11}$$

that will be used later. Next, we define an addition on this set. For abbreviation, we denote $\boxplus = +^{\mathbb{Z}_2[X]/(X^8+_2X^4+_2X^3+_2X+_21)}_{|\mathbb{G}[Y]}$.

$$\begin{aligned}\boxplus : \mathbb{G}[Y] \times \mathbb{G}[Y] \to \mathbb{G}[Y], \ [a_3, a_2, a_1, a_0] \boxplus [b_3, b_2, b_1, b_0]\\ := \left[a_3 +^{\mathbb{Z}_2}_{|\mathbb{Z}_2[X]_8} b_3, a_2 +^{\mathbb{Z}_2}_{|\mathbb{Z}_2[X]_8} b_2, a_1 +^{\mathbb{Z}_2}_{|\mathbb{Z}_2[X]_8} b_1, a_0 +^{\mathbb{Z}_2}_{|\mathbb{Z}_2[X]_8} b_0\right].\end{aligned}$$

Example 6.31.

$$A(Y) = [03_{(16)}, 01_{(16)}, 01_{(16)}, 02_{(16)}],\ B(Y) = [54_{(16)}, 74_{(16)}, 90_{(16)}, 14_{(16)}].$$

$$\begin{aligned} &A(Y) \boxplus B(Y) \\ &\quad = [03_{(16)}, 01_{(16)}, 01_{(16)}, 02_{(16)}] \boxplus [54_{(16)}, 74_{(16)}, 90_{(16)}, 14_{(16)}] \\ &\quad = [00000011_{(2)}, 00000001_{(2)}, 00000001_{(2)}, 00000010_{(2)}] \\ &\qquad \boxplus [01010100_{(2)}, 01101100_{(2)}, 10010000_{(2)}, 00010100_{(2)}] \\ &\quad = [01010111_{(2)}, 01101101_{(2)}, 10010001_{(2)}, 00010110_{(2)}] \\ &\quad = [57_{(16)}, 6d_{(16)}, 91_{(16)}, 16_{(16)}]. \end{aligned}$$

A multiplication is defined by an ordinary multiplication operation modulo $\tilde{N}(X) = X^4 +_2 1$. For abbreviation, we denote

$$\boxdot = \cdot^{\mathbb{Z}_2[X]/(X^4+_2 1)}.$$

Since we have polynomials of degree three after raw multiplication without modulo computation, we obtain a polynomial of degree six.

$$[c_6, c_5, c_4, c_3, c_2, c_1, c_0] = [a_3, a_2, a_1, a_0] \boxdot [b_3, b_2, b_1, b_0],$$

in which

$$c_k = \sum_{i+j=k} a_i \boxdot_{N(X)} b_j.$$

By calculation, we can denote any coefficient:

$$\begin{aligned} c_0 &= a_0 \boxdot_{\tilde{N}(X)} b_0, \\ c_1 &= a_0 \boxdot_{\tilde{N}(X)} b_1 +^{\mathbb{Z}_2}_{|\mathbb{Z}_2[X]_8} a_1 \boxdot_{\tilde{N}(X)} b_0, \\ c_2 &= a_0 \boxdot_{\tilde{N}(X)} b_2 +^{\mathbb{Z}_2}_{|\mathbb{Z}_2[X]_8} a_1 \boxdot_{\tilde{N}(X)} b_1 +^{\mathbb{Z}_2}_{|\mathbb{Z}_2[X]_8} a_2 \boxdot_{N(X)} b_0, \\ c_3 &= a_0 \boxdot_{\tilde{N}(X)} b_3 +^{\mathbb{Z}_2}_{|\mathbb{Z}_2[X]_8} a_1 \boxdot_{\tilde{N}(X)} b_2 +^{\mathbb{Z}_2}_{|\mathbb{Z}_2[X]_8} a_2 \boxdot_{\tilde{N}(X)} b_1, \\ &\quad +^{\mathbb{Z}_2}_{|\mathbb{Z}_2[X]_8} a_3 \boxdot_{\tilde{N}(X)} b_0, \\ c_4 &= a_1 \boxdot_{\tilde{N}(X)} b_3 +^{\mathbb{Z}_2}_{|\mathbb{Z}_2[X]_8} a_2 \boxdot_{\tilde{N}(X)} b_2 +^{\mathbb{Z}_2}_{|\mathbb{Z}_2[X]_8} a_3 \boxdot_{\tilde{N}(X)} b_1, \\ c_5 &= a_2 \boxdot_{\tilde{N}(X)} b_3 +^{\mathbb{Z}_2}_{|\mathbb{Z}_2[X]_8} a_3 \boxdot_{\tilde{N}(X)} b_2, \text{ and} \\ c_6 &= a_3 \boxdot_{\tilde{N}(X)} b_3. \end{aligned}$$

Because of

$$X^{4i+k} = (X^{4(i-1)+k} +_2 \cdots +_2 X^k) \cdot_2 (X^4 +_2 1) +_2 X^k,$$

for $i \in \mathbb{N}$ and $k \in \mathbb{Z}_4$, we can write

$$X^{4i+k} \bmod (X^4 +_2 1) = X^k \Leftrightarrow X^j \bmod (X^4 +_2 1) = X^{j \bmod 4}.$$

Thus, a multiplication modulo $\tilde{N}(X) = (X^4 +_2 1)$ yields the multiplication $\boxdot_{\tilde{N}(X)} : \mathbb{G}[Y] \times \mathbb{G}[Y] \to \mathbb{G}[Y]$,

$$\begin{aligned}
[d_3, d_2, d_1, d_0] &:= [a_3, a_2, a_1, a_0] \boxdot_{\tilde{N}(X)} [b_3, b_2, b_1, b_0] \\
&= \left[c_3, c_2 +^{\mathbb{Z}_2}_{|\mathbb{Z}_2[X]_8} c_6, c_1 +^{\mathbb{Z}_2}_{|\mathbb{Z}_2[X]_8} c_5, c_0 +^{\mathbb{Z}_2}_{|\mathbb{Z}_2[X]_8} c_4\right] \\
&= \begin{bmatrix} a_0 & a_1 & a_2 & a_3 \\ a_3 & a_0 & a_1 & a_2 \\ a_2 & a_3 & a_0 & a_1 \\ a_1 & a_2 & a_3 & a_0 \end{bmatrix} \begin{bmatrix} b_3 \\ b_2 \\ b_1 \\ b_0 \end{bmatrix}.
\end{aligned} \tag{6.12}$$

The latter term is written down in a notation similar to a matrix multiplication.

Example 6.32.

$$\begin{aligned}
A(Y) &= [03_{(16)}, 01_{(16)}, 01_{(16)}, 02_{(16)}], \\
B(Y) &= [0b_{(16)}, 0d_{(16)}, 09_{(16)}, 0e_{(16)}].
\end{aligned}$$

We calculate $A(Y) \boxdot_{\tilde{N}(X)} B(Y)$.

$c_0 = Y^4 +_2 Y^3 +_2 Y^2 \bmod (Y^4 +_2 1) = Y^3 +_2 Y^2 +_2 1,$

$c_4 = Y^4 +_2 Y^3 +_2 Y^2 +_2 1 \bmod (Y^4 +_2 1) = Y^3 +_2 Y^2,$

$c_1 = Y^4 +_2 Y^3 +_2 Y^2 \bmod (Y^4 +_2 1) = Y^3 +_2 Y^2 +_2 1,$

$c_5 = Y^4 +_2 Y^3 +_2 Y^2 \bmod (Y^4 +_2 1) = Y^3 +_2 Y^2 +_2 1,$

$c_2 = Y^4 +_2 Y^3 +_2 Y^2 +_2 1 \bmod (Y^4 +_2 1) = Y^3 +_2 Y^2 +_2 1,$

$c_6 = Y^4 +_2 Y^3 +_2 Y^2 +_2 1 \bmod (Y^4 +_2 1) = Y^3 +_2 Y^2 +_2 1,$ and

$c_3 = 0.$

It follows

$$\begin{bmatrix} 02_{(16)} & 01_{(16)} & 01_{(16)} & 03_{(16)} \\ 03_{(16)} & 02_{(16)} & 01_{(16)} & 01_{(16)} \\ 01_{(16)} & 03_{(16)} & 02_{(16)} & 01_{(16)} \\ 01_{(16)} & 01_{(16)} & 03_{(16)} & 02_{(16)} \end{bmatrix} \begin{bmatrix} 0b_{(16)} \\ 0d_{(16)} \\ 09_{(16)} \\ 0e_{(16)} \end{bmatrix} = \begin{bmatrix} 00_{(16)} \\ 00_{(16)} \\ 00_{(16)} \\ 01_{(16)} \end{bmatrix},$$

resulting in $B(Y) = A(Y)^{-1}$.

6.3.2.1 *Structure of the AES*

The AES is a cipher system based on rounds and works on 128-bit blocks. That means $\mathcal{P} = \mathcal{C} = \mathbb{Z}_2^{128}$, and in a byte-by-byte manner

$$\begin{aligned} m &= m_0||m_1||\cdots||m_{15}, \; m_i \in \mathbb{Z}_2^8, \text{ and} \\ c &= c_0||c_1||\cdots||c_{15}, \qquad c_i \in \mathbb{Z}_2^8. \end{aligned}$$

Inside the process of encryption or decryption, a block is called a state s and the bits are arranged in a matrix-like form. Initially, we set

$$s = (s_{ij}), \quad s_{ij} = m_{i+4j}, \quad i,j \in \mathbb{Z}_4,$$

in the encryption process. Finally, we set

$$c_{i+4j} = s_{ij}, \quad i,j \in \mathbb{Z}_4.$$

The blocks are connected using one of the block cipher modes of operation. There are three different key sizes possible: 128, 192 or 256 bits. Depending on the key size, there is a different count of rounds:

Label	Key size (ks)	Number of rounds (nr)
AES-128	128	10
AES-192	192	12
AES-256	256	14

For both encryption and decryption, there are four different transformations used:

(Inv)SubBytes	A byte substitution using an S-box,
(Inv)ShiftRows	Shifting rows of the state by different offsets,
(Inv)MixColumns	Mixing the bits within each column of the state, and
AddRoundKey	Adding a round key to the state.

The transformations are executed in the order mentioned above, as observed in Algorithm 6.3.

Algorithm 6.3: The AES encryption base structure

Require: $m \in \mathbb{Z}_2^{128},\ k \in \mathbb{Z}_2^{\mathrm{ks}}$.
Ensure: $c = \mathrm{AES}_k(m) \in \mathbb{Z}_2^{128}$.
$m := m_0||m_1||\cdots||m_{15},\ m_i \in \mathbb{Z}_2^8$.
$s := (s_{ij}), \quad s_{ij} := m_{i+4j}, \quad i, j \in \mathbb{Z}_4$.
$\mathrm{rk} := \mathrm{GenerateRoundKeys}(k, \mathrm{nr})$.
$s := \mathrm{AddRoundKey}(s, \mathrm{rk}_0)$.
for $r := 1$ to $\mathrm{nr} - 1$ **do**
  $s := \mathrm{SubBytes}(s)$.
  $s := \mathrm{ShiftRows}(s)$.
  $s := \mathrm{MixColumns}(s)$.
  $s := \mathrm{AddRoundKey}(s, \mathrm{rk}_r)$.
end for
$s := \mathrm{SubBytes}(s)$.
$s := \mathrm{ShiftRows}(s)$.
$s := \mathrm{AddRoundKey}(s, \mathrm{rk}_{\mathrm{nr}})$.
$c := c_0||c_1||\cdots||c_{15},\ c_i \in \mathbb{Z}_2^8$.
$c_{i+4j} := s_{ij}, \quad i, j \in \mathbb{Z}_4$.
return c.

6.3.2.2 *SubBytes and InvSubBytes*

We change the internal state by Algorithm 6.4.

Algorithm 6.4: SubBytes

Require: $s = (s_{ij}), \quad s_{ij} \in \mathbb{Z}_2^8, \quad i, j \in \mathbb{Z}_4$.
Ensure: $s = (s_{ij}), \quad s_{ij} \in \mathbb{Z}_2^8, \quad i, j \in \mathbb{Z}_4$.
$s_{ij} := \mathrm{Invert}(s_{ij}), \quad i, j \in \mathbb{Z}_4$.
$s_{ij} := \mathrm{AffineTrans}(s_{ij}), \quad i, j \in \mathbb{Z}_4$.
return s.

The subroutine "Invert" works as follows. Each byte s_{ij} represents a polynomial $P(X) \in \mathbb{Z}_2[X]/(X^8 +_2 X^4 +_2 X^3 +_2 X +_2 1)$. Thus, there is an inverse polynomial $P^{-1}(X)$ represented by a bit sequence, which is the result of Invert(s_{ij}). If the input is the Null-polynomial, we define the Null-polynomial as the "inverse element" here. Getting an inverse element is a non-linear operation and provides a strong part of the AES's security. The second subroutine "AffineTrans" is an affine transformation. Again, the input byte represents a polynomial $P(X)$. However, in this case, we use the polynomial $N(X) = X^8 +_2 1$ for modulo operations. Consider two more polynomials,

$$A(X) = X^4 +_2 X^3 +_2 X^2 +_2 X +_2 1 \text{ and } B(X) = X^6 +_2 X^5 +_2 X +_2 1,$$

and define the transformation "AffineTrans"

$$\mathbb{Z}_2[X]_8 \times \mathbb{Z}_2[X]_8 \to \mathbb{Z}_2[X]_8,\ S(X) \mapsto A(X) \cdot^{\mathbb{Z}_2}_{N(X)} S(X) +^{\mathbb{Z}_2}_{|\mathbb{Z}_2[X]_8} B(X)$$

on the commutative ring with identity $\mathbb{Z}_2[X]/(X^8 +_2 1)$.[8]

Example 6.33. Consider

$$P(X) = X^5 +_2 X^3 +_2 X^2 +_2 1 \cong 00101101_{(2)} \cong 45_{(10)} \cong 2d_{(16)}.$$

We see that

$$A(X) = X^4 +_2 X^3 +_2 X^2 +_2 X +_2 1 \cong 00011111_{(2)} \cong 31_{(10)}, \text{ and}$$
$$B(X) = X^6 +_2 X^5 +_2 X +_2 1 \cong 01100011_{(2)} \cong 99_{(10)}.$$

From Example 6.29 we know that

$$P^{-1}(X) = X^6 +_2 X^2 \cong 01000100_{(2)} \cong 68_{(10)}.$$

Hence, we can calculate

$$A(X) \cdot^{\mathbb{Z}_2} P^{-1}(X) = X^{10} +_2 X^9 +_2 X^8 +_2 X^7 +_2 X^5 +_2 X^4 +_2 X^3 +_2 X^2$$

and

$$A(X) \cdot^{\mathbb{Z}_2}_{X^8+_2 1} P^{-1}(X) = X^7 +_2 X^5 +_2 X^4 +_2 X^3 +_2 X +_2 1 \cong 10111011_{(2)}.$$

In the last step, we have to execute a bitwise XOR

$$10111011_{(2)} \oplus 01100011_{(2)} = 11011000_{(2)} \cong 216_{(10)} \cong d8_{(16)}.$$

Thus, we have SubBytes($00101101_{(2)}$) $= 11011000_{(2)}$.

[8]The notation follows the notation of a finite field from Remark 6.22.

Table 6.18 Rijndael S-box (SubBytes).

	0	1	2	3	4	5	6	7	8	9	*a*	*b*	c	*d*	*e*	*f*
0	63	7*c*	77	7*b*	*f*2	6*b*	6*f*	*c*5	30	01	67	2*b*	*fe*	*d*7	*ab*	76
1	*ca*	82	*c*9	7*d*	*fa*	59	47	*f*0	*ad*	*d*4	*a*2	*af*	9*c*	*a*4	72	*c*0
2	*b*7	*fd*	93	26	36	3*f*	*f*7	*cc*	34	*a*5	*e*5	*f*1	71	**d8**	31	15
3	04	*c*7	23	*c*3	18	96	05	9*a*	07	12	80	*e*2	*eb*	27	*b*2	75
4	09	83	2*c*	1*a*	1*b*	6*e*	5*a*	*a*0	52	3*b*	*d*6	*b*3	29	*e*3	2*f*	84
5	53	*d*1	00	*ed*	20	*fc*	*b*1	5*b*	6*a*	*cb*	*be*	39	4*a*	4*c*	58	*cf*
6	*d*0	*ef*	*aa*	*fb*	43	4*d*	33	85	45	*f*9	02	7*f*	50	3*c*	9*f*	*a*8
7	51	*a*3	40	8*f*	92	9*d*	38	*f*5	*bc*	*b*6	*da*	21	10	*ff*	*f*3	*d*2
8	*cd*	0*c*	13	*ec*	5*f*	97	44	17	*c*4	*a*7	7*e*	3*d*	64	5*d*	19	73
9	60	81	4*f*	*dc*	22	2*a*	90	88	46	*ee*	*b*8	14	*de*	5*e*	0*b*	*db*
a	*e*0	32	3*a*	0*a*	49	06	24	5*c*	*c*2	*d*3	*ac*	62	91	95	*e*4	79
b	*e*7	*c*8	37	6*d*	8*d*	*d*5	4*e*	*a*9	6*c*	56	*f*4	*ea*	65	7*a*	*ae*	08
c	*ba*	78	25	2*e*	1*c*	*a*6	*b*4	*c*6	*e*8	*dd*	74	1*f*	4*b*	*bd*	8*b*	8*a*
d	70	3*e*	*b*5	66	48	03	*f*6	0*e*	61	35	57	*b*9	86	*c*1	1*d*	9*e*
e	*e*1	*f*8	98	11	69	*d*9	8*e*	94	9*b*	1*e*	87	*e*9	*ce*	55	28	*df*
f	8*c*	*a*1	89	0*d*	*bf*	*e*6	42	68	41	99	2*d*	0*f*	*b*0	54	*bb*	16

The whole "SubBytes" operation can be represented by an S-box representation. Let the input be given by a hexadecimal representation. By taking the first digit for the row and the second for the column, we obtain the result of the operation. For convenience, the index "$_{(16)}$" indicates a hexadecimal number is omitted. In mathematical notation, we write

$$\mathbb{Z}_2^8 \to \mathbb{Z}_2^8,\ b \mapsto \text{SubBytes}(b). \tag{6.13}$$

To reverse the SubBytes operation we have to first prove that $A(X)$ is invertible modulo $N(X) = X^8 +_2 1$. The extended Euclidean algorithm yields

$$1 = (1 +_2 X +_2 X^2) \cdot^{\mathbb{Z}_2}_{X^8+_2 1} N(X) + \underbrace{(X +_2 X^3 +_2 X^6)}_{A^{-1}(X)} \cdot^{\mathbb{Z}_2}_{X^8+_2 1} A(X).$$

Hence, we can define the affine transformation "InvAffineTrans"

$$\begin{aligned} &\mathbb{Z}_2[X]_8 \times \mathbb{Z}_2[X]_8 \to \mathbb{Z}_2[X]_8, \\ &\qquad \tilde{S}(X) \mapsto A^{-1}(X) \cdot^{\mathbb{Z}_2}_{N(X)} (\tilde{S}(X) -^{\mathbb{Z}_2}_{|\mathbb{Z}_2[X]_8} B(X), \end{aligned}$$

and determine $P(X)$ by inverting $\tilde{S}(X)$ in $\mathbb{Z}_2[X]/(X^8 +_2 X^4 +_2 X^3 +_2 X +_2 1)$. Again, this can be combined in the inverse S-box representation.

Algorithm 6.5: InvSubBytes

Require: $s = (s_{ij}), \quad s_{ij} \in \mathbb{Z}_2^8, \quad i, j \in \mathbb{Z}_4.$
Ensure: $s = (s_{ij}), \quad s_{ij} \in \mathbb{Z}_2^8, \quad i, j \in \mathbb{Z}_4.$
$s_{ij} :=$ InvAffineTrans$(s_{ij}), \quad i, j \in \mathbb{Z}_4.$
$s_{ij} :=$ Invert$(s_{ij}), \quad i, j \in \mathbb{Z}_4.$
return s.

6.3.2.3 *ShiftRows and InvShiftRows*

We modify the internal state using Algorithm 6.6. The bytes in the rows of the state are circularly shifted by different offsets, except for the first row that remains unchanged.

Algorithm 6.6: ShiftRows

Require: $s = (s_{ij}), \quad s_{ij} \in \mathbb{Z}_2^8, \quad i, j \in \mathbb{Z}_4.$
Ensure: $\tilde{s} = (\tilde{s}_{ij}), \quad \tilde{s}_{ij} \in \mathbb{Z}_2^8, \quad i, j \in \mathbb{Z}_4.$
$\tilde{s}_{ij} := s_{i,(j+i) \bmod 4}, \quad i \in \{1, 2, 3\}, j \in \mathbb{Z}_4.$
return $\tilde{s}$.

The inverse shift operation has to first cancel the shift, which can be done by Algorithm 6.7 because

$$s_{ij} = s_{i,(((j+i) \bmod 4)-i) \bmod 4}.$$

Algorithm 6.7: InvShiftRows

Require: $s = (s_{ij}), \quad s_{ij} \in \mathbb{Z}_2^8, \quad i, j \in \mathbb{Z}_4.$
Ensure: $\tilde{s} = (\tilde{s}_{ij}), \quad \tilde{s}_{ij} \in \mathbb{Z}_2^8, \quad i, j \in \mathbb{Z}_4.$
$\tilde{s}_{ij} := s_{i,(j-i) \bmod 4}, \quad i \in \{1, 2, 3\}, j \in \mathbb{Z}_4.$
return $\tilde{s}$.

6.3.2.4 *MixColumns and InvMixColumns*

Let $s = (s_{ij})$ be the state and $S_{ij}(X)$ be the corresponding polynomial to s_{ij}. By using the polynomial (6.11),

$$A(Y) = [03_{(16)}, 01_{(16)}, 01_{(16)}, 02_{(16)}],$$

from the set $\mathbb{G}[Y] := \mathbb{Z}_2[X]/(X^8 +_2 X^4 +_2 X^3 +_2 X +_2 1)[Y]_4$ of polynomials over $\mathbb{Z}_2[X]/(X^8 +_2 X^4 +_2 X^3 +_2 X +_2 1)$, we define "MixColumns" in terms of

$$\mathbb{G}[Y] \times \mathbb{G}[Y] \to \mathbb{G}[Y],$$
$$\begin{bmatrix} s_{3,j} \\ s_{2,j} \\ s_{1,j} \\ s_{0,j} \end{bmatrix} \mapsto \underbrace{\begin{bmatrix} 02_{(16)} & 01_{(16)} & 01_{(16)} & 03_{(16)} \\ 03_{(16)} & 02_{(16)} & 01_{(16)} & 01_{(16)} \\ 01_{(16)} & 03_{(16)} & 02_{(16)} & 01_{(16)} \\ 01_{(16)} & 01_{(16)} & 03_{(16)} & 02_{(16)} \end{bmatrix}}_{A} \begin{bmatrix} s_{3,j} \\ s_{2,j} \\ s_{1,j} \\ s_{0,j} \end{bmatrix}$$

for every $j \in \mathbb{Z}_4$. From Example 6.32, we see that $A(Y)$ is invertible, i.e.,

$$A^{-1}(Y) = [0b_{(16)}, 0d_{(16)}, 09_{(16)}, 0e_{(16)}],$$

and thus, we get "InvMixColumns" by

$$\mathbb{G}[Y] \times \mathbb{G}[Y] \to \mathbb{G}[Y],$$
$$\begin{bmatrix} s_{3,j} \\ s_{2,j} \\ s_{1,j} \\ s_{0,j} \end{bmatrix} \mapsto \begin{bmatrix} 0e_{(16)} & 09_{(16)} & 0d_{(16)} & 0b_{(16)} \\ 0b_{(16)} & 0e_{(16)} & 09_{(16)} & 0d_{(16)} \\ 0d_{(16)} & 0b_{(16)} & 0e_{(16)} & 09_{(16)} \\ 09_{(16)} & 0d_{(16)} & 0b_{(16)} & 0e_{(16)} \end{bmatrix} \begin{bmatrix} s_{3,j} \\ s_{2,j} \\ s_{1,j} \\ s_{0,j} \end{bmatrix}$$

for every $j \in \mathbb{Z}_4$. "MixColumns" and "InvMixColumns" are each a special kind of Hill cipher. Let $[A_i]$ be the ith row of the matrix A

beginning with index zero. Then, "MixColumns" can be written in pseudocode by Algorithm 6.8.

Algorithm 6.8: MixColumns

Require: $s = (s_{ij}), \quad s_{ij} \in \mathbb{Z}_2^8, \quad i, j \in \mathbb{Z}_4.$

Ensure: $\tilde{s} = (\tilde{s}_{ij}), \quad \tilde{s}_{ij} \in \mathbb{Z}_2^8, \quad i, j \in \mathbb{Z}_4.$

$i := 3.$

$j := 0.$

while $j < 4$ **do**

  while $i > -1$ **do**

$$\tilde{s}_{ij} := [A_{3-i}] \begin{bmatrix} s_{3j} \\ s_{2j} \\ s_{1j} \\ s_{0j} \end{bmatrix}.$$

    $i := i - 1.$

    $j := j + 1.$

  end while

end while

return $\tilde{s}$.

6.3.2.5 *Generating the Round Keys*

The given key has to be expanded, such that there is another key for each round. Algorithm 6.9 shows the proceeding. There are three internal functions inside the process. "RotWord" is the function

$$(\mathbb{Z}_2^8)^4 \to (\mathbb{Z}_2^8)^4, \quad \begin{bmatrix} a \\ b \\ c \\ d \end{bmatrix} \mapsto \begin{bmatrix} b \\ c \\ d \\ a \end{bmatrix}.$$

"SubWord" takes a four-byte input and applies the Rijndael S-box from Table 6.18 to each of the bytes. At last, "Rcon" is a four-byte word that always remains constant. Let "hex" calculate the hexadecimal representation of a polynomial and $h_{(16)} = \text{hex}(X^{i-1} \bmod (X^8 +_2 X^4 +_2 X^3 +_2 X +_2 1))$. We note

$$\mathbb{Z} \to \mathbb{Z}_2^{32}, \; i \mapsto \text{Rcon}(i) := h_{(16)} || 00_{(16)} || 00_{(16)} || 00_{(16)}.$$

Algorithm 6.9: GenerateRoundKeys

Require: $k \in \mathbb{Z}_2^{\text{ks}}, \text{nr}$.
Ensure: $\text{rk} \in \mathbb{Z}_2^{\text{nr}+1,128}$.
$\text{nk} := \text{ks}/32$.
$t \in \mathbb{Z}_2^{32}$.
$\text{key} \in \mathbb{Z}_2^{4\cdot\text{nk},8}$
$\text{rk} \in \mathbb{Z}_2^{\text{nr}+1,128}$.
$w \in \mathbb{Z}_2^{4\cdot(\text{nr}+1),32}$.
$i := 0$.
while $i < 4 \cdot \text{nk}$ **do**
  $\text{key}_i := k_{8\cdot i}||k_{8\cdot i+1}||k_{8\cdot i+2}||k_{8\cdot i+3}||k_{8\cdot i+4}||k_{8\cdot i+5}||k_{8\cdot i+6}||k_{8\cdot i+7}$.
  $i := i + 1$.
end while
$i := 0$.
while $i < \text{nk}$ **do**
  $w_i := \text{key}_0||\text{key}_1||\text{key}_2||\text{key}_3$.
  $i := i + 1$.
end while
$i := \text{nk}$.
while $i < 4 \cdot (\text{nr} + 1)$ **do**
  $t := w_{i-1}$
  if $i \bmod \text{nk} = 0$ **then**
    $t := \text{SubWord}(\text{RotWord}(t)) \oplus \text{Rcon}(i/\text{nk})$.
  else if $\text{nk} > 6$ **and** $i \bmod \text{nk} = 4$ **then**
    $t := \text{SubWord}(t)$.
  end if
  $w_i := w_{i-\text{nk}} \oplus t$.
  $i := i + 1$.
end while
$i := 0$.
while $i < 4 \cdot \text{nr} + 1$ **do**
  $\text{rk}_i := w_{4\cdot i}||w_{4\cdot i+1}||w_{4\cdot i+2}||w_{4\cdot i+3}$.
  $i := i + 1$.
end while
return rk.

6.3.2.6 *AddRoundKey*

Adding the round key is an XOR operation. The round key is first put into a 4×4 matrix of bytes. The state is then XOR-ed with the corresponding elements of the matrix. This can be done by Algorithm 6.10.

Algorithm 6.10: AddRoundKey

Require: $s = (s_{ij}),\quad s_{ij} \in \mathbb{Z}_2^8,\quad i, j \in \mathbb{Z}_4,\ \mathrm{rk} \in \mathbb{Z}_2^{128}.$
Ensure: $\tilde{s} = (\tilde{s}_{ij}),\quad \tilde{s}_{ij} \in \mathbb{Z}_2^8,\quad i, j \in \mathbb{Z}_4.$

```
i := 0.
j := 0.
while i < 4 do
    while j < 4 do
        s̃_ij := s_i,j ⊕ rk_{8·i+32·j} || rk_{8·i+32·j+1} || ··· || rk_{8·i+32·j+7}.
        j := j + 1.
        i := i + 1.
    end while
end while
return s̃.
```

Security of AES

If we look at the security of the AES, we can check the strict avalanche criteria by performing empirical studies that both criteria have been met.

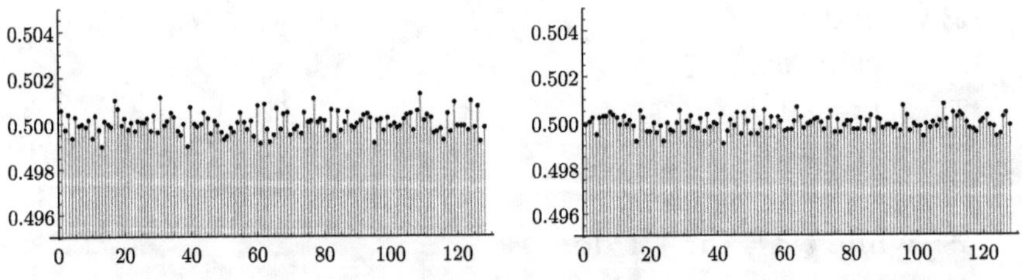

Figure 6.3 Strict avalanche criterion for the AES: Empirical probabilities of bit changes of the 128 output bits resulting from bit flips in the message (left) with a fixed key or in the key (right) with a fixed message.

6.4 Pohlig–Hellman Exponentiation Cipher

So far, two entities have to meet each other to exchange a secret key before cryptography can be performed. In the 1970s, some cryptographers explored going around this step. One of the first ciphers resulting from this exploration was an exponentiation cipher invented by Pohlig[9] and Hellman.[10] Though this did not solve the problem it is a classical private-key cipher system. Let $p \in \mathbb{N}$ be a prime number. We state $\mathcal{P} = \mathcal{C} = \mathbb{Z}_p$ and for now, $\mathcal{K} = \mathbb{Z}_p^\times$. By defining

$$e_k : \mathbb{Z}_p \to \mathbb{Z}_p,\ m \mapsto e_k(m) := m^k \bmod p, \tag{6.14}$$

we can encrypt a plaintext m given the parameters p and k. Let $c = e_k(m)$ be a ciphertext. How can we recover the plaintext? If $m = 0$, there is no issue because $m = 0 \Leftrightarrow c = 0$. Otherwise, Fermat's little theorem 3.86 tells us that for any $m \in \mathbb{Z}_p^\times$

$$m^{p-1} \bmod p = 1, \text{ or rather } m^p \bmod p = m.$$

Hence, we can look for some $k' \in \mathcal{K}$ satisfying

$$m = c^{k'} \bmod p = (m^k)^{k'} \bmod p = m^{k \cdot k'} \bmod p \text{ and } k \cdot k' \equiv_{p-1} 1.$$

The latter means that $k \cdot k' = z \cdot (p-1) + 1$ for some $z \in \mathbb{Z}$. Since not all of the k's have inverse elements modulo $p - 1$, we have to restrict the possible keys to $\mathcal{K} = \mathbb{Z}_{p-1}^\times$.

Definition 6.34. Let p be a prime number, $\mathcal{P} = \mathcal{C} = \mathbb{Z}_p$, $\mathcal{K} = \mathbb{Z}_{p-1}^\times$, $e_k(m) = m^k \bmod p$ and $d_{k'}(c) = c^{k'} \bmod p$, satisfying $k \cdot k' \equiv_{p-1} 1$. Then, the cipher system $(\mathcal{P}, \mathcal{C}, \mathcal{K}, \mathcal{E}, \mathcal{D})$ is called the *Pohlig–Hellman exponentiation cipher.*

[9]Steven Pohlig (1952–2017).

[10]Martin E. Hellman, born 1945.

There are $\phi(p-1)$ good keys for this cipher. In the best case, we have $p-1 = 2 \cdot q$, where q is prime and then we obtain $\phi(p-1) = q-1 = \frac{p-3}{2}$ such keys. If p is large enough, we will be secured against a brute-force ciphertext-only attack. If someone has a plaintext-ciphertext pair (m, c), they would have to solve the problem of finding any k' with

$$c^{k'} \bmod p = m,$$

which we normally write as a logarithmic problem

$$k' = \log_c(m).$$

However, the challenge here is finding a whole number k'. We call this the *discrete logarithm* and this creates a large problem that will be discussed in Chapter 7. Since we have to represent the plaintext in $\mathbb{Z}_p$, we can put together many letters in practice. This means that the Pohlig–Hellman exponentiation cipher is a block cipher.

Algorithm 6.11: Pohlig–Hellman encryption and decryption

Require: Prime p, secret key $k \in \mathbb{Z}_{p-1}^{\times}$, plaintext $m \in \mathbb{Z}_p$.
Ensure: Ciphertext c, decrypted plaintext m'.

1: $c := e_k(m) = m^k \bmod p$.
2: $k' := k^{-1} \bmod p - 1$.
3: $m' := d_{k'}(c) = c^{k'} \bmod p$.
4: **return** c, m'.

Example 6.35. The message "SECURITY" from Σ_{Lat}^8 has to be encrypted using a block size of two. The blockwise coding according to Example 2.13 results in a whole number representation. For example, SE $\to (18, 4) \to 26 \cdot 18 + 4 = 472$. Since $26^2 = 676$, we can choose the prime $p = 677$. Firstly, $\phi(p-1) = \phi(2^2 \cdot 13^2) = 2 \cdot 13 \cdot 12 = 312$ and the size of the key space is $|\mathcal{K}| = 312$. Further, by choosing $k = 431$ ($\text{GCD}(431, 676) = 1$), the "key for decryption" gets

$$k' = 527, \quad 1 = \underbrace{-149}_{\equiv_{676} 527} \cdot 431 + 95 \cdot 676.$$

Messages	SE	CU	RI	TY
m_i (encoded)	472	72	450	518
$c_i = m_i^{431} \bmod 677$	170	3	50	599
Decoded ciphertexts	GO	AD	BY	XB
$c_i^{527} \bmod 677$	472	72	450	518

Security of the exponentiation cipher

The Pohlig–Hellman exponentiation cipher is considered secure as long as it is hard to calculate the discrete logarithm. Another question is whether there are numbers $a, u \in \mathbb{Z}_p$ with $a \not\equiv_p u$ and $a^k \bmod p = u^k \bmod p$. However, if there are such numbers, we multiply the equation by k', resulting in

$$\begin{aligned} a^k \bmod p = u^k \bmod p &\Leftrightarrow \left(a^k\right)^{k'} \bmod p = \left(u^k\right)^{k'} \bmod p \\ &\Leftrightarrow a \bmod p = u \bmod p, \end{aligned}$$

which contradicts the assumption. Any $a \in \mathbb{Z}_p$ generates a different $a^k \bmod p$. Furthermore, the cipher system satisfies both the strict message avalanche criterion and the strict key avalanche criterion from Definition 5.25.

Example 6.36. Based on a 128-bit prime number, the resulting (binary) sequences show a probability of 50% for a bit change. This happens in both situations: a fixed key with bit flips in the message or a fixed message with bit flips in the key. The data shown here is empirically based on 2^{12} randomly chosen messages and keys.

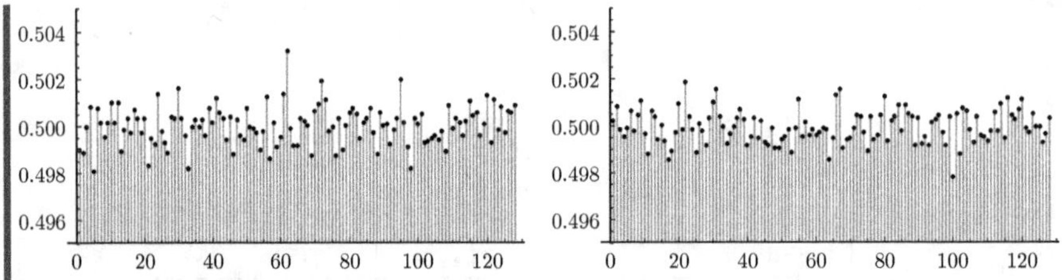

Figure 6.4 Strict avalanche criterion for the Pohlig–Hellman exponentiation cipher: Empirical probabilities of bit changes of the 128 output bits resulting from bit flips in the message (left) with a fixed key or in the key (right) with a fixed message.

Some problems will occur if we use the same k more than once. From $c_1 = m_1^k \bmod p$ and $c_2 = m_2^k \bmod p$, it follows $c_1 \cdot c_2 \bmod p = (m_1 \cdot m_2)^k \bmod p$. Given any "real" plaintext-ciphertext pair (m_1, c_1) and a "fabricated" plaintext-ciphertext pair (m_2, p_2), we can get a desired encryption for m. This can be prevented by randomizing the key k.

Chapter 7

Components of Public-Key Cryptosystems

Note 7.1. In this chapter, the requirements are:

- being familiar with basics of number theory, see Section 1.1, and
- being familiar with basics about groups and rings, see Section 3.1.

Selected literature: See (Hoffstein *et al.*, 2008; Stamp and Low, 2007; Stinson, 2005; Vaudenay, 2006).

Diffie[1] and Hellman mention a "brink of a revolution in cryptography" in (Diffie and Hellman, 1976, p. 644). In a private-key cryptosystem, a secret key $k \in \mathcal{K}$ is used to encrypt a message $m \in \mathcal{P}$ using an encryption function e on the sender's part, i.e., $e : \mathcal{P} \to \mathcal{C}$, $m \mapsto c := e_k(m)$. The receiver processes the decryption d using the same key to recover the original plaintext, $d : \mathcal{C} \to \mathcal{P}$, $c \mapsto m = d_k(c)$. Perfect secrecy can only be attained by a cryptosystem if the corresponding random variables are independent. The only known cryptosystem capable of perfect secrecy is a one-time pad. However, we know from Section 5.2.3 that this system is inefficient because the

[1]Whitfield Diffie, born 1944.

key has to provide as much uncertainty as the plaintext does. This means that the key has to be as long as the plaintext.

There are two main problems with private-key cryptography. Firstly, since each entity has to possess the key, there needs to be a secure channel for distributing the key. Just-in-time communication needs to establish an exchange of a key. Secondly, exactly one entity has to be able to exhibit provable knowledge for authenticity or non-repudiation. If a common key is used, two entities can at least be the origin of this knowledge. Furthermore, n entities need to have $\binom{n}{2} = \frac{n(n-1)}{2}$ different keys before the exchange can be secure. To solve these problems, there are two possibilities: (1) Exchanging the secret key on a so-called public-key distribution system and (2) using a public-key cryptosystem. The latter is characterized by the use of different keys at both the sender's and receiver's side. The receiver prepares a pair of keys, a public key and a corresponding private key. The public key has open read access and will be used by the sender for encryption. The private key is at the receiver and is intended for the decryption process. Third parties should not be able to estimate the private key, even though they might know the used cryptosystem and possess the public key.

7.1 Public-Key Distribution

Three years before Diffie and Hellman's revolutionary paper, Merkle,[2] a student of Hellman, was already concerned about the security of the key distribution channel. Although these ideas were not published until 1978 in (Merkle and Hellman, 1978), they already influenced his teacher Hellman.

7.1.1 *Merkle's puzzle*

In using a private-key cipher, there usually needs to be a secret exchange of the secret key between two entities. Therefore, if this communication is intercepted, the secrecy will be over. Merkle's idea was

[2]Ralph C. Merkle, born in 1952.

to drop the demanded secrecy and to assume complete interception. Let us think about two entities that agree on using a specific private-key cryptosystem, an identifying feature c and perhaps a key-limited cryptosystem that has a key space $\mathcal{K}$ of size n. One entity creates a number n of possible keys $k_1, \ldots, k_n$, each provided with a unique ID $i_1, \ldots, i_n$, and encrypts each sequence

$$i_j, k_j, c \text{ by } c_j = e_{f_j}(i_j, k_j, c),$$

where all $f_j \in \mathcal{K}$ are disjoint in pairs. Merkle calls such a sequence a "puzzle".[3] The communication partner receives all the resulting ciphertexts $c_1, \ldots, c_n$ and has to decrypt exactly one randomly chosen ciphertext, for instance, c_q. As expected, $n/2$ trials are performed on average during this brute-force attack, which can be done fast. After checking the identifying feature c they can resend the ID i_q and both entities know the secret key k_q for the actual communication. An adversary may explicitly know all of the puzzles and the transmitted ID. All they need to do to get the wanted key is to decrypt an average $n/2$ of the messages where each costs $n/2$ shots on average. This results in a square effort of $n/2 \cdot n/2$ trials. Alternatively, that may be enough, i.e., if a fast computer can do 10^{13} en- or decryptions a second,[4] we may create 2^{56} different puzzles using the DES from Section 6.2. The counterpart solves the problem within two hours, but the adversary needs 2^{110} shots to break the right puzzle. That means

$$\frac{2^{110}}{10^{13} \cdot 3600 \cdot 24 \cdot 365} = 4 \cdot 10^{12}$$

years, which is quite difficult. Against this backdrop, a large amount of time, space and capacity is needed for creating, storing and transmitting the data, indicating that this method is impractical. However, this is a necessary intermediate step that provides the inspiration to invent the important key agreement process of Diffie–Hellman.

[3]See (Merkle and Hellman, 1978, p. 296).

[4]The computer can break the DES in two hours using a brute-force attack.

Example 7.2. For example, we use an affine block cipher from Definition 4.18 with block size $t = 2$. Let $c = 90$ and $n = 10$. Let the keys $k_j = (k_{j1}, k_{j2}, k_{j3}, k_{j4})$ consist of four integers. For example, we create the following ten puzzles $(i_j, k_{j1}, k_{j2}, k_{j3}, k_{j4}, c)$:

$$(5, 11, 20, 22, 7, 90),\ (6, 16, 12, 19, 10, 90),\ (1, 4, 16, 6, 23, 90),$$
$$(7, 8, 7, 8, 13, 90),\ (4, 6, 12, 20, 22, 90),\ (9, 23, 4, 4, 7, 90),$$
$$(2, 11, 12, 0, 14, 90),\ (8, 9, 16, 21, 3, 90),\ (3, 8, 15, 9, 11, 90) \text{ and}$$
$$(0, 25, 3, 16, 1, 90).$$

For executing the affine block cipher, we encode the puzzles using letter sequences, i.e.,

$(5, 11, 20, 22, 7, 90)$
$\mapsto$ FIVEELEVENTWENTYTWENTYTWOSEVENNINETY
$(6, 16, 12, 19, 10, 90)$
$\mapsto$ SIXSIXTEENTWELVENINETEENTENNINETYZZZ.

and by introducing a padding with Z's if the sequence is too short, like in the second row. The following table shows the key (A, b) of the affine linear block cipher in the first column, and the second column contains the plaintext over the ciphertext.

Key	Plaintext / Ciphertext
DOIT,WK	FIVEELEVENTWENTYTWENTYTWOSEVENNINETY TULUGRQZIDXIIDZUXIIDZUXIEWQZIDRGNIZU
UVVX,PS	SIXSIXTEENTWELVENINETEENTENNINETYZZZ XIVFINLPELZNORZFBHVTLPELLPCSGRATGFAA
VSBX,RN	ONEFOURSIXTEENSIXTWENTYTHREENINETYZZ ZOJCVTWCBEUUXETHKFFXIVFGCVRFSCYOQMEP
ZZBK,BQ	SEVENEIGHTSEVENEIGHTTHIRTEENNINETYZZ FWCZKRNGBFFWCZKRNGBFBBCMEXKUGFKRKPDF
XAGJ,CF	FOURSIXTWELVETWENTYTWENTYTWONINETYZZ NFUSADLCORVAQSORPUIIORPUIIODPZPPXXFQ
TQDF,GX	NINETWENTYTHREEFOURFOURSEVENNINETYZZ RYFERIEWXSLLDQGIUJTVUJTICKEWRYFEXSXP
TPAZ,YN	TWOELEVENTWELVEZEROFOURTEENNINETYZZZ NRMJHJPJKUIJCSHORWBISTIUEJYAHAVUXOQO
CJPF,LL	EIGHTNINESIXTEENTWENTYONETHREENINETY NHIGKXOOZFAMHEGGNQGGFAAAIKWTDNFMVSFA
IJFS,DS	THREEEIGHTFIFTEENNINEELEVENNINETYZZZ KFTTTGRKWFLFGVTGQFCGTGXPZNQFCGYQEQMV
RAST,TC	ZEROTWENTYFIVETHREESIXTEENONENINETYZ CIWCEIJJEUAKMOEJWUJAZLEEJJXHJJZDJTLZ

Now, let the counterpart decrypt the seventh ciphertext using the key LJAZ, CN. They transmit ID 2 and both participants can work together.

7.1.2 *Diffie–Hellman key agreement*

Inspired by Merkle's idea, "New Directions in Cryptography"[5] had a deep impact on further development and research. Diffie and Hellman's method of exchanging a secret key is still being used, though there are still some disadvantages concerning its implementation. However, as we demonstrated, computational security will be granted if the number of Merkle's puzzles is appropriately large. Merkle had shared his ideas with Diffie and Hellmann before their article was published.[6] The latter applied the idea of computational fast examination on one side and computational hard examination on the another. They considered the modular exponentiation and proposed the following (communication) Protocol 7.1.

Protocol 7.1: Diffie–Hellman key agreement

Require: Prime number p, $\langle g \rangle = \mathbb{Z}_p^{\times}$.

Ensure: Secret key x_{AB}.

1: A chooses $x_A \in \{2, \ldots, p-2\}$ at random and computes $y_A := g^{x_A} \bmod p$.

2: B chooses $x_B \in \{2, \ldots, p-2\}$ at random and computes $y_B := g^{x_B} \bmod p$.

3: y_A gets transferred to B, y_B gets transferred to A.

4: A computes
$x_{AB} := y_B^{x_A} \bmod p = (g^{x_B} \bmod p)^{x_A} \bmod p = g^{x_B x_A} \bmod p.$

5: B computes
$x_{AB} := y_A^{x_B} \bmod p = (g^{x_A} \bmod p)^{x_B} \bmod p = g^{x_A x_B} \bmod p.$

6: **return** x_{AB} is a common secret key of A and B.

---

[5]See (Diffie and Hellman, 1976).

[6]See (Holden, 2017, p. 208).

This was the first method using the discrete logarithm. If we know the numbers p, g, $y_A = g^{x_A} \bmod p$ or $y_B = g^{x_B} \bmod p$, we have to solve one of the equations

$$g^{x_A} \bmod p = y_A \text{ or } g^{x_B} \bmod p = y_B$$

for some $x_A, x_B \in \mathbb{Z}_p$. After solving this, we can calculate x_{AB}, which is called the *Diffie–Hellman problem* and the core task is to solve the discrete logarithm, for example, according to Algorithm 7.4. We will soon see that it is possible to quickly compute y_A and y_B, but backward computing the discrete logarithm is slow.

Example 7.3. Let $p = 633825300151008188895770717987$ and $g = 2$ be given. Then, we can compute the public keys and the common secret key of A and B using the private keys $x_A = 126584$ and $x_B = 18544165841641$.

Entity	Public keys y_A and y_B	Common secret key x_{AB}
A	376929335322892368661007761494	476180515590621878051279928148
B	132382496838821719107940371914	476180515590621878051279928148

It is possible to get an overflow while computing the example, which is due to the big exponent. Thus, it is necessary to use an efficient algorithm for computing the modular power, according to Algorithm 7.3.

A smaller example can be performed by hand: $p = 17$, $g = 3$, $x_A = 7$ and $x_B = 9$. We obtain

$$y_A = 3^7 \bmod 17 = 11, \; y_B = 3^9 \bmod 17 = 14.$$

Next, A and B compute their common secret key by

$$x_{AB} = 14^7 \bmod 17 = 6 = 11^9 \bmod 17.$$

Since

$$\begin{aligned} y_A^{x_B} \bmod p &= (g^{x_A})^{x_B} \bmod p = g^{x_A \cdot x_B} \bmod p \\ &= g^{x_B \cdot x_A} \bmod p = (g^{x_B})^{x_A} \bmod p = y_B^{x_A} \bmod p, \end{aligned}$$

both entities have the same key and we say that the Diffie–Hellman key agreement ensures a mutual key establishment. However, how can we find the requested for generator in Algorithm 7.1? Fortunately, there are $\phi(p-1)$ generators according to the considerations of Theorem 3.67. If we know the prime factorization of $p-1$ according to Theorem 1.29, we can do it using Theorem 7.4.

Theorem 7.4. *Let p be prime. For $g \in \mathbb{Z}_p^\times$, it applies $\mathcal{L}(g) = \mathbb{Z}_p^\times \iff g^{\frac{p-1}{q_j}} \bmod p \neq 1$ for each prime divisor q_j of $p-1$.*

Proof. Let $m = \mathrm{ord}_{\mathbb{Z}_p^\times}(g)$, i.e., $m \mid p-1$, according to Corollary 3.34. Furthermore, consider the notation $p-1 = q_i \cdot Q_i$ for each prime divisor q_i of $p-1$ referred to in Theorem 1.29. It follows

$$\begin{aligned}\mathcal{L}(g) \neq \mathbb{Z}_p^\times &\Leftrightarrow m < p-1 \Leftrightarrow p-1 = v \cdot m \text{ for } v \in \mathbb{Z}, v \neq 1\\ &\Leftrightarrow p-1 = q_i \cdot Q_i = v \cdot m\\ &\Leftrightarrow \exists i : \; m \mid q_i \vee m \mid Q_i.\end{aligned}$$

If m divides the number q_i, there is any j satisfying $p-1 = q_j \cdot Q_j$ and $q_i \mid Q_j$ or q_i is a divisor of Q_i. In any case,

$$\begin{aligned}p-1 = q_i \cdot Q_i = v \cdot m &\Leftrightarrow \exists j : p-1 = q_j \cdot Q_j \wedge m \mid Q_j\\ &\Leftrightarrow p-1 = q_j \cdot Q_j = q_j \cdot k_j \cdot m \text{ for } k_j \in \mathbb{Z}\\ &\Leftrightarrow (p-1)/q_j = Q_j = k_j \cdot m\\ &\Leftrightarrow g^{\frac{p-1}{q_j}} \bmod p\\ &\quad = g^{k_j \cdot m} \bmod p = (g^m)^{k_j} \bmod p = 1. \quad \square\end{aligned}$$

If $p > 2$ is prime and $\mathcal{L}(g) = \mathbb{Z}_p^\times$, we have $g^{\frac{p-1}{2}} \bmod p \neq 1$. Squaring this equation yields

$$\left(g^{\frac{p-1}{2}}\right)^2 \bmod p = g^{p-1} \bmod p = 1.$$

A polynomial $P(X) = X^2 - 1 \in \mathbb{Z}_p[X]$ has two zeros: 1 and $p-1$, since $P(1) = 1^2 - 1 \bmod p = 0$ and $P(p-1) = p^2 - 2 \cdot p + 1 - 1 \bmod p = 0$. Thus,

$$g^{\frac{p-1}{2}} \bmod p \in \{1, p-1\}. \tag{7.1}$$

Since $g^{\frac{p-1}{2}} \bmod p \neq 1$, $g^{\frac{p-1}{2}} \bmod p = p-1$. This is a necessary condition for g being a generator of $\mathbb{Z}_p^\times$.

Example 7.5. In Example 7.3, we used the 100-bit prime number

$$p = 633825300151008188895770717987$$

and $g = 2$. Factorizing $p-1$ results in

$$p - 1 = 2 \cdot 316912650075504094447885358993.$$

Is $g = 2$ really a generator of $\mathbb{Z}_p^\times$? Using Theorem 7.4 we calculate

$$2^{316912650075504094447885358993} \bmod p = p - 1 \neq 1, \text{ and}$$
$$2^2 \bmod p = 4 \neq 1.$$

This proves that $g = 2$ is a generator of $\mathbb{Z}_p^\times$, i.e., $\mathcal{L}(2) = \mathbb{Z}_p^\times$.

Factorizing large numbers can be a big challenge. Example 7.5 is somewhat special. There is a prime number that is arrestingly composite. If q is prime and $p = 2 \cdot q + 1$ is likewise prime, then q is called a *Sophie Germain prime*[7] and p is called a *safe prime.* For such a safe prime, the process of testing for a generator is quite easy.

There is one major problem using the Diffie–Hellman key exchange, a *man in the middle attack.* If an adversary intercepts the communication between A and B, they may be able to join up in circuit. Consider such an entity named M (Mallory), who knows the common parameters of this communication, i.e., p and g. M now chooses any $x_M \in \{2, \ldots, p-2\}$ and establishes two separate key agreements. One is between A and M and the other between M and B. M uses x_M for both and generates x_{AM} and x_{BM}. A and B do not know what happened. They assume that they have established a connection with each other. However, M can now intercept

[7]Sophie Germain (1776–1831)

and manipulate the whole communication, which was thought to be secure. Therefore, there is no assurance of who A or B are communicating with. We have to ensure a so-called *mutual entity authentication*, i.e., the two communicating entities are authenticated to each other.

7.1.3 *Authentication and key establishment*

Since no participant can be sure about its counterpart in a Diffie–Hellman key exchange, a type of mutual authentication is necessary. One possibility is to make use of a trusted third party denoted by TP. Specifically, an actor whom both A and B trust. Furthermore, A has established a long-term key x_{ATP} with TP. Likewise B has established a long-term key x_{BTP} with TP. The authentication and key establishment are carried out in a five-pass process.[8] A and B need to generate nonces, i.e., random numbers that are used just once, as previously mentioned in Section 2.3.1.

Protocol 7.2: ISO9798-2-like key establishment and entity authentication

---

Require: Numbers x_A and x_B, random numbers r_A, r'_A and r_B, long term keys x_{ATP} and x_{BTP}, consistent with a cryptosystem convention.

Ensure: Secret key x_{AB} and mutual authentication between A and B.

1: B chooses r_B at random and sends $r_B||x_B$ to A.
2: A chooses r_A at random and sends $r_A||r_B||x_A||x_B$ to TP.
3: TP sends $e_{x_{ATP}}(r_A||x_{AB}||x_B)||e_{x_{BTP}}(r_B||x_{AB}||x_A)$ to A.
4: A decrypts and verifies the first part, chooses r'_A at random and sends $e_{x_{BTP}}(r_B||x_{AB}||x_A)||e_{x_{AB}}(r'_A||r_B)$ to B.
5: B decrypts and verifies the first part and sends $e_{x_{AB}}(r_B||r'_A||x_A)$ to A.
6: A decrypts and verifies the message.
7: **return** x_{AB} (a common secret key of A and B).

---

[8] According to (ISO/IEC, 1999).

Example 7.6. Again, we use the 100-bit prime number

$$p = 633825300151008188895770717987$$

and the numbers

$$\begin{aligned} x_A &= 126584, \\ x_B &= 18544165841641, \\ r_A &= 271149513617780391754181210084, \\ r_{A'} &= 364286903851281840123597028475, \\ r_B &= 723613620816743175125370043353, \\ x_{ATP} &= 135574756808890195877090605043, \text{ and} \\ x_{BTP} &= 140111474217722 7865757. \end{aligned}$$

For the sake of simplicity, we choose the Pohlig–Hellman exponentiation cipher from Section 6.4 with the ECB mode for all communications. TP generates

$$x_{AB} = 507320713019169990711111705871.$$

While running Protocol 7.2, A is using $x_{ATP}^{-1} \bmod p-1 = 299948207074515187213928653767$ and B is using $x_{BTP}^{-1} \bmod p-1 = 294518757836023955473076901645$. The protocol goes as follows.

$$B \xrightarrow[r_B||x_B]{723613620816743175125370043353||18544165841641} A$$

$$A \xrightarrow[r_A||r_B||x_A||x_B]{\substack{271149513617780391754181210084||723613620816743175125370043353|| \\ 126584||18544165841641}} TP$$

$$TP \xrightarrow[e_{x_{ATP}}(r_A||x_{AB}||x_B)||e_{x_{BTP}}(r_B||x_{AB}||x_A)]{\substack{320962224792050698199411371466||544686955012504456999719992040|| \\ 596735785294444161082761596772||349431751380216933545222440949|| \\ 394291725069277903030405279467||940466358619661718565333351073}} A$$

$$A \xrightarrow[e_{x_{BTP}}(r_B||x_{AB}||x_A)||e_{x_{AB}}(r'_A||r_B)]{\substack{349431751380216933545222440949||394291725069277903030405279467|| \\ 940466358619661718565333351073||628750887868218013290793385377|| \\ 482385919541575729668253720788}} B$$

$$B \xrightarrow[e_{x_{AB}}(r_B||r'_A||x_A)]{\substack{482385919541575729668253720788||628750887868218013290793385377|| \\ 629490343067847515332903644161}} A$$

7.2 One-way Functions

The two different approaches, an exponentiation cipher by Pohlig–Hellman and a key distribution by Diffie–Hellman, are based on the same idea. The calculation is easy but reverse engineering is much more difficult. This approach was identified at the beginning of the computer age.

Convention 7.7 (One-way function). A *one-way function* $f : X \to Y$ is a function that meets two properties:

- There is an efficient method for computing $y = f(x)$ for every $x \in X$, and
- There is no efficient method for computing $x = f^{-1}(\{y\})$ for almost every $y \in Y$.

In 1874, Jevons[9] addressed such a problem. He wrote[10]:

> "Can the reader say what two numbers multiplied together will produce the number 8616460799? I think it's unlikely that anyone but myself will ever know; for they are two large prime numbers, and can only be re-discovered by trying in succession a long series of prime divisors until the right one be fallen upon. The work would probably occupy a good computer for many weeks, but it did not occupy me many minutes to multiply the two factors together."

However, there was no evidence that such a function exists. Alternatively, there are some candidates for one-way functions that are not disproved to be such functions.

7.2.1 *Discrete exponentiation and logarithm*

In many situations, it is necessary to compute large powers of a number a modulo any other number n. This can be done by sequentially

[9] William S. Jevons (1835–1882).
[10] See (Jevons, 1875, p. 12).

multiplying a by itself and computing the remainder,

$$a^x \bmod n = ((((a \cdot_n a) \cdot_n a) \cdot_n a) \ldots) \cdot_n a, \quad x \in \mathbb{N}. \tag{7.2}$$

The 2-adic representation

$$x = b_0 + b_1 \cdot 2 + b_2 \cdot 2^2 + \cdot \ldots \cdot b_l 2^l,$$
$$b_1, \ldots, b_l \in \{0, 1\}, \quad l = \lfloor \log_2(x) \rfloor,$$

of x might help to simplify the procedure. By that, we can compute

$$\begin{aligned} a^x \bmod n &= a^{b_0 + b_1 \cdot 2 + b_2 \cdot 2^2 + \cdot \ldots \cdot b_l 2^l} \bmod n \\ &= a^{b_0} \cdot_n a^{b_1 \cdot 2} \cdot_n a^{b_2 \cdot 2^2} \cdot_n \cdots \cdot_n a^{b_l \cdot 2^l} \\ &= a^{b_0} \cdot_n \left(a^{2^1}\right)^{b_1} \cdot_n \left(a^{2^2}\right)^{b_2} \cdot_n \cdots \cdot_n \left(a^{2^l}\right)^{b_l}. \end{aligned}$$

The factors $a^{2^i} \bmod n = (a^{2^{i-1}})^2 \bmod n$ can be easily computed by squaring the factor before. Together, there are at most

$$2(l+1) = 2\lceil \log_2(x) \rceil \tag{7.3}$$

multiplications necessary.

Algorithm 7.3: Square-and-multiply algorithm

Require: $n, x \in \mathbb{N}$, $a \in \mathbb{Z}$.
Ensure: $y = a^x \bmod n$.

$a_1 := a;\ x_1 := x,\ y := 1.$
while $x_1 \neq 0$ **do**
  while $(x_1 \bmod 2) = 0$ **do**
    $x_1 := x_1/2.$
    $a_1 := (a_1 \cdot a_1) \bmod n.$
  end while
  $x_1 := x_1 - 1.$
  $y := (y \cdot a_1) \bmod n.$
end while
return y.

Example 7.8. As in Example 3.53, we compute the power 2^{10} mod 3.

a_1	x_1	y
2	10	1
$2 \cdot 2 \bmod 3 = 1$	$10/2 = 5$	1
1	$5 - 1 = 4$	$1 \cdot 1 \bmod 3 = 1$
$1 \cdot 1 \bmod 3 = 1$	$4/2 = 2$	1
$1 \cdot 1 \bmod 3 = 1$	$2/2 = 1$	1
1	$1 - 1 = 0$	$1 \cdot 1 \bmod 3 = \mathbf{1}$

A slightly more complex example is $5^{11} \bmod 21 = (5^1 \cdot 4^1 \cdot 16^0 \cdot 4^1) \bmod 21 = 17$.

a_1	x_1	y
5	11	21
5	$11 - 1 = 10$	5
$5 \cdot 5 \bmod 21 = 4$	$10/2 = 5$	5
$4 = 1$	$5 - 1 = 4$	$5 \cdot 4 \bmod 21 = 20$
$4 \cdot 4 \bmod 21 = 16$	$4/2 = 2$	20
$16 \cdot 16 \bmod 21 = 4$	$2/2 = 1$	20
4	$1 - 1 = 0$	$20 \cdot 4 \bmod 21 = \mathbf{17}$

At last, Algorithm 7.3 needs 15 steps to compute $5^{573} \bmod 587 = 216$.

At this point we make a short excursion to show the possible savings. By using the floating-point operations per second (*flops*) measure, we assume one flop each for addition, subtraction or multiplication and four flops for division. The modulo operation can be thought of as a division followed by a multiplication and an addition, i.e., six flops.

Example 7.9. $n = 574 = 1+2^2+2^3+3^4+2^5+2^9$. If we apply (7.2), a computer has to do 573 multiplications and modulo operations, i.e., $573 \cdot (1 + 6) = 4011$ flops. In contrast, if we were to use Algorithm 7.3, the computer will have to do $(6+9) \cdot 7 = 15 \cdot 7 = 105$ flops, which is clearly less than before.

Remembering the Pohlig–Hellman exponentiation cipher from Definition 6.34, the challenge is to find the key k in a known-plaintext environment. Given a prime number p, any $a \in \mathbb{Z}_p$ and any key $k \in \mathbb{Z}_{p-1}^{\times}$, it is not difficult to compute

$$b = a^k \bmod p$$

by using Algorithm 7.3.

Problem 7.10 (Computing the discrete logarithm in $\mathbb{Z}_p$). Given a prime number p, $a \in \mathbb{Z}_p$ and $b \in \mathbb{Z}_p$, find the unique integer k with $1 \le k \le p-2$, such that

$$a^k \bmod p = b, \text{ i.e. } k =: \log_a(b).$$

We assume a to be a generator of $\mathbb{Z}_p^{\times}$ to ensure that there is a unique solution. A simple method to find the exponent k is to count all possible values starting with $x = 0$, see Example 7.11.

Example 7.11.

$$p = 257, \ a = 51, \ b = 111, \ x = \log_{51}(111) = 188$$

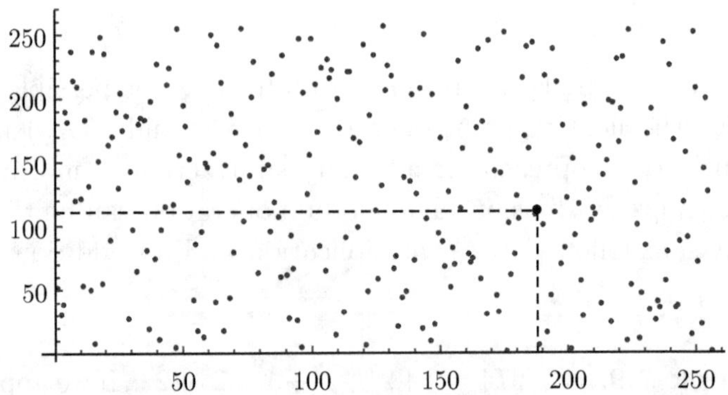

Figure 7.1 Determining the pre-image of the discrete logarithm.

As soon as there is a match, we are ready. On average, $\frac{p}{2}$ multiplications and modulo operations must be performed while four values a, b, p and $a^x \bmod p$ are stored. This method is unsatisfactory because the bit sizes of p are too large in practice.

A better way of calculating the discrete logarithm originates from Shanks.[11] By setting $m = \lceil\sqrt{p}\rceil$ and

$$k = q \cdot m + r, \quad q, r \in \mathbb{Z}_m,\ 0 \le q \cdot m + r \le m^2 - 1,$$

i.e., the set $\mathbb{Z}_p$ is covered and all possible exponents are reached, we calculate

$$b = a^k \bmod p = a^{q \cdot m + r} \bmod p \Rightarrow (a^m)^q \bmod p = b \cdot a^{-r} \bmod p.$$

Let $\alpha = a^m \bmod p$. Comparing the members of the set of the so-called "babysteps",

$$B = \{(b \cdot a^{-r} \bmod p, r);\ r \in \mathbb{Z}_m\},$$

with those of the set of the "giantsteps",

$$G = \{(\alpha^q \bmod p, q);\ q \in \mathbb{Z}_m\},$$

we will find a match. This is because a is a generator of $\mathbb{Z}_p^\times$ and for each b there are numbers $i, j \in \mathbb{Z}_p$ satisfying $j \cdot m + i = \log_a(b)$ due to the construction. Let $(y, i) \in B$ and $(y, j) \in G$ be such a matching. Then,

$$(a^m)^j \bmod p = b \cdot a^{-i} \bmod p \Leftrightarrow a^{m \cdot j + i} \bmod p = b.$$

It follows $a^{m \cdot j + i - k} \bmod p = 1$ and $m \cdot j + i - k = u \cdot \phi(p) = u \cdot (p-1)$ for any $u \in \mathbb{Z}$. This means $j \cdot m + i \equiv_p k$.

Corollary 7.12 (Discrete logarithm by Shanks). *The method of Shanks, denoted in Algorithm 7.4 as a babystep-giantstep algorithm, computes the discrete logarithm* $\log_a(b)$ *mod* p *for a given prime* p*, a generator* a *of* $\mathbb{Z}_p^\times$ *and a number* $b \in \mathbb{Z}_p^\times$*.*

---

[11] Daniel Shanks (1917–1996).

Algorithm 7.4: Babystep-giantstep algorithm

Require: Prime p, generator $a \in \mathbb{Z}_p^\times$, i.e., $\mathcal{L}(a) = \mathbb{Z}_p^\times$ and $b \in \mathbb{Z}_p^\times$.
Ensure: $k = \log_a(b)$.
$m := \lceil \sqrt{p-1} \rceil$.
$B := \{(b \cdot a^{-i} \bmod p, i) = (b \cdot a^{p-1-i} \bmod p, i); i = 0, \ldots, m-1\}$.
$G := \{(a^{m \cdot j} \bmod p, j); j = 0, \ldots, m-1\}$.
Find $(y, i) \in B$ and $(y, j) \in G$ with the same first component.
$k = \log_a(b) := (m \cdot j + i) \bmod (p-1)$.
return k.

Example 7.13. We compute $\log_{51}(111) \bmod 257$: $m = 17$,

$$\begin{aligned} B = \{&(111,0), \mathbf{(108,1)}, (244,2), (161,3), (240,4), (171,5), (215,6), \\ &(105,7), (123,8), (78,9), (62,10), (102,11), (2,12), (252,13), \\ &(141,14), (33,15), (46,16)\}, \text{ and} \\ G = \{&(1,0), (151,1), (185,2), (179,3), (44,4), (219,5), (173,6), \\ &(166,7), (137,8), (127,9), (159,10), \mathbf{(108,11)}, (117,12), \\ &(191,13), (57,14), (126,15), (8,16)\}. \end{aligned}$$

There is a match in $i = 1$ and $j = 11$. Thus, we obtain $k = m \cdot j + i \bmod 257 = 17 \cdot 11 + 1 \bmod 257 = 188$.

If a is not a generator of $\mathbb{Z}_p^\times$, the discrete logarithm may not exist. Only b's that are producible by a work. Alternatively, such a situation reduces the effort. We can replace the values $p-1$ in the first and last step by $\operatorname{ord}_{\mathbb{Z}_p^\times}(a)$ in Algorithm 7.4. A great disadvantage of Shanks' method is the need for intensive main memory. The Pohlig–Hellman method is somewhat less memory intensive. Knowledge about the factorization of $p-1$ is required according to Theorem 1.29. At this point, let p be prime again and a be a generator of $(\mathbb{Z}_p^\times, \cdot_p, 1)$. Given a factorization

$$\phi(p) = p - 1 = \prod_{j=1}^{l} p_j^{\alpha_j},$$

we define

$$p_{p_j} = \frac{p-1}{p_j^{\alpha_j}}, \quad a_{p_j} = a^{p_{p_j}} \bmod p \text{ and } b_{p_j} = b^{p_{p_j}} \bmod p. \tag{7.4}$$

The order of a_{p_j} is

$$\operatorname{ord}_{\mathbb{Z}_p^\times}(a_{p_j}) \overset{\text{Cor. 3.28}}{=} \frac{p-1}{\operatorname{GCD}\left(p-1, {}^{p-1}/_{p_j^{\alpha_j}}\right)} = p_j^{\alpha_j}.$$

By regarding

$$\begin{aligned} a_{p_j}^k \bmod p = a^{p_{p_j} \cdot k} \bmod p &= \left(a^k\right)^{p_{p_j}} \bmod p \\ &= b^{p_{p_j}} \bmod p = b_{p_j}, \end{aligned}$$

$b_{p_j} \in \mathcal{L}(a_{p_j})$. Since $(\mathcal{L}(a_{p_j}), \cdot_{p|\mathcal{L}(a_{p_j})}, 1)$ is cyclic according to Example 3.66,

$$k_{p_j} = k \bmod p_j^{\alpha_j}.$$

Because all p_j are mutual relatively prime numbers due to their construction, we can apply the Chinese remainder theorem 3.77 to the system of congruences

$$k \equiv_{p_1^{\alpha_1}} k_{p_1} \ldots k \equiv_{p_l^{\alpha_l}} k_{p_l}$$

for obtaining k. The effort is reduced to prime powers.

Algorithm 7.5: Pohlig–Hellman algorithm

Require: Prime p, generator $a \in \mathbb{Z}_p^\times$, i.e., $\mathcal{L}(a) = \mathbb{Z}_p^\times$, and $b \in \mathbb{Z}_p^\times$.

Ensure: $k = \log_a(b)$.

$\phi(p) = p - 1 = \prod_{j=1}^{l} p_j^{\alpha_j}$.

$p_{p_j} := \frac{p-1}{p_j^{\alpha_j}}, \quad a_{p_j} := a^{p_{p_j}} \bmod p$ and $b_{p_j} := b^{p_{p_j}} \bmod p$.

$k_{p_j} :=$ shanks(a_{p_j}, b_{p_j}, p), $j = 1, \ldots, l$.

$k = \log_a(b) :=$ Chinese temainder$(\{(k_{p_j}, p_j^{\alpha_j});\ j = 1, \ldots, l\})$.

return k.

Corollary 7.14 (Pohlig–Hellman algorithm). *The Pohlig–Hellman method denoted in Algorithm 7.5 computes the discrete logarithm* $\log_a(b) \bmod p$ *for a given prime* p*, a generator* a *of* $\mathbb{Z}_p^\times$ *and a number* $b \in \mathbb{Z}_p^\times$*.*

Example 7.15. Remember Example 7.13. Since $p-1 = 256 = 2^8$, $a_2 = a$ and $b_2 = b$. Thus, there is no improvement using the Pohlig–Hellman algorithm.

We calculate $k = \log_{51}(111) \bmod 271$. $270 = 2^1 \cdot 3^3 \cdot 5^1$.

$$p_2 = \frac{270}{2} = 135, \quad a_2 = 51^{135} \bmod 271 = 270,$$

$$b_2 = 111^{135} \bmod 271 = 270,$$

$$p_3 = \frac{270}{3^3} = 10, \quad a_3 = 51^{10} \bmod 271 = 83,$$

$$b_3 = 111^{10} \bmod 271 = 238,$$

$$p_5 = \frac{270}{5} = 54, \quad a_5 = 51^{54} \bmod 271 = 10,$$

$$b_5 = 111^{54} \bmod 271 = 1.$$

We have to solve $k_2 = \log_{270}(270) \bmod 271$, $k_3 = \log_{83}(238) \bmod 271$ and $k_5 = \log_{10}(1) \bmod 271$. We obtain $k_2 = 1$ and $k_5 = 0$ quickly. To get k_3, we call the method of Shanks: $m = \left\lceil \sqrt{\mathrm{ord}_{\mathbb{Z}_{271}^\times}(83)} \right\rceil = \lceil \sqrt{27} \rceil = 6$. Next, we calculate

$$B = (238,0), (140,1), (178,2), (25,3), (206,4), \mathbf{(169{,}5)},$$
$$G = (1,0), (258,1), \mathbf{(169{,}2)}, (242,3), (106,4), (248,5)$$

and $m \cdot 2 + 5 \bmod 27 = 17$. Finally, we apply the Chinese remainder theorem to solve

$$k \equiv_2 1, \ k \equiv_{27} 17 \text{ and } k \equiv_5 0$$
$$\Rightarrow k = 1 \cdot 1 \cdot 135 + 17 \cdot (-8) \cdot 10 + 0 \cdot (-1) \cdot 54 \bmod 270 = 125.$$

Example 7.16. Figure 7.2 shows the time required in the calculation of the discrete logarithm as a function of the bit length of p.

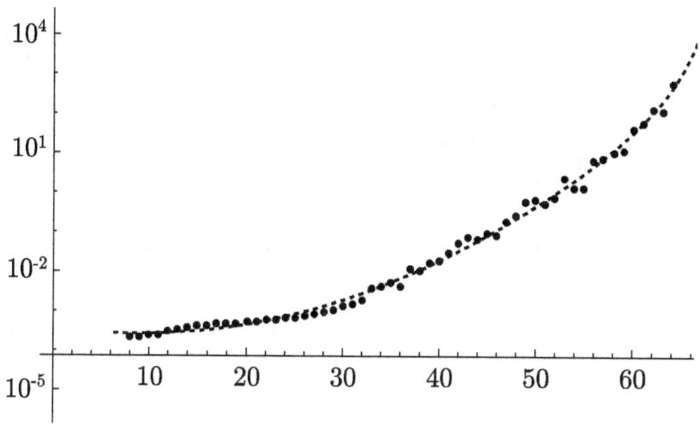

Figure 7.2 Pohlig–Hellman time complexity relying on the number of bits.

The dotted line indicates a regression function adapted to the data based on a theoretical estimation of time complexity due to (Buchmann, 2012).

There are improvements to the Pohlig–Hellman algorithm and slightly faster algorithms for calculating the discrete logarithm, for example, see the *index calculus method* in (Stinson, 2005). However, there is currently no known and accepted algorithm fast enough to solve the problem quickly, though this does not refer to the quantum algorithm of Shor, which requires sufficient large quantum computers that are currently unavailable.[12]

7.2.2 *Squaring and square roots modulo n*

Given any integer $n \in \mathbb{N}$, $n \geq 2$, and any $x \in \mathbb{N}_0$, the value

$$a = x^2 \bmod n \tag{7.5}$$

can be computed by one multiplication and modulo operation. In reverse, consider any $n \in \mathbb{N}$ and an integer $\tilde{a} \in \mathbb{Z}$. Is it possible to

[12]cf. (Nielsen and Chuang, 2011).

find a corresponding $x \in \mathbb{N}$ satisfying Equation (7.5) by processing $a = \tilde{a} \bmod n \in \mathbb{Z}_n$? If there exists such a value x, the value $\tilde{a}$ will be called a *quadratic residue* modulo n and we denote $x = \sqrt{a}$. Otherwise, a will be called a *quadratic nonresidue* modulo n. If $x = q \cdot n + r$, $r \in \mathbb{Z}_n$, it follows

$$\begin{aligned} x^2 \bmod n &= (q \cdot n + r)^2 \bmod n = q^2 \cdot n^2 + 2 \cdot q \cdot n \cdot r + r^2 \bmod n \\ &= r^2 \bmod n. \end{aligned}$$

We can restrict a and x to be in $\mathbb{Z}_n$. Now, we assume that $p = n$ is an odd prime, $a, x \in \mathbb{Z}_p$, to examine two cases. Let a be a quadratic residue modulo p. Since there is a corresponding value x, we obtain a second solution of Equation (7.5) by

$$\begin{aligned} (p - x)^2 \bmod p &= p^2 - 2 \cdot p \cdot x + x^2 \bmod p \\ &= x^2 \bmod p \\ &= a. \end{aligned} \tag{7.6}$$

If $a = 0$, then $x = 0$ and $p - x = p \notin \mathbb{Z}_p$. We therefore have just one solution. Otherwise, $p - x$ is different from x because from $p - x = x$ it follows $p = 2 \cdot x$. However, p is an odd integer according to the above assumption. There are no more solutions because if we were to interpret Equation (7.5) as a task to find a root of the polynomial

$$P(X) = X^2 - a \bmod p \in \mathbb{Z}_p[X],$$

we obtain at most two solutions from $\mathbb{Z}_p$, according to Corollary 6.24. If a is any quadratic nonresidue modulo p, there are no solutions.

Corollary 7.17. *Given an odd prime $p > 2$ and $a \in \mathbb{Z}_p^\times$. Then x^2 mod $p = a$ has two solutions if a is a quadratic residue modulo p, and no solution if a is a quadratic nonresidue modulo p.*

We define

$$R_n = \{a \in \mathbb{Z}_n^\times;\ a \text{ is a quadratic residue modulo } n\}$$

for our further considerations. Since p is prime, there must be a generator g of the cyclic group $(\mathbb{Z}_p^\times, \cdot_p, 1)$ with $a = g^u \bmod p$ due to Corollary 3.88. If $a \notin R_p$, then u must be odd, $u = 2 \cdot k + 1$, because $a = g^{2k} \bmod p = (g^k)^2 \bmod p \in R_p$, otherwise. Because $a \in \mathbb{Z}_p^\times$, we can use Equation (7.1) and Fermat's little theorem 3.86 for obtaining

$$a^{\frac{p-1}{2}} \bmod p = \begin{cases} (x^2)^{\frac{p-1}{2}} \bmod p = x^{p-1} \bmod p \overset{(3.86)}{=} 1, & a \in R_p, \\ (g^{2 \cdot k+1})^{\frac{p-1}{2}} \bmod p = g^{\frac{p-1}{2}} \bmod p \overset{(7.1)}{=} p-1, & a \notin R_p. \end{cases}$$

For $1 \equiv_p a^{\frac{p-1}{2}} \equiv_p g^{\frac{u}{2} \cdot (p-1)}$, it applies $\frac{u}{2} \in \mathbb{Z}$, i.e., $a \in R_p$.

Corollary 7.18. *Given an odd prime $p > 2$ and $a \in \mathbb{Z}_p^\times$. Then,*

$$a \in R_p \Leftrightarrow a^{\frac{p-1}{2}} \textit{ mod } p = 1 \textit{ and } a \notin R_p \Leftrightarrow a^{\frac{p-1}{2}} \textit{ mod } p = p-1.$$

It follows that for $a, b \in R_p$, the product $a \cdot b$ is also in R_p. Similarly, if $a, b \notin R_p$ the product $a \cdot b$ will also be in R_p.

Example 7.19. Let $a = 4$ and $p = 5$. We try all the possible values of $x \in \mathbb{Z}_5$, $x^{\frac{5-1}{2}} \bmod 5 = x^2 \bmod 5$:

$$0^2 \bmod 5 = 0,\ 1^2 \bmod 5 = 1, \quad 2^2 \bmod 5 = 4,$$
$$3^2 \bmod 5 = 4,\ 4^2 \bmod 5 = 1.$$

We obtain $R_5 = \{1, 4\}$.

Assuming u is even, $u = 2 \cdot k$, $k \in \{1, \ldots, \frac{p-1}{2}\}$, we know

$$a = g^{2 \cdot k} \bmod p = (\underbrace{g^k \bmod p}_{x})^2 \bmod p = x^2 \bmod p \in R_p.$$

In reverse, $a \in R_p$, i.e., $a = x^2 \bmod p$ and $x = g^k$ mod p for some $k \in \mathbb{Z}_p^\times$ yields

$$a = x^2 \bmod p = \left(g^k\right)^2 \bmod p = g^{2 \cdot k \bmod p-1} \bmod p.$$

However, $2 \cdot k \equiv_{p-1} 2 \cdot \left(\frac{p-1}{2} + k\right)$ yields the restriction $k \in \left\{1, \ldots, \frac{p-1}{2}\right\}$ without loss.

Corollary 7.20.

$$a \in R_p \Leftrightarrow a = g^{2 \cdot k} \; mod \; p, \; k \in \left\{1, \ldots, \frac{p-1}{2}\right\}.$$

Thus, we get $\frac{p-1}{2}$ *quadratic residues modulo p.*

It is a low-budget affair to find a root $x \in \mathbb{Z}_p^\times$ for a given quadratic residue modulo p.

Theorem 7.21 (Square root modulo p). *Let $p > 2$ be prime and $a \in \mathbb{Z}_p^\times$ be a quadratic residue modulo p. Then, Algorithm 7.6 returns an $x \in \mathbb{Z}_p^\times$ with x^2 mod $p = a$.*

Proof. For a given $a \in R_p$, we apply (7.6): $x^2 \bmod p = a$ and $(p - x)^2 \bmod p = a$. If we randomly choose any $v \in \mathbb{Z}_p^\times$ in Algorithm 7.6, v is a quadratic nonresidue modulo p with probability $\frac{1}{2}$, according to Corollary 7.20. Let

$$p - 1 = q \cdot 2^l \text{ and } 2^{l+1} \nmid p - 1 \text{ for } l, q \in \mathbb{N}_0, \; q \text{ odd}.$$

Define $a_1 = a$. There is a smallest $k_1 \in \mathbb{N}_0$ with $a_1^{q \cdot 2^{k_1}} \bmod p = 1$ and $k_1 \leq l$. At worst, $k_1 = l$ and

$$a_1^{q \cdot 2^{k_1}} \bmod p = a_1^{q \cdot 2^l} \bmod p = a_1^{p-1} \bmod p \overset{(3.86)}{=} 1.$$

We look at the sequence

$$a_{n+1} = a_n \cdot v^{2^{l-k_n}} \bmod p :$$

$$\begin{aligned}
a_{n+1}^{q \cdot 2^{k_n - 1}} \bmod p &= \left(a_n \cdot v^{2^{l-k_n}}\right)^{q \cdot 2^{k_n - 1}} \bmod p \\
&= a_n^{q \cdot 2^{k_n - 1}} \cdot v^{q \cdot 2^{l-1}} \bmod p \\
&= a_n^{q \cdot 2^{k_n - 1}} \cdot v^{\frac{p-1}{2}} \bmod p \\
&= a_n^{q \cdot \frac{2^{k_n}}{2}} \cdot (-1) \bmod p \\
&= (-1) \cdot (-1) \bmod p \\
&= 1.
\end{aligned}$$

Algorithm 7.6: Find a square root modulo p

Require: $p > 2$ prime, $a \in \mathbb{Z}_p^\times$ quadratic residue modulo p.
Ensure: $x \in \mathbb{Z}_p^\times$ with $x^2 \bmod p = a$, i.e., $x = \sqrt{a}$.

```
Choose any v ∈ Z_p^×, such that v^((p−1)/2) mod p = p − 1,
  i.e., v ∉ R_p.
Calculate l, q ∈ N_0 with p − 1 = q · 2^l and 2^(l+1) ∤ p − 1.
a_1 := a, n := 1.
Find the smallest k_1 ≥ 0 with a_1^(q·2^(k_1)) mod p = 1.
while k_n ≠ 0 do
    a_(n+1) := a_n · v^(2^(l−k_n)) mod p.
    Find the smallest k_(n+1) ≥ 0 with a_(n+1)^(q·2^(k_(n+1))) mod p = 1.
    n := n + 1.
end while
r_n := a_n^((m+1)/2) mod p.
for i := n − 1, i > 0 do
    r_i := r_(i+1) (v^(2^(l−k_i−1)))^(−1) mod p.
    i := i − 1.
end for
return x := r_1.
```

Thus, $k_{n+1} \leq k_n - 1 < k_n$ can always be found based on the choice of the quadratic nonresidue v, such that $l \geq k_1 > k_2 > \ldots > k_n > k_{n+1} > \ldots \geq 0$. Consequently, there is an integer $m \leq l + 1$ with $k_m = 0$ and

$$1 = a_m^{q \cdot 2^{k_m}} \bmod p = a_m^q \bmod p.$$

Multiplying the last equation by a_m yields

$$a_m \cdot a_m^q \bmod p = a_m^{q+1} \bmod p = a_m \text{ and } \left(a_m^{\frac{q+1}{2}}\right)^2 \bmod p = a_m.$$

Hence, $r_m = a_m^{\frac{q+1}{2}} \bmod p$ is a square root of the quadratic residue a_m. By defining

$$r_i = r_{i+1} \left(v^{2^{l-k_i-1}}\right)^{-1} \bmod p$$

for $i = m-1, \ldots, 1$, we obtain $r_i^2 \bmod p = a_i$, which gets proven by induction. If $i = m$, the statement is correct. Now, assume the statement is right for $i+1 < m$. Then, it follows

$$\begin{aligned} r_i^2 \bmod p &= r_{i+1}^2 \cdot \left(\left(v^{2^{l-k_i-1}} \right)^{-1} \right)^2 \bmod p \\ &\overset{\text{i.hyp.}}{=} a_{i+1} \cdot \left(\left(v^{2^{l-k_i-1}} \right)^2 \right)^{-1} \bmod p \\ &= a_{i+1} \cdot \left(v^{2^{l-k_i}} \right)^{-1} \bmod p \\ &= a_i \cdot v^{2^{l-k_i}} \cdot \left(v^{2^{l-k_i}} \right)^{-1} \bmod p \\ &= a_i. \end{aligned}$$

Thereby we proved that $r_1^2 \bmod p = a_1 = a$. Thus, $x = r_1$ is one of the square roots searched for. □

Example 7.22.

$$p = 17,\ a = 8 \in R_{17},\ \text{since } 8^8 \bmod 17 = 1.$$

$p - 1 = 16 = 1 \cdot 2^4 \Rightarrow q = 1,\ l = 4$. Let $v = 5$, $v^8 \bmod 17 = 16$.

$n = 1 : a_1 = 8,\ 8^2 \bmod 17 = 13,\ 8^3 \bmod 17 = 16,\ 8^4 \bmod 17 = 1$
$\Rightarrow k_1 = 3,$

$n = 2 : a_2 = 8 \cdot 5^2 \bmod 17 = 13,\ 13^2 \bmod 17 = 16,\ 13^4 \bmod 17 = 1$
$\Rightarrow k_2 = 2,$

$n = 3 : a_3 = 13 \cdot 5^4 \bmod 17 = 16,\ 16^2 \bmod 17 = 1$
$\Rightarrow k_3 = 1,$

$n = 4 : a_4 = 16 \cdot 5^8 \bmod 17 = 1$
$\Rightarrow k_4 = 0,$

$i = 4 : r_4 = 1,$
$i = 3 : r_3 = 1 \cdot (5^4)^{-1} \bmod 17 = 4,$
$i = 2 : r_2 = 4 \cdot (5^2)^{-1} \bmod 17 = 9,$ and
$i = 1 : r_1 = 9 \cdot (5^1)^{-1} \bmod 17 = 12.$

Check: $12^2 \bmod 17 = 144 \bmod 17 = 8$ and $5 = 17 - 12$ is also a solution.

It is possible to get the square root much easier. If $p \equiv_4 3$, we obtain

$$a^{\frac{p-1}{2}} \bmod p = 1 \Rightarrow a^{\frac{p-1}{2}+1} \bmod p = a^{\frac{p+1}{2}} \bmod p = a.$$

Since $p \equiv_4 3$, $\frac{p+1}{2}$ is even. Thus,

$$\left(a^{\frac{p+1}{4}}\right)^2 \bmod p \overset{x=a^{\frac{p+1}{4}}}{=} x^2 \bmod p = a. \tag{7.7}$$

We go one step further and look at prime powers. Let x be a square root modulo a prime power p^n, $p > 2$. It follows

$$x^2 \equiv_{p^n} a \Rightarrow x^2 - a = q \cdot p^n \Rightarrow x^2 - a = (q \cdot p^{n-1}) \cdot p \Rightarrow x^2 \equiv_p a,$$

and x is a square root of a modulo p. In reverse, if x is a square root of a modulo p, what about the square root of a modulo p^n? Firstly, we have to prove that $a \in \mathbb{Z}_{p^n}^{\times}$. Since $\mathrm{GCD}(a, p) = 1$, we can write $1 = u \cdot a + v \cdot p$. We obtain

$$\begin{aligned} v^n \cdot p^n = (v \cdot p)^n = (1 - u \cdot a)^n &= \sum_{k=0}^{n} \binom{n}{k} 1^k \cdot (-u \cdot a)^{n-k} \\ &= \sum_{k=0}^{n-1} \binom{n}{k} 1^k \cdot (-u \cdot a)^{n-k} + 1 \\ &= a \cdot \sum_{k=0}^{n-1} \binom{n}{k} 1^k \cdot (-u)^{n-k} \cdot a^{n-k-1} + 1. \end{aligned}$$

Hence, $\mathrm{GCD}(a, p^n) = 1$.

Theorem 7.23 (Computing square roots modulo p^n). *Assume any prime power p^n, $p > 2$, and a quadratic residue $a \in \mathbb{Z}_{p^n}^{\times}$ modulo p^n satisfying*

$$x_0^2 \equiv_p a$$

for some $x_0 \in \mathbb{Z}_p^{\times}$. Then, there exists a unique number $x \in \mathbb{Z}_{p^n}^{\times}$ with

$$x^2 \equiv_{p^n} a \text{ and } x \equiv_p x_0.$$

Proof. We show the existence by induction on a running index k. Interestingly, we use Newton's[13] method for calculating zeros and accordingly define the iteration

$$\begin{aligned} x_{k+1} &= x_k - (x_k^2 - a) \cdot ((2 \cdot x_k)^{-1} \bmod p^k) \bmod p^{k+1} \\ &= x_k \cdot (2^{-1} \bmod p^k) + a \cdot ((2 \cdot x_k)^{-1} \bmod p^k) \bmod p^{k+1}. \end{aligned}$$

Since $a \in \mathbb{Z}_{p^k}^{\times}$, we get $x_k \cdot x_k \bmod p^k \in \mathbb{Z}_{p^k}^{\times}$, and an appropriate $x_k \in \mathbb{Z}_{p^k}^{\times}$ and its inverse element does in fact exist. Moreover, the values x_k and x_{k+1} match modulo p^k. Squaring the equation yields

$$\begin{aligned} x_{k+1}^2 &\equiv_{p^{k+1}} x_k^2 \cdot 2^{-2} + 2 \cdot x_k \cdot 2^{-1} \cdot a \cdot (2 \cdot x_k)^{-1} + a^2 \cdot (2 \cdot x_k)^{-2} \\ &\equiv_{p^{k+1}} 2^{-2} \cdot (x_k^4 + 2 \cdot a \cdot x_k^2 + a^2) \cdot x_k^{-2} \\ &\equiv_{p^{k+1}} 2^{-2} \cdot (x_k^2 - a)^2 \cdot x_k^{-2} + a, \end{aligned}$$

where we calculate modulo p^k on the right side. By subtracting a on both sides we obtain

$$x_{k+1}^2 - a \equiv_{p^{k+1}} (x_k^2 - a)^2 \cdot (2^{-2} \cdot x_k^{-2} \bmod p^k).$$

The induction base is given by the assumption for x_0. The statement applies to k, i.e., $x_k^2 - a = q \cdot p^k$ for some $q \in \mathbb{N}$. Then, we obtain

$$\begin{aligned} x_{k+1}^2 - a &\equiv_{p^{k+1}} (x_k^2 - a)^2 \cdot (2^{-2} \cdot x_k^{-2} \bmod p^k) \\ &\overset{\text{i.hyp.}}{\equiv}_{p^{k+1}} (q \cdot p^k)^2 \cdot (2^{-2} \cdot x_k^{-2} \bmod p^k) \\ &\equiv_{p^{k+1}} 0 \quad \Leftrightarrow 2 \cdot k \geq k+1 \Leftrightarrow k \geq 1. \end{aligned}$$

Next, consider two different solutions x, y with $x^2 \equiv_{p^n} y^2$ and $x - y \bmod p^n = r$. This yields

$$(x + y) \cdot (x - y) \equiv_{p^n} 0.$$

Since $x \equiv_p x_0 \equiv_p y$, it follows $x + y \equiv_p 2 \cdot x_0$ and $(x + y) \cdot (x - y) = (2x_0 + qp) \cdot r \equiv_{p^n} 0 \equiv_p 0$, i.e., $2x_0 r \bmod p = 0$. Since p is prime and $x_0 \neq 0$, it remains $r = 0$. Thus, the solution is unique, $x = y$. □

[13] Isaac Newton (1643–1727).

In the same way as in Corollary 7.18, we make a statement about quadratic residues modulo a prime power p^n. We recall $\mathrm{GF}(p^n)$ being a field, $|\mathbb{Z}_{p^n}^\times| = p^{n-1} \cdot (p-1)$, and we use Euler's theorem 3.84.

Corollary 7.24. *Given an odd prime $p > 2$ and $a \in \mathbb{Z}_{p^n}^\times$. Then, we obtain*

$$a \in R_{p^n} \Leftrightarrow a^{\frac{p^{n-1}\cdot(p-1)}{2}} \mod p = 1,$$

$$a \notin R_{p^n} \Leftrightarrow a^{\frac{p^{n-1}\cdot(p-1)}{2}} \mod p = p-1.$$

If $a \in R_{p^n}$ and $x^2 \mod p^n = a$, there is a second square root $p^n - x$. Otherwise, if $a \notin R_{p^n}$, there is no square root.

Since an odd n is not necessarily a prime power, we will talk about a commutative ring with identity, i.e., $(\mathbb{Z}_n, +_n, \cdot, 0, 1)$. Thus, we have to decompose the problem first. If the decomposition

$$n = p_1^{\alpha_1} \cdot \ldots \cdot p_k^{\alpha_k}$$

of n is known, we can consider the actual problem of computing square roots modulo n.

Problem 7.25 (Computing square roots modulo n). Given any positive composite odd integer n and an integer $a \in \mathbb{Z}_n^\times$, find an integer $x \in \mathbb{Z}_n^\times$, if possible, such that

$$x^2 \bmod n = a, \text{ i.e., } x = \sqrt{a}.$$

If $a \notin R_n$, there is no solution to the problem. Assume $a \in R_n$. There is an $x \in \mathbb{Z}_n^\times$ satisfying $x^2 \bmod n = a$. Because of the decomposition of n, we can resolve the problem into subproblems. From

$$x^2 - a = q \cdot n = q \cdot p_1^{\alpha_1} \cdot \ldots \cdot p_k^{\alpha_k} = \left(q \cdot \prod_{i \neq j} p_i^{\alpha_i}\right) \cdot p_j^{\alpha_j},$$

it follows $x^2 - (a \bmod p_j^{\alpha_j}) \equiv_{p_j^{\alpha_j}} 0$. Instead of solving the main problem, we have to first solve the subproblems

$$x^2 \bmod p_j^{\alpha_j} = a \bmod p_j^{\alpha_j}, \quad j \in \{1, \ldots, k\}.$$

However, this can be done using Algorithm 7.6 and Theorem 7.23, respectively, resulting in solutions x_{j1} and $x_{j2} = p_j^{\alpha_j} - x_{j1}$. After that, we have to find a solution x satisfying all of the equations

$$x \bmod p_j^{\alpha_j} = x_j, \tag{7.8}$$

where $x_j \in \{x_{j1}, x_{j2}\}$. These subproblems go according to the application 3.14 of the Chinese remainder theorem 3.77 and yield 2^k different solutions at most.

Example 7.26.

$n = 221 = 13 \cdot 17,\ a = 55,\ x_1 = 87,\ x_2 = 100,\ x_3 = 121,\ x_4 = 134.$

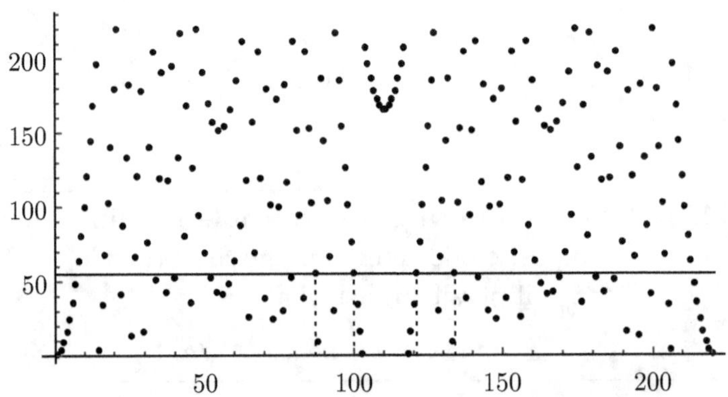

Figure 7.3 Four different square roots modulo 221.

For example, 55 mod 13 = 3 and 9^2 mod 13 = 3, 55 mod 17 = 4 and 15^2 mod 17 = 4. We have to solve the congruences

$$x \equiv_{13} 9 \text{ and } x \equiv_{17} 15,$$

resulting in $x = 100$. Finally, for checking purposes, we calculate $87^2 \bmod 221 = 100^2 \bmod 221 = 121^2 \bmod 221 = 134^2 \bmod 221 = 55$.

Without factorizing n, we try the possible values for x. We write down the procedure of finding square roots modulo a typically composite n in Algorithm 7.7.

Algorithm 7.7: Square roots modulo n

Require: Odd $n \in \mathbb{N}$, $a \in R_n$.

Ensure: $x \in \mathbb{Z}_n$ with $x^2 \bmod n = a$.

1: Find the decomposition of n: $n = p_1^{\alpha_1} \cdot \ldots \cdot p_k^{\alpha_k}$.

2: Solve the subproblems

$$x^2 \bmod p_j^{\alpha_j} = a \bmod p_j^{\alpha_j}, \quad j \in \{1, \ldots, k\},$$

using Algorithm 7.6 or rather Theorem 7.23, resulting in solutions x_{j1} and $x_{j2} = p_j^{\alpha_j} - x_{j1}$.

3: By applying the Chinese remainder algorithm 3.2, find a solution x satisfying all of the equations

$$x \bmod p_j^{\alpha_j} = x_j$$

where $x_j \in \{x_{j1}, x_{j2}\}$.

4: Set x to be one of the at most 2^k solutions.

5: **return** x.

Example 7.27.

$$n = 221 = 13 \cdot 17 = p \cdot q, \ a = 1.$$

We obtain the two simple square roots $x_1 = 1$, $x_2 = 220$. We calculate the third solution by

$$\begin{aligned} &x_3 \equiv_p p - 1 \text{ and } x_3 \equiv_q 1 \\ \Leftrightarrow &x_3 = p \cdot (p^{-1} \bmod q) - q \cdot (q^{-1} \bmod p) \bmod n = 103 \end{aligned}$$

and finally, $x_4 = n - x_3 = 118$.

7.2.3 *Multiplying prime powers and their factorization*

Given some prime numbers $p_1, \ldots, p_k$ and exponents $\alpha_1, \ldots, \alpha_k \in \mathbb{N}$, we can easily compute the product

$$n = \prod_{j=1}^{k} p_j^{\alpha_j}.$$

Alternatively, it is difficult to get a factorization for a given number n, according to Equation (1.5). An easy but very expensive way is to test all possible prime numbers up to a fixed boundary $b \geq 2$. If the fraction can be fully canceled, the tested number is a prime factor. Example 7.28 shows this method.

Example 7.28 (Trial division).

$$n = 253 = 11 \cdot 23,\ b = 31$$

p	2	3	5	7	11	13	17	19	23	29	31
n/p	$253/2$	$253/3$	$253/5$	$253/7$	23	$253/13$	$253/17$	$253/19$	11	$253/29$	$253/31$

The method is called *trial division.* If a factor p_1 is found, we can start this method again by looking at $n_1 = n/p_1$, beginning at prime p_1 and so on until $n_k = 1$. The resulting p_j form an increasing series. In the worst case, the trial division needs to do about $\sqrt{n}$ divisions. Assuming the possibility of 10^{13} divisions per second and $n = 2^{512} \approx 10^{154}$, we need approximately

$$\frac{2^{256}}{10^{13} \cdot 3600 \cdot 24 \cdot 365} = 3.7 \cdot 10^{56}$$

years for factorizing n.

Problem 7.29 (Factorizing positive integers). Given a positive integer $n \in \mathbb{N}$, find prime numbers $p_1, \ldots, p_k$ and appropriate integers $\alpha_1, \ldots, \alpha_k$, such that

$$n = p_1^{\alpha_1} \cdot \ldots \cdot p_k^{\alpha_k},$$

corresponding to the Fundamental Theorem of Arithmetic 1.29.

Pollard[14] considered a method to find a factor p of an odd n in 1974. Consider a prime factor p of n. By choosing an $x \in \mathbb{Z}_n^\times$ and a suitable

[14] *cf.* (Pollard, 1974).

$k \in \mathbb{N}$ satisfying

$$x^k \bmod n \neq 1 \text{ and } x^k \bmod p = 1,$$

we can conclude that k is no multiple of $\phi(n)$, but $x^k - 1$ is a multiple of p, such that

$$z = \text{GCD}(x^k - 1 \bmod n, n) | n. \tag{7.9}$$

Since $\text{GCD}(x, p) = 1$ because of $x \in \mathbb{Z}_n^\times$ and since k is a multiple of $p - 1$ because of $x^k \bmod p = 1$, we can possibly guess a suitable k. For this purpose, we look at the factorization of $p - 1$,

$$p - 1 = \prod_{j=1}^{l} p_j^{\alpha_j}.$$

Now, we choose a bound $b \in \mathbb{N}$ and calculate values

$$\alpha_b(q) = \max\{i \in \mathbb{N};\ q^i \leq b\}$$

for all primes less than or equal to b and set

$$k = \prod_{\substack{q \leq b \\ q \text{ prime}}} q^{\alpha_b(q)}.$$

If the unknown $p - 1$ has powers of prime factors all smaller than b, then $p - 1$ is a divisor of k. Otherwise, we have to try a higher bound. The method works only if the prime factors of $p - 1$ are small enough. Because it is consuming to calculate all of the $\alpha_b(q)$, we have to simplify the procedure plainly. Firstly, we use $x = 2$, which always yields $\text{GCD}(x, n) = 1$ for composite n. Secondly, the construction tells us that at best

$$p - 1 = \prod_{j=1}^{l} p_j^{\alpha_j} \,\Bigg|\, \prod_{\substack{q \leq b \\ q \text{ prime}}} q^{\alpha_b(q)} \,|b!\,. \tag{7.10}$$

The last relation in (7.10) is valid because the q's are relatively prime numbers of each other. We denote $k = b! = (p - 1) \cdot Q$. Thus, we can compute

$$x^k \bmod n = 2^{b!} \bmod n = 2^{2 \cdot 3 \cdot \ldots \cdot b} \bmod n.$$

If $x^k \bmod p = 1$, we use Equation 7.9 again. The result z can be a composite number. Next, we have to continue by investigating z and n/z.

Algorithm 7.8: Pollard's $p-1$ factorizing algorithm

Require: Odd $n \in \mathbb{N}$, bound $b \in \mathbb{N}$.
Ensure: A non-trivial divisor z of n or a fail (-1).

```
1: x := 2.
2: for i = 2 to b do
3:     x := x^i mod n.
4: end for
5: z := GCD(x − 1, n).
6: if 1 < z < n then
7:     return z.
8: end if
9: return −1.
```

Corollary 7.30 (Pollard's $p-1$ factorizing algorithm). *The method of Pollard, denoted in Algorithm 7.8, computes a divisor z of a given odd n, or it fails and has to be restarted with a higher bound b.*

Example 7.31.

$$n = 253 = 11 \cdot 23,\ b = 6$$

The sequence of x in Steps 1–4 of Algorithm 7.8 is

$$(2, 4, 64, 27, 12, 78).$$

We compute $\mathrm{GCD}(78-1, 253) = \mathrm{GCD}(7 \cdot 11, 11 \cdot 23) = 11$ and obtain the factor $11|253$. Another example:

$$n = 70698786003409,\ b = 1000.$$

After Step 4 of Algorithm 7.8, we obtain

$$x = 54091116376397.$$

We compute $z = \mathrm{GCD}(x-1, n) = 698887751$. We go on with z and $n/z = 101159$, which is already a prime. Furthermore, the largest of all simple prime factors of the order $\mathrm{ord}_{\mathbb{Z}^{\times}_{698887751}}(2)$ is 277. Thus, we have to reduce the bound to a lower threshold here, i.e., $b = 270$. A recall of the algorithm with the parameters

$$n = 698887751 \text{ and } b = 270$$

yields

$$x = 296397719$$

and $z = \mathrm{GCD}(x-1, n) = 131$, which is prime. Additionally, $n/z = 5335021$ is prime. In total, we obtain

$$70698786003409 = 131 \cdot 101159 \cdot 5335021.$$

Stirling's approximation[15] tells us that $b! \approx \sqrt{2\pi \cdot b}\,(b/e)^b$. By using this and Equation (7.3) we can consider the effort of Pollard's method by estimating

$$2\log_2\left(\sqrt{2\pi \cdot b}\,(b/e)^b\right) \approx 2b\log_2(b).$$

multiplications and modulo operations. Indeed, this method works for numbers that are not large, but the problem is that the method only works if for a factor p of n the number $p-1$ happens to be a product of small primes. This is a very interesting property of a number that we will soon use again.

Definition 7.32. An integer $m \in \mathbb{N}$ is called b-smooth if all of its prime factors are less than or equal to b. The function

$$\psi : \mathbb{N} \times \mathbb{N} \to \mathbb{N},\ \psi(n, b) = |\{m \in \{2, \ldots, n\};\ m \text{ is } b\text{-smooth}\}|$$

counts all the b-smooth numbers smaller than any given n.

[15] James Stirling (1692–1770).

Example 7.33.

Integer	2	3	4	5	6	7	8	9	10	11	12	13	14	15
Factorization	2	3	2^2	5	$2 \cdot 3$	7	2^3	3^2	$2 \cdot 5$	11	$2^2 \cdot 3$	13	$2 \cdot 7$	$3 \cdot 5$

We obtain $\psi(15, 7) = |\{2, 3, 4, 5, 6, 7, 8, 9, 10, 12, 14, 15\}| = 12$.

We want to factorize n by another method. For this, consider any odd $n = p \cdot Q$, where p is a prime number. Defining

$$x = \frac{p + Q}{2} \text{ and } y = \frac{p - Q}{2},$$

we can calculate $x^2 - y^2 = (x - y) \cdot (x + y) = Q \cdot p = n$. Initially, we obtain $x^2 = n + y^2$ by rearrangement. Given any y, we can try to find a matching x. We can also allow multiples of n in the equation, i.e., $x^2 = k \cdot n + y^2$, $k \in \mathbb{N}$. However, $x - y$ and $x + y$ are divisors of $k \cdot n$. Thus, we have to compute $\mathrm{GCD}(x - y, n)$ and $\mathrm{GCD}(x + y, n)$ because factors of k could be factors of $x - y$ or $x + y$.

Example 7.34.

$$n = 2491 = 47 \cdot 53.$$

We try to find a square number, a *perfect square*:

y	1	2	3	4	5	6	7	8	9
$n + y^2$	2492	2495	2500	2507	2516	2527	2540	2555	2572
x^2			50^2						
$9n + y^2$	22420	22423	22428	22435	22444	22455	22468	22483	22500
x^2									150^2

It follows from the first two rows that $x - y = 47$, $x + y = 53$. The second equation yields $x - y = 141$ and $x + y = 159$. We obtain $\mathrm{GCD}(141, 2491) = 47$ and $\mathrm{GCD}(159, 2491) = 53$.

This generalization shows us how to investigate the problem in another way to find distinct numbers x, y satisfying

$$x^2 \equiv_n y^2.$$

However, this can be like finding a needle in the haystack. In Example 7.34, we are lucky to get $9n + 9^2 = 22500 = 150^2$. Thus, we take a special approach. Looking at the factorization of a perfect square, we see that every prime factor's exponent is even. Normally, for a given y we obtain no such situation by computing the factorization of $y^2 \bmod n$. However, we can combine several such squares together in the hope that the factorization of the outcome results in only even exponents, i.e.,

$$\begin{aligned} &y_1^2 \bmod n = a_1, \ldots, y_u^2 \bmod n = a_u \\ \Rightarrow &(y_{i_1} \cdot \ldots \cdot y_{i_v})^2 \equiv_n a_{i_1} \cdot \ldots \cdot a_{i_v} = p_{i_1}^{2\alpha_1} \cdot \ldots \cdot p_{i_w}^{2\alpha_w}. \end{aligned}$$

The greatest common divisor of the sum or difference of such numbers and n could be a proper factor of n.

Example 7.35.

$$17^2 \bmod 87 = 28 = 2^2 \cdot 7,\ 18^2 \bmod 87 = 63 = 3^2 \cdot 7.$$

Combining this we obtain $n = 87$,

$$\begin{aligned} 306^2 \bmod 87 &= (17 \cdot 18)^2 \bmod 87 \\ &= 45 \\ &= 28 \cdot 63 \bmod 87 = (2 \cdot 3 \cdot 7)^2 \bmod 87 = 42^2 \bmod 87. \end{aligned}$$

Then, $\mathrm{GCD}(306 - 42, 87) = 3$ and $\mathrm{GCD}(306 + 42, 87) = 87$. We have found one proper factor of n.

The prime factors could be very large. Thus, we can restrict the factor's size by specifying a barrier b which must not be exceeded by both prime numbers and prime powers. We collect them in the *factor base* B,

$$B = \{q \in \mathbb{N}; q \text{ is prime or a prime power and } q \leq b\}.$$

To get a reasonable choice of different squares, we consider the function

$$f_n : \mathbb{N} \to \mathbb{N}, t \mapsto f_n(t) = (\underbrace{\lfloor\sqrt{n}\rfloor + t}_{y_t})^2 \bmod n$$

and try to factorize the values by only the primes or prime powers in B. We can do this more efficiently using an adaption of the sieve of Eratosthenes 1.27. Since a quadratic equation has zero, one (modulo 2) or two solutions, we can test one after the other to see whether

$$f_n(t) \equiv_q 0, \quad q \in B.$$

If there is any t doing so, $f_n(t+k\cdot q)$ works, too. Thus, we can divide $f_n(t)$, $f_n(t+p)$, $f_n(t+2p), \ldots$ by q. If q is a prime power, we can divide by the underlying prime number. After finishing all the q's from B, some of the resulting numbers are cut to 1. Such numbers are B-smooth and we can use them to assemble a number whose factorization is based even on prime powers.

Example 7.36. $n = 2491$, $\lfloor\sqrt{n}\rfloor = 49$, B={2,3,4,5,7,8,9,11}.

y	1	2	3	4	5	6	7	8	9	10
$(\lfloor\sqrt{n}\rfloor + y)^2 \bmod n$	9	110	213	318	425	534	645	758	873	990
2	9	**55**	213	**159**	425	**267**	645	**379**	873	**495**
3	**3**	55	71	**53**	425	89	**215**	379	291	**165**
2^2	3	55	71	53	425	89	215	379	291	165
5	3	**11**	71	53	**85**	89	**43**	379	291	**33**
7	3	11	71	53	85	89	43	379	291	33
2^3	3	11	71	53	85	89	43	379	291	33
3^2	**1**	11	71	53	85	89	43	379	**97**	**11**
11	1	**1**	71	53	85	89	43	379	97	**1**
	↑ 50	↑ 51								↑ 59

Now, we can take

$$\underbrace{(51 \cdot 59)}_{3009}{}^2 \equiv_{2491} (2\cdot 5\cdot 11)\cdot(2\cdot 3^2\cdot 5\cdot 11) \equiv_{2491} \underbrace{(2\cdot 3\cdot 5\cdot 11)}_{330}{}^2$$

and this leads to

$$\mathrm{GCD}(2491, 3009 - 330) = 47 \text{ and } \mathrm{GCD}(2491, 3009 + 330) = 53.$$

However, these are just the factors searched for.

In Example 7.36, it is easy to recognize which combination of B-smooth numbers leads to even exponents. In general, we have to consider the following situation:

$$y_t^2 \bmod n = a_t = \prod_{j=1}^{k} p_j^{\alpha_{tj}}, \quad p_j^{\alpha_{tj}} \in B \cup \{1\}.$$

If p_j is no factor of a_t, the exponent α_{tj} will be set to zero. By multiplying all numbers we obtain

$$\prod_{t=1}^{s} y_t^2 = \left(\prod_{t=1}^{s} y_t\right)^2 \equiv_n \prod_{j=1}^{k} p_j^{\sum\limits_{t=1}^{s} \alpha_{tj}}.$$

Because we are looking for perfect squares, we cannot choose any number a_t. Thus, we introduce a flag value $f_t \in \{0, 1\}$ that decides whether a_t is selected or not:

$$\left(\prod_{t=1}^{s} y_t\right)^{2f_t} \equiv_n \prod_{j=1}^{k} p_j^{\sum\limits_{t=1}^{s} \alpha_{tj} \cdot f_t}.$$

If the exponents of each p_j get even, we have a solution. Now, we can solve this problem by solving a system of equations for f_t in $\mathbb{F}_2$:

$$\sum_{t=1}^{s} \alpha_{tj} \cdot f_t \bmod 2 = 0, \quad j = 1, \ldots, k.$$

Example 7.37. We continue Example 7.36. After the sieving process, we obtain three candidates.

$p_j \backslash a_t$	9	110	990
2	0	1	1
3	2	0	2
5	0	1	1
7	0	0	0
11	0	1	1

.

The system of equations gets

$$\begin{pmatrix} 0 & 1 & 1 \\ 0 & 0 & 0 \\ 0 & 1 & 1 \\ 0 & 0 & 0 \\ 0 & 1 & 1 \end{pmatrix} \cdot \begin{pmatrix} f_1 \\ f_2 \\ f_3 \end{pmatrix} \equiv_2 \begin{pmatrix} 0 \\ 0 \\ 0 \end{pmatrix}.$$

The general solution for this system is

$$\mathbb{L} = \left\{ \lambda \cdot \begin{pmatrix} 1 \\ 0 \\ 0 \end{pmatrix} +_2 \mu \cdot \begin{pmatrix} 0 \\ 1 \\ 1 \end{pmatrix} \; ; \; \lambda, \mu \in \mathbb{F}_2 \right\}.$$

By choosing $\lambda = 0$ and $\mu = 1$, we obtain the solution from Example 7.36.

Let $L(n) = e^{\sqrt{\log n \cdot (\log(\log(n)))}}$. It can be shown that if $b = L(n)^{1/\sqrt{2}}$ and $s \approx 2L(n)$, for example, $y_t \in (\lfloor\sqrt{n}\rfloor - L(n), \lfloor\sqrt{n}\rfloor + L(n)) \cap \mathbb{N}$, we have a good chance to factorize n. The effort is approximately about $c \cdot L(n)$ divisions where c is a constant. Further details can be found in (Hoffstein *et al.*, 2008; Stamp and Low, 2007; Pomerance, 1996). If an integer n is composite, we compute square roots modulo n by decomposing n. However, this is hard work. Thus, we can use a quadratic function in the role of a one-way function.

Example 7.38 (Rabin function). Let $n = p \cdot q$ be the product of two primes p and q. Define a system of functions by

$$f_n : \mathbb{Z}_n \to \mathbb{Z}_n, \; x \mapsto f_n(x) = x^2 \bmod n.$$

For any fixed n, such a one-way function is called a *Rabin function*.

7.2.4 *Binary subset sum problems*

Consider a set $x = (x_1, \ldots, x_n) \in \mathbb{N}^n$ of n integers. Take corresponding weights $w_j \in \{0, 1\}$ and compute

$$f_x : \mathbb{F}_2^n \to \mathbb{N}, (w_1, \ldots, w_n) \mapsto f_x(w_1, \ldots, w_n) := \sum_{j=1}^{n} w_j x_j.$$

This is easy, however, recovering the weights w_j is hard.

Problem 7.39 (Subset sum problem). Given a positive integer $s \in \mathbb{N}$ and a tuple of positive integers $x = (x_1, \dots, x_n) \in \mathbb{N}^n$, find weights $w_j \in \{0, 1\}$, such that

$$s = \sum_{j=1}^{n} w_j x_j.$$

Since there is no indication about how many and which integers to use, we have to consider all possible combinations of numbers. Therefore, we have to compute

$$\sum_{j=1}^{n} \binom{n}{j} = 2^n - 1$$

different sums at the worst. In the same way, as done with the brute-force attack in Section 2.6, we can estimate the average number of trials before success. If all possible $2^n - 1$ sequences are assumed to be equally likely, we have an expected number of trials of

$$\frac{2^n - 1 + 1}{2} = 2^{n-1}$$

following Equation (2.11). We can do even better. For this purpose, we take elements of two power sets in the following manner:

$$\mathcal{P}_1 = \mathcal{P}(\{1, \dots, \lfloor n/2 \rfloor\}) \text{ and } \mathcal{P}_2 = \mathcal{P}(\{\lfloor n/2 \rfloor + 1, \dots, n\}).$$

After this, we calculate for all possible sets $I \in \mathcal{P}_1$ and $J \in \mathcal{P}_2$ two lists each of length $2^{n/2}$,

$$L_{\mathcal{P}_1} = \left\{ \sum_{i \in I} x_i;\ I \in \mathcal{P}_1 \right\} \text{ and } L_{\mathcal{P}_2} = s - \left\{ \sum_{j \in J} x_j;\ J \in \mathcal{P}_2 \right\}.$$

Since

$$s = \sum_{j=1}^{n} w_j x_j = \sum_{i=1}^{\lfloor n/2 \rfloor} w_i x_i + \sum_{j=\lfloor n/2 \rfloor + 1}^{n} w_j x_j,$$

the effort for finding the right weights is approximately $2^{n/2}$.

Example 7.40.

$$x = (202, 404, 159, 419, 391, 133, 670, 403), \quad s = 1884.$$

Depending on the order of the different sequences of bits, the following plot of all 256 different sums can be generated.

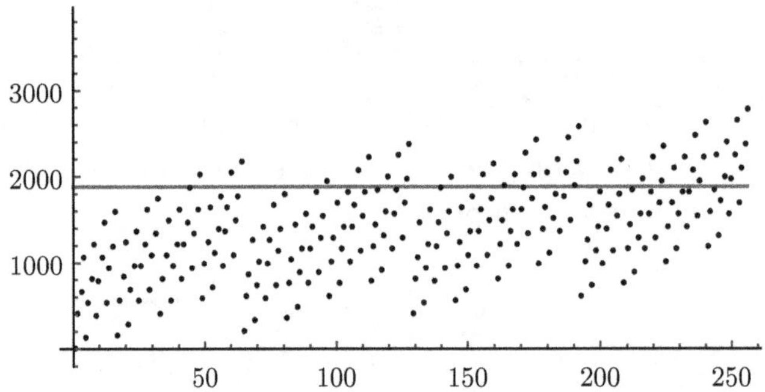

Figure 7.4 Problem of inverting the subset sum.

The vector x can address the numbers 1883, 1884 and 1896 near s. Here, the sequence number 90 (01011010) does the trick.

Finding the weights can be done by investigating the $2 \cdot 2^4 = 32$ elements of two power sets.

L_1	$\sum_{x \in L_1} x$	L_2	$1884 - \sum_{x \in L_2} x$
$\emptyset$	0	$\emptyset$	1884
{202}	202	{391}	1493
{404}	404	{133}	1751
{159}	159	{670}	1214
{419}	419	{403}	1481
{202, 404}	606	{391, 133}	1360
{202, 159}	361	**{391, 670}**	**823**
{202, 419}	621	{391, 403}	1090
{404, 159}	563	{133, 670}	1081
{404, 419}	**823**	{133, 403}	1348
{159, 419}	578	{670, 403}	811
{202, 404, 159}	765	{391, 133, 670}	690
{202, 404, 419}	1025	{391, 133, 403}	957
{202, 159, 419}	780	{391, 670, 403}	420
{404, 159, 419}	982	{133, 670, 403}	678
{202, 404, 159, 419}	1184	{391, 133, 670, 403}	287

7.3 Trapdoor One-way Functions in Public-key Cipher Systems

Let f be a one-way function. We will not be able to use it directly for encrypting a message as the receiver of the encrypted message will not be able to decrypt it, though it is possible. To make life easier for the receiver, some additional information can be included, which enables them to perform the process. Such information is called *trapdoor information*.

Convention 7.41 (Trapdoor one-way function). A one-way function $f : X \to Y$ is called a *trapdoor one-way function* if $x = f^{-1}(y)$ is easy to compute by using only given trapdoor information.

Based on the studies of Diffie and Hellman (1976), the intention was to use a trapdoor one-way function for encrypting and decrypting messages. In this way, a public-key cipher system can be defined.

Definition 7.42 (Public-key cipher system). A cipher system $(\mathcal{P}, \mathcal{C}, \mathcal{K}, \mathcal{E}, \mathcal{D})$ is called a *public-key cipher system* if $\mathcal{E}$ is a system of trapdoor one-way functions.

In the next chapter, we will discuss public-key cipher systems suitable for any of the presented one-way functions.

- Merkle–Hellman knapsack based on the subset sum problem,
- Rabin cipher based on the square root problem,
- RSA cipher based on the factoring problem and
- El-Gamal cipher and Elliptic curve cipher based on the discrete logarithm problem.

Example 7.43. The final example shows the idea behind trapdoor information. Let $n = 253$. If an entity B encrypts any plaintext m by using the Rabin function f_{253} resulting in $c = f_{253}(m) = 36$, any receiver A of the ciphertext has to decrypt it. This would be difficult without any knowledge of the composition of n. However, the real communication partner A of B is in a good starting position by previously setting this parameter. Since A knows that $n = 11 \cdot 23$, they can decrypt the ciphertext using Algorithm 7.7 for solving

$$m_1^2 \equiv_{11} 36\ (\equiv_{11} 3) \text{ and } m_2^2 \equiv_{23} 36\ (\equiv_{11} 13).$$

For example, they obtain $m_1 = 5$ and $m_2 = 17$. In step two, they make use of the Chinese remainder theorem 3.77, solving

$$m \equiv_{253} 5 \text{ and } m \equiv_{253} 17.$$

The result here is $m = 247$, which could be a candidate for being the searched plaintext.

Chapter 8

Public-Key Ciphering

Note 8.1. In this chapter, the requirements are:

- being familiar with basics of number theory, see Section 1.1,
- knowing the multiplication cipher, see Section 4.2.2,
- being able to calculate with polynomials, see Section 6.3.1, and
- being familiar with components of public-key cryptosystems, see Chapter 7.

Selected literature: See (El Gamal, 1985; Hoffstein *et al.*, 2008; Menezes and Vanstone, 1993; Stinson, 2005).

A public-key cipher system is an alternative for private-key ciphering. If entity A wants to send data to entity B in this context, B has to publish a public key $k_{\text{a,pub}}$ that A can use to encrypt the data. Since B owns the private key $k_{\text{a,priv}}$, only B can decrypt the received data. Illustration Figure 8.1 shows this principle of public-key ciphering.

Based on the one-way functions presented in Section 7.2, cryptographers tested many public-key cipher systems, including trapdoor information. The following sections provide an overview of the basic principles and achievements on this topic.

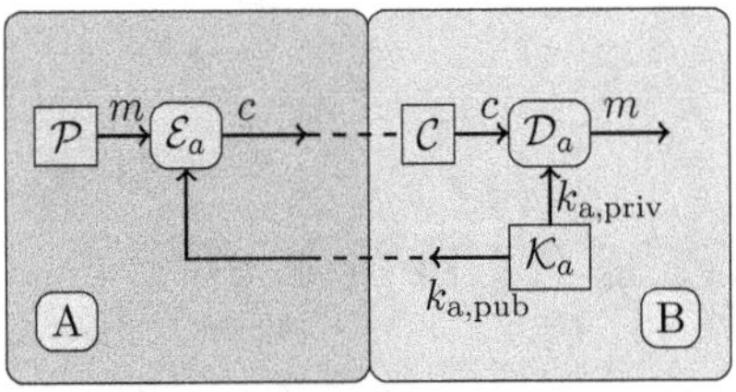

Figure 8.1 Public-key cipher system.

8.1 Merkle–Hellman Knapsack Cipher System

Invented in 1978,[1] the Merkle–Hellman knapsack cipher system and its variants itself are no longer secure. For example, the basic idea that we discussed here was broken by Shamir in 1982.[2] The cipher system is based on the subset sum problem 7.39. Since this problem is difficult, we introduce a trapdoor information. A sequence of positive numbers $x_1, \ldots, x_n \in \mathbb{N}$ is called "superincreasing" if every element of the sequence is greater than the sum of all previous elements,

$$x_{i+1} > \sum_{j=1}^{i} x_j, \quad 1 \leq i \leq n-1.$$

By induction we can show that $x_n \geq 2^{n-2} \cdot (x_1 + 1)$. By starting with $x_2 \geq 2^0 \cdot (x_1 + 1)$, we process the induction step by showing that $x_{n+1} \geq 2^{n-1} \cdot (x_1 + 1)$.

$$\begin{aligned} x_{n+1} &\geq \sum_{j=1}^{n} x_j + 1 = \sum_{j=2}^{n} x_j + x_1 + 1 \\ &\stackrel{\text{i.hyp.}}{\geq} \sum_{j=2}^{n} 2^{j-2} \cdot (x_1 + 1) + x_1 + 1 = (x_1 + 1) \cdot \left(1 + \sum_{q=0}^{n-2} 2^q\right) \\ &= (x_1 + 1) \cdot \left(1 + \frac{1 - 2^{n-1}}{1 - 2}\right) = (x_1 + 1) \cdot 2^{n-1}. \end{aligned} \tag{8.1}$$

Solving the subset sum problem based on a superincreasing sequence is simple. Suppose a superincreasing sequence $x_1, \ldots, x_n$, weights

[1] See (Merkle and Hellman, 1978).
[2] See (Shamir, 1982).

$w_1, \ldots, w_n$ and the sum

$$s = \sum_{j=1}^{n} w_j x_j \leq \sum_{j=1}^{n} x_j.$$

We have to determine y_j, such that $y_j = w_j$ for any $j = 1, \ldots, n$, and prove this by downward induction. For this purpose, we reduce the sum each time we have set y_j to be one by x_j, say $s_{j-1} = s_j - x_j$ starting at $s_n = s$. For the case $j = n$, we consider that $y_n = 0$ if $s < x_n$. Otherwise, we set $y_n = 1$ because $s \geq x_n > \sum_{j=1}^{n-1} x_j$ and we do not reach s anymore. The inductive hypothesis is that $y_j = w_j$ for all $j \geq k+1$ for any fixed k. Now, we look at stage k. Until now, the sum has been reduced to

$$s_k = s - \sum_{j=k+1}^{n} y_j x_j = \sum_{j=1}^{n} w_j x_j - \sum_{j=k+1}^{n} y_j x_j \overset{\text{i.hyp.}}{=} \sum_{j=1}^{k} w_j x_j.$$

If $w_k = 1$, we obtain $s_k \geq x_k$ and determine $y_k = 1$. Otherwise, if $w_k = 0$, it follows

$$s_k = \sum_{j=1}^{k} w_j x_j = \sum_{j=1}^{k-1} w_j x_j < x_k \Rightarrow y_k = 0.$$

In each case we get $y_k = w_k$ and this finishes the proof. Furthermore, we obtain a unique solution.

Corollary 8.2. *If* $(x_1, \ldots, x_n)$ *is a superincreasing sequence, the subset sum problem can easily be solved by Algorithm* 8.1.

Example 8.3. $s = 28$, $x = (1, 2, 4, 9, 22, 40)$.

$$w_6 = 0 \overset{28<40}{\rightarrow} w_5 = 1 \overset{28\geq 22}{\rightarrow} w_4 = 0 \overset{6<9}{\rightarrow} w_3 = 1 \overset{6\geq 4}{\rightarrow} w_2 = 1 \overset{2\geq 2}{\rightarrow} w_1 = 0 \overset{0<1}{.}$$

Since $s_0 = 0$, there is the unique solution $w = (0, 1, 1, 0, 1, 0)$, $2 + 4 + 22 = 28$.

At this point, we know that the subset sum problem is difficult to solve, but in the presence of a superincreasing sequence, the weights of the subset sum problem can be recovered easily. We can use this

Algorithm 8.1: Superincreasing subset sum problem.

Require: $s \in \mathbb{N}$, $x = (x_1, \ldots, x_n) \in \mathbb{N}^n$ superincreasing sequence.
Ensure: $w = (w_1, \ldots, w_n) \in \{0, 1\}^n$ with $s = \sum_{j=1}^{n} w_j x_j$ or no solution.

$s_n := s$.
for $j = n$ **to** 1 **do**
  $w_j := 0$.
  if $s_j \geq x_j$ **then**
    $w_j := 1$.
    $s_{j-1} := s_j - x_j$.
  end if
end for
if $s_0 = 0$ **then**
  $w := (w_1, \ldots, w_n)$.
  return w.
end if
return -1.

fact for generating a cipher system. If the private key is a superincreasing sequence and the public key is not, but depending on the private key, we win. To reach this, we introduce trapdoor information given by a multiplication modulo n. Assume a superincreasing sequence $(x_1, \ldots, x_n)$, a prime $p > \sum_{i=1}^{n} x_i$ and $1 < a < p - 1$. The magnitude of p can be estimated by

$$\begin{aligned} p > \sum_{i=1}^{n} x_i &\overset{(8.1)}{\geq} x_1 + \sum_{i=2}^{n} 2^{i-2} \cdot (x_1 + 1) \\ &= x_1 + (x_1 + 1) \cdot (2^{n-1} - 1) = 2^{n-1} \cdot (x_1 + 1) - 1. \end{aligned} \tag{8.2}$$

Next, we define

$$y_i = a \cdot x_i \bmod p.$$

Any plaintext encoded by a binary sequence $(w_1, \ldots, w_n)$ of block size n can get encrypted by

$$s = \sum_{i=1}^{n} w_i \cdot y_i \leq \sum_{i=1}^{n} y_i \leq n \cdot (p - 1).$$

In principle, anyone who wants to decrypt the ciphertext has to solve the subset sum problem. However, if we use the trapdoor information, we can decrypt and recover the plaintext.

$$\hat{s} = a^{-1} \cdot s \bmod p \equiv_p a^{-1} \cdot \sum_{i=1}^{n} w_i \cdot y_i \equiv_p \sum_{i=1}^{n} w_i \cdot a_i^{-1} \cdot y_i \equiv_p \sum_{i=1}^{n} w_i \cdot x_i.$$

Since $0 \leq \hat{s}, \sum_{i=1}^{n} w_i \cdot x_i \leq p-1$, we obtain equality $\hat{s} = \sum_{i=1}^{n} w_i \cdot x_i$. The use of Algorithm 8.1 allows the decryption.

Definition 8.4 (Merkle–Hellman knapsack). Let $x = (x_1, \ldots, x_n)$ be any superincreasing sequence, $p > \sum_{i=1}^{n} x_i$ prime and $a \in \mathbb{Z}_p^{\times}$. Say, $\mathcal{P} = \mathbb{F}_2^n$ and $\mathcal{C} = \mathbb{Z}_{n(p-1)}$. After calculating $y = (y_1, \ldots, y_n) = a \cdot (x_1, \ldots, x_n) \bmod p$, we set

$$\mathcal{K}_a = \{(p, a, x, y)\},$$

$$k_{\text{a,pub}} = (y, p) \text{ and } k_{\text{a,sec}} = (a, p).$$

Denoting Algorithm 8.1 by "supsubS" we define

$$e_{k_{\text{a,pub}}}(m_1, \ldots, m_n) = \sum_{i=1}^{n} m_i \cdot y_i, \; d_{k_{\text{a,sec}}}(c) = \text{supsubS}(a^{-1} \cdot c \bmod p).$$

Example 8.5.

$$x = (1, 2, 4, 9, 22, 40, 81, 165, 344, 700), \; p = 1373, \; a = 480.$$

We apply $\mathcal{P} = \mathbb{F}_2^{10}$ and $\mathcal{C} = \mathbb{Z}_{13720}$. The plaintext

"SECURITY"

has to get encoded to ten bits each block. We therefore use two letters, each encoded by five bits, resulting in

$$18, 4 \to (1, 0, 0, 1, 0, 0, 0, 1, 0, 0),$$

$$2, 20 \to (0, 0, 0, 1, 0, 1, 0, 1, 0, 0),$$

$$17, 8 \to (1, 0, 0, 0, 1, 0, 1, 0, 0, 0),$$

$$19, 24 \to (1, 0, 0, 1, 1, 1, 1, 0, 0, 0).$$

For enciphering we need the public key

$$\begin{aligned} k_{\text{a,pub}} = (y, p) &= (a \cdot x \bmod p, p) \\ &= ((480, 960, 547, 201, 949, 1351, 436, 939, \\ &\quad 360, 988), 1373). \end{aligned}$$

We obtain

$$\begin{aligned} c_1 &= 480 + 201 + 939 = 1620, \\ c_2 &= 201 + 1351 + 939 = 2491, \\ c_3 &= 480 + 949 + 436 = 1865, \\ c_4 &= 480 + 201 + 949 + 1351 + 436 = 3417. \end{aligned}$$

For decrypting we calculate $a^{-1} \bmod p = 123$,

$$\hat{c}_1 = a^{-1} \cdot c_1 \bmod p = 175.$$

and accordingly, $\hat{c}_2 = 214$, $\hat{c}_3 = 104$ and $\hat{c}_4 = 153$. Running through Algorithm 8.1 yields the correct plaintext.

However, there is a catch to the story[3]: this cipher system is insecure. To understand how this is possible, we have to rewrite the subset sum problem 7.39. Therefore, we use the $n \times n$ identity matrix I_n and inflate our problem:

$$\underbrace{\left(\begin{array}{ccc|c} & & & 0 \\ & I_n & & \vdots \\ & & & 0 \\ \hline y_1 & \cdots & y_n & -s \end{array}\right)}_{M} \cdot \underbrace{\left(\begin{array}{c} w_1 \\ \vdots \\ w_n \\ \hline 1 \end{array}\right)}_{\tilde{w}} = \underbrace{\left(\begin{array}{c} w_1 \\ \vdots \\ w_n \\ \hline 0 \end{array}\right)}_{\hat{w}}.$$

The last line is exactly our problem equation; the first n equations are identities. The advantage of this notation is as follows. Since the columns m_i of the matrix M are linear independent, we know that $\tilde{w}$ is a unique solution for the LGS $Mx = \hat{w}$. The components of w are just 0 or 1. Therefore, all of the possible vectors reached by the

[3]See (Stamp, 2011).

columns of M can be written as

$$\mathcal{L}_{\mathbb{F}_2}(m_1, \ldots, m_{n+1}) = \left\{ M \cdot \begin{pmatrix} x \\ 1 \end{pmatrix};\ x \in \mathbb{F}_2^n \right\}$$

$$\subset \mathcal{L}_{\mathbb{Z}}(m_1, \ldots, m_{n+1}) = \left\{ \sum_{i=1}^{n+1} \lambda_i \cdot m_i;\ \lambda_i \in \mathbb{Z} \right\}.$$

$\mathcal{L}_{\mathbb{Z}}(m_1, \ldots, m_{n+1})$ is called a *lattice*. The vectors reached by the basis $\{m_1, \ldots, m_{n+1}\}$ using linear combinations, as defined in $\mathcal{L}_{\mathbb{F}_2}$, may have an Euclidean norm of magnitude $p \approx 2^{n-1}(x_1 + 1)$. Instead, the vector $\hat{w}$ possesses an Euclidean norm that is smaller or equal to $\sqrt{n}$. Such a vector is called a *short vector*. There is a polynomial-time algorithm[4] for finding such short vectors called the Lenstra–Lenstra–Lovász (LLL) lattice basis reduction algorithm[5] from 1982. The LLL algorithm works under two great ideas. The columns of M are an independent spanning set consisting of integer components. The first idea is to find a new basis of the underlying lattice using an adaption of the Gram–Schmidt process.[6] While the Gram–Schmidt process is orthogonalizing linear independent vectors by

$$m_i^\star = m_i - \sum_{j=1}^{i-1} \underbrace{\frac{m_i^T m_j^\star}{m_j^{\star T} m_j^\star}}_{\mu_{ij}} \cdot m_j^\star,$$

and while it shortens the magnitudes,[7] i.e., $m_i^{\star T} m_i^\star \leq m_i^T m_i$, the adaption uses a rounding function $\lfloor \mu_{ij} \rceil$ for obtaining integer vectors during the whole process. $\lfloor . \rceil$ means rounding off to the next integer. Thus, orthogonality is not entirely achieved, though size reduction will also be achieved if $\mu_{ij} \leq 0.5$ for all i, j. The second idea is to change the order of the new basis vectors by arranging them according to their magnitude. This would be achieved by the

[4]cf. (Bremner, 2011).
[5]A. Leenstra, born 1946, H. Leenstra, born 1949, and L. Lovász, born 1948.
[6]cf. (Lang, 1987).
[7]cf. (Bremner, 2011, p. 55ff).

so-called Lovász condition:

$$
\begin{aligned}
&(\lambda - \mu_{i,i-1}^2)||m_{i-1}^\star||^2 \leq ||m_i^\star||^2, \quad \frac{1}{4} < \lambda < 1 \\
\Leftrightarrow\ &||m_i^\star + \mu_{i,i-1} m_{i-1}^\star||^2 \geq \lambda ||m_{i-1}^\star||^2.
\end{aligned}
$$

The last line means that the magnitude of the complementary representation of the orthogonal projection of m_i on $\{m_1^\star, \dots, m_{i-1}^\star\}$ is at most as large as the one of m_{i-1} scaled by factor λ. If the Lovász condition is not true, the two vectors will be exchanged. Leenstra, Leenstra and Lovász showed that their algorithm would finish in polynomial time. Since short basis vectors are found and $\hat{w}$ is one of very few short vectors, the chances of finding this vector is reasonably high.

Example 8.6. We use Example 8.5 for modeling the Matrix M as

$$
M = \left(\begin{array}{cccccccccc|c}
1 & 0 & 0 & 0 & 0 & 0 & 0 & 0 & 0 & 0 & 0 \\
0 & 1 & 0 & 0 & 0 & 0 & 0 & 0 & 0 & 0 & 0 \\
0 & 0 & 1 & 0 & 0 & 0 & 0 & 0 & 0 & 0 & 0 \\
0 & 0 & 0 & 1 & 0 & 0 & 0 & 0 & 0 & 0 & 0 \\
0 & 0 & 0 & 0 & 1 & 0 & 0 & 0 & 0 & 0 & 0 \\
0 & 0 & 0 & 0 & 0 & 1 & 0 & 0 & 0 & 0 & 0 \\
0 & 0 & 0 & 0 & 0 & 0 & 1 & 0 & 0 & 0 & 0 \\
0 & 0 & 0 & 0 & 0 & 0 & 0 & 1 & 0 & 0 & 0 \\
0 & 0 & 0 & 0 & 0 & 0 & 0 & 0 & 1 & 0 & 0 \\
0 & 0 & 0 & 0 & 0 & 0 & 0 & 0 & 0 & 1 & 0 \\
\hline
480 & 259 & 518 & 114 & 45 & 273 & 325 & 688 & 385 & 221 & -1282
\end{array}\right).
$$

Given $\lambda = 0.75$, the LLL algorithm does not provide a satisfactory result. By setting $\lambda = 0.85$, we obtain the new basis represented by the matrix

$$
\tilde{M} = \begin{pmatrix}
-1 & \mathbf{1} & -1 & 1 & 0 & 0 & 0 & 0 & 2 & 0 & 1 \\
1 & \mathbf{0} & -1 & 0 & 0 & 0 & 1 & -1 & 1 & 0 & -1 \\
0 & \mathbf{0} & 1 & 0 & 0 & -1 & 0 & 0 & -1 & 1 & -1 \\
0 & \mathbf{1} & 0 & -1 & 0 & 0 & 0 & 0 & -1 & 1 & 1 \\
0 & \mathbf{0} & 0 & -1 & 0 & 0 & 1 & 1 & 0 & 0 & -2 \\
0 & \mathbf{0} & 0 & 1 & -2 & -1 & 0 & 1 & -1 & 0 & 1 \\
0 & \mathbf{0} & 0 & 0 & 1 & 1 & 0 & 1 & -1 & 0 & 0 \\
0 & \mathbf{1} & 0 & 1 & 0 & 1 & -1 & 0 & 1 & -1 & 0 \\
0 & \mathbf{0} & 0 & 0 & 0 & 0 & 1 & -1 & 1 & -1 & 0 \\
1 & \mathbf{0} & 1 & 0 & 1 & -1 & 0 & 0 & 1 & 2 & 0 \\
0 & \mathbf{0} & 0 & 0 & 0 & 1 & 1 & -1 & 1 & 1 & 0
\end{pmatrix}.
$$

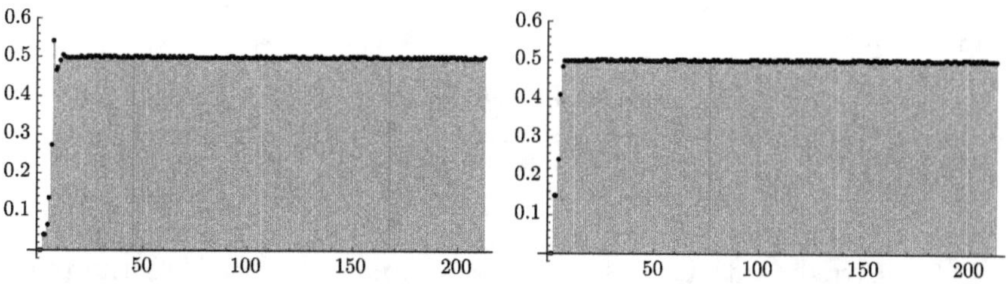

Figure 8.2 Strict avalanche criterion for knapsack: empirical probabilities of bit changes resulting from bit flips in the (128-bit) message (left) with fixed key or in the key (right) with fixed message.

Since we know that $\hat{w}$ has 0 as its last component and that all other components must be elements from $\mathbb{F}_2$, the second column will deliver us a suitable vector. After a proof, this gets confirmed.

It is clear now that the Merkle–Hellman knapsack is not secure. A further weakness is the failure of proving the strict avalanche criterion for the highest bits, both for the private key and message. The highest bits are away from the 50% mark, as shown in Figure 8.2.

8.2 Rabin Cipher System

In 1979, the Rabin[8] cipher system was invented[9] and has been proven to be secure against a chosen-plaintext attack, as long as factoring is difficult. Here, the trapdoor information is the decomposition of a public known integer n into two different prime factors.

Definition 8.7 (Rabin cipher). Let $n = p \cdot q$ be a product of two distinct primes and $p, q \equiv_4 3$. Given $\mathcal{P} = \mathcal{C} = \mathbb{Z}_n$, $b \in \mathbb{Z}_n$, we set

$$\mathcal{K}_a = \{(n, p, q, b);\ p, q \text{ prime},\ n = p \cdot q, b \in \mathbb{Z}_n\},$$
$$k_{\text{a,pub}} = (n, b) \text{ and } k_{\text{a,sec}} = (p, q, b),$$

[8]Michael O. Rabin, born 1931.

[9]See (Stinson, 2005).

and define

$$e_{k_{\text{a,pub}}}(m) = m \cdot (m+b) \bmod n,\ d_{k_{\text{a,sec}}}(c) = \sqrt{b^2 \cdot 4^{-1} + c} - b \cdot 2^{-1} \bmod n.$$

We have to show that it is actually a cipher system. We therefore use the substitution $m = m_1 - b \cdot 2^{-1} \bmod n$ and omit the mention of the modulo operation inside the proof.

$$\begin{aligned} d_{k_{\text{a,sec}}}(e_{k_{\text{a,pub}}}(m)) &= \sqrt{b^2 \cdot 4^{-1} + m \cdot (m+b)} - b \cdot 2^{-1} \\ &= \sqrt{b^2 \cdot 4^{-1} + (m_1 - b \cdot 2^{-1}) \cdot (m_1 - b \cdot 2^{-1} + b)} \\ &\quad - b \cdot 2^{-1} \\ &= \sqrt{m_1^2 + m_1 \cdot \underbrace{(-b \cdot 2^{-1} - b \cdot 2^{-1} + b)}_{\equiv_n 0} \underbrace{+ b^2 \cdot 4^{-1} + b^2 \cdot 2^{-1} \cdot 2^{-1} - b^2 \cdot 2^{-1}}_{\equiv_n 0}} - b \cdot 2^{-1} \\ &= \sqrt{m_1^2} - b \cdot 2^{-1} \\ &= m. \end{aligned}$$

Finding the roots is shortened here because there are up to four different solutions since $n = p \cdot q$. This can also be interpreted as meaning that e_k is not an injective function. To see this, let $z \in \mathbb{Z}_n$ be any of the four solutions of $x^2 \bmod n = 1$ calculated by Equation (7.8), cf. Example 7.27, i.e.,

Easy	Laborious
$z = 1$	or $z = q \cdot (q^{-1} \bmod p) +_n p \cdot (p^{-1} \bmod q) \cdot (q-1)$
	$= q \cdot (q^{-1} \bmod p) -_n p \cdot (p^{-1} \bmod q)$
or $z = n - 1$	or $z = q \cdot (q^{-1} \bmod p) \cdot (p-1) +_n p \cdot (p^{-1} \bmod q)$
	$= p \cdot (p^{-1} \bmod q) -_n q \cdot (q^{-1} \bmod p)$

Then, we obtain (again omitting modulo n) while abbreviating $v = z \cdot (m + b \cdot 2^{-1}) - b \cdot 2^{-1}$

$$\begin{aligned} e_{k_{\text{a,pub}}}(v) &= (z \cdot (m + b \cdot 2^{-1}) - b \cdot 2^{-1}) \\ &\quad \cdot ((z \cdot (m + b \cdot 2^{-1}) - b \cdot 2^{-1}) + b) \\ &= z^2(m + b \cdot 2^{-1})^2 - 2 \cdot b \cdot 2^{-1} \cdot z \cdot (m + b \cdot 2^{-1}) \\ &\quad + b \cdot z \cdot (m + b \cdot 2^{-1}) + b^2 \cdot 2^{-1} \cdot 2^{-1} - b^2 \cdot 2^{-1} \\ &= (m + b \cdot 2^{-1})^2 - b^2 \cdot 2^{-1} \cdot 2^{-1} \\ &= m^2 + m \cdot b = m \cdot (m + b) \\ &= e_{k_{\text{a,pub}}}(m). \end{aligned}$$

Since $p, q \equiv_4 3$, we can calculate the four solutions using Equation (7.7). Let c be the received ciphertext. If the process of encryption goes wrong, we would get $c \notin R_p$ or $c \notin R_q$ by application of Corollary 7.18.

Example 8.8. Let $n = 713$ and $b = 25$. For this example, we apply $\mathcal{P} = \mathcal{C} = \Sigma_{\text{Lat}} \cup \{[\}$. This is because $26^2 = 676 < 713 = n < 27^2 = 729$. If we were to take just the 26 letters from Σ_{Lat}, issues will arise at the decoding process. Here, the convention should not use the dummy symbol [. The plaintext

"SECURITY"

should be encrypted by $e_{(713,25)}(m) = m^2 + m \cdot b \bmod n$. We use a block size of two and encrypt the encoded plaintext

$$(m_1, m_2, m_3, m_4) = (490, 74, 467, 537)$$

to the ciphertext

$$(c_1, c_2, c_3, c_4) = (661, 196, 178, 195).$$

For deciphering, we first have to calculate the (four) roots of $\tilde{c}_i = b^2 \cdot 4^{-1} + c_i$ by using the private key $(23, 31, 25)$, i.e., $p = 23$, $q = 31$

and $b = 25$:

	$\tilde{c}_1 = 639$	$\tilde{c}_2 = 174$	$\tilde{c}_3 = 156$	$\tilde{c}_4 = 173$
$c^6 \bmod p$	8	6	8	9
$-c^6 \bmod p$	15	17	15	14
$c^8 \bmod q$	9	9	1	7
$-c^8 \bmod q$	22	22	30	24

Applying the Chinese remainder theorem 3.77, we obtain four solutions for each m_i.

Possible plaintext	Decoded
(260, **74**, 283, **537**)	JR**CU**KN**TY**
(198, 384, 221, 289)	HJOGIFKT
(**490**, 304, **467**, 399)	**SE**LH**RI**OV
(428, 614, 405, 151)	PXWUPAFQ

It is difficult to recognize the right square root for each block of text without any foreknowledge. We can bypass this problem by inserting some redundant information. In this example, we could add the dummy symbol at the end of each block.

S[E[C[U[R[I[T[Y[

We obtain

Possible plaintext	Decoded
(176, 692, 701, 628, 48, 12, 632, **674**)	GOZRZ[XHBVAMXL**Y[**
(52, **134**, 608, **566**, 203, 446, **539**, 612)	BZ**E[**WO**U[**HOQO**T[**WS
(636, 554, **80**, 122, **485**, **242**, 149, 76)	XPUO**C[**EO**R[I[**FOCW
(**512**, 709, 700, 60, 640, 676, 56, 14)	**S[**[HZZCGXTZBCCAO

and the decryption is clearer. Naturally, there are even more sophisticated techniques for implementing this idea.

If the decomposition of n is known, the deciphering can be done by applying Algorithm 7.7. In reverse, consider any $r \in \{1, \ldots, n-1\}$ that can be chosen at random. If $\mathrm{GCD}(n, r) > 1$, we have found a factor of n and decomposing will usually be fast. Thus, let

$\mathrm{GCD}(n, 1) = 1$. From

$$\begin{aligned} & e_{(n,b)}(r - b \cdot 2^{-1} \bmod n) \\ & \quad = (r - b \cdot 2^{-1})^2 + (r - b \cdot 2^{-1}) \cdot b \bmod n \\ & \quad = r^2 - rb + b^2 \cdot 2^{-1} \cdot 2^{-1} + rb - b^2 \cdot 2^{-1} \bmod n \\ & \quad = r^2 - b^2 \cdot 2^{-1} \cdot 2^{-1} \bmod n \end{aligned}$$

we fix $y = r^2 - b^2 \cdot 2^{-1} \cdot 2^{-1} \bmod n$. Assuming that there exists a method for decrypting y to x, i.e., $e_{(n,b)}(x) = x^2 + x \cdot b \bmod n$, we set $z = x + b \cdot 2^{-1} \bmod n$. It follows

$$\begin{aligned} z^2 &= x^2 + x \cdot b + b^2 \cdot 2^{-1} \cdot 2^{-1} \bmod n \\ &= y + b^2 \cdot 2^{-1} \cdot 2^{-1} \bmod n \\ &= r^2 \bmod n. \end{aligned}$$

Now, we know that

$$n \mid z^2 - r^2 = (z - r) \cdot (z + r).$$

We distinguish between two cases. If $z \equiv_n r$, we obtain $n \mid z - r$ and thus, $\mathrm{GCD}(n, z - r) = n$. In addition, if $n \mid z + r$, we obtain $\mathrm{GCD}(n, z + r) = n$. Then again, if $n \nmid z + r$ and $p \mid z + r$, we can calculate

$$\begin{aligned} 2z &= z + r + z - r = k_1 \cdot p + k_2 \cdot p \cdot q = p \cdot (k_1 + k_2 \cdot q) \\ &\Rightarrow p \mid 2z \overset{\mathrm{GCD}(p,2)=1,(1.10)}{\Rightarrow} p \mid z. \end{aligned}$$

This implies $z + r = k_1 \cdot p = k_3 \cdot p + r \Rightarrow r = p \cdot (k_1 - k_3) \Rightarrow p \mid r$, which contradicts the assumption of $\mathrm{GCD}(n, r) = 1$. Thus, $p \nmid z + r$. In the same way, $q \nmid z + r$, which implies $\mathrm{GCD}(n, z + r) \in \{1, n\}$. The same issues will happen if $z \equiv_n -r$. Therefore, these situations are not profitable. Instead, we examine the second case $z \equiv_n w \cdot r$ where w is one of the non-simple square roots of 1, according to Example 7.27. We assume that $w \equiv_p p - 1$, i.e., $w - (p - 1) = k_4 \cdot p$. Then we get

$$k_5 \cdot p \cdot q = k_5 \cdot n = z - w \cdot r = z - (k_4 \cdot p + p - 1) \cdot r = z - r - p \cdot (k_4 \cdot r + r).$$

We obtain $z - r \bmod p = 0$ and thus, $\text{GCD}(n, z - r)$ is a multiple of p, but smaller than n. If we are able to determine a square root, we will ultimately find a prime factor. Since two of the four solutions for the randomly chosen r yield to success, we have a probability of $1/2$ for success. The procedure is according to a chosen plaintext attack, where r can be interpreted as the chosen plaintext and computing a square root is done by a black box. Combined, breaking the Rabin cipher (especially obtaining a square root) is equivalent to breaking the factoring problem. Being able to induce someone to decrypt such a message y, we execute a chosen-ciphertext attack and the Rabin cipher will be broken by this type of attack.

Example 8.9. We continue Example 8.8 with $n = 713$ and $b = 25$, and try a chosen ciphertext attack. Let $r = 444$ be selected at random. We test $\text{GCD}(r, n) = 1$ and set $y = r^2 - b^2 \cdot 2^{-1} \cdot 2^{-1} \bmod n = 370$, since $2^{-1} \bmod n = 357$. After successfully pinging a computer, we receive the decrypted message $x = 199$. We obtain $z = 199 + 25 \cdot 357 \bmod 713 = 568$ and see that $568 \not\equiv_n \pm 444$. This yields $\text{GCD}(713, 568 + 444) = 23$, which is a prime factor of n.

8.3 RSA Cipher System

In 1978, Rivest, Shamir and Adleman[10] invented the RSA cipher system, which was named using the first letters of their surnames. They utilized the problem of factorizing a positive integer $n = p \cdot q$ with $p \neq q$ primes, as mentioned in Problem 7.29, and chose the encryption function

$$e_{(k,n)} : \mathbb{Z}_n \to \mathbb{Z}_n,\ m \mapsto m^k \bmod n,\ k \in \mathbb{Z}_{\phi(n)}^{\times}$$

with the public key (k, n) and private key (k', n), satisfying

$$k \cdot k' = 1 \bmod \phi(n),\ \textit{i.e.}\ k \cdot k' = \alpha \cdot \phi(n) + 1,\ \alpha \in \mathbb{Z}.$$

[10] R. Rivest, born 1947, A. Shamir, born 1952, and L. Adleman, born 1945.

Decryption works with the same function using the private key, i.e., $d_{(k',n)} = e_{(k',n)}$. First, we note that

$$\begin{aligned} d_{(k',n)}(e_{(k,n)}(m)) &= (m^k)^{k'} \bmod n = m^{k\cdot k'} \bmod n \\ &= m^{\alpha\cdot\phi(n)+1} \bmod n = m^{\alpha\cdot(p-1)\cdot(q-1)+1} \bmod n. \end{aligned}$$

In a case-by-case analysis, we show that the ciphering process works.

Case 1: $m = 0$.

$$d_{(k',n)}(e_{(k,n)}(m)) = (0^k)^{k'} \bmod n = 0.$$

Case 2: $m \in \mathbb{Z}_n^\times$.

$$d_{(k',n)}(e_{(k,n)}(m)) = m^{k\cdot k'} \bmod n = (m^{\phi(n)})^\alpha \cdot m \bmod n \overset{(3.84)}{=} m.$$

Case 3: $m \in \mathbb{Z}_n \setminus \{0\}$ and m is a multiple of p or q. Let m be a multiple of p, i.e., $m = \mu \cdot p$. From $\mathrm{GCD}(p, q) = 1$, it follows that $q \nmid m$ and

$$m^{k\cdot k'} \bmod q = (m^{q-1})^{\alpha\cdot(p-1)} \cdot m \bmod q \overset{(3.84)}{=} m \text{ and } m^{k\cdot k'} \bmod p = 0.$$

By the Chinese remainder theorem 3.77, we can solve such a system of two congruences $x \equiv_q m$ and $x \equiv_p 0$, and obtain

$$\begin{aligned} x &\overset{(3.13)}{=} a_1 \cdot \tilde{y}_1 \cdot M_1 + a_2 \cdot \tilde{y}_2 \cdot M_2 \\ &= 0 \cdot q \cdot (q^{-1} \bmod p) + m \cdot p \cdot (p^{-1} \bmod q) \bmod n \\ &= m \cdot p \cdot (p^{-1} \bmod q) \bmod n \\ &\overset{\lambda\in\mathbb{Z}}{=} m \cdot (\lambda \cdot q + 1) \bmod n \\ &\overset{m=\mu\cdot p}{=} (\mu \cdot p \cdot \lambda \cdot q + m) \bmod n \\ &= m. \end{aligned}$$

In the case of m being a multiple of q, we obtain the same result correspondingly.

Corollary 8.10. *For each $m \in \mathbb{Z}_n$, it follows $d_{(k',n)}(e_{(k,n)}(m)) = m$.*

We can now define the *RSA cipher system*.

Definition 8.11 (RSA cipher). Let $n = p \cdot q$ be a product of two distinct primes. Given $\mathcal{P} = \mathcal{C} = \mathbb{Z}_n$, $k \in \mathbb{Z}^{\times}_{\phi(n)}$, we set

$$\mathcal{K} = \{(n, k, k');\ k' = k^{-1} \bmod \phi(n)\},$$
$$k_{\text{a,pub}} = (k, n) \text{ and } k_{\text{a,sec}} = (k', n),$$

and define

$$e_{k_{\text{a,pub}}}(m) = m^k \bmod n,\ d_{k_{\text{a,sec}}}(c) = c^{k'} \bmod n.$$

Knowing p and q implies knowing $\phi(n) = (p-1) \cdot (q-1)$ and $k' = k^{-1} \bmod \phi(n)$ consequently. Alternatively, if n and $\phi(n)$ are known, we can calculate p and q because

$$\begin{aligned} \phi(n) &= (p-1) \cdot (q-1) = p \cdot q - (p+q) + 1 = n + 1 - (p+q) \\ &\Leftrightarrow p + q = n + 1 - \phi(n) \\ (p+q)^2 &= p^2 - 2n + q^2 + 4n = (p-q)^2 + 4n \\ &\overset{p \geq q}{\Leftrightarrow} p - q = \sqrt{(p+q)^2 - 4n} \end{aligned}$$

and we can immediately calculate $(p > q)$

$$p = \frac{p+q}{2} + \frac{p-q}{2} = \frac{1}{2} \cdot (n + 1 - \phi(n)) + \frac{1}{2}\sqrt{(n+1-\phi(n))^2 - 4n}.$$

By solving the factorizing problem, the RSA will be insecure. However, we may not need to solve the factorizing problem, as solving the congruence $m^k \equiv_n c$ for m would suffice. This can be done independently from the factorizing problem.

Example 8.12.

$$n = 925272656494817,\ \phi(n) = 925272595163136.$$

We try to calculate p and q: $n + 1 - \phi(n) = 61331682$.

$$\begin{aligned} p &= \frac{1}{2} \cdot 61331682 + \frac{1}{2} \cdot \sqrt{61331682^2 - 4 \cdot 3701090625979268} \\ &= 30665841 + \frac{1}{2} \cdot 7777184 = 34554433 \\ &\Rightarrow q = 26777249. \end{aligned}$$

Algorithm 8.2: RSA key generation

Require: $n = p \cdot q$ with p, q prim.
Ensure: Public key $k_{\text{a,pub}}$.
$\phi(n) := (p-1) \cdot (q-1)$.
Choose k with $1 < k < \phi(n)$ and $\text{GCD}(k, \phi(n)) = 1$ (public key (k, n)).
$k' := k^{-1} \bmod \phi(n)$ (private key (k', n)).
return (k, n).

Algorithm 8.3: RSA encryption and decryption

Require: For encryption: public key (k, n), plaintext m (encoded by $0 \leq m < n$). For decryption: private key (k', n).
Ensure: Ciphertext c, decrypted plaintext m'.
$c := e_{(k,n)}(m) = m^k \bmod n$.
$m' := d_{(k',n)}(c) = c^{k'} \bmod n$.
return c and m'.

The generated magnitudes of p and q in Algorithm 8.2 are crucial for the security of the RSA process in Algorithm 8.3. There should be 1024 bits (about 310 decimals), each proposed in binary representation. Thus, n has a magnitude of about 2048 bits. For example, the plaintext consists of an 8-bit ASCII representation. Then, 256 symbols are composed to one single block. A longer plaintext is split into parts as usual.

Example 8.13.

$$n = 771767, \ k = 2^{16} + 1 = 65537.$$

We apply $\mathcal{P} = \mathcal{C} = \mathbb{F}_2^{20}$. The plaintext

"SECURITY"

has to be encoded to twenty bits each block. We therefore use four letters, each encoded by five bits resulting in

$$18, 4, 2, 20 \rightarrow \ (1,0,0,1,0,0,0,1,0,0,0,0,0,1,0,1,0,1,0,0) \rightarrow \ 594004,$$
$$17, 8, 19, 24 \rightarrow \ (1,0,0,0,1,0,1,0,0,0,1,0,0,1,1,1,1,0,0,0) \rightarrow \ 565880.$$

For encryption we use the public key

$$k_{\text{a,pub}} = (k, n) = (65537, 771767).$$

We obtain

$$c_1 = 594004^{65537} \bmod 771767 = 686067 \rightarrow U\hat{}\text{`}T\ , \text{ and}$$
$$c_2 = 565880^{65537} \bmod 771767 = 211916 \rightarrow GO\_M.$$

For decryption, we calculate $k' = k^{-1} \bmod \phi(n) = 62297$ and with the private key

$$k_{\text{a,sec}} = (k', n) = (62297, 771767).$$

we calculate

$$\tilde{m}_1 = 686067^{62297} \bmod 771767 = 594004$$
$$\tilde{m}_2 = 211916^{62297} \bmod 771767 = 565880$$

Two significant drawbacks of the RSA yielded a search for another trapdoor one-way function and with it different public-key cipher systems.

1. Once someone succeeds in efficiently performing the prime factorization of natural numbers, the RSA procedure must be replaced immediately. It is then too late to start looking for alternatives.
2. The current algorithms for prime factorization force the cryptographers to use primes with at least 1024 bits. These quantities make encryption and decryption very complex. We are looking for public-key methods that manage with smaller numbers.

We will still show a chosen ciphertext attack on the RSA. Let c be a given ciphertext based on the public key (k, n), i.e., $c = m^k \bmod n$ for some unknown plaintext m. If an attacker can choose any ciphertext z for decryption, they can set $z = c^{-1} \bmod n$. Now, let $\tilde{m}$ be the corresponding plaintext for z. Then,

$$1 = c^{-1} \cdot c \bmod n = z \cdot c \bmod n = \tilde{m}^k \cdot m^k \bmod n = (\tilde{m} \cdot m)^k \bmod n.$$

However, decrypting 1 inevitably yields 1. It follows

$$1 = \tilde{m} \cdot m \bmod n \Leftrightarrow m = \tilde{m}^{-1} \bmod n.$$

Example 8.14.

$$n = 771767,\ k = 2^{16} + 1 = 65537,\ c = 292493.$$

First, we calculate $z = c^{-1} \bmod n = 65611$ and let it decrypt to $\tilde{m} = 612136$, obtaining

$$m = \tilde{m}^{-1} \bmod n = 612136^{-1} \bmod 771767 = 600000.$$

With the same configuration, the same ciphertext is generated each time from the same plaintext, which can be used to guess the plaintext if the amount of possible plaintexts is not too large. To overcome such a situation, we can introduce a probabilistic version of RSA encryption called RSA-OAEP (Optimal Asymmetric Encryption Padding). Here, we show a simplified version, according to Martin's procedure,[11] to get the basic idea. Therefore, we assume that the modulus n is of size s bits. Now, we need two one-way functions $g : \mathbb{F}_2^u \to \mathbb{F}_2^v$ and $h : \mathbb{F}_2^v \to \mathbb{F}_2^u$ fulfilling the condition $s = v + u$. The plaintext comes from $\mathbb{F}_2^v$. An additional element is a randomly chosen number $r \in \mathbb{F}_2^u$. The encryption process consists of three steps.

$$\begin{aligned} a &= m \oplus g(r), \\ b &= r \oplus h(a), \text{ and} \\ \tilde{m} &= a||b \ \rightarrow\ c = \tilde{m}^k \bmod n. \end{aligned}$$

Among other things, we have to recover r for decryption of c. Again, three steps yield the plaintext.

$$\begin{aligned} \tilde{m} &= a||b = c^{k'} \bmod n, \\ r &= r \oplus h(a) \oplus h(a) = b \oplus h(a), \text{ and} \\ m &= m \oplus g(r) \oplus g(r) = a \oplus g(r). \end{aligned}$$

RSA-OAEP is a two-rounded Feistel-like processing due to Section 6.1.

---

[11]See (Martin, 2017).

8.4 El-Gamal Cipher System

The idea behind an El-Gamal cipher is to apply the discrete logarithm problem 7.10. For it, a simple combination of a Diffie–Hellman key agreement from Section 7.1.2 and a simple multiplication cipher from Section 4.2.2 is used.

Let p be prime and g be a generator of the multiplicative group $(\mathbb{Z}_p^\times, \cdot_p, 1)$. An entity A who wants to be entered in a public directory with its own public key chooses an $x_A \in \{2, \dots, p-2\}$ randomly and calculates its public key $k_{\text{a,pub}} = (p, g, y_A)$ by $y_A = g^{x_A} \bmod p \in \mathbb{Z}_p \setminus \{1, g\}$. The corresponding private key is $k_{\text{a,sec}} = (p, x_A)$. If an entity B wants to send a message m to entity A using the public key (p, g, y_A), B has to represent the message in $\mathbb{Z}_p$ and choose an integer $x_B \in \mathbb{Z}_p^\times$ randomly. Then, B calculates $y_B = g^{x_B} \bmod p \in \mathbb{Z}_p \setminus \{1, g\}$ and $c = m \cdot y_A^{x_B} \bmod p$.

Entity B only uses a private-key multiplication cipher as a special case of an affine block cipher from Section 4.2.2. The keyspace is given by

$$\mathcal{K} = \{(p, g, x_A, y_A);\ y_A = g^{x_A} \bmod p\}$$

and the encryption key is calculated by $x_{AB} = y_A^{x_B} \bmod p \in \mathbb{Z}_p^\times$. The encryption function is given by

$$e_{p,g,y_A;x_B} : \mathbb{Z}_p \to \{2, \dots, p-2\} \times \mathbb{Z}_p,\ m \mapsto (y_B, c)$$

with $c = m \cdot y_A^{x_B} \bmod p = m \cdot x_{AB} \bmod p$. B sends the ciphertext c and information y_B to the receiver A. Since $c, y_B \leq \mathbb{Z}_p$, the transmitted message is twice as long as the plaintext m.

The original message can be recovered using x_A from the private key. Therefore, we set $z = (y_B^{x_A})^{-1} \bmod p$ and obtain

$$\begin{aligned} c \cdot z \bmod p &= m \cdot y_A^{x_B} \cdot (y_B^{x_A})^{-1} \bmod p \\ &= m \cdot (g^{x_A})^{x_B} \cdot ((g^{x_B})^{x_A})^{-1} \bmod p \\ &= m \cdot (g^{x_B})^{x_A} \cdot ((g^{x_B})^{x_A})^{-1} \bmod p = m \cdot 1 \bmod p = m. \end{aligned}$$

We note the decryption function by $d_{x_A} : \{2, \dots, p-2\} \times \mathbb{Z}_p \to \mathbb{Z}_p$. In this situation

$$z = (y_B^{x_A})^{-1} \bmod p = y_B^{p-1} \cdot (y_B^{x_A})^{-1} \bmod p = y_B^{p-1-x_A} \bmod p$$

can be calculated easily. If we understand $x_{AB} = y_A^{x_B} \bmod p$ as a secure key of a multiplication cipher we get

$$x_{AB} = y_A^{x_B} \bmod p = (g_A^x)^{x_B} \bmod p = (g^{x_B})^{x_A} \bmod p = y_B^{x_A} \bmod p$$

and entity A can calculate x_{AB} using x_A and y_B. The number x_A works as the trapdoor information here. Finally, c can be deciphered. This is exactly the situation that occurs in the Diffie–Hellman key agreement in Section 7.1.2. An attacker who only knows p, g, y_A and y_B has to solve $x_A = \log_g(y_A) \bmod p$ or $x_B = \log_g(y_B) \bmod p$ in order to obtain the private key. In other words, this person needs to solve the Diffie–Hellman problem.

Corollary 8.15. *For each $m \in \mathbb{Z}_p^\times$, it follows*

$$d_{x_A}(e_{(p,g,y_A;x_B)}(m)) = m.$$

We can now define the El-Gamal cipher system.[12]

Definition 8.16 (El-Gamal cipher with $\mathbb{Z}_p^\times$). Let p be prime and g be a generator of $(\mathbb{Z}_p^\times, \cdot_p, 1)$. Given $\mathcal{P} = \mathbb{Z}_p$ and $\mathcal{C} = \{2, \ldots, p-2\} \times \mathbb{Z}_p$, we set

$$\mathcal{K} = \{(p, g, x_A, y_A);\ y_A = g^{x_A} \bmod p\},$$
$$k_{\text{a,pub}} = (p, g, y_A) \text{ and } k_{\text{a,sec}} = (p, x_A),$$

and define

$$e_{p,g,y_A;x_B} : \mathbb{Z}_p \to \{2, \ldots, p-2\} \times \mathbb{Z}_p,$$
$$m \mapsto (g^{x_B} \bmod p, m \cdot y_A^{x_B} \bmod p),$$
$$d_{x_A} : \{2, \ldots, p-2\} \times \mathbb{Z}_p \to \mathbb{Z}_p,\ (y_B, c) \mapsto c \cdot (y_B^{x_A})^{-1} \bmod p.$$

Remark 8.17. (1) p does not need to be prime. Only a cyclic group of a reasonably high order is need and the choices of x_A and y_A are permissible.

(2) Remember: the size of a message is doubled by El-Gamal.

[12]See (El Gamal, 1985).

Algorithm 8.4: El-Gamal key generation with safe prime

Require: $p := 2q + 1$ safe prime, $q \in \mathbb{N}$ prime and $g \in \mathbb{Z}_p^\times$ with $\mathcal{L}(g) = \mathbb{Z}_p^\times$.

Ensure: Public key (p, g, y_A).

Choose $x_A \in \{2, \ldots, p-2\}$ randomly (for the private key).

$y_A := g^{x_A} \bmod p$.

return (p, g, y_A).

Algorithm 8.5: El-Gamal with $\mathbb{Z}_p^\times$

Require: For encryption: public key (p, g, y_A), plaintext m (encoded with $m \in \mathbb{Z}_p$). For decryption: private key (p, x_A).

Ensure: ciphertext $\tilde{c}$, decrypted plaintext m'.

Choose $x_B \in \{2, \ldots, p-2\}$ randomly.

$y_B := g^{x_B} \bmod p$ and $c := m \cdot y_A^{x_B} \bmod p$.

$\tilde{c} := (y_B, c)$.

$z := y_B^{-x_A} \bmod p$.

$m' := c \cdot z \bmod p$.

return $\tilde{c}$ and m'.

Example 8.18.

$$p = 771767,\ g = 458751,\ x_A = 65535,\ x_B = 262145.$$

We apply $\mathcal{P} = \mathbb{Z}_p \approx \mathbb{F}_2^{20}$, $\mathcal{C} = \{2, \ldots, p-2\} \times \mathbb{Z}_p$ and obtain

$$y_A = g^{x_A} \bmod p = 458751^{65535} \bmod 771767 = 84088,$$
$$y_B = g^{x_B} \bmod p = 458751^{262145} \bmod 771767 = 93493.$$

The plaintext

"SECURITY"

has to get encoded to twenty bits each block. We therefore use four letters, each encoded by five bits resulting in

$$18, 4, 2, 20 \rightarrow \quad (1,0,0,1,0,0,0,1,0,0,0,0,0,1,0,1,0,1,0,0) \rightarrow \quad 594004,$$
$$17, 8, 19, 24 \rightarrow \quad (1,0,0,0,1,0,1,0,0,0,1,0,0,1,1,1,1,0,0,0) \rightarrow \quad 565880.$$

For enciphering, we use the public key

$$k_{\text{a,pub}} = (p, g, y_A) = (771767, 65537, 84088).$$

We obtain $x_{AB} = y_A^{x_B} \bmod p = 492258$ and

$$c_1 = m_1 \cdot x_{AB} \bmod p = 594004 \cdot 492258 \bmod 771767 = 742644 \\ \to WVHU,$$

$$c_2 = m_2 \cdot x_{AB} \bmod p = 565880 \cdot 492258 \bmod 771767 = 363346 \\ \to, LC[S.$$

The messages $(93493, 742644)$ and $(93493, 742644)$ are transmitted. For decrypting, using the private key we calculate

$$k_{\text{a,sec}} = (p, x_A) = (771767, 65535),$$

the value $z = y_B^{p-1-x_A} \bmod p = 210711$ and

$$\tilde{m}_1 = 742644 \cdot 210711 \bmod 771767 = 594004, \text{ and}$$

$$\tilde{m}_2 = 363346 \cdot 210711 \bmod 771767 = 565880.$$

Trapdoor information gets transmitted in addition to the ciphertext. However, the same configuration is used for each block in Example 8.18. The decryption process uses the same private key (p, x_A). Thus, an attacker could recover any plaintext without any knowledge about the private key if they have one plaintext-ciphertext pair.

Example 8.19. Consider the plaintext-ciphertext pair $(m_2, c_2) = (565880, 363346)$ where the ciphertext $c_1 = 742644$ and $p = 771767$ are known. Then, it follows

$$c_1 \cdot c_2^{-1} \bmod p = c_1 \cdot c_2^{p-2} \bmod p = m_1 \cdot y_A^{x_B} \cdot m_2^{p-2} \cdot y_A^{x_B(p-2)} \bmod p \\ = m_1 \cdot m_2^{p-2} \bmod p.$$

Thus, we obtain $m_1 = c_1 \cdot c_2^{-1} \cdot m_2 \bmod p$. Working off the example, we get

$$m_1 = 742644 \cdot 363346^{-1} \cdot 565880 \bmod 771767 = 594004.$$

Any new plaintext should be encrypted by a new configuration. Alternatively, we do not want to change the public key configuration, which remains to change y_B constantly. This can be done by randomizing y_B. If x_B is equally likely from $\{2, \ldots, p-2\}$ each time and y_A is a generator of $(\mathbb{Z}_p^\times, \cdot_p, 1)$, the possible values of (y_B, c) are equally likely to be chosen from $\mathbb{Z}_p \setminus \{1, g\} \times \mathbb{Z}_p^\times$. El-Gamal behaves like a probabilistic scheme.

El-Gamal is not limited to $(\mathbb{Z}_p^\times, \cdot_p, 1)$. All of the operations can be implemented on other groups. To generalize, there are two aspects to consider:

- The basic principle of solving the discrete logarithm problem 7.10 must be maintained.
- The group operations must be executable with little effort, for reasons of efficiency.

8.5 Elliptic Curve Cipher Systems

In Section 8.4, we applied the discrete logarithm problem 7.10 to the multiplicative group $(\mathbb{Z}_p^\times, \cdot_p, 1)$. Similarly, we can apply it to any other cyclic group. For example, if we look at the additive group $(\mathbb{Z}_p, +_p, 0)$ where p is prime, the operation according to the exponential function is defined in Section 3.1.1, namely

$$e_g : \mathbb{Z}_p \to \mathbb{Z}_p,\ x \mapsto \begin{cases} x \cdot_p g = g +_p \cdots +_p g, & x \neq 0, \\ 0, & x = 0. \end{cases}$$

There, g is a generator, i.e., $\mathcal{L}(g) = \{k \cdot g \bmod p;\ k \in \mathbb{Z}_p\} = \mathbb{Z}_p$. In the group $(\mathbb{Z}_p, +_p, 0)$, all elements $g \in \mathbb{Z}_p \setminus \{0\}$ are generators according to Theorem 3.59. Since all elements in $\mathcal{L}(g)$ are pairwise distinct, the mapping e_g with $g \in \mathbb{Z}_p \setminus \{0\}$ is bijective, too. Thus, there is an inverse function corresponding to the discrete logarithm

$$d_g : \mathbb{Z}_p \to \mathbb{Z}_p,\ x \mapsto d_g(x) \text{ with } e_g(d_g(x)) = x.$$

The problem of the discrete logarithm in $(\mathbb{Z}_p, +_p, 0)$ is: find any x satisfying $x \cdot_p g = c$, given a logarithmic basis $g \in \mathbb{Z}_p \setminus \{0\}$ and some $c \in \mathbb{Z}_p$. The solution is $x = g^{-1} \cdot_p c$, where g^{-1} is the multiplicative inverse element of g in $\mathbb{Z}_p^\times$. Since the inverse element can be easily calculated by the extended Euclidean algorithm, this group is not useful for cryptographical applications.

Example 8.20.

$$(\mathbb{Z}_{23}, +_{23}, 0);\ g = 17.$$

$\mathcal{L}(g) = \mathbb{Z}_{23}$. Given $x_A = 5$, we obtain $y_A = 17 \cdot 5 \bmod 23 = 16$. The public key is $(23, 17, 16)$ and the private key is $(23, 5)$. The message $m = 11$ combined with $x_B = 2$ yields $y_B = 17 \cdot 2 \bmod 23 = 11$ and $c = 11 + 16 \cdot 2 \bmod 23 = 20$, i.e., $\tilde{c} = (11, 20)$. For decryption, we calculate $z = -(11 \cdot 5) \bmod 23 = 14$. The recovered plaintext is then $20 + 14 \bmod 23 = 11$. Another possibility is to calculate x_B: $x_B = g^{-1} \cdot_p x_{AB} = 19 \cdot_{23} 11 = 2$. Finally, $m = c - y_A \cdot x_B \bmod p = 20 - 16 \cdot 2 \bmod 23 = 11$.

Hence, we have to look for other finite cyclic groups in which the discrete logarithm problem is not computationally solvable. We obtain alternative commutative additive groups using elliptic curves. To prepare this term, we have to investigate plane affine curves.

Remark 8.21. In the style of Definition 6.5, we denote a polynomial consisting of more variables $X_1, \ldots, X_k$ with coefficients $a_{i_1 \ldots i_k}$ by

$$P(X_1, \ldots, X_k) = \sum_{i_1, \ldots, i_k > 0} a_{i_1 \ldots i_k} X_1^{i_1} \cdot \cdots \cdot X_k^{i_k},\ i_1 + \cdots + i_k < \infty.$$

Definition 8.22 (Plane affine curve). Let $(\mathbb{F}, +, \cdot, 0, 1)$ be a field and

$$f : \mathbb{F} \times \mathbb{F} \to \mathbb{F},\ (x, y) \mapsto f(x, y) = \sum_{i,j > 0} a_{ij} x^i y^j, \quad a_{ij} \in \mathbb{F},$$

be the evaluation of a polynomial consisting of two variables satisfying $a_{ij} \neq 0$, for finitely as many a_{ij} as possible. Then,

$$\tilde{C}_f(\mathbb{F}) = \{(x, y) \in \mathbb{F} \times \mathbb{F};\ f(x, y) = 0\}$$

is called a *plane affine curve* over $\mathbb{F}$.

We now look at polynomial with degree 3 and $a_{ijk} = 0$, for $i + j + k \neq 3$,

$$\begin{aligned} g &: \mathbb{F}^3 \to \mathbb{F},\ (x, y, z) \mapsto g(x, y, z), \\ g(x, y, z) &= a_{300}x^3 + a_{210}x^2y + a_{201}x^2z + a_{120}xy^2 \\ &\quad + a_{111}xyz + a_{102}xz^2 + a_{030}y^3 + a_{021}y^2z \\ &\quad + a_{012}yz^2 + a_{003}z^3. \end{aligned}$$

Such a polynomial is called homogeneous of degree 3. For every zero $(x_0, y_0, z_0) \in \mathbb{F}^3$ of g, the scaled tuple $(\lambda x_0, \lambda y_0, \lambda z_0)$ yields

$$\begin{aligned} g(\lambda x_0, \lambda y_0, \lambda z_0) &= a_{300}(\lambda x_0)^3 + a_{210}(\lambda x_0)^2(\lambda y_0) + a_{201}(\lambda x_0)^2(\lambda z_0) \\ &\quad + \cdots + a_{012}(\lambda y_0)(\lambda z_0)^2 + a_{003}(\lambda z_0)^3 \\ &= \lambda^3 g(x_0, y_0, z_0) = 0, \end{aligned}$$

evaluating g again. This enables us to define an equivalence relation

$$\begin{aligned} &(x_0, y_0, z_0) \sim (u, v, w) \\ \Leftrightarrow\ &(u, v, w) = (\lambda x_0, \lambda y_0, \lambda z_0) \text{ for any } \lambda \in \mathbb{F} \setminus \{0\} \end{aligned}$$

and (x_0, y_0, z_0) is a representative of a representative class that we denote by $[x_0 : y_0 : z_0]$.

Definition 8.23 (Plane projective curve). A *plane projective curve* is the quotient set

$$C_g(\mathbb{F}) = \{[x_0 : y_0 : z_0];\ g(x_0, y_0, z_0) = 0\} = (\mathbb{F}^3 \setminus \{(0, 0, 0)\})/\sim,$$

i.e., the set of the representative classes of $\sim$.

For special mapping

$$\begin{aligned} \tilde{f} : \mathbb{F}^2 \to \mathbb{F},\ \tilde{f}(x, y) &= a_{300}x^3 + a_{210}x^2y + a_{201}x^2 + a_{120}xy^2 + a_{111}xy \\ &\quad + a_{102}x + a_{030}y^3 + a_{021}y^2 + a_{012}y + a_{003} \\ &= g(x, y, 1), \end{aligned} \tag{8.3}$$

it is possible to define an injective mapping

$$i : \tilde{C}_{\tilde{f}}(\mathbb{F}) \to C_g(\mathbb{F}),\ i(x, y) = [x : y : 1].$$

This is because from $i(x, y) = i(x', y')$, it follows $[x : y : 1] = [x' : y' : 1]$ and $x = tx'$, $y = ty'$, $1 = t1$, thus, $t = 1$ and $x = x'$, $y = y'$. Applying this mapping, we can interpret $\tilde{C}_{\tilde{f}}(\mathbb{F})$ as a subset of $C_g(\mathbb{F})$. $\tilde{C}_{\tilde{f}}(\mathbb{F})$ gets embedded into the plane projective curve $C_g(\mathbb{F})$ based on the mapping i. Beyond that, there are more zeros of g that cannot be achieved by i evaluated at any element of $\tilde{C}_{\tilde{f}}(\mathbb{F})$. Combined, these are the equivalence classes $[u : v : 0]$ for some $u \neq 0$ or $v \neq 0$, $u, v \in \mathbb{F}$ and

$$g(u, v, 0) = a_{300}u^3 + a_{210}u^2v + a_{120}uv^2 + a_{030}v^3 = 0.$$

Finally, we obtain

$$C_g(\mathbb{F}) = i(\tilde{C}_{\tilde{f}}(\mathbb{F})) \cup \{[u : v : 0];\ g(u, v, 0) = 0\}.$$

Let g be a homogeneous polynomial of degree 3. A plane projective curve $C_g(\mathbb{F})$ is singular at the point $[x_0 : y_0 : z_0]$ if all partial derivatives of g will disappear, i.e.,

$$\frac{\partial g}{\partial x}(x_0, y_0, z_0) = \frac{\partial g}{\partial y}(x_0, y_0, z_0) = \frac{\partial g}{\partial z}(x_0, y_0, z_0) = 0. \tag{8.4}$$

We have to calculate the derivation of the polynomial in a natural way. If $C_g(\mathbb{F})$ has no singular point, it is called *non-singular*. We look into a special class of homogeneous polynomials of degree 3.

Definition 8.24 (Elliptic curve over $\mathbb{F}$). An *elliptic curve* is a non-singular plane projective curve $C_{g_{\mathcal{W}}}(\mathbb{F})$ on a field $(\mathbb{F}, +, \cdot, 0, 1)$ at which $g_{\mathcal{W}}$ is the Weierstraß-polynomial[13]

$$g_{\mathcal{W}}(x, y, z) = y^2z + a_1xyz + a_3yz^2 - x^3 - a_2x^2z - a_4xz^2 - a_6z^3$$

with $a_1, a_2, a_3, a_4, a_6 \in \mathbb{F}$.

[13]Karl Weierstraß (1815–1891).

Remark 8.25. (1) In the Weierstraß polynomial, $a_{210} = a_{120} = a_{030} = 0$. Thus, $g_{\mathcal{W}}(u, v, 0) = -u^3 = 0 \Leftrightarrow u = 0$ and

$$C_{g_{\mathcal{W}}}(\mathbb{F}) = i(\tilde{C}_{\tilde{f}_{\mathcal{W}}}(\mathbb{F})) \cup \{[0:1:0]\}$$

at which $\tilde{f}_{\mathcal{W}}(x, y) = y^2 + a_1xy + a_3y - x^3 - a_2x^2 - a_4x - a_6$.

(2) As the only one, the "point" $[0:1:0]$ cannot be identified by an element from $\tilde{C}_{\tilde{f}_{\mathcal{W}}}(\mathbb{F})$. From now on, we abbreviate it: $\mathcal{O} := [0:1:0]$. $\mathcal{O}$ is not singular, since

$$\frac{\partial g_{\mathcal{W}}}{\partial z}(0, 1, 0) = 1 \neq 0.$$

For a point $[x:y:1] \in C_{g_{\mathcal{W}}}(\mathbb{F}) \setminus \{[0:1:0]\}$, we calculate

$$\begin{aligned}
\frac{\partial g_{\mathcal{W}}}{\partial x}(x, y, z) &= a_1yz - 3x^2 - 2a_2xz - a_4z^2 \\
&\overset{z=1}{=} a_1y - 3x^2 - 2a_2x - a_4, \\
\frac{\partial g_{\mathcal{W}}}{\partial y}(x, y, z) &= 2yz + a_1xz + a_3z^2 \\
&\overset{z=1}{=} 2y + a_1x + a_3, \\
\frac{\partial g_{\mathcal{W}}}{\partial z}(x, y, z) &= y^2 + a_1xy + 2a_3yz - a_2x^2 - 2a_4xz - 3a_6z^2 \\
&\overset{z=1}{=} y^2 + a_1xy + 2a_3y - a_2x^2 - 2a_4x - 3a_6,
\end{aligned}$$

and can see that

$$\frac{\partial g_{\mathcal{W}}}{\partial x}(x, y, 1) = \frac{\partial \tilde{f}_{\mathcal{W}}}{\partial x}(x, y) \text{ and } \frac{\partial g_{\mathcal{W}}}{\partial y}(x, y, 1) = \frac{\partial \tilde{f}_{\mathcal{W}}}{\partial y}(x, y),$$

and also

$$\begin{aligned}
\frac{\partial g_{\mathcal{W}}}{\partial z}(x, y, 1) &= -x \cdot \frac{\partial g_{\mathcal{W}}}{\partial x}(x, y, 1) - y \cdot \frac{\partial g_{\mathcal{W}}}{\partial y}(x, y, 1) + 3g(x, y, 1) \\
&= -x \cdot \frac{\partial \tilde{f}_{\mathcal{W}}}{\partial x}(x, y) - y \cdot \frac{\partial \tilde{f}_{\mathcal{W}}}{\partial y}(x, y) + 3\tilde{f}_{\mathcal{W}}(x, y).
\end{aligned}$$

It follows that a point $[x:y:1] \in C_{g_{\mathcal{W}}}(\mathbb{F}) \setminus \{[0:1:0]\}$ is singular iff the partial derivations of $f_{\mathcal{W}}$ disappear in the point $(x, y) \in \tilde{C}_{\tilde{f}_{\mathcal{W}}}(\mathbb{F})$.

Henceforth, we only discuss plane projective curves over $\mathbb{R}$ or $\mathbb{F}_p$, where $p > 3$ is prime. Thus, $\mathbb{F}$ at least holds the elements $0, 1, 2 = 1+1, 3 = 1+1+1$. For convenience, we write $\frac{1}{q^k}$ instead of $q^{-k} \bmod p$ for $q \in \{2, 3\}$. If we look at the linear and thus bijective transformation

$$\tilde{\tau} : C_{g_{\mathcal{W}}}(\mathbb{F}) \to C_{g_{\mathcal{W}}}(\mathbb{F}),\ \tau([x:y:z]) = \left[x : y - \frac{1}{2}(a_1 x + a_3 z) : z\right],$$

$$\tilde{\tau} = \begin{pmatrix} 1 & 0 & 0 \\ -\frac{1}{2}a_1 & 1 & -\frac{1}{2}a_3 \\ 0 & 0 & 1 \end{pmatrix}, \quad \det(\tilde{\tau}) = 1,$$

we can simplify the Weierstraß polynomial to

$$\tilde{g}_{\mathcal{W}}(x, y, z) = y^2 z - x^3 - a_2' x^2 z - a_4' x z^2 - a_6' z^3,$$

at which $a_2' = a_2 + \frac{1}{4}a_1^2$, $a_4' = a_4 + a_1 a_3$ and $a_6' = a_6 + \frac{1}{4}a_3^2$.

Example 8.26 (Curve 25519). Let $p = 2^{255} - 19$. Look at $C_{\tilde{g}_{\mathcal{W}}}(\mathbb{F}_p)$ and

$$\tilde{g}_{\mathcal{W}}(x, y, z) = y^2 z - x^3 - 486662 x^2 z - x z^2.$$

Since

$$\frac{\partial \tilde{g}_{\mathcal{W}}}{\partial x}(x, y, z) \overset{z=1}{=} -3x^2 - 2 \cdot 486662 x - 1 \overset{!}{=} 0 \bmod p$$

$$\Leftrightarrow x_{1,2} = -3^{-1} \cdot 486662 \pm \sqrt{486662^2 - 3} \bmod p \text{ and further}$$

$$(486662^2 - 3)^{\frac{p-1}{2}} = p - 1 \neq 1$$

$\Rightarrow$no square root exists according to Corollary 7.18;

there is no singular point. Thus, $C_{\tilde{g}_{\mathcal{W}}}(\mathbb{F}_p)$ is an elliptic curve.

Again, we can simplify by bijective linear transforming

$$\hat{\tau} : C_{g_{\mathcal{W}}}(\mathbb{F}) \to C_{g_{\mathcal{W}}}(\mathbb{F}),\ \tau([x:y:z]) = \left[x - \frac{1}{3}a_2' z : y : z\right],$$

$$\hat{\tau} = \begin{pmatrix} 1 & 0 & -\frac{1}{3}(a_2 + \frac{1}{4}a_1^2) \\ 0 & 1 & 0 \\ 0 & 0 & 1 \end{pmatrix}, \quad \det(\hat{\tau}) = 1,$$

obtaining

$$\hat{g}_{\mathcal{W}}(x, y, z) = y^2 z - x^3 - axz^2 - bz^3, \tag{8.5}$$

at which $a = a'_4 - a'^2_2$ and $b = a'_6 - \frac{1}{3}a'_2 a'_4 + \frac{2}{27}a'^3_2$. In future discussions, this will be called the *short Weierstraß polynomial*

$$\hat{f}_{\mathcal{W}}(x, y) := \hat{g}_{\mathcal{W}}(x, y, 1) := y^2 - x^3 - ax - b$$

for defining an elliptic curve. Furthermore, we use $\Delta = \frac{a^3}{27} + \frac{b^2}{4}$ to decide whether singular points exist or not. To see this, consider $[x : y : 1] \in C_{g_{\mathcal{W}}}(\mathbb{F})$ to be a singular point, i.e., $y = 0, x^2 = -\frac{a}{3}$ and $\hat{g}_{\mathcal{W}}(x, y, 1) = \hat{f}_{\mathcal{W}}(x, y) = 0$. If $a = 0$, we obtain $x = 0$ and thus, $b = 0$ and $\Delta = 0$. Otherwise ($a \neq 0$), it follows

$$0 = x^3 + ax + b = -\frac{a}{3} \cdot x + ax + b = \frac{2}{3}ax + b$$

$$\Rightarrow x = -\frac{3b}{2a} \Rightarrow x^2 = -\frac{a}{3} = \frac{9b^2}{4a^2} \Rightarrow -\frac{a^3}{27} = \frac{b^2}{4} \Rightarrow \Delta = 0.$$

Conversely, let $\Delta = 0$. We show that there exists at least one singular point $(x, y) \in C_{g_{\mathcal{W}}}(\mathbb{F})$. Such a point $(x, y) \in \mathbb{F}^2$ has to ensure $y = 0$ and $x^2 = -\frac{a}{3}$ for being a singular point. Then, we obtain

$$\begin{aligned}
& y^2 - x^3 - ax - b \overset{y=0}{=} -x^3 - ax - b \Rightarrow x(x^2 + a) = -b \\
\Rightarrow \quad & \frac{1}{4}x^2(x^2 + a)^2 = \frac{b^2}{4} \Rightarrow \frac{1}{4}x^2(x^2 + a)^2 = -\frac{a^3}{27} \\
\Rightarrow \quad & -\frac{27}{4}(x^6 + 2ax^4 + a^2x^2) = -\frac{27}{4}\left(-\frac{a^3}{27} + \frac{2a^3}{9} - \frac{a^3}{3}\right) \\
& = \frac{1}{4}(a^3 - 6a^3 + 9a^3) = a^3 \Rightarrow (x, y) \in C_{g_{\mathcal{W}}}(\mathbb{F}).
\end{aligned}$$

Corollary 8.27. *There exists a singular point in $C_{g_{\mathcal{W}}}(\mathbb{F})$ iff $\Delta = \frac{a^3}{27} + \frac{b^2}{4} = 0$, or rather $C_{g_{\mathcal{W}}}(\mathbb{F})$ is an elliptic curve iff $\Delta \neq 0$.*

Remark 8.28. Depending on the choice of a and $\mathbb{F}$ it is sometimes not true for $-\frac{a}{3}$ to be a perfect square or quadratic residue modulo p. One possibility is to consider a field extension where all elements are perfect squares, for example, $\mathbb{C}$ instead of $\mathbb{R}$. However, this would go beyond the scope of this book.

Example 8.29. Let $p = 2^{255} - 19$ again. Look at $C_{\tilde{g}_{\mathcal{W}}}(\mathbb{F}_p)$ and

$$\tilde{g}_{\mathcal{W}}(x, y, z) = y^2 z - x^3 - 486662x^2 z - xz^2$$

from Example 8.26. Transforming to a short Weierstraß polynomial yields

$$a = -38597363079105398474523661669562635951089994888546854679819194669383323180713,$$

$$b = -21442979488391888041402034260868131083938886049192697044343911659998354615 13.$$

Since

$$\frac{a^3}{27} + \frac{b^2}{4} \bmod p = 64328938465175664124206102782604393251816658147578091133031991115485364623 81 \neq 0,$$

there is no singular point.

Let $p = 31$. Look at $C_{\hat{g}_{\mathcal{W}}}(\mathbb{F}_p)$ and

$$\hat{f}_{\mathcal{W}}(x, y) = y^2 - x^3 - 18x + 2 \quad (a = 18, b = -2).$$

Since $\frac{a^3}{27} + \frac{b^2}{4} \bmod p = 6^3 + 1 \bmod p = 0$, there is a singular point. We calculate

$$x = \pm\sqrt{-\frac{a}{3}} = \pm\sqrt{25} = \pm 5$$

and check $(5, 0) \notin C_{\hat{g}_{\mathcal{W}}}(\mathbb{F}_p)$, but $(26, 0) \in C_{\hat{g}_{\mathcal{W}}}(\mathbb{F}_p)$. $(26, 0)$ is a singular point and $C_{\hat{g}_{\mathcal{W}}}(\mathbb{F}_p)$ is not an elliptic curve.

We define

$$E_{\mathbb{F}}(a, b) = \{(x, y) \in \mathbb{F}^2;\ y^2 = x^3 + ax + b\} \cup \mathcal{O},$$

Algorithm 8.6: Arithmetic on elliptic curves

Require: Elliptic curve $E_{\mathbb{F}}(a,b)$, a point $P_1 = (x_1, y_1) \in E_{\mathbb{F}}(a,b)$ and maybe a point $P_2 = (x_2, y_2) \in E_{\mathbb{F}}(a,b)$.

Ensure: $P_3 = P_1 \oplus P_2$ or determining $-P_1$.

if P_2 is not present **then**
  $P_3 := -P_1$. $\{-\mathcal{O} := \mathcal{O}$ and $-P_1 := (x_1, -y_1)\}$
else if $P_1 = \mathcal{O}$ or $P_2 = \mathcal{O}$ **then**
  $P_3 := \mathcal{O} \oplus P_2 := P_2$ and $P_3 := P_1 \oplus \mathcal{O} := P_1$. $\{\mathcal{O}$ id. element$\}$
else if $P_1 = -P_2$ **then**
  $P_3 := P_1 \oplus P_2 := \mathcal{O}$.
else if the previous steps will not apply **then**

$$x_3 := \lambda^2 - x_1 - x_2, \quad y_3 := \lambda(x_1 - x_3) - y_1 \text{ with } \lambda \in \mathbb{F} \text{ and}$$

$$\lambda := \begin{cases} \frac{y_2 - y_1}{x_2 - x_1} & P_1 \neq P_2, \\ \frac{3x_1^2 + a}{2y_1} & P_1 = P_2, \end{cases}, \quad P_3 := (x_3, y_3)$$

end if
return P_3.

denoting an elliptic curve over $\mathbb{F}$. This set can be extended to an algebraic structure. By specifying an addition

$$\oplus : E_{\mathbb{F}}(a,b) \times E_{\mathbb{F}}(a,b) \to E_{\mathbb{F}}(a,b),$$

the structure $(E_{\mathbb{F}}(a,b), \oplus, \mathcal{O})$ yields an abelian additive group.[14] The intention is to take two (distinct) points P_1 and P_2 on the curve and take the line through the points. This line cuts the elliptic curve at another point, except in some special cases. Then, the reflection on the x-axis yields the result P_3 of the addition. Point $\mathcal{O}$ is the identity element.

[14]For further details and a proof of the group properties, see (Silverman, 1986) and (Kaliski, 1988).

Example 8.30. Given the elliptic curve $E_{\mathbb{R}}(3, 22)$ characterized by equation $y^2 = x^3 + 3x + 22$ with the discriminant $\Delta = 122 > 0$, take a look at the three situations represented by the following pictures.

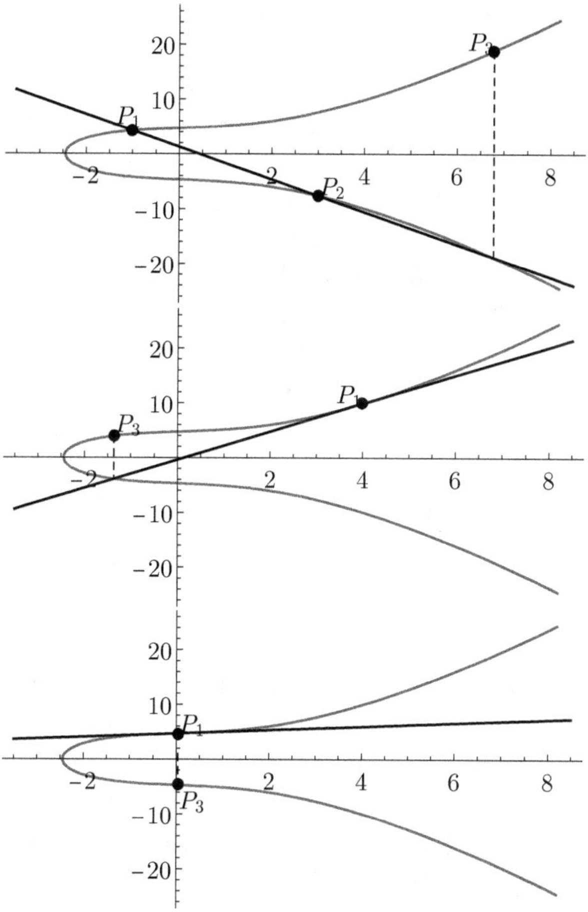

Figure 8.3 Three cases of addition on elliptic curves over $\mathbb{R}$.

The typical situation is to take two different points (and $P_2 \neq -P_1$) and reflect the cutting point on the x-axis (first case). The second case shows the addition $P_1 \oplus P_1$. We use the tangent on $E_{\mathbb{R}}(3, 22)$ at this point. The third case is even more special. It takes an inflectional tangent on a point of inflection.

With that, we can reformulate the addition by $P_1 \oplus P_2 \oplus P_3 = \mathcal{O}$. Algorithm 8.6 shows the arithmetic steps on this group. Steps 2 and 3, $-\mathcal{O} := \mathcal{O}$ and $-P_1 := (x_1, -y_1)$, are just definitions. The algorithm is to be understood as a sequence that has to be processed in succession. As soon as a point is applied, the rest can be ignored.

Let us have a closer look on the elliptic curves $E_{\mathbb{Z}_p}(a, b)$ based on the field $(\mathbb{Z}_p, +_p, \cdot_p, 0, 1)$ where $p > 3$ is prime. The intuition behind the addition $\oplus_p$ gets lost but the arithmetic continues to work. The rules get fully transferred from $\mathbb{R}$ to $\mathbb{Z}_p$ with respect to the modulo operations. The number of elements in the group can be estimated. Since we look for quadratic residues modulo p, we know from Corollary 7.20 that there are $\frac{p-1}{2}$ such numbers. Each such number has two square roots. Thus, we can expect approximately p points on $E_{\mathbb{Z}_p}(a, b)$. By the Theorem[15] of Hasse,[16] the number of elements can be limited by

$$p + 1 - 2\sqrt{p} \leq |E_{\mathbb{Z}_p}(a, b)| \leq p + 1 + 2\sqrt{p}. \tag{8.6}$$

By variation of a and b, all of the possible values for $|E_{\mathbb{Z}_p}(a, b)|$ can be achieved.

Example 8.31. Let $p = 23$. Depending on the choice of a and b, between 15 and 33 points on the elliptic curve are possible. We choose $a = 3$ and $b = 22$ and obtain the following 33 points, considering the equation $y^2 = x^3 + 3 \cdot x + 22 \bmod 23$:

$$\mathcal{O}, (1,7), (1,16), (2,17), (2,6), (3,14), (3,9), (4,11), (4,12), (5,22),$$
$$(5,1), (6,7), (6,16), (7,15), (7,8), (8,11), (8,12), (11,11), (11,12),$$
$$(13,21), (13,2), (14,5), (14,18), (16,7), (16,16), (17,15), (17,8),$$
$$(20,20), (20,3), (21,10), (21,13), (22,15), (22,8).$$

---

[15] See (Silverman, 1986) for the proof.
[16] Helmut Hasse (1898–1979).

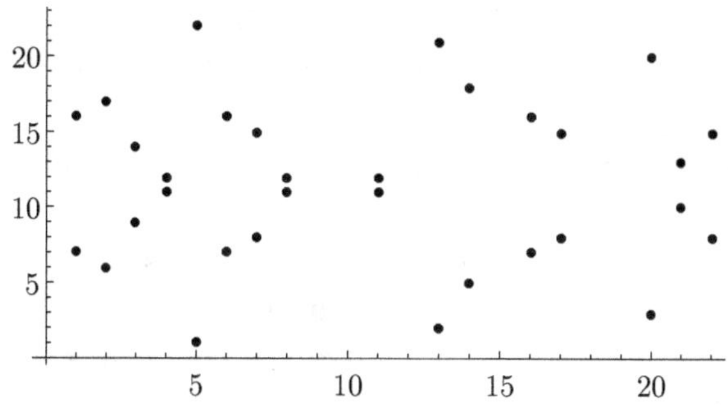

Figure 8.4 Elliptic curve $E_{\mathbb{Z}_{23}}(3, 22)$ over $\mathbb{Z}_{23}$.

All of the points (except $\mathcal{O}$) are appearing in pairs due to the square root modulo p being calculated. As an example, we notice the following additions:

$$\begin{aligned}
(7,8) &\oplus_{23} (7,15) = \mathcal{O}, \\
(7,8) &\oplus_{23} (7,8) \ = (11,12),\ \lambda = 18, \\
(11,12) &\oplus_{23} (7,8) \ = (6,16),\ \ \lambda = 1, \\
(11,12) &\oplus_{23} (7,15) = (7,8),\ \ \ \lambda = 5.
\end{aligned}$$

To determine all the points of an elliptic curve $E_{\mathbb{Z}_p}(a, b)$, we can use each possible value for $x \in \mathbb{Z}_p$ successively and test whether it is a quadratic residue modulo p. If so, an associated y can be found. If $x^3 + ax + b \bmod p = 0$, we obtain $y = 0$ and the point $(x, 0) \in E_{\mathbb{Z}_p}(a, b)$. If we add any point $g \in E_{\mathbb{Z}_p}(a, b)$ n times together, we abbreviate by

$$n \odot_p g := \underbrace{g \oplus_p \cdots \oplus_p g}_{n \text{ times}} .$$

In the same way as we used the square-and-multiply algorithm 7.3, we now can fasten the operation $n \odot_p g$. We just have to replace the multiplication in Steps 5 and 8 by the addition $\oplus_p$ (doubling in Step 8). By choosing any $g \in E_{\mathbb{Z}_p}(a, b)$, we can look at the subgroup generated by $\mathcal{L}(g)$. Let $n = \mathrm{ord}_{E_{\mathbb{Z}_p}(a,b)}(g)$ be the order of g. From Lagrange's Theorem 3.33, we know that $h = {|E_{\mathbb{Z}_p}(a,b)|}/{n}$ is an integer, and for our cryptographic purposes it should be as small as possible.

Elliptic Curve Diffie–Hellman (ECDH)
The Diffie–Hellman key agreement protocol allows entities to establish a common secret key over an insecure channel. The procedure is described in Section 7.1.2. Elliptic curve Diffie–Hellman (ECDH) is also a key agreement protocol that works in the same manner as the Diffie–Hellman protocol. However, it is based on the group $(E_{\mathbb{Z}_p}(a,b), \oplus_p, \mathcal{O})$ instead of the group $(\mathbb{Z}_p^\times, \cdot_p, 1)$. Given the parameters (p, a, b, g, n, h) defined, the two entities must each own a pair consisting of a private key and a public key. Hence, the private key of A is any number x_A in $\{1, \ldots, n-1\}$. The public key is supplemented by the point

$$y_A = x_A \odot_p g \in E_{\mathbb{Z}_p}(a,b).$$

In this way, A and B can establish their common secret key by

$$\begin{aligned} x_{AB} &= x_B \odot_p y_A = x_B \odot_p (x_A \odot_p g) = (x_B \cdot_p x_A) \odot_p g \\ &= x_A \odot_p (x_B \odot_p g) = x_A \odot_p y_B. \end{aligned}$$

An attacker has to solve the Diffie–Hellman problem applied to elliptic curves, i.e., compute x_{AB} after solving $u \odot_p g = y_A$ for some u, or $v \odot_p g = y_B$ for some v.

Example 8.32.

$$p = 23, a = 3, b = 22,\ y^2 = x^3 + 3 \cdot x + 22 \bmod 23.$$

Let $x_A = 5$, $x_B = 12$, $g = (7,8)$. We obtain $\mathcal{L}(g) = E_{\mathbb{Z}_{23}}(3,22)$ and

$$y_A = 5 \odot_p (7,8) = (14,18),\ y_B = 12 \odot_p (7,8) = (8,11) \text{ and}$$

$$x_{AB} = 12 \odot_p (14,18) = 5 \odot_p (8,11) = (20,20).$$

El-Gamal and Elliptic curves
Consider the parameters (p, a, b, g, n, h) for a Diffie–Hellman key exchange. If we transfer the El-Gamal cipher to elliptic curves, we must represent a message m by a point on $E_{\mathbb{Z}_p}(a,b)$. Let $m \in E_{\mathbb{Z}_p}(a,b)$, then we encrypt it to $c = m \oplus_p x_B \odot_p y_A$ and send back the cipher message (y_B, c).

For decrypting, we calculate $z = -(x_A \odot_p y_B) = -x_{AB}$ using the common secret key and obtain the original message m. That is because

$$\begin{aligned} d_{(E_p(a,b),x_A)} = c \oplus_p z &= m \oplus_p (x_B \odot_p y_A) \oplus_p (-(x_A \odot_p y_B)) \\ &= m \oplus_p (x_B \odot_p y_A) \oplus_p (-(x_A \odot_p (x_B \odot_p g))) \\ &= m \oplus_p (x_B \odot_p y_A) \oplus_p (-(x_B \odot_p x_A \odot_p g)) \\ &= m \oplus_p (x_B \odot_p y_A) \oplus_p (-(x_B \odot_p y_A)) \\ &= m. \end{aligned}$$

The cipher message (y_B, c) consists of four numbers in $\mathbb{Z}_p$, but the plaintext m has to be represented in $E_{\mathbb{Z}_p}(a, b)$. From Hasse's estimation (8.6), this means approximately p possible plaintexts corresponding to a ratio of 4 to 1 in length. Another problem is the mapping between a plaintext and a point on the elliptic curve.

Example 8.33. We continue Example 8.32. The plaintext

"SECURITY"

gets encoded to $(18, 4, 2, 20, 17, 8, 19, 24)$. We try to use the first components of the points of the elliptic curve. However, there are no points with the first value $18, 19$ or 24. Instead, we order the points by component-by-component ordering, starting with the first component. The last point is $\mathcal{O}$. Furthermore, we apply the alphabet

$$\Sigma_{\text{Latext}} = \Sigma_{\text{Lat}} \cup \{.,!,?,\ ,\,,;,:\},$$

and encode each symbol corresponding to the specified position in the alphabet. We obtain the encoded plaintext

$$(13, 2), (3, 9), (2, 6), (14, 5), (11, 12), (5, 1), (13, 21), (17, 8).$$

Encryption using the value $x_{AB} = (20, 20)$ yields

$$(6, 16), (4, 12), (7, 8), (1, 16), (5, 1), (4, 11), (21, 13), (2, 6),$$

which gets decoded to

$$(11, 7, 12, 1, 8, 6, 29, 2) \rightarrow \text{"LHMBIG,C"}.$$

Here, we are lucky not to get the encrypted point $\mathcal{O}$ for which there is no symbol. For decryption, we need to calculate $-x_{AB} = (20,3)$ to finally get back the right plaintext. For example, $(6,16) \oplus_{23} (20,3) = (13,2)$.

In practice, the two difficulties of the 4-to-1 text expansion and mapping of the plaintext to points on the elliptic curve are too big. Thus, the method must be adapted. Menezes and Vanstone[17] have modified the method by simply masking the encryption by an elliptic curve. We now do not need to represent the data as exact points on an elliptic curve.

Definition 8.34 (Adapted El-Gamal with $E_{\mathbb{Z}_p}(a,b)$). Let (p,a,b,g,n,h) be the parameters for a Diffie–Hellman key exchange using an elliptic curve $E_{\mathbb{Z}_p}(a,b)$. Given $\mathcal{P} = \mathbb{Z}_p^\times \times \mathbb{Z}_p^\times$, $\mathcal{C} = E_{\mathbb{Z}_p}(a,b) \times \mathbb{Z}_p \times \mathbb{Z}_p$, $x_A, x_B \in \{1,\dots,n-1\}$, we set

$$\begin{aligned}\mathcal{K} = \{&(p,a,b,g,n,h,x_A,y_A,x_B);\\ &p \text{ prime }, \frac{a^3}{27} + \frac{b^2}{4} \neq 0, h \leq 4,\\ &x_A \in \{1,\dots,n-1\}, y_A = x_A \odot_p g, x_B \in \{1,\dots,n-1\},\\ &k_{\text{a,pub}} = (p,a,b,g,y_A), \text{ and}\\ &k_{\text{a,priv;A}} = (p,x_A), k_{\text{a,priv;B}} = (p,x_B),\end{aligned}$$

and define $y_B = x_B \odot_p g$, $x_{AB} = (k_1,k_2) = x_B \odot_p y_A = x_A \odot_p y_B$ and

$$\begin{aligned}e_{k_{\text{a,pub}}}(m_1,m_2) &= (y_B, k_1 \cdot_p m_1, k_2 \cdot_p m_2),\\ d_{k_{\text{a,priv,A}}}(y_B,c_1,c_2) &= (k_1^{-1} \cdot_p c_1, k_2^{-1} \cdot_p c_2).\end{aligned}$$

Example 8.35. Again, we choose

$$p = 23, a = 3, b = 22,\ y^2 = x^3 + 3 \cdot x + 22 \bmod 23, x_A = 5, x_B = 12,$$

[17]See in (Menezes and Vanstone, 1993).

obtaining

$$y_A = 5 \odot_p (7,8) = (14,18), \;\; y_B = 12 \odot_p (7,8) = (8,11) \text{ and}$$
$$x_{AB} = (k_1,k_2) = 12 \odot_p (14,18) = 5 \odot_p (8,11) = (20,20).$$

The plaintext

"SECURITY"

gets prepared to $(18,4),(2,20),(17,8),(19,24)$. For example, following Algorithm 8.7, we encrypt

$$c_1 = 20 \cdot_{23} 18 = 15, \;\; c_2 = 20 \cdot_{23} 4 = 11.$$

Finally, we get

$$((8,11),15,11),((8,11),17,9),((8,11),18,22),((8,11),12,20)$$
$$\rightarrow \text{"PLRJSWMU"}.$$

Remark 8.36. The same problems exist with this version of El-Gamal, as mentioned in Example 8.19. Consider an attacker has information about one plaintext-ciphertext component pair, i.e., $(m_{21}, c_{21}) = (2,17)$, and any corresponding ciphertext component, i.e., $c_{11} = 15$. Without any change at x_B, the attacker can recover the plaintext by $m_{11} = c_{11} \cdot_p c_{21}^{-1} \cdot_p m_{21}$. In the last example, we obtain $m_{11} = 15 \cdot_{23} 17^{-1} \cdot_{23} 2 = 18$.

Example 8.37. The ASCII code (7 bit for each symbol) serves as the basis. We choose $E_{18743}(3,22)$, $g = (12,338)$ and $x_A = 20$, and obtain $y_A = 20 \odot_{18743} (12,338) = (8308,8072)$. Since $p = 18743$, we can encrypt four symbols together. Firstly, we encode

"SE" $\rightarrow$ 10693, "CU" $\rightarrow$ 8661, "RI" $\rightarrow$ 10569, "TY" $\rightarrow$ 10841.

To encrypt the message $(10693, 8661)$, let $x_B = 1000$. Then, $(k_1,k_2) = 1000 \odot_{18743} (8308,8072) = (16553,18311)$. The encrypted message (y_B, c_1, c_2) is obtained by $y_B = 1000 \odot_{18743} (12,338) = (7977,18734)$, $c_1 = 16553 \cdot_{18743} 10693 = 11080$ and $c_2 = 18311 \cdot_{18743} 8661 = 7048$, together $((7977,18734),11080,7048)$. To get around the mentioned problem in Remark 8.36, we choose $x_B = 14102$ and obtain $((7872, 3379), 12361, 10329)$ for the last two plaintext blocks, respectively.

To decrypt the first block, we calculate $20 \odot_{18743} (7977, 18734) = (16553, 18311) = (k_1, k_2)$. Thus, we calculate $k_1^{-1} \bmod p = 659$ and $k_2^{-1} \bmod p = 5163$. The decrypted message is $(11080 \cdot_{18743} 659, 7048 \cdot_{18743} 5163) = (10693, 8661)$.

While applying the adapted El-Gamal cipher with elliptic curves, the last example shows that the ciphertext will be twice as long as the plaintext. Starting with two numbers representing the plaintext, we obtain ciphertext consisting of four numbers. It is not necessary to consider a mapping between the plaintext and the points of an elliptic curve. Thus, the two problems mentioned could be solved.

Algorithm 8.7: Adapted El-Gamal with $E_{\mathbb{Z}_p}(a, b)$

Require: Elliptic curve $E_{\mathbb{Z}_p}(a, b)$, public key $k_{\text{a,pub}} = (p, a, b, g, y_A)$, private keys $k_{\text{a,priv;A}} = (p, x_A)$, $k_{\text{a,priv;B}} = (p, x_B)$, as in Definition 8.34, message $m = (m_1, m_2) \in \mathbb{Z}_p^\times \times \mathbb{Z}_p^\times$.

Ensure: ciphertext $\tilde{c}$, decrypted plaintext m'.

1: $y_B := x_B \odot_p g$.
2: $x_{AB} := (k_1, k_2) := x_B \odot_p y_A$.
3: $(c_1, c_2) := (k_1 \cdot_p m_1, k_2 \cdot_p m_2)$.
4: $\tilde{c} := (y_B, c_1, c_2)$.
5: $x_{AB} := (\tilde{k}_1, \tilde{k}_2) := x_A \odot_p y_B$.
6: $m' := (\tilde{k}_1^{-1} \cdot_p c_1, \tilde{k}_2^{-1} \cdot_p c_2)$.
7: **return** $(\tilde{c}, m')$.

Chapter 9

Message Digests

Note 9.1. In this chapter, the requirements are:

- being familiar with basics of number theory, see Section 1.1,
- being able to apply basic probability concepts, see Section 1.2.
- knowing modern private-key ciphering, see Section 6, and
- knowing concepts of a message digest function, see Section 2.5.2.

Selected literature: See (Chaum *et al.*, 1992; Damgård, 1989; Dang, 2013; Stinson, 2005).

We have already seen examples for creating a message digest in Section 2.5.2. The aim was to identify whether data would be changed in any way, e.g., in their transmission, which achieves the security goal of data integrity.

A random change like a bit flip can be recognized. The basic principle was shown with the ISBN-13-code. However, this code has a weakness: for example, if the change happens intentionally because there are many such codes owning the same message digest. Such a match is called a *collision* and is not desired in cryptological applications. We distinguish between two types of message digest generation: (1) a message digest function $h : \mathcal{P} \to \Sigma^n$ taking only the input data for generating the message digest is called a hash function, and (2) a message authentication code is a message digest obtained by a message digest function $h_k : \mathcal{P} \to \Sigma^n$, which includes a key. The latter is often based on private-key cipher systems.

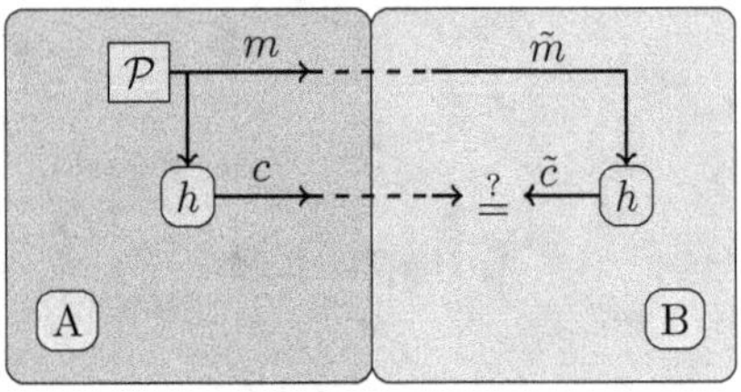

Figure 9.1 Integrity check by cryptographical hash functions.

9.1 Message Detection Codes

In computer science, there is the class of *hash functions* mapping messages with variable bit lengths to messages with fixed bit lengths. It is a matter of fingerprinting a message. Figure 9.1 shows the idea of integrity checking data using a cryptographical hash function. A further criterion is to enable a simple and fast execution.

Two additional and very important properties revolve around avoiding certain kinds of collisions and performing the strict avalanche criteria.

Definition 9.2 (Cryptographical hash function). Given $n \in \mathbb{N}$, a *cryptographical hash function* is a message digest function

$$h : \mathcal{P} \to \Sigma^n$$

satisfying the strict avalanche criteria and the so-called *strongly collision-free* property, which reads that it is computationally infeasible to find messages $x, y \in \mathcal{P}$, such that from $x \neq y$ it follows $h(x) = h(y)$. The resulting value is called a *modification detection code* or a *hash value* in short form. Consider $x, y \in \mathcal{P}$ with $x \neq y$. If $h(x) = h(y)$, we talk about a *collision*.

For example, the *Adler-32* hash algorithm[1] is not applicable for cryptographical purposes and is not its intended use. Namely, it does not satisfy the strongly collision-free property, as well as the

[1]See RFC 1950 and (Deutsch and Gailly, 1996).

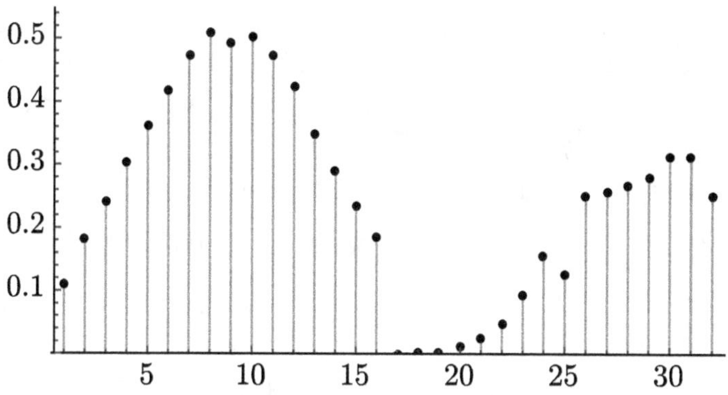

Figure 9.2 Adler32 fails under the strict message avalanche criterion.

strict message avalanche criterion. It yields a collision if any message gets changed at byte k by adding value q, at byte $k+1$ by adding value $-2q$, and finally at byte $k+2$ by adding value q again. Moreover, the algorithm fails under the strict message avalanche criterion. Figure 9.2 shows this issue.

An example of a cryptographical hash function is the Chaum–van Heijst–Pfitzmann hash function (Chaum *et al.*, 1992), based on Problem 7.10, which attempts to calculate the discrete logarithm.

Theorem 9.3 (Chaum–van Heijst–Pfitzmann hash function). *Given a safe prime $p = 2q+1$ and two generators $g_1, g_2 \in \mathbb{Z}_p$ of $(\mathbb{Z}_p^\times, \cdot_p, 1)$, define the cryptographical hash function*

$$h : \mathbb{Z}_q^2 \to \mathbb{Z}_p, \quad (x, y) \mapsto h(x, y) := g_1^x \cdot g_2^y \ mod\ p. \tag{9.1}$$

The function h is strongly collision-free if the discrete logarithm $\log_{g_1}(g_2)$ cannot be computed efficiently.

Proof. Since $\mathbb{Z}_q \subset \mathbb{Z}_p$, the set $\mathbb{Z}_q^2$ is a language over $\mathbb{Z}_p$. Suppose h is not strongly collision-free, i.e., it is computationally feasible to determine a collision

$$(x, y) \neq (u, v) \text{ and } h(x, y) = h(u, v),$$

for $0 \leq x, y, u, v \leq q-1$. We then obtain

$$g_1^x \cdot g_2^y \equiv_p g_1^u \cdot g_2^v \Leftrightarrow g_1^{x-u} \equiv_p g_2^{v-y}.$$

Since $p-1 = 2\cdot q$ with q prime, $d = \mathrm{GCD}(v-y, p-1)$ takes on one of four values, $d \in \{1, 2, q, 2\cdot q\}$. If $y = v$, we obtain $d = 2\cdot q$. This results in $g_1^{x-u} \equiv_p g_2^{v-y} = 1 \Leftrightarrow x = u$, which contradicts the assumption of $(x,y) \neq (u,v)$. Because $-q < v-y < q$, we observe $d \neq q$. There are two possible values remaining for d.

Case 1, $d = 1$: Let $w = (v-y)^{-1} \bmod p-1$. It follows

$$g_2 \equiv_p g_2^{(v-y)\cdot w} \equiv_p g_1^{(x-u)\cdot w} \Rightarrow \log_{g_1}(g_2) = (x-u)\cdot(v-y)^{-1} \bmod p-1.$$

Case 2, $d = 2$: Since q is even and $p-1 = 2\cdot q$, we get $\mathrm{GCD}(v-y, q) = 1$. Let $w = (v-y)^{-1} \bmod q$, i.e., $(v-y)\cdot w = k\cdot q+1$ for some $k \in \mathbb{Z}$. Using the fact that $\mathcal{L}(g_2) = \mathbb{Z}_p^{\times}$, it follows

$$g_1^{(x-u)\cdot w} \equiv_p g_2^{(v-y)\cdot w} \equiv_p g_2^{k\cdot q+1} \overset{(7.1)}{\equiv_p} (-1)^k \cdot g_2 \equiv_p \pm g_2.$$

If $g_1^{(x-u)\cdot w} \equiv_p -g_2$, we can use $g_1^q \bmod p = p-1$ because of $\mathcal{L}(g_1) = \mathbb{Z}_p^{\times}$ for obtaining the discrete logarithm $\log_{g_1}(g_2)$.

Each possible case yields the discrete logarithm $\log_{g_1}(g_2)$. □

Example 9.4.

$p = 179 = 2\cdot 89 + 1, g_1 = 2, g_2 = 23, x = 31, y = 77, u = 19, v = 85.$

From Theorem 7.4 we see that $\mathcal{L}(g_1) = \mathcal{L}(g_2) = \mathbb{Z}_p^{\times}$. Now,

$$h(x,y) = 2^{31}\cdot 23^{77} \bmod 179 = 42 = 2^{19}\cdot 23^{85} \bmod 179 = h(u,v)$$

yields a collision. Since $\mathrm{GCD}(v-y, p-1) = \mathrm{GCD}(-22, 178) = 2$, we calculate

$$w = 8^{-1} \bmod 89 = 78 \text{ and } 2^{12\cdot 78+89} \bmod 179 = 23$$
$$\Rightarrow \log_2(23) = 12\cdot 78 + 89 \bmod 178 = 135.$$

The verification with Shanks' Algorithm 7.4 is successful.

The Chaum–van Heijst–Pfitzmann hash function has two disadvantages: (1) its execution is slow because of the modular exponentiations, and (2) it has a finite domain.

Merkle–Damgård design

If we consider finite domain cryptographical hash functions, we have to extend them to permit messages of any length. The idea is to make a block-wise operation that will guarantee it to be strongly collision-free if the basic hash function is as such.[2] In this context, we assume cryptographical hash functions to be bit-by-bit operations, i.e., $h : \mathbb{Z}_2^k \to \mathbb{Z}_2^n$ where $k \geq n+2$. We extend h to a cryptographical hash function $h^* : \bigcup_{i=k+1}^{\infty} \mathbb{Z}_2^i \to \mathbb{Z}_2^n$. Consider $x \in \mathbb{Z}_2^w$, i.e., $|x| = w > k$. We divide x into sequences of length $k-n-1$, and denote $w = q \cdot (k-n-1) + r$, $r \in \mathbb{Z}_{k-n-1}$. Say we obtain v sequences $x = x_1||x_2||\ldots||x_v$ at which $x_i \in \mathbb{Z}_2^{k-n-1}, |x_i| = k-n-1$, for $i \in \{1, \ldots, v-1\}$ and

$$|x_v| = \begin{cases} k-n-1, & r = 0, \\ r, & r \neq 0, \end{cases} \qquad v = \left\lceil \frac{w}{k-n-1} \right\rceil.$$

Let us save the sequence by a function $y : \mathbb{Z}_2^w \to (\mathbb{Z}_2^{k-n-1})^{v+1}$, $x \mapsto y(x) = y_1||\ldots||y_v||y_{v+1}$, $y_i = x_i$, $i \in \{1, \ldots, v-1\}$. We may have to enlarge the last sequence x_v by inserting $d = k-n-1-r \in \{1, \ldots, k-n-2\}$ zeros, $y_v = x_v||0^d$ to obtain the full length. Let y_{v+1} be the binary representation of d pre-padded by zeros, such that $|y_{v+1}| = k-n-1$. Suppose that $y(x) = y(x')$ for some $x, x' \in \mathbb{Z}_2^w$. It follows that $x_i = x_i'$ for $i \in \{1, \ldots, v-1\}$. If $x_v \neq x_v'$, one has either one or too many zeros. However, this would change the value of d and thus, $y_{v+1} \neq y_{v+1}'$, in opposition to the assumption, and we get $x = x'$. The function y is injective. We now define the sequence

$$cv_1 = h(\underbrace{0^{n+1}||y_1}_{\text{length is } k}), \quad cv_{i+1} = h(\underbrace{cv_i||1||y_{i+1}}_{\text{length is } k}), \ i \in \{1, \ldots, v\}. \tag{9.2}$$

The cv_i's are called *chaining values*. If we set $h^*(x) = cv_{v+1}$, we have a candidate for a cryptographical hash function with an input message of any length. However, we have to investigate the strongly collision-free property of h^*.

---

[2]Following (Stinson, 2005).

Theorem 9.5. *Let $h : \mathbb{Z}_2^k \rightarrow \mathbb{Z}_2^n$ be a cryptographical hash function where $k \geq n + 2$ and $h^* : \bigcup_{i=k}^{\infty} \mathbb{Z}_2^i \rightarrow \mathbb{Z}_2^n$, as defined by the last chaining value from Equation (9.2). Then, h^* is a cryptographical hash function, assuming that the strict message avalanche criterion is fulfilled.*

Proof. Suppose h^* is not strongly collision-free, i.e., we find some x, x' with $x \neq x'$ and $h^*(x) = h^*(x')$. Looking at

$$y(x) = y_1 || \dots || y_{v+1} \text{ and } y(x') = y'_1 || \dots || y'_{v'+1}$$

with associated values d, d' and chaining values. We distinguish between three cases:

Case 1: $|x| \not\equiv_{k-n-1} |x'|$: this means $d \neq d'$, and $y_{v+1} \neq y'_{v'+1}$ and yields

$$h(cv_v || 1 || y_{v+1}) = cv_{v+1} = h^*(x) = h^*(x') = cv'_{v'+1} = h(cv'_{v'} || 1 || y_{v'+1}), \tag{9.3}$$

which is a collision for h since $y_{v+1} \neq y_{v'+1}$.

Case 2: $|x| \equiv_{k-n-1} |x'|$ and $|x| = |x'|$: we have $v = v'$ and $y_{v+1} = y'_{v+1}$ and we first obtain the same result as in Equation (9.3), $h(cv_v || 1 || y_{v+1}) = h(cv'_v || 1 || y_{v'+1})$. If $cv_v \neq cv'_{v'}$, we have found a collision for h. Otherwise, assume $cv_v = cv'_{v'}$. We take a step back to

$$h(cv_{v-1} || 1 || y_v) = h(cv'_{v-1} || 1 || y_{v'}).$$

Either we find a collision for h or $cv_{v-1} = cv'_{v-1}$ and $y_v = y'_v$, which can be worked on iteratively. The last step yields

$$h(0^{n+1} || y_1) = cv_1 = cv'_1 = h(0^{n+1} || y'_1).$$

If $y_1 \neq y'_1$, we find a collision for h. Otherwise, assume $y_1 = y'_1$. Putting everything together, we obtain $y_i = y'_i$ for all $i \in \{1, \dots, v+1\}$ and $y(x) = y(x')$. However, y is injective and thus, $x = x'$. This is a contradiction.

Case 3: $|x| \equiv_{k-n-1} |x'|$ and $|x| \neq |x'|$: We assume $v' > v$ and start proceeding as in Case 2. Finally, if no collision arises, we get to the point

$$h(0^{n+1}||y_1) = cv_1 = cv'_{v'-v+1} = h(0^{n+1}||1||y'_{v'-v+1}).$$

However, the $(n+1)$th bit of the left argument is 0 and the $(n+1)$th argument of the right side is 1 and this yields a collision for h. □

It follows that h^* is a cryptographical hash function if h is as well. The design structure is named[3] the *Merkle–Damgård structure* after Merkle and Damgård.[4]

Remark 9.6. (1) A weakness of this approach is that one collision generates many collisions. If two different data q and $\tilde{q}$ yield $h(q) = h(\tilde{q})$, it follows $h(q||p) = h(\tilde{q}||p)$ for any p:

$$\mathrm{cv}_i = h(\mathrm{cv}_{i-1}, y_i) = h(h(\mathrm{cv}_{i-2}, y_{i-1}), y_i). \tag{9.4}$$

(2) The initial value cv_0 need not be 0^n and can be any other value. The middle bit in the initial step has to be zero.

One-way property

A cryptographical hash function $h : \mathcal{P} \to \Sigma^n$ makes it difficult to find a collision. In this context we prove two different requirements.

Firstly, for a given message m, it should not be possible to easily find any message $x \neq m$ with $h(x) = h(m)$. This is called *weakly collision-free*. If it happens nonetheless, we will get a collision for h by m and x. Thus, h cannot be strongly collision-free. Alternatively, a strongly collision-free hash function does not show this behavior and is weakly collision-free.

The second point is that for a given message m we should be able to quickly calculate the message digest $z = h(m)$. However, finding a pre-image of z and possibly also a collision should be very hard.

[3]See (Damgård, 1989, pp. 216ff.).
[4]Ivan B. Damgård, born 1956.

This is accordingly to the one-way function from Convention 7.7. Suppose that for a randomly chosen message m and $z = h(m)$, it is easy to find any $x \in h^{-1}(\{z\})$, i.e., $h(x) = z$ and h is not one-way. If $m \neq x$, we get a collision. Otherwise, there is a miss. What is the probability for finding such a collision in this way? We call two members x, y of $\mathcal{P}$ equivalent, i.e., $x \sim y$ if $h(x) = h(y)$. This yields an equivalence relation. Since $|\Sigma^n| = |\Sigma|^n$ is finite, we will get a finite number of equivalence classes. Let $C = \{[m] = \{x \in \mathcal{P};\ x \sim m\}\}$. Then, $|C| \leq |\Sigma|^n$. Assume $|\mathcal{P}| < \infty$ is finite. The probability of finding a collision (denoted by 1 here) for h, given an equivalence class $[m]$, is $\mathbb{P}(\{1\}|\{[m]\}) = \frac{|[m]|-1}{|[m]|}$ and we obtain

$$\mathbb{P}(\{1\}) \overset{(1.9)}{=} \sum_{[m]\in C} \mathbb{P}(\{1\}|\{[m]\}) \cdot \mathbb{P}(\{[m]\}) = \sum_{[m]\in C} \frac{|[m]|-1}{|[m]|} \cdot \frac{|[m]|}{|\mathcal{P}|}$$

$$= \sum_{[m]\in C} \frac{|[m]|-1}{|\mathcal{P}|} = \frac{|\mathcal{P}| - |C|}{|\mathcal{P}|} \geq 1 - \frac{|\Sigma|^n}{|\mathcal{P}|}.$$

Consider a cryptographical hash function candidate $h : \mathbb{Z}_2^k \to \mathbb{Z}_2^n$, $k \geq n+2$ due to Theorem 9.5, as we mostly use $\Sigma = \mathbb{Z}_2$. Consequently, $|\mathcal{P}| = 2^k \geq 2^{n+2} \geq 2^n = |\Sigma|^n$. This means that the message should be at least two bits larger than the message digest, which is arguable. Then, we obtain $\mathbb{P}(\{1\}) \geq 1 - \frac{1}{4} = \frac{3}{4}$. Hence, there is a fast way to find a collision and a cryptographical hash function h is not strongly collision-free.

Corollary 9.7. *Any cryptographical hash function is weakly collision-free and a one-way function.*

Birthday paradoxon

Let n be the output length of a cryptographical hash function $h : \mathbb{Z}_2^k \to \mathbb{Z}_2^n$. Suppose that each bit sequence has the same probability of occurrence. How many sequences have to be checked for obtaining a collision with a probability greater than $\frac{1}{2}$? To answer this, let $r = 2^n$. Overall, there are r^k possibilities for choosing any sequence of n bits by k-fold sampling. If it is desired to choose a different sequence each time, there are first r, then $r-1$, $r-2$, and until $r-k+1$ possible sequences remaining. The probability of choosing k different sequences from r^k in total results in

$$\mathbb{P}_r(\{k\}) = \frac{r \cdot (r-1) \cdot (r-2) \cdot \ldots \cdot (r-k+1)}{r^k}.$$

The complementary probability represents the selection of at least one duplicate and is assumed to have the value $b \in (0,1)$:

$$\begin{aligned}
b &= 1 - \frac{r \cdot (r-1) \cdot (r-2) \cdot \ldots \cdot (r-k+1)}{r^k} \\
&= 1 - \left(1 \cdot \frac{r-1}{r} \cdot \frac{r-2}{r} \cdot \ldots \cdot \frac{r-k+1}{r}\right) \\
&= 1 - \left(\left(1 - \frac{1}{r}\right) \cdot \left(1 - \frac{2}{r}\right) \cdot \ldots \cdot \left(1 - \frac{k-1}{r}\right)\right) \\
&\geq 1 - \left(e^{-1/r} \cdot e^{-2/r} \cdot \ldots \cdot e^{-(k-1)/r}\right) \\
&= 1 - e^{-\frac{k(k-1)}{2r}}. \qquad (9.5)
\end{aligned}$$

The estimation is valid because of

$$e^{-u/r} = \sum_{i=0}^{\infty} \frac{(-\frac{u}{r})^i}{i!} = 1 - \frac{u}{r} + \frac{(\frac{u}{r})^2}{2} - \frac{(\frac{u}{r})^3}{6} \pm \ldots \geq 1 - \frac{u}{r}, \quad 0 < u < r.$$

For a given n, we look for k, such that the probability is at least b. Thus, we have to solve the following inequality in k:

$$\begin{aligned}
1 - b &\leq e^{-\frac{k(k-1)}{2r}} \\
\Leftrightarrow \ln(1-b) &\leq -\frac{k(k-1)}{2 \cdot 2^n} \\
\Leftrightarrow 2^{n+1} \ln(1-b) &\leq -k(k-1) \\
\Leftrightarrow 0 &\geq k^2 - k + 2^{n+1} \ln(1-b) \\
\Rightarrow k &= 1/2 + \sqrt{1/4 - 2^{n+1} \ln(1-b)}.
\end{aligned}$$

This yields a (positive) k at about $k \approx \sqrt{-2 \ln(1-b)}\sqrt{2^n}$.

Example 9.8. We need approximately 77,000 trials to find at least one collision for a 32-bit message digest with a probability of $\frac{1}{2}$. By trying it 200,000 times, the probability increases to 0.99. It requires a number of trials on the order of 10^{19}, or rather 10^{24}, after using 128-bit or 160-bit message digests without additional information. This is computationally very difficult or infeasible.

MD5 message digest

One of the most famous Merkle–Damgård designs is the message digest algorithm 5 (MD5) md5 : $\mathbb{Z}_2^* \to \mathbb{Z}_2^{128}$ that maps any bit sequence to a bit sequence of length 128 bits. Consider data $m \in \mathbb{Z}_2^b$,

$$m = m_0 m_1 \dots m_{b-1},$$

of any length. Firstly, m has to be padded to a length of 448 mod 512 by 1-0-padding, resulting in $\tilde{m}_e$. Next, the binary representation of b gets fitted to 64 bits and is added to the data, $m_e = \tilde{m}_e || (b_{(2)} \bmod 2^{64})$. The whole length is now divisible by 512. The preparation ends by partitioning them into 32-bit blocks,

$$m_e = m_0 m_1 \dots m_{N-1},$$

at which N is a multiple of 16. An initialization vector of 128 bits,

$$\text{IV} = A||B||C||D,$$

with $A = 0x67452301$, $B = 0xefcdab89$, $C = 0x98badcfe$ and $D = 0x10325476$ is created, and the four non-linear functions

$$g_0 : (\mathbb{F}_2^{32})^3 \to \mathbb{F}_2^{32}, (X, Y, Z) \mapsto g_0(X, Y, Z) = (X \wedge Y) \vee (\neg X \wedge Z),$$
$$g_1 : (\mathbb{F}_2^{32})^3 \to \mathbb{F}_2^{32}, (X, Y, Z) \mapsto g_1(X, Y, Z) = (X \wedge Z) \vee (Y \wedge \neg Z),$$
$$g_2 : (\mathbb{F}_2^{32})^3 \to \mathbb{F}_2^{32}, (X, Y, Z) \mapsto g_2(X, Y, Z) = X \oplus Y \oplus Z,$$
$$g_3 : (\mathbb{F}_2^{32})^3 \to \mathbb{F}_2^{32}, (X, Y, Z) \mapsto g_3(X, Y, Z) = Y \oplus (X \vee \neg Z),$$

are introduced. Furthermore, we need 64 values T_k, $k = 1, \dots, 64$, with

$$T_k := \lfloor \underbrace{4294967296}_{2^{32}} \cdot |\sin(k)| \rfloor, \; k \in \{1, \dots, 64\}.$$

Table 9.1 shows all the resulting values.

Table 9.1 The values $T_k = \lfloor 2^{32} \cdot |\sin(k)| \rfloor$.

3614090360,	3905402710,	606105819,	3250441966,
4118548399,	1200080426,	2821735955,	4249261313,
1770035416,	2336552879,	4294925233,	2304563134,
1804603682,	4254626195,	2792965006,	1236535329,
4129170786,	3225465664,	643717713,	3921069994,
3593408605,	38016083,	3634488961,	3889429448,
568446438,	3275163606,	4107603335,	1163531501,
2850285829,	4243563512,	1735328473,	2368359562,
4294588738,	2272392833,	1839030562,	4259657740,
2763975236,	1272893353,	4139469664,	3200236656,
681279174,	3936430074,	3572445317,	76029189,
3654602809,	3873151461,	530742520,	3299628645,
4096336452,	1126891415,	2878612391,	4237533241,
1700485571,	2399980690,	4293915773,	2240044497,
1873313359,	4264355552,	2734768916,	1309151649,
4149444226,	3174756917,	718787259,	3951481745

The blocks of m_e are each used two times. This happens in sequence, but after a permutation $\sigma(k)$, which is shown in Table 9.2.

Table 9.2 The permutation $\sigma(k)$ of the MD5.

0	1	2	3	4	5	6	7	8	9	10	11	12	13	14	15
1	6	11	0	5	10	15	4	9	14	3	8	13	2	7	12
5	8	11	14	1	4	7	10	13	0	3	6	9	12	15	2
0	7	14	5	12	3	10	1	8	15	6	13	4	11	2	9

The core of the algorithm consists of a 64-time iteration where non-linear functions g_0 to g_3 are used. A cyclic left shift s_k according to Table 9.3 follows.

Table 9.3 Shift values s_k for the cyclic left shift.

7	12	17	22	7	12	17	22	7	12	17	22	7	12	17	22
5	9	14	20	5	9	14	20	5	9	14	20	5	9	14	20
4	11	16	23	4	11	16	23	4	11	16	23	4	11	16	23
6	10	15	21	6	10	15	21	6	10	15	21	6	10	15	21

The whole process is shown in Algorithm 9.1. It is a simplified version of MD5 as it is not considered that the bytes of each sequence are represented in little-endian, i.e., the byte of the smallest order will start.

Algorithm 9.1: MD5

Require: Data $m \in \mathbb{Z}_2^b$, $b \in \mathbb{N}$, further A, B, C, D, T, σ, s.
Ensure: 128-bit message digest MD5(m).

$d := 447 - b \bmod 2^9$.
$l := b_{(2)} \bmod 2^{64}$ (64-bit binary representation of b).
Create $m_e = m_0||m_1||\dots||m_{N-1} := m||1||\underbrace{0\dots0}_{d \text{ times}}||l$ from m.
$(S_1, S_2, S_3, S_4) := (A, B, C, D)$.
for $i := 0$ **to** $N/16 - 1$ **do**
  for $j := 0$ **to** 15 **do**
    $x_j := m_{i \cdot 16 + j}$
  end for
  $(U, V, W, X) := (S_1, S_2, S_3, S_4)$.
  for $k := 0$ **to** 63 **do**
    $t := U + g_{\lfloor k/16 \rfloor}(V, W, X) + x_{\sigma(k)} + T_k \bmod 2^{32}$.
    $t := t \lll s_k$.
    $t := (V + t) \bmod 2^{32}$.
    $(U, V, W, X) := (X, t, V, W)$.
  end for
  $(S_1, S_2, S_3, S_4) := (S_1 +_{2^{32}} U, S_2 +_{2^{32}} V, S_3 +_{2^{32}} W, S_4 +_{2^{32}} X)$.
end for
return MD5$(m) = S_1||S_2||S_3||S_4$.

Remark 9.9. (1) MD5 follows the Merkle–Damgård structure starting with an initial value $\mathrm{CV}_0 = A||B||C||D$ and the compression function

$$h_{\mathrm{MD5}} : \mathbb{Z}_2^{641} \to \mathbb{Z}_2^{128}, (S_1||S_2||S_3||S_4||1||m_{i\cdot 16}||\ldots||m_{i\cdot 16+15})$$
$$\mapsto \mathrm{cv}_{i+1} = h(\underbrace{S_1||S_2||S_3||S_4}_{\mathrm{cv}_i}||1||\underbrace{m_{i\cdot 16}||\ldots||m_{i\cdot 16+15}}_{y_{i+1}}).$$

In doing so, $m_{i\cdot 16}||\ldots||m_{i\cdot 16+15} \in \mathbb{Z}_2^{512}$ is 512 bits long and $\mathrm{MD5}(p) = \mathrm{cv}_{N/16}$. In the first step we have to change the middle bit from one to zero.

(2) As stated earlier, one collision block is enough to attack the whole method. This has been shown a number of times. For example, Wang[5] indicated that MD5 is no longer recommended. There are other Merkle–Damgård-based secure hash algorithms (SHA). A current version of such a cryptographical hash function can be found at the Federal Information Processing Standards Publication FIPS PUB 180-4.[6]

(3) However, MD5 fulfills the strict message avalanche criterion. As an example, Figure 9.3 shows the probabilities of change of the output bits of MD5 while testing approximately 2^{15} randomly chosen messages.

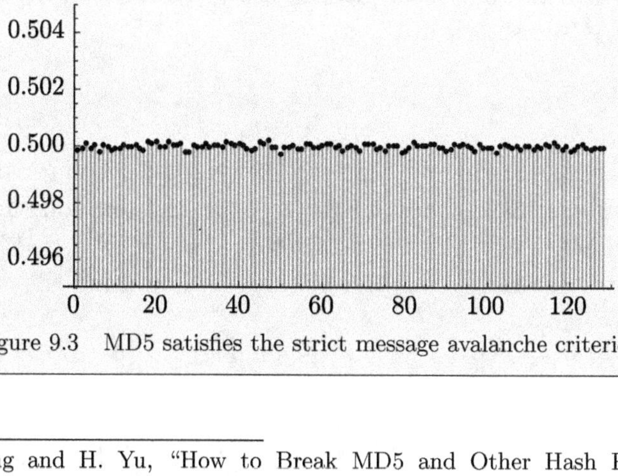

Figure 9.3 MD5 satisfies the strict message avalanche criterion.

[5] X. Wang and H. Yu, "How to Break MD5 and Other Hash Functions", http://merlot.usc.edu/csac-f06/papers/Wang05a.pdf.

[6] (Dang, 2013) and https://nvlpubs.nist.gov/nistpubs/FIPS/NIST.FIPS.180-4.pdf.

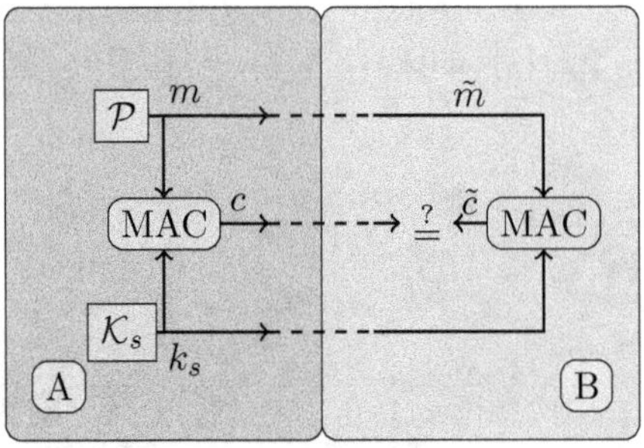

Figure 9.4 Message authentication code generation.

9.2 Message Authentication Codes

Cryptographical hash functions may be weak as long as tampering is performed until a meaningful collision is found. The proof of integrity is more difficult for any instance when transferring data to another instance and enabling an integrity check at the same time. To provide more security, we can use a *message authentication code* (MAC) instead. In addition, a usually secret key k_s is added to the process of generating a message digest. The key k_s and data p are used in the function as input variables. Its aim is to prevent an attacker from inferring with the key from given pairs $(p_i, \mathrm{MAC}_{k_s}(p_i))$. The basic idea of MACs is shown in Figure 9.4.

CBC-MAC

The use of a key suggests a private-key cipher system instead of a cryptographical hash function. In fact, this is often done in practice by returning the last block of an encryption process $e_{k_s}(p)$ in a CBC cipher block chaining mode, for example, while using the AES.

Example 9.10. Given data $m = m_0||m_1||\ldots||m_N$ with block size n, let

$$\mathrm{MAC}_{k_s} : \mathbb{Z}_2^* \to \mathbb{Z}_2^n,\ \mathrm{MAC}_{k_s}(m) = e_{k_s}(\underbrace{m_0 \oplus m_1 \oplus \cdots \oplus m_N}_{\Delta(m)})$$

be a message authentication code. Suppose $(m, \text{MAC}_{k_s}(m))$ is known. Let $q = q_0||q_1||\ldots||q_{N-1}$ be arbitrary with the same block size as m and $q_N = \Delta(q) \oplus \Delta(m)$. Then, it follows

$$\text{MAC}_{k_s}(q||q_N) = e_{k_s}(\Delta(q||q_N)) = \text{MAC}_{k_s}(m).$$

This MAC is independently insecure from the used private-key cipher system.

CMACs (Cipher MAC) are an extension of MACs. Here, the key is first used for a CBC-MAC. Two temporary keys are then generated from the one key by encrypting $e_{k_s}(0\ldots0)$, left shift cycling and perhaps applying an XOR operation.[7] Such a message authentication code is currently considered secure.[8]

9.3 Hash-based Message Authentication Codes

A MDC-MAC is a MAC based on cryptographical hash functions. Data and the key act as an input of a hash function.

Example 9.11 (Naive MDC-MAC with MD5). Given data $m \in \mathbb{Z}_2^{\times}$ and a key k_s, we want to use MD5$(k||m)$ for checking the integrity. However, MD5$(k||m)$ can be attacked. To see this we look at

$$m_e = \underbrace{k_s||m||\underbrace{10\ldots0}_{d+1 \text{ bit}}}_{\equiv 448 \bmod 512}||l,$$

according to Algorithm 9.1, where l is the bit length of $m \bmod 2^{64}$. We generate any $q \in \mathbb{Z}_2^{512}$ with

$$q = \underbrace{10\ldots0}_{d+1 \text{ bit}}||l||q_0,$$

[7]See (Iwata and Kurosawa, 2003).
[8]See (Dworkin, 2016a).

where $q_0 \in \mathbb{Z}_2^{447-d \bmod 2^9}$ is arbitrary. Then, it follows from Equation (9.4)

$$\text{MD5}(k||m||q) = \text{cv}_{i+1} = h_{\text{MD5}}(\underbrace{\text{MD5}(k||m)}_{\text{cv}_i}||1||q_0||\underbrace{10\ldots0}_{d+1 \text{ bit}}||\tilde{l}).$$

An attacker can equip new data with a valid MAC without knowing the key if the size of m is larger than 65 bits.

This approach and similar approaches are bad for practice. The hash-based MAC (HMAC) is an MDC-MAC whose key is more scattered around the data. Given a cryptographical hash function h with an output size of n bits, in RFC 2104,[9] the method

$$\text{HMAC}_{k_s}(m) = h(k_s \oplus \text{opad}||h(k_s \oplus \text{ipad}||m))$$

is recommended. There, two constant values, ipad $= 0x36\ldots36$ and opad $= 0x5c\ldots5c$, are used where the bytes are each repeated $n/8$ times. The key may get enlarged to size n bits by padding it with zeros or it gets shortened by hashing. Figure 9.5 shows the process of generating a HMAC and integrity checking.

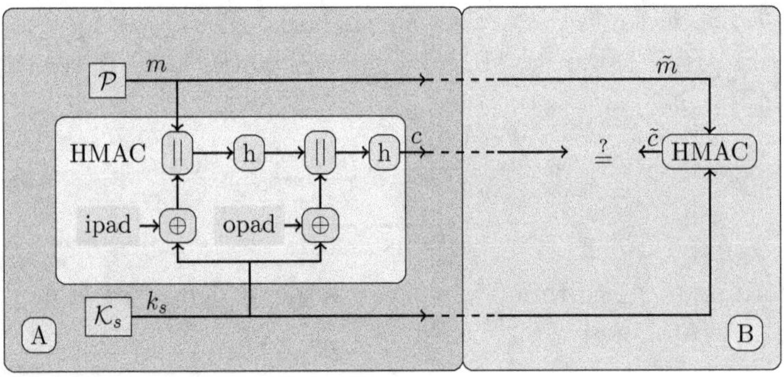

Figure 9.5 Hash Message Authentication Code (HMAC) generation.

[9]Request for Comments, https://www.ietf.org/rfc/rfc2104.txt.

Chapter 10

Digital Signatures

Note 10.1. In this chapter, the requirements are:

- being familiar with basics of number theory, see Section 1.1,
- being familiar with extended basics of algebra, see Sections 3.1 and 3.2,
- being able to apply basic probability concepts, see Section 1.2, and
- knowing modern public-key ciphering, see Chapter 8.

Selected literature: See (Coutinho, 1999; El Gamal, 1985; Hoffstein *et al.*, 2008).

A *digital signature* is a type of a digital code that is attached to an electronically transmitted document to verify the origin of the data. For that, the entity (sender) needs a secret usable for signing. Apart from that, another entity (receiver) needs a corresponding public review mechanism. Public-key cipher systems can be useful for this purpose because the required concept is intrinsically contained in such a system. The sender owns a private key and is the only one who knows it. All other entities have a public key. Instead of encrypting with the public key, the sender who signs the data can reverse the process by "decrypting" data with the private key. The public key is then used to "encrypt" the data. This requires the public-key cipher system to be reversible in that sense,

$$m = e_{k_{\text{a,pub}}}(\underbrace{d_{k_{\text{a,priv}}}(m)}_{s}). \tag{10.1}$$

Such data origin authentication includes an integrity check in case of success. From another perspective, we can use such a scheme to make someone accountable for their actions. It also concerns the security goal of non-repudiation if a third entity gets involved.

10.1 Types of Signature Generation

There are two fundamental methods in generating a digital signature.[1] A *digital signature with recovery* signs the data itself. The verification is done by comparing the unencrypted data with the data processed by the public key.

A *digital signature with an appendix* signs a message digest of the data. The advantage is that only a few bits have to be signed. Since the computation complexity is very high using public-key cipher systems, this is a very important aspect. The verification can be done by processing the signed data with the public key and then comparing

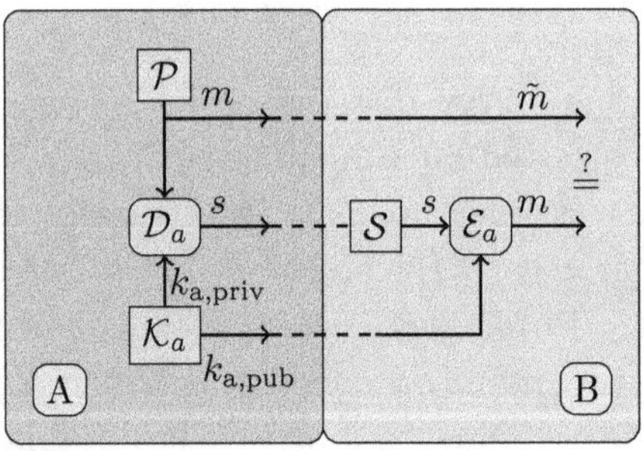

Figure 10.1 Digital signature with recovery.

[1]See (Coutinho, 1999).

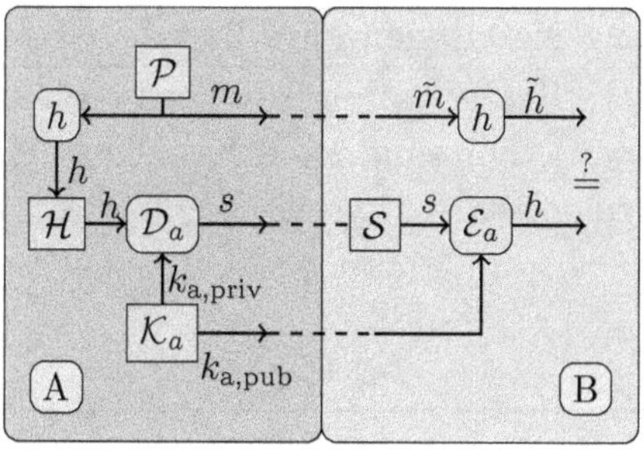

Figure 10.2 Digital signature with an appendix.

the result with the message digest of the original message, which does not have to be transferred. This version is mostly used.

10.2 RSA-Based Digital Signature

The RSA cipher system from Section 8.3 is one of the most used and important methods for generating a digital signature. Because

$$e_{k_{\text{a,pub}}}(m) = m^k \bmod n,\ d_{k_{\text{a,priv}}}(c) = c^{k'} \bmod n,$$

we can verify Equation (10.1), namely

$$\begin{aligned} d_{k_{\text{a,priv}}}(e_{k_{\text{a,pub}}}(m)) &= m^{k_{\text{a,pub}} \cdot k_{\text{a,priv}}} \bmod n \\ &= m^{k_{\text{a,priv}} \cdot k_{\text{a,pub}}} \bmod n = e_{k_{\text{a,pub}}}(d_{k_{\text{a,priv}}}(m)) = m. \end{aligned}$$

Only the roles of the keys get reversed.

Algorithm 10.1: RSA key generation

Require: $n = p \cdot q$ with p, q prime.
Ensure: Public key (k, n).
1: $\phi(n) := (p-1) \cdot (q-1)$.
2: Choose k with $1 < k < \phi(n)$ and $\text{GCD}(k, \phi(n)) = 1$ (public key (k, n)).
3: $k' := k^{-1} \bmod \phi(n)$ (private key (k', n)).
4: **return** (k, n).

Algorithm 10.2: Digital signature based on RSA

Require: For verifying: public key (k, n), plaintext m (encoded by $0 \leq m < n$). For signing: private key (k', n).

Ensure: Signed message s, verifying plaintext m'.

1: $s := d_{(k',n)}(m) = m^{k'} \bmod n$.
2: $m' := e_{(k,n)}(s) = s^k \bmod n$.
3: **return** s and m'.

If the public key is accepted as a verification key, the authenticity of the signature can be proven. Instead, if the public key originates from another instance, it can foist signed data on the first entity.

Example 10.2. We choose $p = 131$ and $q = 139$. This yields $n = 18209$. It is $\phi(18209) = 17940$ and because of $\text{GCD}(17, 17940) = 1$, we can use $k = 17$ as an appropriate public key ingredient. Let $m = 9682$ be the message to be signed. For this purpose, we need a private key supported by k' satisfying $k \cdot k' = 1 \bmod 17940$. We obtain $k' = 10553$ and thus m gets signed to

$$s = m^{k'} \bmod 18209 = 9682^{10553} \bmod 18209 = 8873.$$

For verification we calculate

$$m' = s^k \bmod 18209 = 8873^{17} \bmod 18209 = 9682.$$

The digital signature is accepted.

Based on two digital signatures $s_1 = m_1^{k_{\text{a,priv}}} \bmod n$ and $s_2 = m_2^{k_{\text{a,priv}}} \bmod n$, it applies

$$s = s_1 \cdot s_2 \bmod n = (m_1^{k_{\text{a,priv}}} \cdot m_2^{k_{\text{a,priv}}}) \bmod n = (m_1 \cdot m_2)^{k_{\text{a,priv}}} \bmod n$$

and s is a valid digital signature of $m = m_1 \cdot m_2 \bmod n$. This is a weakness of digital signatures with recovery. If such a digital signature of a message m should be generated, we can first choose a message $m_1 \in \mathbb{Z}_n$ with $m \neq m_1$ and then calculate a message $m_2 = (m \cdot m_1^{-1}) \bmod n$. If both messages get signed to s_1 and s_2, we obtain a valid digital signature s for m. This is a chosen plaintext attack. By using a digital signature with an appendix, we can avoid this problem because a cryptographical hash function usually does not satisfy

$$h(m_1) \cdot h(m_2) = h(m_1 \cdot m_2).$$

10.3 El-Gamal Based Digital Signature

The El-Gamal cipher system does not fulfill the requirements of Equation (10.1). However, the idea of using discrete logarithm as a one-way function makes sense with El-Gamal.[2] The key generation can be used without modification. For this purpose, we mention two statements that are clear in principle. Let $(G, *, e_*)$ be a group and $g \in G$ with $n = \mathrm{ord}_G(g)$. If $u = q \cdot n$, $q \in \mathbb{Z}$, it follows

$$\overset{u}{\ast} g = \overset{n \cdot q}{\ast} g = \overset{q}{\ast} \underbrace{\left(\overset{n}{\ast} g \right)}_{e_*} = e_*.$$

Vice versa, if $\overset{u}{\ast} g = e_*$ and $u = q \cdot n + r$, $q \in \mathbb{Z}, r \in \mathbb{Z}_n$, it applies

$$e_* = \overset{u}{\ast} g = \overset{q \cdot n + r}{\ast} g = \underbrace{\overset{n \cdot q}{\ast} g}_{e_*} * \overset{r}{\ast} g = \overset{r}{\ast} g.$$

It follows $r = 0$ and $u = q \cdot n$. A special case occurs if we set $u = k - l$ for some $k, l \in \mathbb{Z}$. This yields $\overset{k}{\ast} g = \overset{l}{\ast} g$.

Corollary 10.3. *Let $(G, *, e_*)$ be a group and $g \in G$.*

(1) *Let $u \in \mathbb{Z}$. Then, we obtain $\overset{u}{\ast} g = e_*$ iff u is divisible by $\mathrm{ord}_G(g)$.*

(2) *Let $k, l \in \mathbb{Z}$. Then, we obtain $\overset{k}{\ast} g = \overset{l}{\ast} g$, iff $k \equiv_{\mathrm{ord}_G(g)} l$.*

[2]See (El Gamal, 1985).

Algorithms 10.3 and 10.4 show the proceeding by signing a message based on El-Gamal.

Algorithm 10.3: El-Gamal signature key generation with safe prime

Require: $p := 2q + 1$ safe prime, $q \in \mathbb{N}$ prime and $g \in \mathbb{Z}_p^\times$ with $\mathcal{L}(g) = \mathbb{Z}_p^\times$.
Ensure: Public key (p, g, y_A).
1: Choose $x_A \in \{2, \ldots, p-2\}$ randomly (private key).
2: $y_A := g^{x_A} \bmod p$.
3: **return** (p, g, y_A).

Algorithm 10.4: Digital signature based on El-Gamal

Require: For signing: private key x_A, data m (encoded with $m \in \mathbb{Z}_p$). For verifying: public key (p, g, y_A).
Ensure: Signed message $\tilde{s}$, verifying plaintext $z_1 \equiv_p z_2$?
1: Choose $x_B \in \{2, \ldots, p-2\}$ with $\mathrm{GCD}(x_B, p-1) = 1$.
2: $y_B := g^{x_B} \bmod p$.
3: Calculate $x_B^{-1} \bmod (p-1)$.
4: $s := x_B^{-1} \cdot (m - x_A \cdot y_B) \bmod (p-1)$.
5: $\tilde{s} := (m, y_B, s)$.
6: $z_1 := y_A^{y_B} \cdot y_B^s \bmod p$.
7: $z_2 := g^m \bmod p$.
8: **return** $\tilde{s}, z_1 == z_2$.

From Step 3 onwards in Algorithm 10.4, there is nothing in common with the El Gamal cipher system in Section 8.4. Thus, we have to show that it works.

Theorem 10.4. *According to Algorithms* 10.3 *and* 10.4, *a tuple* $\tilde{s} = (m, y_B, s)$ *is a valid digital signature due to El-Gamal iff*

$$y_A^{y_B} \cdot y_B^s \bmod p = g^m \bmod p.$$

Proof. Let $p, g, y_A, x_A, m, x_B, y_B$ and s be given due to Algorithms 10.3 and 10.4.

"$\Rightarrow$": If $\tilde{s}$ is a valid digital signature, it follows

$$\begin{aligned} y_A^{y_B} \cdot y_B^s \bmod p &= g^{x_A \cdot y_B} \cdot g^{x_B \cdot (x_B^{-1}(m - x_A \cdot y_B)) \bmod (p-1)} \bmod p \\ &\overset{\text{Cor. 10.3}}{=} g^{x_A \cdot y_B} \cdot g^{x_B \cdot (x_B^{-1}(m - x_A \cdot y_B))} \bmod p \\ &= g^{x_A \cdot y_B} \cdot g^{m - x_A \cdot y_B} \bmod p \\ &= g^m \bmod p. \end{aligned} \tag{10.2}$$

"$\Leftarrow$": Let $y_A^{y_B} \cdot {y_B}^s \bmod p = g^m \bmod p$ for any (m, y_B, s) and $x_B = \log_g(y_B)$. Firstly, it follows from Corollary 10.3

$$g^{x_A \cdot y_B + x_B \cdot s \bmod \mathrm{ord}_G(g)} \equiv_p g^m.$$

Since $\mathcal{L}(g) = \mathbb{Z}_p^{\times}$, we obtain $x_A \cdot y_B + x_B \cdot s \equiv_{p-1} m$. Consequently, $\mathrm{GCD}(x_B, p-1) = 1$ yields

$$\begin{aligned} x_A \cdot y_B + x_B \cdot s &\equiv_{p-1} m \\ x_B \cdot s &\equiv_{p-1} m - x_A \cdot y_B \\ s &\equiv_{p-1} x_B^{-1} \cdot (m - x_A \cdot y_B). \end{aligned}$$

By defining $s = x_B^{-1} \cdot (m - x_A \cdot y_B) \bmod (p-1)$, we obtain a valid digital signature. □

Example 10.5. We use the same key as in Example 8.18, the public key is $(p, g, y_A) = (18743, 15, 16385)$ and the private key is $x_A = 17333$. Given $x_B = 5553$, $\mathrm{GCD}(5553, 18742) = 1$ and the data $m = 9682$ to be signed, e.g., the message digest of a message, we obtain

$$\begin{aligned} y_B &= 15^{5553} \bmod 18743 = 13702, \\ x_B^{-1} \bmod p &= 3743, \text{ and} \\ s &= 3743 \cdot (9682 - 17333 \cdot 13702) \bmod 18742 = 12562. \end{aligned}$$

This yields the digital signature $(m, y_B, s) = (9682, 13702, 12562)$. The verification is done by calculating

$$\begin{aligned} g^m \bmod p &= 15^{9682} \bmod 18743 = 12614, \\ x_B^{-1} \bmod p &= 3743, \text{ and} \\ y_A^{y_B} \cdot y_B{}^s \bmod p &= 16385^{13702} \cdot 13702^{12652} \bmod 18743 = 12614. \end{aligned}$$

The digital signature seems to be valid.

Since x_B in Algorithm 10.4 is chosen randomly, just as it was provided in the El-Gamal cipher in Algorithm 8.5, we can interpret the signature generation as a randomized process.

There is a similar weakness as in the RSA-based digital signature. If the same x_B is used twice for generating signatures s_1 and s_2, we can calculate

$$s_1 - s_2 \equiv_{p-1} x_B^{-1} \cdot (m_1 - x_A \cdot y_B - (m_2 - x_A \cdot y_B)) \equiv_{p-1} x_B^{-1} \cdot (m_1 - m_2).$$

If $\text{GCD}(m_1 - m_2, p - 1) = 1$, we can compute x_B^{-1}. We next obtain from Step 4 in Algorithm 10.4

$$x_A \equiv_{p-1} y_B^{-1} \cdot (m_1 - x_B \cdot s_1).$$

A second issue is the same as for RSA: the data should be a message digest to avoid calculating valid digital signatures from the product of two signed messages.

10.4 Digital Signature Standard

The El-Gamal based digital signature requires three exponentiations for verification. A few modifications of this method saves one exponentiation. This yields the *digital signature standard* (DSS). First, we have to generate a prime q meeting $2^{159} < q < 2^{160}$. This means q is a 160-bit number. A second prime p is then determined, fulfilling

$$2^{511+64 \cdot u} < p < 2^{512+64 \cdot u} \text{ for any } u \in \{1, \ldots, 8\} \text{ and } q \mid p - 1.$$

The length of p is between 512 and 1024 bits and is divisible by 64. The property $q \mid p - 1$ enables the use of a special property from number theory. Consider a finite field $(\mathbb{F}, \oplus, \odot, e_\oplus, e_\odot)$, $|\mathbb{F}| = n$, and the corresponding cyclic group $(\mathbb{F}^\times, \odot, e_\odot)$ based on the unity elements of $\mathbb{F}$. Let $d \mid n-1 = |\mathbb{F}^\times|$. By picking any generator $a \in \mathbb{F}^\times$, the element

$$b = \bigodot^{\frac{n-1}{d}} a \in \mathbb{F}^\times \text{ yields } \mathrm{ord}_{\mathbb{F}^\times}(b) \overset{\text{Cor. 3.28}}{=} \frac{n-1}{\mathrm{GCD}(n-1, \frac{n-1}{d})} = d.$$

b generates a subgroup $(\mathcal{L}(b), \odot, e_\odot)$ where $\mathcal{L}(b)$ contains d elements. From Corollary 3.70, it follows that this group has $\phi(d)$ generators.

Corollary 10.6. *Given the group $(\mathbb{F}^\times, \odot, e_\odot)$ of unity elements of a finite field $(\mathbb{F}, \oplus, \odot, e_\oplus, e_\odot)$ and a generator $a \in \mathbb{F}^\times$. If $|\mathbb{F}| = n$ and $d \mid n-1$, there is a subgroup of order d containing $\phi(d)$ generators.*

Now, let $g \in \mathbb{Z}_p^\times$ be a generator of $(\mathbb{Z}_p^\times, \cdot, 1)$ and $g_q = g^{\frac{p-1}{q}} \bmod p$. From Corollary 10.6, g_q is a generator of $\mathcal{L}(g_q)$ of order q. We choose a number $x_A \in \{1, \ldots, q-1\}$ and calculate

$$y_A = g_q^{x_A} \bmod p.$$

We have determined a public key (p, q, g_q, y_A) and a private key x_A. After choosing a number $x_B \in \{1, \ldots, q-1\}$ randomly, we calculate

$$y_B = (g_q^{x_B} \bmod p) \bmod q$$

and define the last part of the signature by

$$s = x_B^{-1} \cdot (m + x_A \cdot y_B) \bmod q$$

at which x_B^{-1} is to be taken modulo q. In doing so, (m, y_B, s) is the digital signature. In a similar way to El-Gamal, we can verify the signature. y_B and s should be from the set $\{1, \ldots, q-1\}$ and we have to check

$$y_B = ((g_q^{s^{-1} \cdot m \bmod q} \cdot y_A^{y_B \cdot s^{-1} \bmod q}) \bmod p) \bmod q. \tag{10.3}$$

Since

$$g_q^{s^{-1} \cdot m \bmod q} \cdot y_A^{y_B \cdot s^{-1} \bmod q} \equiv_p g_q^{s^{-1} \cdot (m + y_B \cdot x_A) \bmod q} \equiv_p g_q^{x_B},$$

we obtain a valid signature if the equality in Equation (10.3) holds.

The method reduces the effort because we now have to do two exponentiations instead of three with El-Gamal. The same two issues known from the RSA and El-Gamal remain: (1) we must not use the same x_B twice, and (2) we must not use the messages themselves, but a message digest thereof.

Algorithms 10.5 and 10.6 show the proceeding by signing a message based on the adapted El-Gamal signature.

Algorithm 10.5: DSS signature key generation with two primes

Require: A prime q meeting $2^{159} < q < 2^{160}$ and a prime $2^{511+64 \cdot u} < p < 2^{512+64 \cdot u}$ for any $u \in \{1, \ldots, 8\}$ with $q \mid p-1$.

Ensure: Public key (p, q, g_q, y_A).

```
Choose any generator g ∈ Z_p^× and calculate g_q := g^((p−1)/q) mod p.
Choose x_A ∈ {1, ..., q − 1} randomly (private key).
y_A := g_q^(x_A) mod p.
return (p, q, g_q, y_A).
```

Algorithm 10.6: Digital Signature based on DSS

Require: For signing: private key x_A, data m (encoded with $m \in \{1, \ldots, q-1\}$). For verifying: public key (p, q, g_q, y_A).

Ensure: Signed message $\tilde{s}$, verifying plaintext $y_B \equiv_p z$?

```
Choose x_B ∈ {1, ..., q − 1}.
Calculate y_B := (g_q^(x_B) mod p) mod q.
s := x_B^(−1) · (m + x_A · y_B) mod q.
s̃ := (m, y_B, s).
if y_B, s ∈ {1, ..., q − 1} then
    z := ((g_q^(s^(−1)·m mod q) · y_A^(y_B·s^(−1) mod q)) mod p) mod q.
    return s̃, y_B == z.
else
    return s̃, FALSE.
end if
```

Example 10.7. Again, we start with the same configuration as in Examples 8.18 and 10.5,

$$p = 18743,\ g = 15,\ x_A = 17333,\ x_B = 5553 \text{ and } m = 9682.$$

Since $p = 2 \cdot 9371 + 1$ is a safe prime, we define $q = 9371$ and obtain

$$g_q = 15^2 \bmod 18743 = 225 \text{ and } y_A = 225^{17333} \bmod 18743 = 12236.$$

The public key is $(p, q, g_q, y_A) = (18743, 9371, 225, 12236)$ and the private key is $x_A = 17333$. Given $x_B = 5553$ and the data $m = 9682$ to be signed, e.g., the message digest of a message, we obtain

$$\begin{aligned} y_B &= (225^{5553} \bmod 18743) \bmod 9371 = 5545, \\ x_B^{-1} &\equiv_q 3743 \\ s &= 3743 \cdot (9682 + 17333 \cdot 5545) \bmod 9371 = 3514. \end{aligned}$$

This yields the digital signature $(m, y_B, s) = (9682, 5545, 3514)$. The verification is done by calculating

$$\begin{aligned} s^{-1} &\equiv_q 9363 \\ x_B^{-1} &\equiv_q 3743 \\ 5545 &\overset{!}{=} (225^{9363 \cdot 9682 \bmod 9371} \cdot 12236^{9363 \cdot 5545 \bmod 9371} \bmod 18743) \\ &\qquad \bmod 9371 = 5545. \end{aligned}$$

The digital signature seems to be valid.

Chapter 11

Primality Tests and Pseudo Random Numbers

Note 11.1. In this chapter, the requirements are:

- being familiar with basics of number theory, see Section 1.1,
- being familiar with extended basics of algebra, see Sections 3.1 and 3.2, and
- knowing the problems of computing square roots and factorizing, see Sections 7.25 and 7.29.

Selected literature: See (Blum *et al.*, 1986; Hoffstein *et al.*, 2008; Pollard, 1974; Shoup, 2009).

Prime numbers play a very important role in cryptological applications. For example, they are required by

- Private-key systems: the AES in Section 6.3 using the finite field $GF(2^8)$ and the Pohlig–Hellman exponentiation cipher in Section 6.4 using a prime modulus,
- Public-key systems: the Diffie–Hellman key agreement in Section 7.1.2 using any prime modulus, problems of applying one-way functions in Section 7.2, such as computing the discrete logarithm, computing square roots and factoring positive integers,
- Mechanisms for inserting trapdoor information: the Merkle–Hellman knapsack in Section 8.1 using a prime modulus for

undoing the mixing operation, the Rabin cipher in Section 8.2 and the RSA in Section 8.3 using a composite modulus based on two primes, and the El-Gamal in Section 8.4 using a prime modulus or a finite prime field,

- Creating message digests: the Chaum–van Heijst–Pfitzmann hash function in Section 9.1 using a safe prime,
- Creating digital signatures: RSA in Section 10.2, the El-Gamal in Section 10.3 and the DSS in Section 10.4 using two prime moduli.

For preparing such systems, we have to do two basic tasks: (1) we must choose prime numbers, and (2) we must check whether a given number is a prime number. For the task of choosing a prime number p, we consider that the prime should have a predetermined bit length n, i.e., $2^{n-1} < p \leq 2^n$. From the prime number theorem 1.28 we know that the approximate number of primes is

$$\begin{aligned}\pi(2^n) - \pi(2^{n-1}) &\approx \frac{2^n}{\ln(2^n)} - \frac{2^{n-1}}{\ln(2^{n-1})} = \frac{(n-1)\cdot 2^n - n\cdot 2^{n-1}}{n\cdot(n-1)\cdot\ln(2)}\\ &= \frac{2^{n-1}\cdot(n-2)}{n\cdot(n-1)\cdot\ln(2)}.\end{aligned} \tag{11.1}$$

If we choose any n bit number randomly, the probability of being a prime number is

$$\mathbb{P}(\text{“prime”}) = \frac{\frac{2^{n-1}\cdot(n-2)}{n\cdot(n-1)\cdot\ln(2)}}{2^n - 2^{n-1}} = \frac{n-2}{n\cdot(n-1)\cdot\ln(2)} \approx \frac{1}{n\cdot\ln(2)}.$$

We are interested in the expected number of (Bernoulli) trials needed to obtain a prime number (success). This random experiment X follows a geometric distribution with parameter $w = \mathbb{P}(\text{“prime”})$ of success. The expectation of a geometric distribution is $\mathbb{E}_w[X] = \frac{1}{w}$. Thus, we expect

$$\mathbb{E}_w[X] = \frac{1}{w} = n\cdot\ln(2)$$

trials here. This is linear in the length n of bits. If the test of whether a number is prime or not is executed fast enough, we can apply Algorithm 11.1 to choose a prime of bit length n.

Algorithm 11.1: Random prime of bit length n

Require: Bit length n.

Ensure: Randomly chosen prime p of bit length n.

$x := 1$.
while x is not prime **do**
  Choose x with $2^{n-1} < x \leq 2^n$.
end while
return $p := x$.

11.1 Primality Tests

Algorithm 11.1 is quite efficient if the primality test is alike. For the purpose of primality testing, there is a deterministic method to test for primality. This test is called *AKS*[1] and provides a pool of similar methods based on the same idea. However, in practice the AKS test is much slower than the probabilistic Miller–Rabin primality test, see (Hoffstein *et al.*, 2008). We will examine the latter in the subsequent sections. Sometimes, there are number theoretic possibilities to make a final decision for primality. For example, the sequence (1.3) from Corollary 1.24 helps to decide.

Example 11.2.

$$p = 1902996923607946508077714625932660181843662165.$$

Since $3 \cdot p + 1 = 4^{76}$ is a power of 4, the number $p = a_{76}$ is composite due to Corollary 1.24. In fact,

$$p = 5 \cdot 17 \cdot 229 \cdot 457 \cdot 1217 \cdot 148961 \cdot 174763 \cdot 524287 \cdot 525313 \\ \cdot 24517014940753.$$

However, this is a special case and we need a more common method.

---

[1] See (Agrawal *et al.*, 2002).

11.2 Fermat Test

One of the simplest tests for primality is the *Fermat's primality test*. It is based on Fermat's little theorem 3.86,

$$p \text{ prime } \Rightarrow \text{ for all } a \in \mathbb{Z}_p^\times, \text{ it applies } a^{p-1} \bmod p = 1.$$

The contraposition,

$$\text{there is any } a \in \mathbb{Z}_p^\times \text{ applying } a^{p-1} \bmod p \neq 1 \Rightarrow p \text{ not prime},$$

can be used to test a given number p for primality.

Example 11.3.

$$p = 341 (= a_5 \text{ due to sequence (1.3)}).$$

Since $\mathrm{GCD}(2, p) = 1$, we start testing with $a = 2$: $2^{340} \bmod 341 = 1$. We call p *pseudo prime* to the base $a = 2$, since p is composite. Moving forward with $a = 3$ ($\mathrm{GCD}(3, p) = 1$), we obtain $2^{340} \bmod 341 = 56 \neq 1$, indicating that p is not prime.

By choosing an $a \notin \mathbb{Z}_p^\times$, it is proven that p is not prime. Algorithm 11.2 shows the procedure in summary. Unfortunately, there are numbers p for which all of the relatively prime numbers with reference to p let p become a pseudo prime to each of them. Such numbers p are

---

Algorithm 11.2: Fermat primality test

Require: Candidate $p \in \mathbb{N}$, $p > 2$.
Ensure: Decision whether p is composite or maybe prime.

Choose a with $1 < a < p$.
if $\mathrm{GCD}(a, p) \neq 1$ **then**
    return p is composite.
end if
if $a^{p-1} \bmod p \neq 1$ **then**
    return p is composite.
end if
return p is maybe prime.

---

called a *Carmichael number.*[2] The smallest Carmichael number is $561 = 3 \cdot 11 \cdot 17$. Consequently, this test is not a valid test.

11.3 Miller–Rabin Primality Test

A probabilistic test for primality is a test that can decide whether a given number is composite or maybe prime. From Corollary 7.18, we know that the two solutions of $x^2 \equiv_p 1$ for an odd prime p are 1 and $p-1$. After choosing any $1 < a < p$, we write

$$1 \overset{\text{Fermat}}{\equiv_p} a^{p-1} \equiv_p \left(a^{\frac{p-1}{2}}\right)^2 \Rightarrow a^{\frac{p-1}{2}} \bmod p \in \{1, p-1\}.$$

This yields a more strict version of Fermat's little theorem. Let $p \in \mathbb{N}$ be a candidate for an odd prime number. By defining the largest number

$$t = \max\{r \in \mathbb{N};\ 2^r \mid n-1\} > 1,$$

for which 2^t is dividing $p-1$, we can determine $q = \frac{p-1}{2^t} > 1$.

Theorem 11.4. *Let $p \in \mathbb{N}$ be prime and $a \in \mathbb{Z}$ with GCD$(a,p) =$ 1. Furthermore, let t and q be defined just like before. Then, either*

$$a^q \equiv_p 1$$

or

$$\text{there is any } r \in \{0, 1, \ldots, t-1\} \text{ with } a^{2^r \cdot q} \equiv_p p-1.$$

Proof. Let $a \in \mathbb{Z}$ with GCD$(a,p) = 1$; $|\mathbb{Z}_p^\times| = p - 1 = 2^t \cdot q$ because p is prime. The order $e = \text{ord}_{\mathbb{Z}_p^\times}(a)$ divides $p - 1 = 2^t \cdot q$, i.e.,

$$2^t \cdot q = e \cdot z, \quad 0 < z < n-1 \text{ and } \text{ord}_{\mathbb{Z}_p^*}(a^q) \overset{\text{Cor. 3.28}}{=} \frac{e}{\text{GCD}(e,q)}.$$

$\Rightarrow\ e = 2^t \cdot q \cdot z^{-1}$, $\text{ord}_{\mathbb{Z}_p^\times}(a^q) = \frac{2^t \cdot q \cdot z^{-1}}{\text{GCD}(2^t \cdot q \cdot z^{-1}, q)} = 2^t \cdot z^{-1} \in \{1, \ldots, p-1\}$. With $2^t \cdot q = (z \cdot q) 2^t z^{-1} = z \cdot (2^t \cdot z^{-1}) \cdot q$, it applies z^{-1}

[2]Named after Robert D. Carmichael (1879–1967).

to be a power of 2. It follows that $k = \text{ord}_{\mathbb{Z}_p^\times}(a^q) = 2^l$ for any $l \in \{0, \dots, t\}$.

$$l = 0: \qquad k = 1 \Rightarrow a^q \equiv_p 1,$$

$$1 \leq l \leq t : k > 1 \Rightarrow \text{ord}_{\mathbb{Z}_p^\times}(a^{2^{l-1} \cdot q}) = \frac{2^l}{\text{GCD}(2^l, 2^{l-1})} = 2.$$

It remains to be decided which numbers $b \in \mathbb{Z}_p^\times$ have order 2. It is clear that $b^2 \bmod n = 1$ or rather $n \mid b^2 - 1 = (b-1) \cdot (b+1)$. Thus, n divides either $(b-1)$ or $(b+1)$ due to the proof of Theorem 1.29. Since n is prime, we obtain $b = n - 1$ and $n \mid b + 1 = n$. However, there is just one such element $b \in \mathbb{Z}_n^\times$: $n - 1$. It follows for $r = l - 1$ that $a^{2^r \cdot q} \equiv_p p - 1$, $0 \leq r < t$. □

One of the two conditions for a unity element $a \in \mathbb{Z}_p^\times$ is necessary for p being prime. Thus, a is a witness for the compositeness of p if the conditions are not fulfilled.

Example 11.5. Let $n = 21$ and $n - 1 = 20 = 2^2 \cdot 5$, and thus, $t = 2$ and $q = 5$. $a = 2$ yields $2^5 \bmod 21 = 11$ for $r = 0$ and $2^{5 \cdot 2} \bmod 21 = 16$ for $r = 1$. Hence, 2 is a witness for the compositeness of 21.

Let $n = 11$ and $n - 1 = 10 = 2 \cdot 5$, and thus, $t = 1$ and $q = 5$. $a = 2$ yields $2^5 \bmod 11 = 10$ and 11 is still a candidate for primality. Similarly, we obtain for $a = 3$ and $a = 7$: $3^5 \bmod 11 = 1$ and $7^5 \bmod 11 = 10$. The probability for falsely accepting 11 as a prime is smaller than 0.016.

Algorithm 11.3 yields a safe decision about the compositeness of $p > 2$. With k-fold repetition of the test using k different and randomly chosen bases, there is a probability[3] smaller than $\frac{1}{4^k}$ for falsely accepting a number to be prime. The idea is to show that approximately $\frac{p-1}{4}$ numbers yield a pseudo-primality if p is composite.

[3]See (Stinson, 2005). For a proof, see (Shoup, 2009).

Algorithm 11.3: Miller–Rabin primality test

Require: Candidate $p \in \mathbb{N}$, p odd.
Ensure: Decision whether p is composite or maybe prime.

```
t := 0,  q := 0,  i := p − 1.
while i mod 2 ≠ 1 do
    i := i/2.
    t := t + 1.
end while
q := (p − 1)/2^t
Choose a number a with 1 < a < p randomly.
if GCD(a, p) ≠ 1 then
    return  p is composite.
end if
e := 0,  b := a^q mod p.
if b = 1 then
    return  p is maybe prime.
end if
while b ≠ ±1 mod p   &&   e < t − 1 do
    b := b^2 mod p,;
    e := e + 1.
end while
if b ≠ p − 1 mod p then
    return  p is composite.
end if
return  p is maybe prime.
```

11.4 Pseudorandom Number Generators

We have seen that cryptological applications require random ingredients in many situations. Thus, we must be able to generate *random numbers* in time. Besides physical possibilities, a real application needs to use a deterministic algorithm that returns random numbers. Such algorithms produce pseudorandom numbers and the algorithm is called a pseudorandom number generator (PRNG) or a deterministic random bit generators (DRBG).

Definition 11.6. A *pseudorandom bit generator* (PRBG) is a deterministic algorithm that when given a truly-random binary sequence of length n, outputs a binary sequence of length larger than n, which appears to be random. The input to the PRBG is called the seed and the output is called a *pseudorandom bit sequence.*

11.4.1 *Linear congruence generator*

A very simple but fast and effective possibility is the *linear congruence generator* (LCG). Given any integer $n \in \mathbb{N}$, integers $b \in \mathbb{Z}_n$, $a \in \mathbb{Z}_n^\times$ and a seed $x_0 \in \mathbb{Z}_n$, we start an iterative process by

$$x_{i+1} := a \cdot x_i + b \bmod n. \tag{11.2}$$

In fact, this is a very fast and effective method to produce many pseudo random numbers if n is large enough. For example, this is a suitable method for simulation projects, but it should not be used for cryptology. To understand this, consider the sequence $(x_i)_{i \in \mathbb{N}_0}$ and define

$$\begin{aligned} y_{i+1} := x_{i+1} - x_i \bmod n &= a \cdot x_i + b - (a \cdot x_{i-1} + b) \bmod n \\ &= a \cdot (x_i - x_{i-1}) \bmod n \\ &= a \cdot y_i \bmod n, \end{aligned} \tag{11.3}$$

for $i \in \mathbb{N}$. Assume for the moment that $y_i^{-1} \bmod n$ exists. Since

$$y_{i+1} \equiv_n a \cdot y_i \equiv_n a^2 \cdot y_{i-1} \equiv_n \dots \equiv_n a^i \cdot y_1,$$

we can compute $a \equiv_n y_{i+1} \cdot y_i^{-1}$ and

$$y_{i+1} \equiv_n (y_{i+1} \cdot y_i^{-1})^i \cdot y_1 \Rightarrow \underbrace{y_1 \cdot y_{i+1}^{i-1} - y_i^i}_{=q \cdot n,\ q \in \mathbb{Z}} \equiv_n 0. \tag{11.4}$$

Thus, just a few members of the sequence yield multiples of n. Taking their greatest common divisor, we will quickly obtain n. From Equation (11.3), we can estimate a. From Equation (11.2), we can estimate b. The estimators can be used to test and predict the sequence. Therefore, the LCG is very insecure.

Example 11.7. Let the following starting sequence of numbers generated by an LCG with unknown parameters be given as:

$$19, 20, 31, 46, 52.$$

After calculating the y_i's, $1, 11, 15, 6$, we try to get n by choosing i from $\{2, 3\}$ successively:

$$y_1 \cdot y_3 - y_2^2 = 1 \cdot 15 - 11^2 = -106 \text{ and}$$
$$y_1 \cdot y_4^2 - y_3^3 = 1 \cdot 46^2 - 31^3 = -3339.$$

From (11.4), these numbers are multiples of n. Hence, we get a candidate for n by computing their greatest common divisor:

$$n = \text{GCD}(-106, -3339) = 53.$$

Since $y_2 = a \cdot y_1 \bmod n$, we obtain $a = 11$. After this, we can compute $b = 23$. In fact, these are the right parameters that can be shown by checking the values here. If this does not work, we need to involve more y_i's to get a better result.

11.4.2 *Blum–Blum–Shub generator*

A better method is to use the results from public-key cryptography. Problem 7.25 of finding square roots modulo n is a suitable base for defining a PRNG. This problem is the same as Problem 7.29 where a composite number is factorized. We cannot determine a square root by using Algorithm 7.7 until we factorize n.

A very well-known and accepted PRNG is the BBS generator[4] described in Algorithm 11.4, which is also known as a "$x^2 \bmod n$" generator. We need a *Blum number* $n = p \cdot q$ with $p \bmod 4 = 3 = q \bmod 4$ and $p \neq q$ prime each. How many such numbers exist? Let $\pi_{a,b}(n)$ be the number of primes smaller than or equal to $n \in \mathbb{N}$, given by the shape of $a \cdot k + b$ where $a, b \in \mathbb{N}$, $\text{GCD}(a, b) = 1$ and $k \in \{0, \ldots, \lfloor \frac{x-b}{a} \rfloor\}$. C.-J. Poussin,[5] who found a proof of the prime number theorem 1.28, proved that this number is proportional

[4]See (Blum *et al.*, 1986) or (McAndrew, 2011).

[5]Charles-Jean de La Vallée Poussin (1866–1962).

Algorithm 11.4: BBS bit-generator

Require: Primes $p \neq q$ with $p, q \equiv_4 3$ and $p-1, q-1, p+1$ and $q+1$ possess at least one large prime factor, $k \in \mathbb{N}$.

Ensure: Pseudo random number given by a bit sequence $x_1 \ldots x_k$, $x_i \in \{0, 1\}$.

$n := p \cdot q$

Choose a seed $a \in \mathbb{N}$ with $\mathrm{GCD}(a, n) = 1$ randomly.

$a_0 := a^2 \bmod n$

$i := 0$.

while $i < k$ **do**

  $a_{i+1} := a_i^2 \bmod n$.

  Take the least significant bit (lsb) of a_{i+1}: $x_{i+1} := a_{i+1} \bmod 2$.

  $i := i + 1$.

end while

return $x_1 \ldots x_k$.

to $\pi(n)$,

$$\pi_{a,b}(n) \sim \frac{1}{\phi(a)} \cdot \frac{n}{\log n} \text{ with } \phi(1) = 1.$$

By setting $a = 4$ and $b = 3$, we obtain $\pi_{4,3}(n) \sim \frac{1}{\phi(4)} \cdot \frac{x}{\log x} = \frac{1}{2} \cdot \frac{n}{\log n}$. Thus, since $\pi_{1,0}(n) = \pi(n) \sim \frac{n}{\log n}$, half of all primes have this shape. A cryptoanalytical attack would be useless.

Let p be prime. If $(p-1)$ and $(p+1)$ possess at least one large prime factor, p is called a *strong prime*. Applying such primes can be used to manage some cryptoanalytical attacks. Thus, their application is required in Algorithm 11.4.

The decomposition of n allows us to calculate the sequence $(a_i)_{i \in \mathbb{N}}$. Further predictions $a_{k+1}, a_{k+2}, \ldots$ of bits are only possible by knowing p, q and a_k. If the values are known, Algorithm 7.7 results in at most four possible solutions. Additional information about the predecessors will yield the right solution.

An inappropriate choice of a and n in Algorithm 11.4 yields patterns in the bit sequences, which undermine the security of the whole sequence. We can see this in Example 11.8.

Example 11.8 (A too short cycle). Let $p = 7$, $q = 11$ and $n = p \cdot q = 77$ be given. Further, let $a = 3 \in \mathbb{Z}_n^\times$. First, this yields $a_0 = 9$. We can generate a pseudo random number of bit length $k = 32$ by

i	a_i	bit sequence	a_i mod 2	a_i^2 mod 77
0	9	0001001	**1**	4
1	4	0000100	**0**	16
2	16	0010000	**0**	25
3	25	0011001	**1**	9
4	9	0001001	**1**	4
5	4	0000100	**0**	16
6	16	0010000	**0**	25
7	25	0011001	**1**	9
⋮	⋮	⋮	⋮	⋮

Starting at a_0, we obtain the repetitive sequence

$$10011001100110011001100110011001_{(2)} = 2576980377.$$

Continuing to a length of 1024 bits and drawing an image of size 32×32, we obtain the following pattern (dark area $\widehat{=}1$, bright area $\widehat{=}0$):

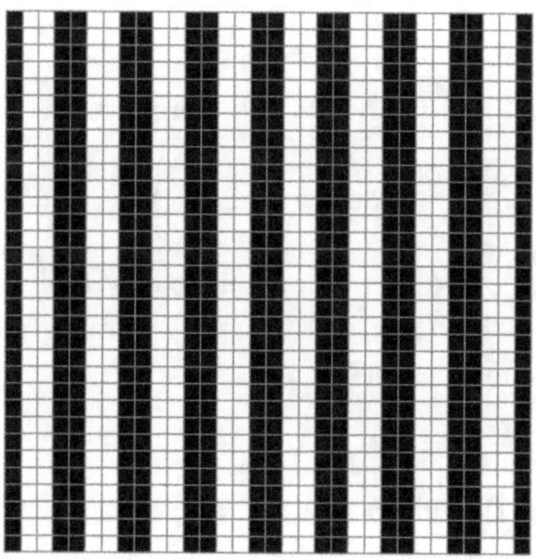

Figure 11.1 Short pattern in a BBS-generated "random" bits sample.

The bit length in Example 11.8 is disadvantageously chosen because there is a short cycle in the generated bit sequence. This is because the order of $a = 3$ is small. Look at the group of residue classes relatively prime to n, $(\mathbb{Z}_n^\times, \cdot_n, 1)$. Consider that the decomposition of n and in particular $\phi(n)$ is known,

$$\phi(n) = \prod_{d|\phi(n)} d^{\alpha(d)},$$

with the multiplicities $\alpha(d)$ of each of the prime factors d. We can calculate the order of any member $a \in G$ of any group $(G, *, e_*)$ then.

Theorem 11.9. *For each prime divisor d of the group order $|G|$ of a group $(G, *, e_*)$, let $\beta(d) \in \mathbb{N}_0$ be the biggest number, such that $a^{|G|/d^{\beta(d)}}$ mod $n = 1$ for any $a \in G$. Then, we obtain $0 \leq \beta(d) \leq \alpha(d)$ and*

$$ord_G(a) = \prod_{d||G|} d^{\alpha(d)-\beta(d)}.$$

Proof. Since $\text{ord}_G(a)$ divides the order $|G|$, it is of the shape $\prod_{d||G|} d^{\gamma(d)}$ with $0 \leq \gamma(d) \leq \alpha(d) - \beta(d)$ for all $d \mid |G|$. Because of the definition of $\beta(d)$, it even applies $\gamma(d) = \alpha(d) - \beta(d)$ for all $d \mid |G|$. □

The sequence $(a_i)_{i\in\mathbb{N}_0}$ produces the elements of the set

$$\left\{a^{2^i \bmod \text{ord}_{\mathbb{Z}_n^\times}(a)} \bmod n;\ i \in \mathbb{N}_0\right\} \subset \mathcal{L}(a^2) \subset \mathcal{L}(a).$$

The length of the cycle can be calculated by looking at the exponent $2^i \bmod \text{ord}_{\mathbb{Z}_n^\times}(a)$. Let $z = \text{ord}_{\mathbb{Z}_n^\times}(a)$. Assuming $p \equiv_4 3$ and $q \equiv_4 3$, we obtain for some $u, v \in \mathbb{N}$

$$\phi(n) = (p-1)(q-1) = (4u+3-1)(4v+3-1) = 4(2u+1)(2v+1).$$

From Fermat's little theorem 3.86, we get

$$\begin{aligned} &a^{\frac{\phi(n)}{2}} \bmod p \\ &\quad = a^{(p-1)\cdot\frac{q-1}{2}} \bmod p = 1 = a^{(q-1)\cdot\frac{p-1}{2}} \bmod q = a^{\frac{\phi(n)}{2}} \bmod q \end{aligned}$$

and thus, we use the Chinese remainder theorem 3.77, which results in

$$a^{\frac{\phi(n)}{2}} \bmod n = 1.$$

It follows that $a^{\frac{\phi(n)}{4}} \bmod n$ has up to four solutions. A quarter of the cases gives the solution 1, which means $\beta(2) = 2$ according to Theorem 11.9. In this case, the order z is odd and we can calculate the cycle length by $\text{ord}_{\mathbb{Z}_z^\times}(2)$. Otherwise, we have to find the periodicity in the sequence $(2^i \bmod z)_{i\in\mathbb{N}}$. This can be done by looking at the value $w = a^{\lceil \log_2(z) \rceil} \bmod z$ and by searching the next in size index i satisfying $2^i \bmod z = w$.

Example 11.10 (Calculating the cycle length). Taking the parameters of Example 11.8, we obtain $\phi(77) = 60 = 2^2 \cdot 3 \cdot 5$. Applying $a = 3$, we get $f(2) = 1$, $f(3) = 0$ and $f(5) = 0$, and thus, $\text{ord}_{\mathbb{Z}_{77}^\times}(3) = 2^{2-1} \cdot 3^{1-0} \cdot 5^{1-0} = 30$ is even. Since $2^5 \equiv_{30} 2^9$, the number of cycle-free elements of this set is 4. Therefore, the values are repeated cyclically.

We can achieve an improved situation by choosing much larger values for p and q and a smart choice of a.

Example 11.11. We ask the BBS generator for 32-bit random numbers by applying the primes

$$p = 59649589127497231 \text{ and } q = 57046892006851290050051.$$

In the first try we choose

$$a = 711619272922836708998775809547944493 7$$

possessing the small order

$$z = \text{ord}_{\mathbb{Z}_n^\times}(a) = 2110.$$

By setting $w = 2^{11} - z = 1986$, we obtain a periodicity of $i = 420$. Since we want to generate 32-bit random numbers, these numbers recur every $\text{LCM}(32,420)/32 = 105$ values. The left image in Figure 11.2 shows the first 1024 generated bits. The periodicity is approximately 420 bits. The image on the right also shows 1024 generated

32-bit random numbers recurring every 105 numbers recognizable by the pattern.

Figure 11.2 Still recognizable pattern in a BBS-generated "random" bits sample based on large primes.

In Figure 11.3, we choose $a = 9$, which possesses a much better order

$$z = \text{ord}_{\mathbb{Z}_n^\times}(a) = 170141183460469268672855492761953 18075.$$

This yields $i = \text{ord}_{\mathbb{Z}_z^\times}(2) = 742714218980839061155288878 60$ and a periodicity of 185678554745209765288822219 65 for the generated 32-bit random numbers. Both corresponding images show no recognizable pattern.

Figure 11.3 No recognizable pattern in a BBS-generated "random" bits sample based on large primes.

In practice, the BBS has two disadvantages: (1) it is very slow to generate sufficient pseudorandom numbers, and (2) it is necessary to use a large modulus n and choose a seed that possesses a large enough order. Hence, other approaches are often used. For example, the so-called HMAC_DRBG[6] based on a HMAC from Section 9.3 is recommended.

[6]See NIST SP 800-90A, http://nvlpubs.nist.gov/nistpubs/SpecialPublications/NIST.SP.800-90Ar1.pdf.

Bibliography

Articles

Agrawal, M., N. Kayal, and N. Saxena (2002). "PRIMES is in P". In: *Anns. Math.* 2, pp. 781–793 (cit. on p. 337).

Blum, L., M. Blum, and M. Shub (1986). "A Simple Unpredictable Pseudo Random Number Generator". In: *SIAM J. Comput.* 15.2, pp. 364–383. ISSN: 0097-5397. DOI:10.1137/0215025. URL: http://dx.doi.org/10.1137/0215025 (cit. on pp. 335, 343).

Cleary, J., and I. Witten (1984). "Data Compression Using Adaptive Coding and Partial String Matching". In: *IEEE Tran. on Communications* 32.4, pp. 396–402. ISSN: 0090-6778. DOI:10.1109/TCOM.1984.1096090 (cit. on p. 171).

Dang, Q. (2013). "Changes in Federal Information Processing Standard (FIPS) 180-4, Secure Hash Standard". In: *Cryptologia* 37.1, pp. 69–73, DOI:10.1080/01611194.2012.687431. URL: https://doi.org/10.1080/01611194.2012.687431 (cit. on pp. 319, 307).

Deutsch, P., and J.-L. Gailly (1996). "RFC1950 — ZLIB Compressed Data Format Specification, Version 3.3". In: URL: https://www.rfc-editor.org/info/rfc1950 (cit. on p. 308).

Diffie, W., and M. Hellman (1976). "New Directions in Cryptography". In: *IEEE Trans. Inf. Theor.* 22.6, pp. 644–654, ISSN: 0018-9448. DOI:10.1109/TIT.1976.1055638. URL: http://dx.doi.org/10.1109/TIT.1976.1055638 (cit. on pp. 225, 229, 265).

Kerckhoffs, A. (1883). "La Cryptographie Militaire". In: *Journal des Sciences Militaires* 9, pp. 5–83 (cit. on p. 61).

Massey, J. L. (1988). "An Introduction to Contemporary Cryptology". In: *Proc. of the IEEE* 76.5, pp. 533–549. DOI:10.1109/5.4440 (cit. on pp. 151, 155, 157, 168, 180).

Menezes, A. J., and S. A. Vanstone (1993). "Elliptic Curve Cryptosystems and their Implementation". In: *J. Cryptol.* 6.4, pp. 209–224. ISSN: 0933-2790. DOI:10.1007/BF00203817. URL: http://dx.doi.org/10.1007/BF00203817 (cit. on pp. 267, 304).

Merkle, R., and M. Hellman (1978). "Hiding Information and Signatures in Trapdoor Knapsacks". In: *IEEE Trans. on Info. Theor.* 24.5, pp. 525–530. ISSN: 0018-9448. DOI:10.1109/TIT.1978.1055927 (cit. on pp. 226, 227, 268).

Merkle, R. C. (1978). "Secure Communications over Insecure Channels". In: *Commun. ACM* 21.4, pp. 294–299. ISSN: 0001-0782. DOI:10.1145/359460.359473. URL: http://doi.acm.org/10.1145/359460.359473 (cit. on p. 226).

Pollard, J. M. (1974). "Theorems on Factorization and Primality Testing". In: *Proceedings of the Cambridge Philosophical Society* 76, p. 521. DOI:10.1017/S0305004100049252 (cit. on pp. 254, 335).

Pomerance, C. (1996). "A Tale of Two Sieves". In: *Notices Amer. Math. Soc.* 43, pp. 1473–1485 (cit. on p. 262).

Rejewski, M. (1981). "How Polish Mathematicians Broke the Enigma Cipher". In: *Anns. History of Computing* 3.3, pp. 213–234. ISSN: 0164-1239. DOI: 10.1109/MAHC.1981.10033 (cit. on p. 124).

Takahira, R., K. Tanaka-Ishii, and L. Debowski (2016). "Entropy Rate Estimates for Natural Language — A New Extrapolation of Compressed Large-Scale Corpora". In: *MDPI Entropy* 18, p. 16 (cit. on p. 171).

Books

Applebaum, D. (2008). *Probability and Information: An Integrated Approach.* 2nd edn. Cambridge University Press. DOI:10.1017/CBO9780511755262 (cit. on pp. 1, 16).

Baigneres, T., *et al.* (2006). *A Classical Introduction to Cryptography Exercise Book.* New York: Springer. ISBN: 0-387-27934-2 (cit. on p. 58).

Biggs, N. (2008). *Codes.* London: Springer, X, 273 S. ISBN: 978-1-84800-272-2 (cit. on pp. 23, 25).

Bremner, M. R. (2011). *Lattice Basis Reduction — An Introduction to the LLL Algorithm and its Applications.* Boca Raton, Fla: CRC Press. ISBN: 978-1-439-80702-6 (cit. on p. 273).

Buchmann, J. (2004). *Introduction to Cryptography* New York: Springer. ISBN: 9781441990037. DOI:10.1007/978-1-4419-9003-7. URL: http://dx.doi.org/10.1007/978-1-4419-9003-7 (cit. on p. 192).

——— (2012). *Introduction to Cryptography.* 2nd ed. New York: Springer, p. 281. ISBN: 978-1468404982 (cit. on pp. 67, 243).

Coutinho, S. C. (1999). *The Mathematics of Ciphers: Number Theory and RSA Cryptography.* CRC Press. ISBN: 1568810822. URL: https://www.crcpress.com/The-Mathematics-of-Ciphers-Number-Theory-and-RSA-Cryptography/Coutinho/p/book/9781568810829 (cit. on pp. 323, 324).

Cover, T. M., and J. A. Thomas (2006). *Elements of Information Theory.* Hoboken, NJ: Wiley-Interscience (cit. on pp. 151, 171).

Dixon, M. R., L. A. Kurdachenko, and I. Ya. Subbotin (2010). *Algebra and Number Theory.* New Jersey: John Wiley and Son. ISBN: 978-0-470-49636-7 (cit. on p. 3).

Durbin, J. R. (2009). *Modern Algebra.* 6th ed. Hoboken, NJ: Wiley, XIII, 335 S. ISBN: 0-470-38443-3 (cit. on pp. 67, 75).

Fano, R. M. (1961). *Transmission of Information: A Statistical Theory of Communications.* MIT Press. URL: https://archive.org/details/TransmissionOfInformationAStatisticalTheoryOfCommunication%20RobertFano (cit. on pp. 155, 164).

Hardy, G. H., *et al.* (2008). *An Introduction to the Theory of Numbers.* Oxford: Oxford University Press. ISBN: 9780199219865. URL: https://books.google.de/books?id=rey9wfSaJ9EC (cit. on pp. 1, 12, 67, 96).

Hellman, M. E. (1977). *An Extension of the Shannon Theory Approach to Cryptography,* Vol. 23. IEEE Press, pp. 289–294. DOI:10.1109/TIT.1977.1055709 (cit. on p. 171).

Hoffstein, J., J. Pipher, and J. H. Silverman (2008). *An Introduction to Mathematical Cryptography.* 1st ed. Springer. ISBN: 9780387779935 (cit. on pp. 1, 57, 119, 179, 188, 225, 262, 267, 323, 335, 337).

Holden, J. (2017). *The Mathematics of Secrets.* Princeton University Press. ISBN: 9781400885626. DOI:10.1515/9781400885626. URL: http://dx.doi.org/10.1515/9781400885626 (cit. on pp. 179, 187, 229).

ISO/IEC, 9798-2 (1999). *Information Technology–Security Techniques — Entity Authentication.* ISO (cit. on p. 233).

Jevons, W. S. (1875). *The Principles of Science: A Treatise on Logic and Scientific Method.* Bd. 1. Macmillan. URL: https://archive.org/details/theprinciplesof00jevoiala/page/n8 (cit. on p. 235).

Kaliski, B. S. (1988). *Elliptic Curves and Cryptography.* MIT, Laboratory for Computer Science, p. 169 (cit. on p. 298).

Kullback, S. (1997). *Information Theory and Statistics.* Dover Publications. ISBN: 9780486696843. URL: https://books.google.de/books?id=luHcCgAAQBAJ (cit. on p. 160).

Küster, M. W. (2006). *Geordnetes Weltbild.* Tübingen: Niemeyer, XV, 712 S. ISBN: 3-484-10899-1 (cit. on p. 26).

Lang, S. (1984). *Algebra.* 2nd ed. Reading, Mass: Addison-Wesley, XV, 714 S. ISBN: 0-201-05487-6 (cit. on pp. 67, 131).

——— (1987). *Linear Algebra* Springer. ISBN: 9780387964126. URL: https://books.google.de/books?id=0DUXym7QWfYC (cit. on pp. 116, 273).

Li, Y., and H. Niederreiter, eds. (2008). *Coding and Cryptology — Proceedings of the First International Workshop (Coding Theory and Crytology),* Vol. 4. Singapore: World Scientific Publishing. ISBN: 9812832238. URL: https://www.worldscientific.com/worldscibooks/10.1142/6915 (cit. on p. 57).

Lidl, R., and H. Niederreiter (1996). *Finite Fields.* Cambridge: Cambridge University Press. ISBN: 9780521392310. DOI:DOI:10.1017/CBO9780511525926. URL: https://www.cambridge.org/core/books/finite-fields/75BDAA74ABAE713196E718392B9E5E72 (cit. on pp. 179, 192, 201).

Mahalingam, R. (2014). *Symmetric Cryptographic Protocols.* Cham: Springer, p. 234. ISBN: 978-3-319-07583-9 (cit. on p. 43).

Mariconda, C. (2016). *Discrete Calculus.* 103. Cham: Springer, xxi, 659 Seiten. ISBN: 978-3-319-03037-1 (cit. on p. 124).

Martin, K. M. (2017). *Everyday Cryptography.* 2nd ed. Oxford: Oxford University Press, p. 674. ISBN: 978-0-19-878801-0 (cit. on pp. 23, 43, 65, 119, 142, 285).

McAndrew, A. (2011). *Introduction to Cryptography with Open-Source Software.* CRC Press (cit. on p. 343).

Nielsen, M. A., and I. L. Chuang (2011). *Quantum Computation and Quantum Information: 10th Anniversary Edition.* New York: Cambridge University Press. ISBN: 9781107002173 (cit. on p. 243).

Proakis, J. G. (2008). *Digital Communications.* 5th ed. Boston: McGraw-Hill, XVIII, 1150 S. ISBN: 978-0-07-126378-8 (cit. on pp. 23, 36, 55).

Ross, S. (2014). *Introduction to Probability Models.* 11th ed. Boston: Academic Press, p. 784. ISBN: 978-0-12-407948-9. DOI:https://doi.org/10.1016/B978-0-12-407948-9.00012-8. URL: http://www.sciencedirect.com/science/article/pii/B9780124079489000128 (cit. on pp. 1, 16).

Shannon, C. E. (1949). *Communication Theory of Secrecy Systems.* New York: AT & T, p. 60 (cit. on pp. 29, 151, 152, 164, 176, 180).

Shoup, V. (2009). *A Computational Introduction to Number Theory and Algebra.* 2nd ed. Cambridge University Press. ISBN: 978-0521516440 (cit. on pp. 335, 340).

Silverman, J. H. (1986). *The Arithmetic of Elliptic Curves.* New York: Springer, XII, 400 S. ISBN: 978-0-387-96203-0 (cit. on pp. 298, 300).

Sorge, C., N. Gruschka, and L. L. Lacono, (2013). *Sicherheit in Kommunikationsnetzen.* München: Oldenbourg. ISBN: 978-3-486-72016-7 (cit. on pp. 51).

Stamp, M. (2011). *Information Security.* John Wiley and Sons, Inc. ISBN: 9780470626399, DOI:10.1002/9781118027974. URL: http://dx.doi.org/10.1002/9781118027974 (cit. on p. 272).

Stamp, M., and R. M. Low (2007). *Applied Cryptanalysis.* New Jersey: Wiley. ISBN: 978-0-470-11486-5 (cit. on pp. 64, 65, 225, 262).

Stinson, D. R. (2005). *Cryptography: Theory and Practice.* 3rd ed. Taylor & Francis. ISBN: 9781584885085. URL: https://books.google.de/books?id=Yz55lPEuzckC (cit. on pp. 23, 62, 119, 171, 225, 243, 267, 275, 307, 311, 340).

Tranquillus, G. S. (1918). *Gai Suetoni Tranquilli De vita Caesarum libri I-II: Iulius, Augustus.* Alyn and Bacon (cit. on p. 44).

Vaudenay, S. (2006). *A Classical Introduction to Cryptography.* Springer (cit. on p. 225).

Other

Chaum, D., E. van Heijst, and B. Pfitzmann (1992). "Cryptographically Strong Undeniable Signatures, Unconditionally Secure for the Signer". In: *Advances in Cryptology — CRYPTO '91, Proceedings.* Ed. J. Feigenbaum. Berlin, Heidelberg: Springer, pp. 470–484. ISBN: 978-3-540-46766-3 (cit. on pp. 307, 309).

Damgård, I. B. (1989). "A Design Principle for Hash Functions". In: *Advances in Cryptology — CRYPTO' 89, Proceedings.* Ed. G. Brassard. New York: Springer, pp. 416–427. ISBN: 978-0-387-34805-6 (cit. on pp. 307, 313).

Dworkin, M. J. (2001). *Sp 800-38A 2001 Edition. Recommendation for Block Cipher Modes of Operation: Methods and Techniques.* Tech. rep. Gaithersburg, MD, United States (cit. on p. 149).

——— (2016a). *Sp 800-38B. Recommendation for Block Cipher Modes of Operation: The CMAC Mode for Authentication.* Tech. rep. Gaithersburg, MD, United States: NIST (cit. on p. 321).

——— (2016b). *Sp 800-38G 2001 Edition. Recommendation for Block Cipher Modes of Operation: Methods for Format-Preserving Encryption.* Tech. rep. Gaithersburg, MD, United States (cit. on pp. 119, 149).

Dworkin, M. J., *et al.* (2001). *Federal Inf. Process. Stds. (NIST FIPS) — 197 (AES).* NIST Pubs 197. NIST (cit. on pp. 179, 188).

El Gamal, T. (1985). "A Public Key Cryptosystem and a Signature Scheme Based on Discrete Logarithms". In: *Advances in Cryptology — CRYPTO'84, Proceedings.* New York: Springer, pp. 10–18. ISBN: 0-387-15658-5. URL: http://dl.acm.org/citation.cfm?id=19478.19480 (cit. on pp. 267, 287, 323, 327).

Iwata, T., and K. Kurosawa (2003). "OMAC: One-Key CBC MAC". In: *Fast Software Encryption.* Ed. T. Johansson. Berlin Heidelberg: Springer Berlin, Heidelberg, pp. 129–153 (cit. on p. 321).

Shamir, A. (1982). "A Polynomial Time Algorithm for Breaking the Basic Merkle-Hellman Cryptosystem". In: *23rd Annual Symposium on Foundations of Computer Science.* SFCS'82, pp. 145–152. DOI:10.1109/SFCS.1982.5 (cit. on p. 268).

Webster, A. F., and S. E. Tavares (1986). "On the Design of S-boxes". In: *Advances in Cryptology — CRYPTO'85, Proceedings.* USA: Springer, pp. 523–534. ISBN: 0-387-16463-4. URL: http://dl.acm.org/citation.cfm?id=18262.25423 (cit. on pp. 151, 176).

Index

www.ingramcontent.com/pod-product-compliance
Lightning Source LLC
LaVergne TN
LVHW052029200926
848481LV00005B/1622